GUIDANCE AND COUNSELING SERIES

Roger A. Myers, Consulting Editor

Explorations in Time-Limited Counseling and Psychotherapy
CHARLES J. GELSO AND DEBORAH HAZEL JOHNSON

Vocational Counseling: A Guide for the Practitioner
PATRICIA M. RASKIN

Experiencing Adolescents: A Sourcebook
for Parents, Teachers, and Teens
RICHARD M. LERNER AND NANCY L. GALAMBOS, EDITORS

EXPERIENCING ADOLESCENTS

A Sourcebook
for Parents, Teachers, and Teens

Richard M. Lerner
Nancy L. Galambos
EDITORS

Teachers College, Columbia University
New York and London

Published by Teachers College Press, 1234 Amsterdam Avenue,
New York, NY 10027.

A hardcover edition of this book is published by Garland Publishing, Inc., New
York, NY. It is reprinted here by arrangement with the publisher.

Library of Congress Cataloging-in-Publication Data

Experiencing adolescents.

(Guidance and counseling series)
Bibliography: p.
Includes indexes.
1. Youth.   2. Adolescence.   3. Child development.
I. Lerner, Richard M.   II. Galambos, Nancy L.
III. Series.
HQ796.E885   1987   305.2'35   87-10129
ISBN 0-8077-2884-5 (pbk.)

Manufactured in the United States of America

92 91 90 89 88 87   1 2 3 4 5 6

To Justin Samuel Lerner and
Blair Elizabeth Lerner,
whose adolescence their parents look
forward to experiencing

To Gabriel J. Galambos and
Emily O. Galambos
for their enduring support

CONTENTS

PREFACE

Adolescence is a period of pronounced change and, often, of profound importance for the individual. The young person experiences changes in his or her physical and psychological functioning; new social relationships are also typical during this period. Parents and other caregivers must attune themselves to the changes of adolescents if they are to interact effectively with these youths. Thus, for adults who deal with children developing through this period, adolescence is also a period of adjustment and change.

Often problems arise as part of a person's adolescent experience and/or as part of the experiences an adult has with an adolescent. Some of the required adjustments may be particularly stressful for adolescents and their parents, and thus may create problems. For instance, an adolescent's changing physical and physiological characteristics may require relatively simple adjustments in his or her motor coordination, hygienic habits, and wardrobe. However, the burgeoning sexuality that accompanies the maturational changes of adolescents may require emotional, behavioral, and moral adjustments that prove more problematic for them and their parents.

There are two purposes of this book. First, we wish to present authoritative summaries of what is known about the experience of adolescence, both with respect to the adolescent undergoing the changes of this period and with respect to the parents, teachers, peers, and others in his or her social world. We do this by presenting, first, a general overview of the adolescent experience in the initial chapter of this book and, second, by presenting, in the ten chapters following the first one, more focused discussions of several major areas of adolescent development: physical and physiological changes of adolescence and their psychosocial implications, adolescent sexuality, social relationships in adolescence, child abuse during adolescence, adolescent substance use and abuse, medical problems of adolescence, moral and religious development during adolescence, education during adolescence, vocational and role development in adolescence, and problems of handicapped adolescents.

The second purpose of this book is to discuss the particular problems that may arise during adolescence—among both adolescents and their parents, teachers, and peers—and to identify sources of help that exist to deal with these problems. Thus, in each of the ten chapters following the first one, there exists a section labeled "Sources of Help." Here are listed the names and addresses of existing agencies, committees, and professional resources that are available for consultation concerning the particular problem of that chapter.

To help expand a reader's knowledge about the topics discussed in this book and to provide further information about the problems of adolescence, there exists in each chapter a section labeled "Annotated References." This section follows the "Sources of Help" section, and lists and describes relevant books, articles, or reports which deal specifically with the particular problem discussed in the chapter. Finally, each chapter contains the list of references used by the author or authors of the chapter.

We believe that this book makes an important contribution to the literature on adolescent development, one perhaps not found in any other single volume. That is, to the extent that this book fulfills its two purposes, it will convey what is known about important features of adolescent development to parents, teachers, and adolescents themselves. In addition, it will be a useful reference and guide for these groups in learning of the options available to them in dealing with problems of adolescent development.

There are several people to whom we are grateful for their help in bringing this book from an initial idea to a completed volume. First and foremost, we would like to thank the authors of the chapters in this book. Their scholarship, patience, and cooperation were the key ingredients in making this book a reality. We would also like to express our appreciation to Arthur H. Stickney, Editor-in-Chief of Garland Publishing, for helping us formulate the idea for this book and for providing his invaluable expertise during the process of developing it. In addition, we are grateful to Pamela Chergotis, Editorial Assistant at Garland

Publishing, for her fine work during the production of this book. Rebecca Gorsuch, Kathie Hooven, and Joy Barger are especially deserving of our deep appreciation for their professional and most able secretarial support. The first editor is grateful also for a grant from the John D. and Catherine T. MacArthur Foundation which, in part, supported his work on this volume.

Finally, and not least of all, we thank our families and loved ones. Their devotion, encouragement, and patience throughout this project were invaluable sources of strength and support.

Richard M. Lerner
Nancy L. Galambos
University Park, PA.

1. THE ADOLESCENT EXPERIENCE: A VIEW OF THE ISSUES[1]

Richard M. Lerner and Nancy L. Galambos

For both adolescents and their parents, adolescence is a time of excitement and of anxiety, of happiness and of troubles, of discoveries and of bewilderment, of breaks with the past and yet of continuations of childhood behavior. Adolescence is a period about which much has been written, but, until relatively recently, little has been known. In short, adolescence can be a confusing time—both for the adolescent experiencing this phase of life and for the people who are observing the adolescent's progression through this phase.

Numerous characteristics of the person undergo change during adolescence. Easily visible changes include those involving the developing body and the styles of dress of the adolescent. Also visible is a change in the adolescent's social relationships. For example, the young teenager begins to spend more and more time with peers rather than with family members. Less visible alterations involve inner-biological changes such as the release of hormones into the bloodstream, and modifications in thought or "cognitions." The adolescent's emotional characteristics are also likely to take on a different character.

With all these changes occurring, in many cases quite rapidly, the adolescent begins to wonder who he or she is, and many experience what Erik Erikson has termed an "identity crisis." That is, in order to resolve the issue of identity, many adolescents

[1]The writing of this manuscript was supported in part by a grant to Richard M. Lerner from the John D. and Catherine T. MacArthur Foundation.

1

ask "Who is this person who looks so different, who feels so many different things, and who thinks so differently?" Parents, too, may begin to wonder about the individual that they have raised for so many years. "What kind of adult will my child be?" "Will these next few years be the same as our earlier years together?" Adolescence may be a time wherein some of the parent's dreams or aspirations about the child are realized, or it may be a time of disappointment.

These feelings and events are well known to parents, to teachers, and to the many writers who have romanticized or dramatized the adolescent experience in novels, short stories, or news articles. Indeed, it is commonplace to survey a newsstand and to find a magazine article describing the "stormy years" of adolescence, the new crazes or fads of youth, or the "explosion" of problems with teenagers—for instance, regarding crime or sexuality.

Yet, until the last 15 or so years, when medical, biological, and social scientists began to study intensively the adolescent period, there was relatively little sound scientific information available to verify the romantic, literary characterizations of adolescence. And, the information that did exist was not consistent with the idea that adolescence is a necessarily stormy and stressful period. For instance, many people held the stereotype that because of the supposed rebellion and close contact of adolescents with their friends, parents must be more controlling and prohibitive of their children during this time. In contrast, Albert Bandura (1964) observed that by adolescence most children had so thoroughly adopted parental values and standards that parental restrictions actually were reduced. In addition, Bandura noted that although the storm and stress idea of adolescence implies a struggle by youth to free themselves of dependence on parents, parents begin to train their children in childhood *to be independent*. Finally, Bandura found that the adolescent's choice of friends was not a major source of friction between adolescents and parents. Adolescents tended to form friendships with those who shared similar values. As such, the peers tended to support those standards of the parents that already had been adopted by the adolescents themselves.

Bandura pointed out, however, that these observations do not mean that adolescence is a stressless, problemless period of life. He was careful to note that *no* period of life is free of crisis or adjustment problems, and any period of life may present particular adjustment problems for some people and not for others. Thus, one has to be careful about attributing problems seen in one group of adolescents to all adolescents. To illustrate, in a portion of his study Bandura observed a sample of antisocial boys. Their excessive aggression did lead to their adolescence being associated with storm and stress. However, Bandura found that one could not appropriately view the problems of these boys as resulting just from adolescence. Their problem behaviors were present throughout their childhood as well. However, when the boys were physically smaller, the parents were able to control their aggressive behavior better than they could during adolescence.

From Bandura's (1964) study it may be concluded that: (1) even when storm and stress is seen in adolescence, it is not necessarily the result of events in adolescence, but instead may be associated with prior developments; and (2) storm and stress is not necessarily characteristic of the adolescent period—many possible types of adolescent development can occur. The existence of such different paths through adolescence is supported by the results of other studies.

Offer (1969) found three major routes through the adolescent period. He noted that there is a *continuous-growth* type of development. This involves smooth changes in behavior. Adolescents showing such development were not in any major conflict with their parents and did not feel that parental rearing practices were inappropriate or that parental values were not ones that they themselves did not share. Most adolescents fell into this category. Such a pattern is like the one we have seen Bandura (1964) describe. A second type of pattern is *surgent growth*. Here development involves an abrupt change. Such rapid change does not necessarily involve the turmoil associated with storm and stress. Finally, however, Offer did identify a *tumultuous-growth* type of adolescent development. Here crisis, stress, and problems characterize the period. For such adolescents, "storm and stress" aptly characterizes the nature of their change.

Thus, only for some people is the adolescent period one of storm and stress. Indeed, based on the Bandura (1964) and Offer (1969) studies, it may be assumed that such a tumultuous period is involved with only a minority of adolescents. This conclusion is bolstered by the data of Douvan and Adelson (1966). In their study, as in the previously noted studies, most adolescents shared the basic values of their parents and were satisfied with their family life and the style of treatment by their parents.

We may see then that available data are inconsistent with the stereotype that adolescence is a *generally* stressful and stormy period. But, despite these data, the stereotyped view of the tumultuous nature of adolescence prevails in several quarters (see Adelson & Doehrman, 1980). One reason that the stereotype has resisted eradication is that neither many scientists nor the public have until relatively recently paid adequate attention to what is known scientifically about adolescent development. Indeed, prior to the last 15 years the study of adolescence had been characterized by "scientific neglect" (Adelson & Doehrman, 1980), that is, by a seeming belief among scientists that little development of fundamental importance to adult life occurred during this period (Lerner, 1981). However, (1) due to the theoretical interest of scientists who study life *transitions*—that is, periods, such as adolescence, wherein the person undergoes major physical, cognitive, and social changes (Lerner, 1981); *and* (2) due to the appearance of real problems in adolescence—for example, increasing rates of adolescent drug use, pregnancy, abortion, childbearing, venereal disease, and life-damaging or fatal accidents, scientists have begun to pay increasing attention to this period of life (Adelson, 1980; Hill, in press; Lerner, 1981).

THE PLAN OF THIS BOOK

The purpose of this book is to convey to parents, to other caregivers of youth (e.g., teachers or counselors), and to adolescents themselves what is known about the major changes experienced in adolescence, what problems are involved with respect to these changes, and what can be done to help deal with and, possibly, resolve these problems. For instance, what *are* the changes in sexual feelings and behavior that characterize adolescence? Are there, in fact, problems of pregnancy and of venereal disease that have to be addressed? If so, how can parents and adolescents themselves solve these problems? Similarly, are there actual changes in adolescents' social relationships? Do they really "break ties" with their parents and relate only to other teenagers? If so, is there a "generation gap," and how can such a potential source of conflict be resolved?

In the 10 chapters that follow this one, we discuss the most significant transitions and problems of today's adolescents. In Chapter 2, Tobin-Richards, Boxer, McNeill Kavrell, and Petersen discuss the inner-physiological and outer-physical appearance changes brought on by puberty and describe the significance of these changes for personality and social development. In Chapter 3, Shea discusses the characteristics of adolescent sexuality; she describes how problems of adolescent sexuality, for example, those of inadequate contraceptive protection, pregnancy, or childbearing, can be dealt with through such programs as sex education or community-based Planned Parenthood Centers. Adolescent social relationships are discussed in Chapter 4, by Guerney and Arthur; these authors stress that while there is a change in the focus of adolescents' relationships from parents to peers, there is still little evidence that adolescents totally break their ties with their parents. Indeed, parents are still the main source of influence for issues of major significance to the adolescent (e.g., regarding future educational plans).

In Chapter 5, Burgess and Richardson discuss a growing problem in today's society—the occurrence of violent, abusive, or neglectful treatment of adolescents by their parents. They stress that such abuse and neglect takes several forms, often of a very subtle, psychological character. Another major problem among contemporary adolescents is the increasing incidence of drug and alcohol (substance) use and abuse. Vicary, in Chapter 6, discusses the nature and bases of adolescent substance use and abuse and describes different types of prevention and intervention programs that may help the adolescent to avoid substance use and abuse or to deal with it once it becomes a problem.

Although adolescents are, as a group, quite healthy, there are numerous important medical and health issues that confront them. These are discussed by Pattishall in Chapter 7. This author stresses the important psychological and social aspects of such relatively minor medical problems as acne, and notes that the major cause of death in adolescence—automobile and motorcycle accidents—has strong bases in adolescents' beliefs in their invulnerability. Beliefs of a moral and ethical nature are discussed in Chapter 8, by Kaus, Lonky, and Roodin. These authors describe moral reasoning development in adolescence and indicate how such changes may be related to problems in moral behaviors, for example, cheating and juvenile delinquency. The use of moral education to enhance moral reasoning and behavior is described and evaluated. Chapter 9, by Busch-Rossnagel, also focuses on education, but of the more general type encountered in public or private secondary schools. The author describes several functions of the school: influencing the literacy of the adolescent, effecting the socialization of the adolescent, and providing a means of social change. Particular attention is paid to the problem of school drop-outs.

"Stay in school to get a good job," is a phrase often heard by the adolescent. Vondracek and Schulenberg, in Chapter 10, discuss the development of adolescents' vocational interests and careers. These authors stress that the occupation one chooses during or immediately following adolescence represents the outcome of a long developmental process, one beginning in early childhood. Finally, in Chapter 11, Reidy and McHale discuss handicapped adolescents, and focus on three major aspects of their development: self-concept, peer relations, and sexuality. These authors discuss procedures that parents can follow in assisting their handicapped adolescent to develop adequately in these areas.

All of the chapters following this one are arranged in a similar manner in order to facilitate easy reference to the information of interest and relevance within a chapter. That is, each chapter begins with a relatively non-technical summary of what is known, on the basis of both theory and research, about the topic of that chapter (e.g., about adolescent sexuality or about adolescent social relationships). This introductory section is labeled "Issues and Findings." A second section of each chapter, "Sources of Help," provides information about the agencies, committees, and/or professional resources to which parents, teachers, or adolescents can turn in order to find help in dealing with the specific problems associated with the topic discussed in that chapter. For instance, in the Vondracek and Schulenberg chapter (Chapter 10), on "Adolescents and Careers," the authors present information about where adolescents can find help in obtaining adequate knowledge about a particular career choice, in making career decisions, and in finding a job.

A third section of each chapter, "Annotated Bibliography," includes and briefly describes a list of quite readable and useful books, pamphlets, and/or articles. This list should help interested parents, teachers, and adolescents learn more about the chapter's topic. Finally, each chapter ends with a list of the references cited in the chapter; full bibliographic citations are given so that these sources may be located by interested readers. At the end of the entire book there are two indexes; one index is of the names of people mentioned in the book, and the other is of the major concepts and topics discussed across the chapters of the book.

In sum, the characteristics of adolescent changes and of major problems in adolescence, as identified by scientific theory and research, are discussed in the following chapters. Suggestions are made about the different sources of expertise which might help parents, teachers, and adolescents deal with the problems that they share, and other reading materials that address these problems are described. In short, each succeeding chapter of this book focuses on one segment of the adolescent's experience, and describes what is known about and how one may cope with problems resulting from this feature of the person's development.

Although the chapters of this book separate adolescent development into biological, cognitive, emotional, social, and other categories, our intention is not to suggest that these are unrelated aspects of adolescence. The characteristics that mark adolescence evolve over a period of time, with some changes occurring simultaneously, and others overlapping at some point during the period. For example, the complex thinking abilities that emerge in adolescence enable the adolescent to perceive, think about, and interact with people in new and different ways. Other individuals are seen in more abstract terms, and their emotions can be better recognized by the adolescent. Clearly, the social development of adolescents is related to their cognitive development. In this manner, we can conceive of all aspects of adolescence as the ebb and flow of new and various abilities, perceptions, and feelings that comprise the adolescent's self—the self as seen by the adolescent and by significant others. Before we begin to look at specific characteristics of the adolescent's self in succeeding chapters, it will be useful to describe the general characteristics of the adolescent experience.

THE TRANSITIONS OF ADOLESCENCE: AN OVERVIEW

Adolescence may be defined as that period within the life span when most of the person's physical, psychological, and social characteristics are in a state of transition from what they were in childhood to what they will be in adulthood (Lerner & Spanier, 1980). Simply stated, adolescence is a period of life characterized by several major changes that bring the person from childhood to adulthood.

The most obvious set of changes that the adolescent goes through are anatomical and physiological ones. New hormones are being produced by the endocrine glands, glands that secrete directly into the bloodstream, and these hormones, first, produce alterations in the *primary sexual characteristics* (e.g., the genitals) and, second, lead to the emergence of secondary sexual characteristics (e.g., pubic hair begins to develop in both sexes, breasts develop in females, and pigmented facial hair develops in males). Thus, as a consequence of the new hormones, adolescents begin to look different. In addition, these hormones produce a change in the adolescent's emotional functioning. Simply, new hormones induce sexual changes and produce new drives and new feelings. In combination with changing social influences such as peer pressure and mass media that stress the role of sexuality in society, the adolescent becomes more sexually oriented.

These physical, psychological, and emotional changes are complicated by the fact that the person is also undergoing cognitive changes. New thought capabilities come to characterize the adolescent. That is, prior to adolescence the youth's thought was primarily tied to the concrete physical reality of "what is." For example, the child with a very happy home life will think that all families are happy, whereas the abused child might think the opposite; neither child may have the ability to understand other possibilities. However, the adolescent is capable of dealing with hypothetical and abstract aspects of reality, and indeed becomes focused primarily on thinking in a hypothetical, "what if. . . ?" manner. Thus, the adolescent no longer sees the way the world is organized as the only way it could be. That is, family life, the system of government, the adolescent's status in the peer group, and the rules imposed on him or her are no longer taken as concrete, immutable things. Rather, as the new thought capabilities that allow adolescents to think abstractly, hypothetically, and counterfactually come to predominate their styles of thought, those capabilities allow adolescents to imagine how things could be. These imaginings could relate to government, self, parents' rules, or what he or she will do in life. In short, anything and everything becomes the focus of an adolescent's hypothetical, counterfactual, and imaginary thinking.

For both psychological and sociological reasons, the major focus of the adolescent's concerns becomes the adolescent himself or herself. We have already noted that, psychologically, the adolescent's inner processes are all going through changes; the physical, physiological, emotional, and cognitive components of the person are undergoing major alterations. Now, with any object being able to be thought of in a new, different, hypothetical way, and with the individual so radically changing, it is appropriate for adolescents to focus on themselves to try to understand what is going on.

The person will ask: What is the nature of these changes? What will it do to me? What will I become? Am I the same person that I think I am? As all these uncertainties are being introduced, another set of problems emerges. That is, at the very time that the adolescent experiences all these concerns—at the very time that he or she may be least prepared to deal with further complications and uncertainties—others are imposed. That is, the adolescent in our society typically is asked to make a choice, a decision about what he or she is going to do when grown. Society, perhaps in the form of parents or teachers, asks the adolescent to choose a role.

Thus, as soon as the young adolescent enters junior high or high school, he or she may be asked to choose between a college preparatory or a vocational program. Thus, at about the age of 13 or so, adolescents embark on a path that will affect their lives years and years later.

The expectations that are placed on youth at this age are, in part, a response to the outward changes taking place. The young adolescent appears to be on the brink of adulthood, at least physically. And the cognitive and emotional maturity that becomes gradually more visible, encourages others to look upon the adolescent as an adult-like figure. Thus, we see that just as the adolescent is influenced by parents, peers, teachers, and society, the reverse is also true—that is, the adolescent influences the ways in which others react to him or her. Because of this relationship between society and the adolescent, with society pressing for new behaviors as the adolescent adjusts to changes within and without, it may be very difficult for the adolescent to cope.

Precisely at the time in life when individuals may be least ready to make a long-term choice, they are often required to do so. In order for adolescents to commit themselves to a certain role in society and to adjust to the larger world, they must know their interests, attributes, skills, and capabilities. In short, adolescents have to know themselves, something that is not simple, considering the multiple changes that the adolescent is experiencing. The adolescent must first settle questions about his or her identity before commitment to a social role can be made successfully. When the answers to these questions are not so clear, a feeling of crisis may emerge. As we have already mentioned, Erikson (1959) labels the search for self-definition and self-identification as the *identity crisis.* Successful resolution of this crisis may take years and does not necessarily occur before the adolescent is already following one direction in life.

To summarize, the adolescent—because of the impact of all the changes converging on him or her—may enter a state of crisis and a search for self-definition. Accordingly, the adolescent moves through his or her days attempting to find a place—or role—in society. Such definition will provide a set of rules for beliefs, attitudes, and values (an "ideology") and a prescription for behaviors (a role) that will enable youth to know what they will "do with themselves" in the world. They will try to find out if they can begin to think and behave like someone who occupies a particular role (for example, a doctor, a lawyer, a nurse, or a telephone operator). This search for an ideology and a set of behaviors that match the adolescent's own preferences and that also fulfill a particular role is really a search for the adolescent's "goodness-of-fit" with society.

Often, the adolescent's search for a place in society develops over time and involves testing various possible roles and/or belief systems. To an adult viewing the adolescent's search, the youth may seem lost, maladjusted, or even a "victimizer" of society (Anthony, 1969). Indeed, for some adolescents the crisis of identity involves experimentation with non-traditional life styles, with drugs and alcohol, or with roles that neither they nor their parents believe are ultimately best suited for them. For even fewer adolescents the identity crisis results in the adoption of a "negative identity," that is, a delinquent or an antisocial role (Erikson, 1959). However, most youths, by the time they pass through their adolescent years, have found a place in society (Lerner & Spanier, 1980); they know who they are and what they believe in; and they have begun on a career path which will allow them to make a productive contribution to their society.

CONCLUSIONS: MAJOR FEATURES OF THE ADOLESCENT TRANSITION

What do the general features of the adolescent transition experience imply for the ways in which we should think about adolescents? First, there are several aspects, several dimensions, of this period that have to be kept in mind in order to understand adolescents. Changes occur in biological, cognitive, psychological, and social realms, and these multiple changes have many implications.

Second, the reason that all these aspects must be remembered is that one type of change may be related to others. For instance, changes in the adolescent's body influence his or her personality (see Tobin-Richards, Boxer, McNeill Kavrell, & Petersen, Chapter 2) *and*, at the same time, the adolescent's personality and thought processes affect the likelihood of encountering situations which affect the adolescent physically. As an example of the former, both males and females may have a more negative or positive self-concept, depending upon the age of onset and the duration of puberty. Also, physical changes lead to sexual feelings that may influence interactions with the opposite sex. As an example of the latter, new cognitions that are characteristic of adolescents may result in beliefs that nothing can happen to them and that they are special or invulnerable. Such thoughts may be responsible for high rates of pregnancy, illness, venereal disease, or auto accidents (see Pattishall, Chapter 7). It must be understood then that there is not a one-way influence from physical change to personality, or vice versa. Instead, the various changes that we have mentioned as occurring within the adolescent are related to each other and, together, influence reactions from the environment. Those reactions then feed back to the adolescent to produce further changes in him or her.

A third important feature of adolescence to remember is that adolescents develop in a social context, one comprised of family members, peers, teachers, and counselors. Not only do these people influence the adolescent, but, at the same time, the adolescent affects them. For example, the religious and educational values and beliefs of the parents influence those of the adolescent, but, in turn, adolescents often bring home new ideas, behaviors, and perspectives that parents evaluate and may adopt (see Guerney & Arthur, Chapter 4).

Fourth, adolescence is not an isolated period within the life span. Events in childhood may influence the nature of the adolescent's transition experience. For example, parents' use of drugs and alcohol when the adolescent was a child may increase the likelihood that the individual will later use drugs and alcohol during his or her adolescence (see Vicary, Chapter 6). Likewise, the child-rearing practices of parents throughout his childhood will influence how successful the adolescent is in coping with the demands and pressures of this life stage (Bandura, 1964; Guerney & Arthur, Chapter 4). In turn, events which occur during one's adolescence—having a child during one's adolescence (see Shea, Chapter 3), choosing one or another particular career (see Vondracek & Schulenberg, Chapter 10), coping with a handicap (see Reidy & McHale, Chapter 11), or dropping out of school (see Busch-Rossnagel, Chapter 9)—will affect the nature of the person's life well into, and possibly entirely across, adulthood. This is also shown when one considers the future of abused adolescents (see Burgess & Richardson, Chapter 5) or adolescents who begin a life course that reflects values, behaviors, and beliefs that are not accepted by society as a whole (see Kaus, Lonky, & Roodin, Chapter 8).

In sum, adolescence is a dynamic and complex time of life—one affecting the people with whom the adolescent interacts, and one shaping adolescents themselves as they move beyond this period and into their adult years. Because of the contemporaneous and long-term importance of adolescence, then, it is quite important for the adolescent and for those who deal with him or her to learn: What is known about the nature of the changes comprising this period? What problems can occur as development through adolescence proceeds? And what can be done to deal with, and perhaps solve, these problems? These are the questions we address in the succeeding chapters of this book.

ANNOTATED REFERENCES

Adelson, J. (Ed.). *Handbook of Adolescent Psychology.* New York: Wiley, 1980.

This book is the first handbook specifically devoted to adolescence. It summarizes the major theoretical and empirical contributions to each of the several facets of adolescent development.

Conger, J. J., and Petersen, A. C. *Adolescence and Youth.* 3rd ed. New York: Harper & Row, 1984.

This textbook is a scientifically sophisticated yet readable account of theory and research about adolescence.

Douvan, E., & Adelson, J. *The Adolescent Experience.* New York: Wiley, 1966.

This book describes a major study of adolescent development, and contains considerable information about the nature of adolescent-parent relations. This information suggests that for most adolescents there is little friction between them and their parents.

Johnson, M. (Ed.). *Toward Adolescence: The Middle School Years.* Chicago: University of Chicago Press, 1980.

This book focuses essentially on the early adolescent period (about years 10 to 15), and presents chapters by researchers and practitioners about the biological, psychological, and social aspects of this period.

Lerner, R. M. "Adolescent Development: Scientific Study in the 1980s." *Youth and Society,* 1981, *12,* 251–275.

This article summarizes the nature of, and probable bases for, the surge of interest in the study of adolescence which has characterized the last 15 or so years. In addition, the article contains projections about the directions further theory and research will take.

Lerner, R. M., & Spanier, G. B. *Adolescent Development: A Life-span Perspective.* New York: McGraw-Hill, 1980.

This is another scientifically sophisticated textbook about adolescent development. The authors pay particular attention to the relations between the adolescent and his or her social context. The childhood antecedents and adulthood consequences of adolescence are emphasized.

Lipsitz, J. *Growing Up Forgotten: A Review of Research and Programs Concerning Early Adolescence.* Lexington, MA: D. C. Heath, 1977.

In this important book, the author indicates that little scientific or professional attention had been paid to the particular problems of early adolescence. She argues for the importance of studying this period of life, both for scientific and practical reasons.

REFERENCES

Adelson, J. (Ed.). *Handbook of Adolescent Psychology.* New York: Wiley, 1980.

Adelson, J., & Doehrman, M. J. "The Psychodynamic Approach to Adolescence." In J. Adelson (Ed.), *Handbook of Adolescent Psychology.* New York: Wiley, 1980.

Anthony, J. "The Reaction of Adults to Adolescents and Their Behavior." In G. Caplan & S. Lebovici (Eds.), *Adolescence.* New York: Basic Books, 1969.

Bandura, A. "The Stormy Decade: Fact or Fiction?" *Psychology in the School,* 1964, *1,* 224–231.

Douvan, E., & Adelson, J. *The Adolescent Experience.* New York: Wiley, 1966.

Erikson, E. H. "Identity and the Life Cycle." *Psychological Issues,* 1959, *1,* 18–164.

Hill, J. P. "Early Adolescence: A Research Agenda." *Journal of Early Adolescence*, in press.

Lerner, R. M. "Adolescent Development: Scientific Study in the 1980s." *Youth and Society*, 1981, *12*, 251–275.

Lerner, R. M., & Spanier, G. B. *Adolescent Development: A Life-span Perspective*. New York: McGraw-Hill, 1980.

Offer, D. *The Psychological World of the Teen-ager*. New York: Basic Books, 1969.

2. PUBERTY AND ITS PSYCHOLOGICAL AND SOCIAL SIGNIFICANCE[1]

Maryse H. Tobin-Richards, Andrew M. Boxer, Suzanne A. McNeill Kavrell, and Anne C. Petersen

INTRODUCTION

It is common in our society to hear the terms "adolescence" and "puberty" used interchangeably. In fact, these periods of life are quite distinct conceptually. Puberty is the process of biological change which transforms a child into a physically mature adult. Adolescence is usually thought to begin with puberty and end when the young person takes on adult roles such as work or parenting. The biological changes of puberty are typically completed long before the adolescent makes the transition into adult status in our society.

The changes during puberty occur at a dramatic rate of growth that is second only to the rate of growth of the infant. It is during puberty that a marked change in height usually occurs, along with the development of secondary sex characteristics, including facial and body hair for boys, breast development and body hair for girls, and the maturation of sexual organs for both sexes. The completion of puberty results in the attainment of full reproductive potential and adult appearance.

In our culture, we tend to attribute many adolescent behaviors to the hormonal changes occurring during puberty. In addition, we tend to regard biological processes as unchangeable and inevitable. The biological changes of puberty can, however, be

[1]Preparation of this manuscript was facilitated by National Institute of Mental Health Grant MH30252/MH38142-02 to Anne C. Petersen, Ph.D.

influenced by other factors. Several factors affect behavior during adolescence, the biological changes being only one.

One example of how sociocultural systems affect biological change is seen in the fact that the onset of puberty has begun to occur increasingly earlier since the Industrial Revolution. Evidence from research suggests that this may be a result of improved nutrition and decreases in illness, and that this trend is levelling off as people are nourished at a more optimal level. Thus, in addition to the influence biology has on social and psychological change, biological processes themselves are subject to influence by social cultural processes. Puberty is one biological process where this is especially true.

In this chapter we shall examine the major features of pubertal change and their social-psychological dimensions as adolescents experience them. One's identity as a male or female is thought to be linked to the biological, psychological, and social transformations of puberty; therefore we shall also consider sex role identity during early adolescence and the ways in which puberty may affect the development of sex roles. Following this are an overview of problems relevant to puberty and a brief annotated bibliography for those wishing to learn more about the topics addressed in this chapter.

FEATURES OF PUBESCENT CHANGE
Internal Hormonal Changes

Designated by a set of physical changes, puberty is actually the culmination of a lengthy and complex maturational process which begins before birth (Petersen & Taylor, 1980). In particular, the hormonal systems that mature during puberty are established by birth but then are suppressed for several years. In comparison to other biological changes which occur over the life cycle, the changes during the period we consider puberty are dramatic in both rate and magnitude. As noted earlier, the rate of growth and development occurring during puberty is second only to that which occurs in infancy. A major difference is that infants have little awareness of their changes while adolescents are usually acutely aware of the changes they are experiencing.

In general, the most observable changes of puberty emerge over four years, and begin and end approximately two years earlier for girls than for boys. However, female development does not suddenly accelerate two years ahead of boys during adolescence. Girls are born with slightly more mature skeletons and nervous systems and slowly increase their developmental lead through the years of childhood, so that girls enter puberty with a more mature skeleton than that of boys entering puberty (Hagg & Taranger, 1982).

The physiological mechanisms responsible for pubertal development involve the hormone system. Hormones are powerful and highly specialized chemical substances which affect the metabolic activity of cells and produce growth, differentiation, or changes in the activity of cells (Baird, 1972). Secreted by endocrine glands, hormones are carried through the body in the bloodstream to various cells in the body called receptor cells, which differentially receive the hormonal "message" and act on it. Thus, the receptor cells, for example, the cells which control hair production will respond differently according to the type of hormone and type of cell (such as on the head or under the arms).

During puberty the levels of particular hormones increase sharply, setting into motion the growth of secondary sex characteristics and the increases in body size. Although these physically apparent changes are dramatic, the underlying hormonal process itself is very gradual and lasts much longer, starting between the ages of five and eight years in both sexes (Brook, 1981). The hormonal systems were established prenatally but become activated with puberty through a process not yet completely understood. Some investigators believe that the system is suppressed to maintain low levels of hormones during childhood (Grumbach, Roth, Kaplan, & Kelch, 1974). With puberty, the suppression is gradually released, and hormones in the brain stimulate the production of gonadal hormones such as testosterone in the testes and estrogen in the ovaries (Petersen & Taylor, 1980; Tanner, 1971). It has also been observed that reaching a critical "metabolic level" or fat-to-lean ratio, roughly represented by weight, appears to be correlated with the beginning of puberty in both boys and girls (Frisch, 1980a, 1980b, 1983; Frisch & McArthur, 1974; Frisch, Wyshak, & Vincent, 1980).

Levels of several kinds of two major classes of hormones—androgens and estrogens—as well as other hormones, increase during puberty. Estrogens are responsible for the development of breasts and female genitals, while androgens influence the growth of body hair and male genitals. Although these hormones are produced by both boys and girls, higher levels of estrogens are present in girls and higher levels of androgens are found in boys.

External Physical Changes

The physical changes of puberty have been divided into stages by the pediatrician J. Tanner (1962, 1974). These are illustrated in Figure 1. For each characteristic, the developmental changes typically occur in the same order for every individual. The major changes of puberty include dramatic growth (usually enough to be considered a spurt) in height and weight, growth of pubic and axillary (underarm) hair, facial hair on boys, breasts on girls, and genital development in both boys and girls. Parallel growth in muscle, both on limbs and internal organs such as the heart, also occurs at this time. Other changes during puberty include voice deepening, acne and other skin eruptions, and the development of sebaceous (oily) and apocrine (sweat) glands, the latter producing a body odor not present before puberty. Skin changes result, in part, from the activity of androgen and can occur in both males and females.

Certain physical sex differences emerge and others are enhanced during puberty. After the adolescent growth spurt, boys are taller and heavier than girls, an outcome due primarily to the earlier onset of puberty in girls. The prepubertal, or childhood, growth period involves especially the growth of the long bones in the arms and legs. An earlier puberty terminates this sort of growth sooner. Boys, on the average, grow for two more years than girls before they begin the adolescent growth spurt. This results in shorter stature for girls by the conclusion of the growth spurt. Although the amount of growth which occurs during puberty is

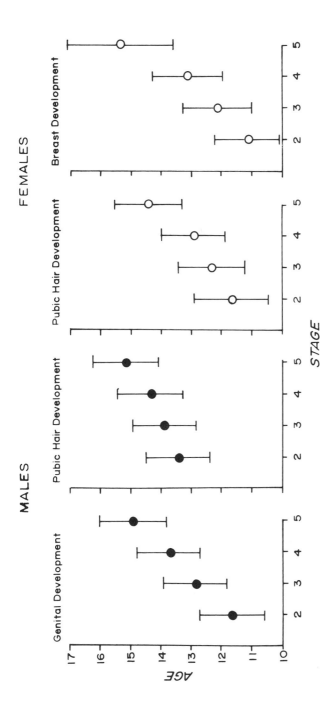

Figure 1. Tanner stages of secondary sex characteristics for males and females. (Reproduced with permission from Petersen and Taylor, 1980.)

21

somewhat greater for boys than girls, most of the sex difference in adult height is caused by longer prepubertal growth (Bock, Wainer, Petersen, Thissen, Murray, & Roche, 1973; Hagg & Taranger, 1982). Although some hormones which control the adolescent growth spurt are different from those that control growth attained prepubertally, the amount of height added during the growth spurt is highly related to the amount of growth attained prior to it (Tanner, 1974). Someone who is tall prior to puberty will generally, though not always, be tall after it.

In addition to the sex difference in height, a sex difference in the ratio of muscle to fat develops with puberty. At the conclusion of puberty boys generally have greater strength and musculature. Succumbing to the strong socioculture pressures to cease what is considered to be masculine activity, girls tend to exercise less, especially from puberty onwards. This may contribute to the sex difference in strength. Recent cross-cultural research has shown that when girls are engaged in strenuous and vigorous exercise throughout childhood, they develop a magnitude of strength similar to boys in our culture (Buchbinder, 1976). Although many of the physical sex differences are due to the differential levels of hormones active in male and female bodies, this provides another example where culture appears to affect biology and modify development in critical ways. Body shape also changes during puberty, with girls developing broader hips and boys broader shoulders (Faust, 1977; Petersen, 1979). Finally, sex differences in degree of body hair emerge with boys generally becoming more hairy than girls (Petersen & Taylor, 1980).

Timing of Changes

As noted above, specific changes occur during puberty and the nature of changes for each characteristic follows a typical sequence. In a small number of individuals a step may be skipped or sometimes, when there is serious illness during puberty, an individual may return to an earlier stage of development. In addition to the typical sequence for each characteristic, there also are typical patterns of timing between characteristics. Figure 2 shows the average length of time for each of these changes and average age when they occur.

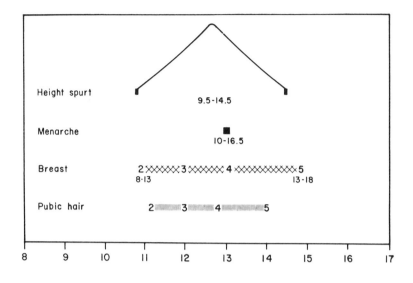

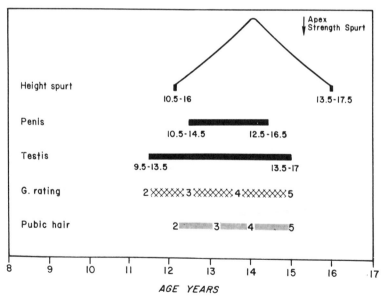

Figure 2. Schematic sequence of events at puberty for an average girl (upper) and boy (lower). The range of ages within which each event may begin and end is given by the numbers placed directly below the start and end of each bar. (Reproduced with permission from Tanner, 1974.)

For girls, beginning breast development is one of the first signs of puberty with the onset of menstruation (menarche) occurring later in the pubertal sequence. Two of the earlier visible changes are the appearance of pubic hair and growth spurt; further development of both of these characteristics continues across the pubertal phase. For boys, pubic hair growth and penis growth frequently initiate the visible pubertal changes. Then axillary hair appears and pubic hair is advanced, while voice change and facial hair generally occur somewhat later (Brook, 1981; Petersen & Taylor, 1980).

In contrast to these normative patterns for both boys and girls, the timing of each physical characteristic relative to the others can vary considerably from individual to individual. For example, it is not unusual for body hair to be developing at the same time and rate as breasts in one girl, while in another, body hair may be developing at a much faster pace than breasts and be almost completed at the same time that breast development continues for an additional year or two. Similar examples could be given for boys. There is a great deal of variation which occurs from one individual to another, something not reflected when one just refers to age averages for these developments.

Not only does the timing of the individual pubertal changes vary, but the timing of the whole pubertal process varies considerably from person to person and between males and females. How fast a child proceeds through puberty does not seem to be related to whether puberty is occurring early or late (Tanner, 1971). Although for girls puberty begins and ends about two years before it does for boys, timing of pubertal onset and completion varies as much as six years for both boys and girls (Hagg & Taranger, 1982). For girls, puberty normally occurs between the ages of eight and eighteen. For boys, puberty normally occurs between the ages of nine and nineteen.

Many have noted a trend for puberty to begin earlier and earlier since at least the turn of the century, and some have expressed concern as to whether this trend will stop. Both boys and girls have been affected by this gradual shift. As mentioned above, the onset of puberty may be associated with a critical "metabolic level" which appears to be roughly represented by weight. Gradually over several generations, nutrition and health care have improved. As a result, people have grown taller and heavier, coming closer to their optimal genetic potentials. The improvement in nutrition and health seem to be the main cause of the earlier pubertal onset, since children now reach this critical metabolic level earlier than in previous periods of history. Given an adequate environment, including such aspects as sufficient nutrition, good medical care, and generally good health, people will grow only as tall as they are genetically programmed to grow. Nutrition and health status for many in America today has reached this level; therefore, both final height attained and the timing of pubertal onset are no longer changing systematically.

Reproduction

A major outcome of puberty for most individuals is the biological ability to reproduce. This reproductive capacity for girls means monthly ovulation and menstruation. For boys, the capacity to reproduce requires the ability to produce sperm and ejaculate seminal fluid (Petersen & Taylor, 1980). Like other aspects of pubertal change, reproductive capacity also develops gradually rather than being a single event. For example, although menarche happens only once, the underlying hormonal and anatomical changes occur over a few years. This more gradual change is reflected initially in the sometimes irregular menstrual cycles which are generally, though not always, *anovulatory*—that is, no egg is released. A few girls, however, are fertile (*ovulatory*) with their very first menstrual cycle. Based on cross-cultural information about the average ages of boys at fatherhood, we might conclude that the onset of reproductive capacity in boys is even more gradual and occurs after the physical changes are completed (Whiting, 1982).

Reciprocal Influences Among Biological, Psychological, and Social Factors

Until recently it had been presumed that biology and psychology interact in a *unidirectional* manner, that is, with biological systems influencing psychological functions in the individual. More recently, however, research has indicated that psychological and social factors also influence biological systems. That the young adolescent is conscious of, and can attribute meaning to, pubertal change contributes to the potential for these factors' influencing biological development. Thus, not only does a child respond psychologically to biological change, but a child's psychological state may, in turn, influence the biological systems. Both the timing and the final outcome of the pubertal process can be affected by a number of social and psychological events, and consequently the time available for height growth is affected. It has been found, for example, that the onset of menarche can be delayed by maintaining a low fat-to-muscle ratio, and therefore can affect the metabolic level as described earlier. Achieved through extensive exercise (at least five hours of training per day) in combination with a restricted diet, the delay of menarche has been maintained by some serious dancers and runners (Frisch, 1980a, 1980b; Frisch, Wyshak & Vincent, 1980).

Another example of the psychological influences on biology is that under conditions of extreme stress, the menstrual cycle may be interrupted or cease completely for a time. This is frequently the case in *anorexia nervosa*, a weight-loss disorder which has been found mainly to affect middle and upper middle class girls. If anorexia nervosa starts early enough and continues long enough during important periods of growth, it approximates a state of near-starvation resulting in stunted growth (Crisp, 1969; Garfinkel & Garner, 1982). Individuals with anorexia nervosa also develop narrower hips and shoulders among other complications (Crisp, 1969). Therefore, the biological cannot be separated from the psychological or social. These biopsychosocial phenomena illustrate the complex interplay among biological, social, and psychological domains of development.

THE SOCIAL PSYCHOLOGY OF PUBERTY
Models of Psychological Adaptation to Puberty

The relationship between pubertal development and adolescent behavior can be viewed from two different perspectives which have emerged in research. The period of adolescence has often been characterized by "storm and stress," as a time when moods and emotions fluctuate wildly and uncontrollably (A. Freud, 1946, 1958; Kestenberg, 1967a, 1967b, 1968). This type of behavior and experience is frequently attributed to the direct effects of hormones on mental processes. This perspective, referred to as the "drive" or "direct-effects" model (Petersen & Taylor, 1980), may attribute more potency to direct hormonal influences on adolescents than is warranted by the available research evidence.

In direct contrast to this perspective is the "mediated effects" model (Petersen & Taylor, 1980), which views adolescent behavior as the result of people's perceptions of and reactions to adolescents, and the attitudes adolescents develop regarding puberty as a result of expectations and responses of these others around them. This perspective, then, attributes behavioral changes more to social psychological processes than to the direct result of hormones and biological drives. Factors such as gender, social class, ethnic group, and parents' experiences of their own adolescence may serve to modify or mediate the psychological and social meanings of puberty. The "social control" perspective is one example of a "mediated effects" model (Miller & Simon, 1980). With this perspective, cultural norms such as those about adolescents' sexual behavior are viewed as especially important as adolescents come to internalize particular ideas and attitudes about how they should act and what others expect from them.

There is a growing literature which highlights the importance of viewing adolescent development within a complex *ecological context*, the term given to the total environment important to adolescents (see, for example, Simmons, Blyth, Van Cleave & Bush, 1979). This context includes various media, such as television, film, and radio. The *social milieu*, a primary aspect of the ecological context, is composed of many institutions, including the school as well as the family. During puberty, adolescents compare themselves to their peers with regard to the changes occurring in their bodies, and this comparison frequently takes place in school. At the same time, they share various conceptions of age-appropriate behavior, regardless of how mature they are biologically. One aspect of ecological context, grade level in school, has been found to be important, often more important than pubertal status, in predicting particular behaviors (Simmons,

Blyth, Carlton-Ford, & Bulcroft, 1982). In a technological society such as ours, where school plays such a major role in the lives of young adolescents, grade in school may have a stronger impact on development than physical maturation, an aspect of adolescence hardly remarked in any consistent way in our society.

Socially shared definitions of the expected course of life strongly influence the self-assessments which boys and girls make (Tobin-Richards, Boxer, & Petersen, 1983). Adolescents develop a set of expectations about their future, for example, the events and experiences which they expect to achieve. Others who are significant to adolescents, for example, parents and teachers, may begin to react differently to them as they mature, changing the socially shared definitions and expectations of the adolescents.

Concepts of Timing

The timing of puberty has been of particular interest in past research. The effects of the timing of physical maturation on the individual's psychological state of mind can be organized into three different approaches. The first approach is based on the idea that individuals internalize a set of "social clocks," involving a sense of which major life events should happen and when they should occur (Neugarten, 1969). Individuals assess themselves against this socially shared time line (Neugarten & Datan, 1973) and may feel themselves to be "on-time" or "off-time" during various periods of their lives with regard to major life events. For adolescents experiencing puberty, this timing comparison appears to be based on the importance of looking mature as well as looking like one's peers.

The second approach is based on the idea that a specific amount of time is needed to complete the development of particular psychological and cognitive functions. According to this perspective, differences between early and late pubertal developers may be a function of the time available for pre-adolescent achievements to be attained (Peskin, 1967).

A third approach proposes that the attainment of adult physical characteristics has significant meaning for adolescents, as well as the adults and peers who are significant to them. Socially shared expectations, responses, and fantasies associated with this stage of physical maturation are viewed as influencing the adolescent's social prestige, role behaviors, social adaptation, and self-concept. Thus, it is expected that an adolescent with a mature body will experience a somewhat different environment, an experience that will influence him/her psychologically in ways different from an age-peer who still appears physically child-like. As pubertal boys and girls mature physically, others in their social world may react differently to them, which then affects a change in their own self-images. The visually apparent changes of puberty have been found to influence patterns of family interaction (Hill, 1980; Lynch, 1981; Steinberg, 1981; Steinberg & Hill, 1978) and alter peer relations (Savin-Williams, 1979), particularly with regard to patterns of intimacy (Douvan & Adelson, 1966) and heterosexual behavior (Simmons, Blyth, VanCleave, & Bush, 1979).

Psychological Sex Differences

Some evidence suggests that during early adolescence, self-concept becomes more negative and less stable than during childhood or late adolescence (Jaquish & Savin-Williams, 1983; Simmons, Blyth, Van Cleave, & Bush, 1979; Simmons & Rosenberg, 1975a, 1975b). Young adolescents appear to feel less happy about themselves relative to adolescents who are younger or older. In particular, girls tend to suffer from a somewhat disturbed self-image which includes lower self-esteem, heightened self-consciousness, and greater instability of self-image. A review of the sex differences research in general reveals that during early adolescence boys start to report higher self-esteem than girls, a difference that continues into adulthood (Petersen, Tobin-Richards, & Crockett, 1982).

Similarly, feelings about the body, or body image, differ for young adolescent boys and girls, with girls seeming to feel less satisfied with their bodies at this stage of life. In the traditional female role, a girl may feel that an attractive body will enhance relationships with boys. Thus, feeling attractive may become

overly important to her. Weight has been found to become a
particularly important component of how a girl feels about her
body. A strong cultural pressure to be tall and slim may contribute
to the finding that the heavier a girl is, or the heavier she thinks
she is, the more dissatisfied she is with both her weight and figure
(Faust, 1983; Simmons, Blyth, & McKinney, 1983; Tobin-Richards,
Boxer, & Petersen, 1983). Greater weight appears to be an important aspect of the negative feelings that girls who mature earlier
experience about their bodies.

As mentioned earlier, past research in this area has been conducted largely on the timing of physical changes and the links
between timing and social psychological factors. Of particular
interest in past research were those children who were late or early
in their physical maturation relative to the maturation of their
peers. Two patterns, differentiated by sex, have emerged from
both past and current research. For boys, being an early maturer,
both in terms of objective evaluations as well as self-perceptions,
is associated with a more positive set of self-perceptions and more
positive evaluations by others. Being late in physical maturation
is associated with a poorer evaluation by the adolescent boys
themselves as well as by others (Jones, 1965; Jones & Bayley, 1950;
Mussen & Jones, 1957). The "on-time" or mid-developers fall
somewhere in between these two extreme groups in their feelings
about themselves and the attitudes others have toward them (Tobin-
Richards, Boxer, & Petersen, 1983). Therefore, maturing early for
a boy has a clear psychological and social advantage, at least
during this period. Once he is beyond adolescence, when physical
maturation has been completed, the social advantages and psychological differences appear to dissipate (Clausen, 1975; Jones,
1965).

When we look at the different physical changes occurring for
boys, the growth of facial hair appears to be one of the most
important visible pubertal changes to a young adolescent boy's
feelings about his physical self (Tobin-Richards, Boxer, & Petersen, 1983). It has been thought that increased physical size with
the accompanying heightened physical prowess might constitute
the most important element to the positive feelings and attitudes
connected with early male puberty (Mussen & Jones, 1957). The

appearance of facial hair is a visually apparent change with powerful symbolic meaning for adult physical status. Thus, the reactions from adults and peers to this physical change may stimulate a change in self-image. The overall positive associations found to occur with early physical maturation for boys may be caused by the favorable social response given to those who have attained adult male physical status. A mature male body brings with it the physical advantage of greater respect from adults, more attention from girls, and leadership roles among peers (Mussen & Jones, 1957).

For girls the picture is quite different. Being in the middle of puberty is related to more positive perceptions of self and more positive evaluations by others (Tobin-Richards, Boxer, & Petersen, 1983). Being early or late, that is, "off-time", is associated with more negative feelings and attitudes. Compared to early maturers, those girls who perceive themselves as late in their pubertal maturation feel better about themselves and are rated by others as having more advantages (Jones & Mussen, 1958; Peskin, 1973; Stolz & Stolz, 1944; Tobin-Richards, Boxer, & Petersen, 1983). Therefore, being average is best and early is worst for girls.

These findings may reflect a mixed social response to the physical maturation of girls. Becoming an adult in this society may not bring with it the same social advantages for a female as it does for a male. Traditionally devoid of several of the social advantages experienced by a similarly maturing boy, such as athletic prowess, leadership roles, and expectations of occupational success (Block, 1978), physical maturation for a girl may carry more explicit sexualized meanings and generate related social responses. This sexualized response, perhaps an unconscious one, may be enacted with restrictions on the pubertal girl's freedoms, with parents becoming concerned with protecting their daughters (Block, 1978). It has been suggested that sexual maturity is more a concern than a joy to parents (Brooks-Gunn & Matthews, 1979). Furthermore, evaluation by peers and adults may rest more on appearance for girls than for boys. As mentioned above, girls report that weight is an important aspect of their perceptions of appearance and more general feelings about themselves. As a girl is further along in puberty and perceives herself as so, she will also tend to perceive herself as heavier and be less satisfied with her weight; this reaction affects her self-image regardless of her actual weight (Tobin-Richards, Petersen, & Boxer, 1983).

There appear to be two different physical ideals for women in this culture. The first ideal, discussed above, is that of a prepubertal look, one of a svelte body, flat chest and long legs (Faust, 1983). In contrast, the second ideal is that of the full-bodied large breasted sexual look representative of the figures displayed in both popular and pornographic media. Here a more mature body is emphasized with particular focus on large breasts. A finding from our own research indicated that the meaning of breast development differs from the other pubertal changes in that the greater the development, the more positive are girls' self-perceptions. Thus, a girl with greater breast development tends to feel more positive about her physical self than a girl who is more flat chested (Tobin-Richards, Boxer, & Petersen, 1983).

The experience of menarche, or first menstruation, appears to arouse ambivalent feelings in girls. Many of these mixed feelings may be culturally determined (Brooks-Gunn & Ruble, 1983; Ruble, 1977). The greater physical maturity signified by menarche may have a positive personal impact, but the positive feelings may be reduced or diffused by a negative interpersonal significance, as girls become increasingly self-conscious, embarrassed, and secretive (Koff, Rierdan, & Jacobson, 1981). One example of the confused cultural messages (Brooks-Gunn & Ruble, 1979; Whisnant, Brett, & Zegans, 1975) are those presented through booklets distributed by sanitary products companies (Logan, 1980; Petersen, 1983). Conveying conflicting ideas about menstruation, they portray it as both a normal noninterruptive aspect of life and, because of sanitation concerns, as something to be constantly attended to and carefully concealed (Whisnant, Brett, & Zegans, 1975). We have found that most of the girls in our research investigation were both happy and frightened by menstruation (Petersen, 1983; Tobin-Richards, Boxer, & Petersen, 1983).

In an examination of the self-reports of puberty given by girls and by their parents, Petersen (1983) found that there was a high degree of agreement with regard to the onset of menarche in the self-reports of daughters with those of their mothers and fathers. The errors which did occur in the reporting of menarche were not random, but related systematically to the significance of the event for the girl. For a very small percentage of girls—all of them early maturers—menarche was an especially troublesome event which was, at least initially, denied in their self-reports of pubertal change.

The difficulty of menarche for early maturers is found consistently by the several research groups that have been studying the experience of menarche. Data from these ongoing projects indicate that earlier maturers felt far more negative about the event than later maturers and that this was related to preparedness for menarche. The better prepared the woman felt she was as a girl, the more positive her memory of the experience of menarche and the less likely she was to experience menstrual distress as an adult (Koff, Rierdan, & Sheingold, 1980; Shainess, 1961). Girls' beliefs about their mothers' menstrual distress are also significant in this regard. Girls who believe that their mothers experience menstrual distress are more likely to anticipate or report being affected by menstrual distress (Brooks-Gunn & Ruble, 1979). As discussed earlier, ambivalence seems best to describe the feelings that girls have about menarche, although some researchers find generally negative feelings and attitudes.

The first ejaculate of seminal fluid frequently is proposed as a male analog to menarche. This generally occurs about a year after the beginning of accelerated penis growth, although there is great variation in the timing of this event. Penis growth is accompanied by the development of seminal vesicles, the prostate, and the bulbourethral glands. Ejaculations during sleep, the so-called "wet dreams" or nocturnal emissions, also occur during this time. In addition, because of high and fluctuating levels of hormones, the occurrence of spontaneous erections may become more frequent. Preadolescent erections often occur in response to a whole array of physical and emotional situations, both sexual and nonsexual in nature. During puberty males begin to respond to physical or psychological stimulation that is culturally defined as sexual. The physiological capacity for erections takes on sexual meanings through both biological changes and experience or learning (Gagnon & Simon, 1973).

First ejaculation is a normative event, but it is one of those events which are hidden (Brim & Ryff, 1980) and most often only discussed among boys in general terms, if at all. While considerable research has been conducted on the event of menarche, little research has investigated the feelings and experiences of pubertal males' first ejaculation. Although first ejaculation may be considered an event comparable to menarche in its implications for reproductive potential, its link to sexual pleasure and functioning is more direct than that of menarche. Indeed, puberty and related issues are often equated with sexuality by adults. Researchers may be reluctant to investigate this topic as well, particularly since it is viewed as such a personal event. Thus, while first ejaculation is a normative event, the sexual meaning associated with it may make investigators reluctant to examine this topic.

The timing of first ejaculation may be quite important to boys, as this event appears to signify an important marker of one's status as a male. For most boys, first ejaculation is associated with some level of orgasmic pleasure, although it is possible to have an ejaculation without orgasm. While many boys may have been prepared for the event through health or sex education courses, the actual experience may stir numerous feelings and fantasies. Although boys talk among themselves about the development of their bodies or their sexual fantasies, they may actually share little information about the personal significance of the first ejaculation or the feelings and thoughts which may result from it.

Although young adolescents can accurately describe the physical changes occurring in their bodies, they have difficulty articulating their feelings about puberty. It becomes clear that a major determinant of the experience of puberty is its social-psychological significance, both to adolescents and to others. Cultural definitions of what is desirable and expectable play an important part in mediating the psychological experience of puberty (see Petersen & Taylor, 1980). For example, for girls one of the most valued aspects of their bodies is facial features (including skin and hair) (Tobin-Richards, Boxer, & Petersen, 1983). For boys, athletic-related strengths and abilities are most frequently valued. For psychological meaning, the growth spurt appears to be a more important aspect of puberty for boys than for girls. For girls, menarche appears to be a more salient pubertal event than the growth spurt.

Puberty is commonly believed to have a powerful role in adolescents' behavior. Whether and how this is actually the case can only be answered by further research. What is clear is that puberty culminates in a dramatic and visually apparent set of changes and that the social and psychological meanings of these changes are important components to understanding the significance of puberty for adolescents and their behavior.

PUBERTY AND SEX ROLES

Many have noted that there are no other distinctions made in society which are as great as the distinction made between male and female. As such, the development and internalization of a sense of oneself as being either male or female is considered crucial to self-concept and identity formation (Kagan, 1964). The description and categorization of individuals as either male or female has particular salience and evokes culturally shared distinctions and expectations, commonly expressed in terms of sex role stereotypes.

The term "sex role" is often employed to identify those stereotypes of behavior and personality characteristics thought to distinguish one sex from the other. More carefully defined, however, sex role denotes behaviors and activities considered appropriate and desirable by society for one sex or the other (Bem, 1974; Katz, 1979; Worell, 1981).

Sex role identity is the degree to which individuals regard themselves as being masculine or feminine and is one component of self-concept (Kagan, 1964). Masculine and feminine identities are defined in terms of qualities considered to be characteristic of males and females (Block, 1973) and are manifested in socially defined sex-appropriate traits, attitudes, and interests (Pleck, 1982). For example, individuals who have a feminine sex role identity experience themselves as possessing attributes which are typically considered to be appropriate for females in our society. Although sex role identity is certainly a psychological construct involving the experience and perception of self, it is embedded within the social context with attendant norms and expectations.

Recent research has demonstrated that masculinity and femininity do not represent opposite ends of a continuum (Bem, 1974; Constantinople, 1973; Spence & Helmreich, 1978). Instead, an individual's sex role identity may contain both masculine and feminine components, a combination which has been labelled "psychological androgyny" (Bem, 1974; Block, 1973; Rebecca, Hefner, & Oleshansky, 1976). The social context plays an important part in sex role identity. Not only does society hold stereotypes as models for what boys and girls should be like, but it also sex-types tasks, skills, and other behaviors as being appropriate for one sex or the other and thus channels behaviors of individuals in those directions (Parsons, 1942). Proscriptions (what one ought *not* do) and prescriptions (what one ought to do) regarding what it means to be male or female are embodied in culturally approved sex role standards, (Kagan, 1964). Sex role identity represents the internalization or assimilation by the individual of these societal attitudes and values.

Differences in male and female psychological development are often conceptualized in terms of an *instrumental versus expressive* dichotomy (Parsons & Bales, 1955). This construct associates masculinity with independence and goal directedness (instrumentality), and femininity with emotional awareness and concern for others (expressiveness). While male status and identity derive from individual qualities and achievements, those of females reside primarily in relationships with others. Research support has been obtained for the salience of the instrumental-expressive distinction in terms of characteristics considered socially desirable in males and females (Bem, 1974; Spence, Helmreich, & Stapp, 1975).

With the introduction of new tasks and demands, sex roles and sex role identity differ across the life course. Therefore, the development of sex role identity and acquisition of sex role behavior begins in infancy and continues throughout life, with both the content of sex roles and sources of influence on them varying at different points of life. Distinctive tasks have salience during different periods of life; adaptation to these tasks may involve change in sex role identity and behavior.

With the transition into early adolescence, the physical distinctions between the sexes become heightened in importance (Brooks-Gunn & Matthews, 1979). As a result of pubertal maturation, developing individuals change dramatically in appearance and hence are perceived and responded to differently by others as well as self. With the development of more adult-like bodies, young adolescents are often expected to behave in accordance with roles they presumably will occupy in adulthood. It is hypothesized that gender-related role expectations intensify during early adolescence and greater emphasis is focused by others on societal proscriptions and prescriptions for appropriate sex-typed behavior (Hill & Lynch, 1983). The new importance of societal expectations and sex typing during this period of rapid biological change has implications for the young adolescent's identity as a male or a female. The emergence of newly expanded cognitive capacities, e.g., self-reflection (Inhelder & Piaget, 1958) enables the adolescent to evaluate who he or she is in a more abstract manner, incorporating culturally defined sex role expectations. Given the multitude of changes occurring during this time of the life course, developmental change in definition and experience of self would be expected.

Katz (1979) has identified early adolescence, with the onset of physiological maturity, as being a time during which dramatic alterations in sex role identity may occur. "Both the physiological and psychological aspects of sexual maturity render much of the previously acquired child sex role obsolete" (Katz, 1979, p. 168). According to this model, the central tasks for girls are: adjustment to menstruation, adjustment to primary and secondary body changes, adjustment to sexual feelings, and a concern with physical attractiveness. For early maturing boys who are experiencing puberty at this time, the tasks are: adjustment to the ability to ejaculate, adjustment to sexual body changes, adjustment to sexual feelings, and although less than girls, concern with physical attractiveness. Prompted by the physiological changes of puberty, the young adolescent focuses on preparation for adult sex roles through the acquisition of concepts regarding appropriate behavior as a potential adult male or female.

The psychological importance of pubertal development for young adolescents is demonstrated by their increased concern about and preoccupation with their changing bodies (Hamburg, 1974). In addition, with the onset of puberty there is an increased tendency to compare onself with culturally defined standards of the "ideal" masculine or feminine body (Brooks-Gunn & Mat-

thews, 1979; McCandless & Coop, 1979; Schonfeld, 1969). Among
both boys and girls, physical attractiveness and self-concept are
significantly related but with the relationship somewhat stronger
for females (Lerner & Karabenick, 1974; Lerner, Karabenick, &
Stuart, 1973). In general, physical appearance becomes more important to girls than boys at this time, and is an important factor
in feminine identity (Bardwick, 1971; Bardwick & Douvan, 1971).

As discussed earlier, considerable research has indicated that
puberty is experienced in different ways by boys and girls and that
the timing of the biological changes does not elicit the same
response in the two sexes (Jones & Mussen, 1958; Mussen & Jones,
1957; Tobin-Richards, Boxer, & Petersen, 1983). While for boys
puberty is an unambiguously positive process, the same does not
hold for girls. Physical maturation in the young adolescent male
brings greater strength, height, and athletic ability, all of which
enhance his standing among both peers and adults. These changes
imply potency and mastery, which are important components of
masculine self-concept (Block, 1979). In addition, they bring the
boy closer to the greater status accorded the adult male in our
society. In contrast, puberty is an ambiguous event for adolescent
girls and is experienced with ambivalence. Although the transition from childhood that accompanies puberty is generally welcomed (Douvan, 1970), the divergence of sex role expectations
becomes more pronounced and female behavior becomes subject
to greater proscriptions (Shepard-Look, 1982).

During adolescence the peer group acts as a socializing agent
by endorsing values which provide guidelines for behavior (Weitz,
1977). Conformity to peer pressure peaks during early adolescence
(Coleman, 1977; Costanzo, 1970; Costanzo & Shaw, 1966), and
conformance rather than independence is the predominant achievement style among girls at this age (Kavrell, 1980). Given the
strong pressures to conform, in particular the strong pressure to
conform to sex role stereotypes, there may be little room for
individual variability. Where variability may exist, it is within
sex appropriate activities or interests. Given the importance of
social desirability and positive responses of others to young
adolescent girls (Bardwick, 1971; Bardwick & Douvan, 1971), de-
viation from stereotypic expectations may be problematic.

SOURCES OF HELP

Adolescents may commonly experience a number of concerns with their changing bodies. These are often normal responses to physical changes, and the accompanying feelings which are elicited may result from confusion or fear with regard to these transformations.

Puberty is marked by rapid physical changes which vary in their timing from individual to individual. Additionally, the outcome of puberty, the adult body, varies from individual to individual. This set of events stimulates an important concern for many adolescents: Am I normal? At the same time the physical changes of puberty stimulate similar questions in the adults involved with young adolescents: Are the changes (or lack of changes) I see in this adolescent a normal part of puberty? For example, during puberty male breasts undergo changes, most of which are temporary. In some boys there is a distinct enlargement of the breasts, sometimes only one breast, about midway through adolescence. This is termed *gynecomastia* and usually reverses itself after about one year (Tanner, 1971). These changes can often frighten and concern boys and even their parents, particularly because they are not expected ones. For girls, the first menstrual cycle may be more irregular than later ones and sometimes accompanied by *dysmenorrhea*, the experience of pain around the time of and during menstruation. Symptoms include cramping, premenstrual tension in the form of headache, backaches, and water retention. The experience of dysmenorrhea varies considerably from individual to individual, with some people never experiencing any symptoms and others experiencing severe discomfort. Another normal concern has to do with a phase of physical awkwardness through which many young adolescents pass. They feel as though they are stumbling over their own feet and can no longer coordinate their hands and arms. Since feet, legs, hands, and arms may actually be growing at somewhat different rates, with feet usually growing first, some limbs may be unusually long or short relative to the rest of them for a period of time. This "gangliness" will pass when the rest of growth catches up.

These concerns are not at all unusual. Changes as significant as those occurring with puberty often stimulate feelings in individuals either experiencing puberty themselves or those in contact with pubertal adolescents. These responses include concerns about changes in feelings, thoughts and behaviors, as well as physical changes. Shifts in certain attitudes, beliefs, fantasies, and feelings occur in response to the physical changes. Behaviors begin to change, too, in the ways that adolescents relate to one another, and in the type and intensity of activities. Most of these shifts are normal. Intervention needs to be considered, however, if the adolescent's behaviors are destructive to themselves or others.

Although many of the worries about normality constitute a healthy part of the process of accommodating to pubertal changes, they should be addressed. There are a number of constructive solutions to these normal concerns. As a parent, educator, or service provider, find out what is available through community agencies. Discussions with experts in adolescent mental and physical health facilities can also help alleviate worries and bring greater understanding of and comfort with pubertal changes. Additionally, a number of excellent books, pamphlets, and films are available to purchase or rent. These provide facts and facilitate discussion. A selection of these materials, as well as addresses for centers which disseminate information regarding literature and films, is included below.

Many adolescents lack information about what pubertal changes involve. Research indicates that the better prepared an individual is, the more positive the experience will be. It is as important to acknowledge and discuss the *feelings* attached to the changes, or anticipated changes, as it is to communicate the facts of puberty. These feelings are influenced by a number of factors, including attitudes toward adulthood and growing up, feelings about being a girl or boy, self-esteem, anxieties about acceptability, and needs for external approval. To insure a more positive experience of puberty, information about and discussion of puberty should occur prior to the beginning of visible pubertal changes. This means that girls need information in the fourth, or no later than the fifth, grade in school. For boys, information could be provided a bit later, but once girls begin developing boys usually have lots of questions. Since many schools provide information later, or not at all, it is very important that parents be ready to discuss puberty. Such discussion is especially important for very early maturing girls, who will not be able to learn from the school or the peer group.

Pubertal changes bring about changes in family relationships. Becoming the size of one's parents probably has a great deal of influence and meaning. The ways in which a child relates to a parent, and a parent to a child, may shift. Suddenly parents and children may be bickering and arguing more than they were before. Changes in family relationships can be caused by changes in both the children and parents. There are also changes in sexuality, the obvious ones having to do with the pubertal changes of the adolescent which, in addition, and for only some parents, stimulate changes related to their feelings about aging. Puberty in children may evoke in parents memories and feelings attached to their own puberty. This re-experiencing of their early adolescence can influence the ways in which parents respond to their children's puberty. There are shifts in needs for independence and autonomy by adolescents. Young adolescents are beginning to change their roles within the family as they, for example, participate more in decision making, exert more influence, take on more responsibilities, and become more independent. Roles need to be renegotiated, and all of these changes can evoke intense feelings in family members which can cause conflict or destructive behavior if not addressed early. Coping with these changes includes trying to discuss them as a family. If these feelings are too difficult to cope with alone, a professional may be of help; for example, a counselor who specializes in early adolescence would be especially useful. The Centers listed in the annotated bibliography may be able to provide additional information.

Sex role and sex role identity may also be changing at this time. Acquiring a woman's or man's body may influence behavior and attitudes about the self which increase conformity to sex role stereotypes. This often invites constriction of options and activities, especially for girls. As family and work roles shift in our society, both men and women are expected to be more active in both spheres of family and work. Early adolescence is an important time for options to remain open. However, it is a time when they often begin to close. Interest and opportunity to enroll in various courses in school and to engage in various activities begin to narrow, restricting future options. For example, a decision by a girl not to continue with advanced mathematics, because it is something that "boys do," could preclude admission to some college programs since most schools require adequate test performance in mathematics.

For girls, early adolescence can be problematic, particularly in the ways that they feel about themselves. As discussed earlier in this chapter, self-esteem tends to become lower during this time, especially for girls. Multiple, simultaneous transitions appear to contribute to these negative feelings in young female adolescents. When, for example, a girl experiences a move from one school to another, begins to menstruate, and begins to date, all in one year, she may feel overwhelmed and less comfortable with herself. These stresses may combine with another problem recently apparent in our culture: eating disorders and concerns with weight. A healthy aspect of puberty is increased fat and weight gain for girls. Unfortunately, this increase in weight is inconsistent with cultural standards of beauty which emphasize thinness. It is important for adults and adolescents to realize that a gain in weight and fat with puberty is natural and healthy.

Major mental and physical health problems are addressed in other chapters. Additionally, the Centers listed below, as well as the books listed in the Annotated References of this chapter, provide information about more severe problems, including topics such as suicide, drug abuse, and venereal disease.

Centers

Center for Adolescent Mental Health. The George Warren Brown School of Social Work. Washington University, St. Louis, Campus Box 1196, St. Louis, Missouri 63130 (314)889-5824.

The main functions of this Center are to gather, synthesize, and disseminate scientifically based information regarding adolescent mental health to a broad range of consumers, including researchers, practitioners, legislators, and the lay public. Among the services offered, the center prepares and distributes a series which reviews the current knowledge about particular areas of interest with regard to adolescent mental health. This is done in such a way as to be of particular use to practitioners and lay people who are interested in mental health services for adolescents. Additionally, the center prepares a series of books that teach children how to cope with key problems that can affect adolescent mental health.

The Center for Early Adolescence. Department of Maternal and Child Health, School of Public Health, University of North Carolina at Chapel Hill, Suite 223, Carr Mill Mall, Carrboro, North Carolina 27510, (919)996-1148.

This center has created a network of national and local organizations to improve services to young adolescents. It serves as a clearing house for information on this age group, develops and sponsors continuing education for professionals and volunteers working with young adolescents, and maintains a pool of consultants to assist agencies and institutions with specific planning and programming requests.

ANNOTATED REFERENCES

Bell, R. *Changing Bodies, Changing Lives: A Book for Teens on Sex and Relationships.* New York: Random House, 1981.

Developed by the authors of *Our Bodies, Ourselves,* this book provides adolescents with accurate and helpful information about physical development, relationships, sex, and emotional health. Its thoughtful and healthy approach encourages teenagers to consider options carefully and to act responsibly.

Brooks-Gunn, J., & Matthews, W. S. *He and She: How Children Develop Their Sex-Role Identity.* Englewood Cliffs, NJ: Prentice-Hall, Inc., 1979.

This book provides a lucid examination of biological, psychological and social factors involved in the development of sex roles up to adulthood. In particular, chapters focusing on pubescence and adolescence offer discussions of the ways in which perceptions of maleness and femaleness are affected by the developmental tasks which are characteristic of those phases of the life cycle.

Gardner-Loulan, J., Lopez, B., & Quackenbush, M. *Period.* San Francisco, CA: New Glide Publications.

Written in a warm, appealing style, this book answers young women's typical concerns about menstruation. It also deals with topics such as excess hair and weight.

Gordon, S., & Conant, R. *You: The Psychology of Enhancing Your Social Life, Love Life, School Life, Work Life, Home Life, Emotional Life, Creative Life, Spiritual Life, Style of Life.* New York: The New York Times Book Co., A Strawberry Hill Book, 1975.

A creatively designed and organized book that helps the teenager to think about and understand him or herself as a whole person. It contains information about how to cope with mental health, sexuality, growing up, and relationships.

REFERENCES

Baird, D. T. "Reproductive Hormones." In C. R. Austin & R. V. Short (Eds.), *Reproduction in Mammals, Book 3: Hormones in Reproduction.* New York and Cambridge: Cambridge University Press, 1972, pp. 1–28.

Bardwick, J. M. *Psychology of Women: A Study of Bio-cultural Conflicts.* New York: Harper & Row, Publishers, 1971.

Bardwick, J. M., & Douvan, E. "Ambivalence: The Socialization of Women." In V. Gornick & B. K. Moran (Eds.), *Women in Sexist Society.* New York: Basic Books, Inc., 1971.

Bem, S. L. "The Measurement of Psychological Androgyny." *Journal of Consulting and Clinical Psychology,* 1974, *42,* 155–162.

Block, J. H. "Conceptions of Sex-roles: Some Cross-cultural and Longitudinal Perspectives." *American Psychologist,* 1973, *28,* 512–526.

Block, J. H. "Another Look at Sex Differentiation in the Socialization Behaviors of Mothers and Fathers." In J. Sherman & F. Denmark (Eds.), *Psychology of Women: Future Directions of Research.* New York: Psychological Dimensions, 1978.

Block, J. H. "Personality Development in Males and Females: The Influence of Differential Socialization." Based on paper presented in the Master Lecture Series, American Psychological Association annual meeting, New York, September 1979.

Bock, R. D., Wainer, H., Petersen, A. C., Thissen, D., Murray, J. S., & Roche, A. F. "A Parameterization of Human Growth Curves." *Human Biology,* 1973, *45,* 63–80.

Brim, O. G., Jr., & Ryff, C. "On the Properties of Life Events." In P. Baltes & O. G. Brim, Jr. (Eds.), *Life-span Development and Behavior. Vol. III.* New York: Academic Press, 1980.

Brook, C. G. "Endocrinological Control of Growth at Puberty." *British Medical Bulletin,* 1981, *37,* 281–285.

Brooks-Gunn, J., & Matthews, W. S. *He and She.* Englewood Cliffs, N.J.: Prentice-Hall, Inc., 1979.

Brooks-Gunn, J., & Ruble, D. N. "The Social and Psychological Meaning of Menarche." Presented at the Society for Research in Child Development Meeting, San Francisco: March 1979 in a symposium on the Psychological Correlates of Puberty.

Brooks-Gunn, J., & Ruble, D. N. "The Experience of Menarche from a Developmental Perspective." In J. Brooks-Gunn & A. C. Petersen (Eds.), *Girls at Puberty: Biological, Psychological and Social Perspectives.* New York: Plenum Press, 1983.

Buchbinder, G. *Man and Woman in the New Guinea Highlands.* Washington, D.C.: American Anthropological Association, 1976.

Clausen, J. A. "The Social Meaning of Differential Physical and Sexual Maturation." In S. E. Dragastin & G. H. Elder, Jr. (Eds.), *Adolescence in the Life Cycle: Psychological Change and Social Context.* New York: John Wiley & Sons, 1975.

Coleman, J. C. "Current Contradictions in Adolescent Theory." *Journal of Youth and Adolescence,* 1977, *7,* 1–11.

Constantinople, A. "Masculinity-Femininity: An Exception to a Famous Dictum?" *Psychological Bulletin,* 1973, *80,* 389–407.

Costanzo, P. R. "Conformity Development as a Function of Self-blame." *Journal of Personality and Social Psychology,* 1970, *14,* 366–374.

Costanzo, P. R., & Shaw, M. E. "Conformity as a Function of Age Level." *Child Development,* 1966, *37,* 967–975.

Crisp, A. H. "Some Skeletal Measurements in Patients with Primary Anorexia Nervosa." *Journal of Psychosomatic Research,* 1969, *13,* 125–142.

Douvan, E. "New Sources of Conflict in Females at Adolescence and Early Adulthood." In J. Bardwick, E. Douvan, M. Horner, & D. Gutman (Eds.), *Feminine Personality and Conflict.* Belmont: Brooks/Cole Publishing Co., 1970.

Douvan, E., & Adelson, J. *The Adolescent Experience.* New York: John Wiley & Sons, 1966.

Faust, M. S. "Somatic Development of Adolescent Girls." *Monographs of the Society for Research in Child Development,* 1977, (1, Serial No. 169).

Faust, M. S. "Alternative Constructions of Adolescent Growth." In J. Brooks-Gunn & A. C. Petersen (Eds.), *Girls at Puberty: Biological, Psychological, and Social Perspectives.* New York: Plenum Press, 1983.

Freud, A. *The Ego and the Mechanisms of Defense.* New York: International Universities Press, 1946.

Freud, A. "Adolescence." *Psychoanalytic Study of the Child*, 1958, *16*, 225–278.

Frisch, R. E. "Fatness, Puberty, and Fertility." *Natural History*, 1980, *89*, 16. (a)

Frisch, R. E. "Pubertal Adipose Tissue: Is It Necessary for Normal Sexual Maturation? Evidence from the Rat and Human Female." *Federation Proceedings*, 1980, *39*, 2395–2400. (b)

Frisch, R. E. "Fatness, Menarche, and Fertility." In S. Golub (Ed.), *Menarche*. New York: D.C. Health, 1983.

Frisch, R. E., & McArthur, J. "Menstrual Cycles: Fatness as a Determinant of Minimum Weight for Height Necessary for Their Maintenance or Onset." *Science*, 1974, *195*, 949–951.

Frisch, R. E., Wyshak, G., & Vincent, L. "Delayed Menarche and Amenorrhea in Ballet Dancers." *New England Journal of Medicine*, 1980, *303*, 17–19.

Gagnon, J. H., & Simon, W. *Sexual Conduct: The Social Sources of Human Sexuality*. Chicago: Aldine Publishing Company, 1973.

Garfinkel, P. E., & Garner, D. M. *Anorexia Nervosa: A Multidimensional Perspective*. New York: Brunner/Mazel, 1982.

Grumbach, M. M., Roth, J. C., Kaplan, S. L., & Kelch, R. P. "Hypothalamic-pituitary Regulation of Puberty: Evidence and Concept Derived from Clinical Research." In M. M. Grumbach, G. D. Grave, & F. E. Mayer (Eds.), *Control of the Onset of Puberty*. New York: Wiley, 1974.

Hagg, U., & Taranger, J. "Maturation Indicators and the Pubertal Growth Spurt." *American Journal of Orthodontics*, 1982, *82*, 299–309.

Hamburg, B. "Early Adolescence: A Specific and Stressful Stage of the Life Cycle." In G. Coelho, D. A. Hamburg, & J. E. Adams (Eds.), *Coping and Adaptation*. New York: Basic Books, 1974.

Hill, J. P. "The Family." In M. Johnson (Ed.), *Toward Adolescence: The Middle School Years. The Seventy-ninth Yearbook of the National Society for the Study of Education*. Chicago: The University of Chicago Press, 1980.

Hill, J. P., & Lynch, M. E. "The Intensification of Gender-related Role Expectancies during Early Adolescence." In J. Brooks-Gunn & A. C. Petersen (Eds.), *Girls at Puberty: Biological, Psychological, and Social Perspectives*. New York: Plenum, 1983.

Inhelder, B., & Piaget, J. *The Growth of Logical Thinking from Childhood to Adolescence*. New York: Basic Books, 1958.

Jaquish, G. A., & Savin-Williams, R. C. "Biological and Ecological Factors in the Expression of Adolescent Self-esteem." *Journal of Youth and Adolescence*, 1983.

Jones, M. C. "Psychological Correlates of Somatic Development." *Child Development*, 1965, *36*, 899–911.

Jones, M. C., & Bayley, N. "Physical Maturing among Boys as Related to Behavior." *Journal of Educational Psychology*, 1950, *41*, 129–148.

Jones, M. C., & Mussen, P. H. "Self-conceptions, Motivations, and Interpersonal Attitudes of Early- and Late-maturing Girls." *Child Development*, 1958, *29*, 491–501.

Kagan, J. "Acquisition and Significance of Sex Typing and Sex Role Identity." In M. L. Hoffman & L. W. Hoffman (Eds.), *Review of Child Development Research, Vol. 1.* New York: Russell Sage, 1964.

Katz, P. "The Development of Female Identity." *Sex Roles*, 1979, *5*, 155–178.

Kavrell, S. M. "Effects of Maternal Employment on Daughters' Psychological Development." Presented in a symposium "Early Adolescent Development: Biopsychosocial Perspectives" at the annual meeting of the American Educational Research Association, Boston, April 1980.

Kestenberg, J. "Phases of Adolescence with Suggestions for a Correlation of Psychic and Hormonal Organizations: Antecedents of Adolescent Organizations in Childhood. Part I." *Journal of the American Academy of Child Psychiatry*, 1967, *6*, 427–463. (a)

Kestenberg, J. "Phases of Adolescence with Suggestions for a Correlation of Psychic and Hormonal Organizations: Antecedents of Adolescent Organizations in Childhood. Part II." *Journal of the American Academy of Child Psychiatry*, 1967, *6*, 577–614. (b)

Kestenberg, J. "Phases of Adolescence with Suggestions for a Correlation of Psychic and Hormonal Organizations. Part III: Puberty, Growth, Differentiation, and Consolidation." *Journal of the American Academy of Child Psychiatry*, 1968, *7*, 108–151. (c)

Koff, E., Rierdan, J., & Jacobson, S. "The Personal and Interpersonal Significance of Menarche." *Journal of the American Academy of Child Psychiatry*, 1981, *20*, 148.

Koff, E., Rierdan, J., & Sheingold, K. "Memories of Menarche: Age and Preparedness as Determinants of Subjective Experience." Paper presented at meetings of the Eastern Psychological Association, Hartford, April 1980.

Lerner, R. M., & Karabenick, S. A. "Physical Attractiveness, Body Attitudes, and Self-concept in Late Adolescence." *Journal of Youth and Adolescence*, 1974, *3*, 7–16.

Lerner, R. M., Karabenick, S. A., & Stuart, J. L. "Relations among Physical Attractiveness, Body Attitudes, and Self-concept in Male and Female College Students." *Journal of Psychology*, 1973, *85*, 119–129.

Logan, D. D. "The Menarche Experience in Twenty-three Foreign Countries." *Adolescence*, 1980, *15*, 247.

Lynch, M. E. "Paternal Androgyny, Daughters' Physical Maturity Level, and Achievement Socialization in Early Adolescence." Unpublished doctoral dissertation, Cornell University, 1981.

McCandless, B. R., & Coop, R. H. *Adolescents: Behavior and Development.* New York: Holt, Rinehart & Winston, 1979.

Miller, P. Y., & Simon, W. "The Development of Sexuality in Adolescence." In J. Adelson (Ed.), *Handbook of Adolescent Psychology.* N.Y.: Wiley & Sons, 1980.

Mussen, P. H., & Jones, M. C. "Self-conceptions, Motivations, and Interpersonal Attitudes of Late- and Early-maturing Boys." *Child Development*, 1957, *28*, 243–256.

Neugarten, B. L. "Continuities and Discontinuities of Psychological Issues into Adult Life." *Human Development*, 1969, *12*, 121–130.

Neugarten, B. L., & Datan, N. "Sociological Perspectives on the Life Cycle." In P. Baltes & K. W. Schaie (Eds.), *Life-span Developmental Psychology: Personality and Socialization.* New York: Academic Press, 1973.

Offer, D., & Howard, K. I. "An Empirical Analysis of the Offer Self-Image Questionnaire for Adolescents." *Archives of General Psychiatry*, 1972, *27*, 529–533.

Parsons, T. "Age and Sex in the Social Structure of the United States." *American Sociological Review*, 1942, 7, 604–616.

Parsons, T., & Bales, R. F. *Family Socialization and Interaction Process.* Glencoe, IL: Free Press, 1955.

Peskin, H. "Pubertal Onset and Ego Functioning." *Journal of Abnormal Psychology*, 1967, *72*, 1–15.

Peskin, H. "Influence of the Developmental Schedule of Puberty on Learning and Ego Development." *Journal of Youth and Adolescence*, 1973, *2*, 273–290.

Petersen, A. C. "Female Pubertal Development." In M. Sugar (Ed.), *Female Adolescent Development.* New York: Brunner/Mazel, 1979.

Petersen, A. C. "Puberty and Its Psychosocial Significance in Girls." In A. J. Dan, E. A. Graham, & C. B. Beecher (Eds.), *The Menstrual Cycle: A Synthesis of Interdisciplinary Research, Vol. 1.* New York: Springer Publishing Co., 1980.

Petersen, A. C. "Menarche: Meaning of Measures and Measures of Meaning." In S. Golub (Ed.), *Menarche: An Interdisciplinary View.* New York: D. C. Heath, 1983.

Petersen, A. C., & Taylor, B. "The Biological Approach to Adolescence: Biological Change and Psychological Adaptation." In J. Adelson

(Ed.), *Handbook of Adolescent Psychology*. New York: John Wiley and Sons, 1980.

Petersen, A. C., Tobin-Richards, M. H., & Crockett, L. "Sex differences." In H. E. Mitzel (Ed.), *Encyclopedia of Educational Research* (Fifth edition). New York: The Free Press, 1982.

Pleck, J. H. *"The Myth of Masculinity."* Cambridge, MA: The MIT Press, 1982.

Rebecca, M., Hefner, R., & Oleshansky, B. "A Model of Sex-role Transcendance." *Journal of Social Issues*, 1976, *32*, 197–206.

Ruble, D. N. "Premenstrual Symptoms: A Reinterpretation." *Science*, 1977, *197*, 291–292.

Savin-Williams, R. "Dominance Hierarchies in Groups of Early Adolescents." *Child Development*, 1979, *50*, 923–935.

Schonfeld, W. A. "The Body and the Body-image in Adolescents." In G. Caplan & S. Lebovici (Eds.), *Adolescence: Psychological Perspectives*. New York: Basic Books, Inc., 1969.

Shainess, N. "A Reevaluation of Some Aspects of Femininity: A Preliminary Report." *Comprehensive Psychiatry*, 1961, *2*, 20–26.

Shepard-Look, D. L. "Sex Differentiation and the Development of Sex Roles." In B. B. Wolman (Ed.), *Handbook of Developmental Psychology*. Englewood Cliffs, NJ: Prentice-Hall, Inc., 1982.

Simmons, R. G., Blyth, D. A., Carlton-Ford, S., & Bulcroft, R. *The Adjustment of Early Adolescents to School and Pubertal Transitions*. Paper presented at the Social Science Research Council Conference on Pubertal and Psychosocial Change, Tucson, Arizona, December 1982.

Simmons, R. G., Blyth, D. A., & McKinney, K. L. "The Social and Psychological Effects of Puberty on White Females." In J. Brooks-Gunn & A. C. Petersen (Eds.), *Girls at Puberty: Biological and Psychosocial Perspectives*. New York: Plenum Press, 1983.

Simmons, R. G., Blyth, D. A., Van Cleave, E. F., & Bush, D. M. "Entry into Adolescence: The Impact of School Structure, Puberty, and Early Dating on Self-esteem." *American Sociological Review*, 1979, *44*, 948–967.

Simmons, R. G., & Rosenberg, F. R. "Sex Differences in the Self-concept in Adolescence." *Sex Roles*, 1975, *1*, 147–159. (a)

Simmons, R. G., & Rosenberg, F. "Sex, Sex-roles and Self-image." *Journal of Youth and Adolescence*, 1975, *4*, 229–258. (b)

Simmons, R. G., Rosenberg, F., & Rosenberg, M. "Disturbance in the Self-image at Adolescence." *American Sociological Review*, 1973, *38*, 553–568.

Spence, J. T., & Helmreich, R. L. *Masculinity and Femininity*. Austin: University of Texas Press, 1978.

Spence, J. T., Helmreich, R. L., & Stapp, J. "Ratings of Self and Peers on Sex-role Attributes and Their Relation to Self-esteem and Conceptions of Masculinity and Femininity." *Journal of Personality and Social Psychology*, 1975, *32*, 29–39.

Steinberg, L. D. "Family Processes at Adolescence: A Developmental Perspective." *Adolescence*, 1981.

Steinberg, L. D., & Hill, J. "Patterns of Family Interactions as a Function of Age, the Onset of Puberty, and Formal Thinking." *Developmental Psychology*, 1978, *14*, 683–684.

Stolz, H. R., & Stolz, L. M. (Eds.). *National Society of the Study for Education (NSSE)*. In *Adolescence* (Part 1) (43rd Yearbook, National Society for the Study of Education.) Chicago: University of Chicago Press, 1944.

Tanner, J. M. *Growth at Adolescence*. Springfield, IL.: Charles C. Thomas, 1962.

Tanner, J. M. "Sequence, Tempo, and Individual Variation in the Growth and Development of Boys and Girls Aged Twelve to Sixteen." *Daedalus*, 1971, *100*, 907–930.

Tanner, J. M. "Sequence and Tempo in the Somatic Changes in Puberty." In M. M. Grumbach, G. D. Grave, & F. E. Mayer (Eds.), *Control of the Onset of Puberty*. New York: Wiley, 1974.

Tobin-Richards, M. H., Boxer, A. M., & Petersen, A. C. "The Psychological Significance of Pubertal Change: Sex Differences in Perceptions of Self during Early Adolescence." In J. Brooks-Gunn & A. C. Petersen (Eds.), *Girls at Puberty: Biological and Psychosocial Perspectives*. New York: Plenum Press, 1983.

Weitz, S. *Sex Roles*. New York: Oxford University Press, 1977.

Whisnant, L., Brett, E., & Zegans, L. "Implicit Messages Concerning Menstruation in Commercial and Educational Materials Prepared for Young Adolescent Girls." *American Journal of Psychiatry*, 1975, *132*, 815–820.

Whiting, J. "Age of Marriage and First Pregnancy Across Cultures." In J. Lancaster and B. Hamberg (Eds.), *School-age Pregnancy and Parenthood*. Chicago: Aldine, in press.

Worell, J. "Life-span Sex Roles: Development, Continuity, and Change." In R. M. Lerner & N. A. Busch-Rossnagel (Eds.), *Individuals as Producers of Their Development: A Life-span Perspective*. New York: Academic Press, 1981.

3. ADOLESCENT SEXUALITY
Judy A. Shea

Adolescent sexuality is one of the central issues of adolescent development. It consumes the thoughts of adolescents as they anticipate, and sometimes worry about, their development and behavior. Similarly, sexuality is an almost constant source of concern for parents, interested in their children's well-being, and educators working with adolescents are very familiar with how sexuality permeates every corner of adolescents' lives. Yet with all of this interest, few issues are more difficult to talk about. It is unclear who should be responsible for guiding the adolescent's learning and behavior, what should be said, and when instruction should take place. Because sexuality presents so many dilemmas, adolescents and adults hold many erroneous, and to some extent exaggerated, notions about the extent and impact of sexual activity. In this chapter some of the facts and issues about adolescent sexual behavior will be reviewed.

ISSUES AND FINDINGS
Sexual Activity

Before we can begin to look at the incidence of behavior, it is important to realize that adolescents' interest and preoccupation with sexuality is not something that just happens overnight. Certainly, physiological and hormonal changes do increase adolescent's awareness of their own sexual maturity. But, sexuality has always been a part of an adolescent's life. When they were young children, a great deal of learning occurred through sometimes subtle messages; such messages were constantly received from parents (Gagnon & Simon, 1973; Laws & Schwartz, 1977).

Later, as adolescents entered school, developed friendships, and perhaps participated in extracurricular functions, the sources of sexual learning and the content of the messages multiplied. Today, adolescents also grow up in a world where television, music, movies, and magazines contain implicit and explicit sexual messages.

The point of this preface is to underscore the complexity of sexual behavior and learning. It is easy to survey what adolescents do. It is far more difficult to understand why they do what they do, be it anything from abstinence to promiscuity. Accordingly, we will first look at the prevalence of sexual activity and then explore some of the possible causes and consequences.

Sexual activity in adolescence, though never rare, is an increasingly common event (Furstenberg, Lincoln, & Menken, 1981). For example, one group of researchers found that the incidence of premarital intercourse increased for women born in each decade between 1920 and 1960, and it has always been more visible for black than white women (Udry, Bauman, & Morris, 1975). Today, adolescents are still engaging in sexual intercourse, and they are doing it at younger ages. Moreover, the gap between blacks and whites is disappearing.

A 1979 survey of urban females between 15 and 19 throughout the United States indicates that by the age of 19, 65% of the white teenage women and nine in ten of the black women had had intercourse at least once (Zelnik & Kantner, 1980). These proportions are significantly higher than those reported for a similar survey in 1971. At that time, only 41% of the white adolescents and 78% of the black adolescents had had intercourse.

When the proportions are broken down by age, it quickly becomes apparent that adolescent women are initiating sexual activity at younger ages. For example, in 1971 one in ten of the white 15-year-olds were sexually active; by 1979 the proportion had nearly doubled to two in ten. Similarly, the proportion of sexually active white 16-year-olds increased from 17% to 35%.

These age changes were foreshadowed in earlier surveys restricted to one part of the country. A study of high school students in Michigan, surveyed in 1970 and 1973, indicates that premarital intercourse was more prevalent in 1973, especially among the youngest adolescent women (Vener & Stewart, 1974). In 1973, 24%

of the 15-year-old girls were sexually active whereas only 13% had had coitus in 1970.

Data about the incidence of sexual activity for adolescent males suggest that the traditional higher rates for males are disappearing also. In the 1973 Michigan study it was found that four in ten of the boys aged 15 and younger had had coitus (Vener & Stewart, 1974). A similar study in Colorado showed slightly lower rates for high school boys. In 1972, 21% of the tenth grade males, 28% of the eleventh grade males and 33% of the twelfth grade males were non-virgins (Jessor & Jessor, 1975). Moreover, in all grades more females than males reported that they had had intercourse; 26% of the tenth grade women, 40% of the eleventh grade women, and 55% of the twelfth grade women.

Among New York City high school males surveyed in 1974, 48% of the whites, 84% of the blacks, and 75% of the hispanics were sexually active (Finkel & Finkel, 1975). These figures are comparable to a 1979 survey of males aged 19 to 21 (Zelnik & Kantner, 1980). By the age of 19, eight in ten of the never married males had had coitus.

The rates of activity speak for themselves. Most urban adolescents will engage in premarital intercourse before the age of 19. While we know less about the incidence of sexual activity for rural adolescents, it appears that sexual activity is more common for them also (Olson, 1980).

Figuring out why adolescents become sexually active is not so cut and dried. Historically, it has been popular to look at sexual activity for females as a way of rebelling against parents (Adams & Gullotta, 1983) or as a means to secure a love relationship (Chilman, 1979). For males, it was the expected thing to do; they were just "sowing their wild oats." Current explanations turn away from individuals and look at the social contexts of adolescents.

Adolescents live in a world where sex has lost its association with morals and marriage. In the past, females were encouraged to reserve sexual intimacy for a future marriage partner, whereas males were apt to behave in line with the double standard which supported sexual activity with anyone except potential marriage partners. Today more and more young men and women are endorsing a standard of permissiveness with affections (Jurich & Jurich, 1974; Reiss, 1967). This means that males and females are

now having sex for the same reason—to establish closeness and
intimacy without a commitment for marriage (Kallen & Stephenson, 1982; Miller & Simon, 1974). This does not mean, however,
that adolescents plan their first intercourse; for most it "just
happens" (Rogel, Zuehkle, Petersen, Tobin-Richards, & Shelton,
1980), although curiosity is a motivating factor (Shea & Freeman,
1983).

Overall, adolescents are adhering to the more liberal sexual
norms of the country. While these norms may be shared by
parents of adolescents, they also create conflicts for them. On one
hand, parents may agree with ideas such as individual choice and
the right to select one's own lifestyle. However, it is doubtful if
many parents would want his or her own adolescent to become
sexually active. Similarly, while parents often feel powerless in
controlling their adolescent's behavior, a large number of parents
simultaneously feel that sexual activity and pregnancy are their
fault—the result of their own lax standards (Yankelovich, 1979).
This frustration may be what too often immobilizes parents and
leads them to withdraw from taking an active role in their adolescents' sexual socialization.

Parents typically do not serve as a source of sex information,
especially for adolescent sons. Surveys with high school and
college youth repeatedly show that parents fall behind peers as
important educators. And, teachers and reading materials have
become more and more important sources of information about
sex related topics (Freeman, Rickels, Huggins, Mudd, Garcia, &
Dickens, 1980; Gebhard, 1977; Spanier, 1976; Zelnik, 1979). Parents
often wait for an adolescent to approach them with questions
(Chess, Thomas, & Cameron, 1976), and white parents especially
are likely to "educate" with books (Rothenberg, 1978).

The lack of initiative by parents is unfortunate because adolescents, realizing what they learn from their peers is often incorrect,
wish that their parents would take a more active role (Bennett &
Dickinson, 1980; Couch, 1967; Dickinson, 1978; Sorenson, 1973).
Moreover, there is some information to show that adolescent
women who learn about sex from their mothers may be more
likely to delay initiating intercourse (Lewis, 1973; Spanier, 1977a;
Thomson, 1982). This last statement must be taken cautiously as
studies also show that while parental involvement may inhibit
sexual activity, partners and peers are usually more influential

(Jorgensen, King, & Torrey, 1980; Thompson & Spanier, 1978). Nevertheless, there is reason to think that parents can have an impact on their adolescents' behaviors.

It is encouraging to see that over the past few years parents, especially mothers, have begun to share the educator role that was abdicated to others outside of the home. A recent survey of mother-daughter pairs points to some interesting findings about sex education in the home (Fox & Inazu, 1980). First, most mothers and daughters agree that they have talked to each other about sex related topics, and they both recall that they have talked about the same things. Nearly all have discussed menstruation and conception. But, sex and birth control, the two topics most closely related to adolescent sexuality and pregnancy, were least likely to be discussed. Second, mothers were more comfortable with the discussions than their daughters, although both mothers and daughters wanted more talks about sex related topics. Third, there were not many differences in the topics discussed or the frequency of talks related to race, the mother's age, religion, or marital status. This means that communication between mothers and daughters is equally likely across most households, be it easy or difficult. However, this was also one study that did not find that communication with mothers was related to the daughters delaying intercourse.

One possible explanation is that the spoken word is much less powerful than nonverbal socialization. In other words, what is said may be less important than how it is said. In fact, these authors found that the quality of the mother-daughter relationship and some of the mothers' behaviors, such as extramarital relationships, were the best predictors of the daughters' behaviors (Inazu & Fox, 1980). Clearly, there is a need to look at the socialization process instead of focusing on specific conversations. It is quite likely that communication about topics like birth control only takes place once parents can no longer ignore the fact that their adolescent is sexually active (Furstenberg, 1971).

Even though it is hard to know how parents can have an impact on their adolescents' sexual behaviors, attitude similarity between adolescents and their parents does suggest that parents are successful in getting their message—or messages, as the case may be—across (Shah & Zelnik, 1981; Thomson, 1982). And, shared attitudes between parents and adolescents are associated with more restrictive behaviors on the part of the adolescent (Shah & Zelnik, 1981). Perhaps more importantly, even if communication does not directly affect behavior, by initiating conversations about sex and birth control, parents can convey a sense of concern and create an atmosphere where the adolescent can approach the parents with his or her questions.

Before moving on to look at contraceptive use, it is important to note that while more and more adolescents are sexually active, they certainly are not promiscuous. The majority have had only one sexual partner (Rogel et al., 1980) and sex is infrequent. Most surveys show that at least half of the adolescents have intercourse less than once a month (Zabin & Clark, 1981; Zelnik & Kantner, 1977).

Adolescent Contraceptive Use

The striking increases in adolescent sexual activity have not been paralleled with better protection from unwanted pregnancies. The following findings highlight the notoriously poor contraceptive habits of adolescents:

- Over half of the sexually active adolescents do not use contraception at first intercourse and one-third never use birth control (Zelnik & Kantner, 1980).
- While the proportions using contraception increased between 1970 and 1980, there was a gradual shift to less effective contraceptive methods (Zelnik & Kantner, 1980).
- The most common birth control practices for adolescents who have not been to a family planning clinic are withdrawal and condoms, although most do not use anything (Alan Guttmacher Institute, 1981).
- The younger a teen is when he or she initiates intercourse, the less likely he or she is to use contraception (Finkel & Finkel, 1975; Zabin, Kantner, & Zelnik, 1979).
- Even when an adolescent woman has gone to a family planning clinic, in the next 15 months, more than half will be at risk of a pregnancy either because they have stopped using their method or they use it incorrectly (Ager, Shea, & Agronow, 1983; Furstenberg, Shea, Allison, Herceg-Baron, & Webb, 1983).

These findings lead to three questions about adolescent contraceptive use: Why don't (more) adolescents use birth control? What can be done to improve use? Who are the adolescents who use contraception?

Why don't adolescents use birth control? As with most questions about adolescent sexual behavior, there is no simple answer to this question. Adolescent females often say "they weren't prepared" or "they just didn't think about it" (Shah, Zelnik, & Kantner, 1975; Rogel et al., 1980). Some researchers have explained these excuses as a denial of sexual activity because of guilt or a refusal to identify oneself as sexually active (Goldsmith, Gabrielson, Gabrielson, Matthews, & Potts, 1972; Rains, 1971).

A related explanation is that adolescents lack the cognitive skills to understand the relationship between intercourse today and a possible pregnancy tomorrow (Baizerman, 1977; Cvetkovich, & Grote, 1981). Adolescents using this reasoning hold the erroneous idea that they are not susceptible to a pregnancy. Their limited perspective about the future also means that they are unable to weigh the costs of a pregnancy and the costs of using birth control against the benefits of not being pregnant, a process that older women go through (Luker, 1975). Indeed, one group of researchers found that while few adolescents could correctly assess the probability of getting pregnant, those that could were better contraceptive users (Smith, Nenney, Weinman, & Mumford, 1982). Moreover, two-thirds of a sample of adolescent girls who did not use contraception gave reasons that indicated they did not think it could happen to them (Zelnik & Kantner, 1979).

A third explanation for adolescents' nonuse of birth control is that adolescents lack the social and communication skills that would enable them to use contraception effectively (Campbell & Barnlund, 1977; Schinke & Gilchrist, 1977). They are often embarrassed or afraid to go to a clinic or doctor (Herold, 1981; Zabin & Clark, 1981). Adolescent couples have difficulty talking to each other about contraception (Scales & Beckstein, 1982; Sorenson, 1973), and they fear talking to their parents because it might expose their sexual activity (Herceg-Baron & Furstenberg, 1982).

Two final explanations for adolescents' failure to use contraception concern their lack of knowledge about sex and birth control and their lack of access to contraception. Many parents

and educators maintain that adolescents would use birth control
if they knew the specific, textbook facts about reproduction and
contraception (Adams & Gullotta, 1983). Others say that contraceptive use could be improved by making contraception more
accessible, by removing the barriers to effective methods of contraception (Dryfoos, 1982; Dryfoos & Heisler, 1978; Jaffe & Dryfoos,
1976).

Each of these explanations has its merits. Because sexuality is
only one part of a complex social and cognitive life, there is a
degree of truth to each. Each explanation also points to an answer
or answers about what can be done to enhance adolescents' use of
contraception and thereby prevent unwanted pregnancies. For
example, skills-training courses have been developed that include
role-playing conversations with sexual partners and conversations
with medical personnel (Schinke & Gilchrist, 1977), and the concepts of risk taking have been applied to birth control use
(Cvetkovich & Grote, 1981). Some of the more ingenious strategies
include developing board games and video games that combine
facts about birth control and pregnancy with hypothetical
decision-making situations (cf. Kuhnen, Chewning, Day, Bosworth, Gustafson, & Hawkins, 1982). Note, however, that little
headway has been made with advertising contraceptives on television or radio even though many restrictive bans have been
removed and numerous other personal products are widely ad-
vertised (Donovan, 1982).

On a small scale, programs such as these may have a positive
impact. How positive the impact is will be hard to know, however, because many educators and counselors do not have the
resources to conduct evaluations. But, there are two strategies that
are being applied across the country: sex education and family
planning clinics.

What can be done to improve use? Over the past fifteen years
sex education has been incorporated, to some degree, in many
school systems throughout the country. Developing and offering
the courses has been a slow, uphill battle. There is often conflict
over the content of the courses, even though a recent Gallup poll
showed that eight in ten adults favor sex education in the schools
and seven in ten support education about birth control (Gallup,
1978a). Currently, 36% of the public schools in the United States

offer sex education as a separate course, and many others incorporate it into health, science, and physical education courses
(Orr, 1982). Clearly there are huge variations in what is offered, as
few states require sex education and most leave the decision up to
local school boards. However, 78% of a sample of sex educators
said the course they taught included information about birth
control and abortion (Orr, 1982).

It is difficult to know how many teens are receiving sex education. Only 43% of a nationwide survey of 13 to 18 year olds said
they had had a sex education course (Gallup, 1978b), whereas
seven in ten of a sample of adolescent females living in metropolitan areas indicated that they had taken a sex education course
(Zelnik & Kim, 1982).

An issue more central than the number is the impact of the
education. On this issue the results are divided. On the pro side,
one finding that stands out is that students who have had a course
have better knowledge than those without sex education (Kirby,
1980; Philliber & Tatum, 1981). More importantly, one group of
researchers found that adolescents with a sex education background were less likely to have ever been pregnant and more
likely to have used contraception the first time they had intercourse (Zelnik & Kim, 1982). Moreover, when parents are involved
in planning the courses, communication between parents and
their children increases as well (Goodman & Goodman, 1976;
Kirby, Peterson, & Brown, 1982). Finally, contrary to the fears of
many opponents of sex education, there is no evidence that taking
a sex education course leads to sexual experimentation.

Lest one get too optimistic, however, on the con, or at least
questionable, side are several other findings. Most studies fail to
show any relationship between taking a sex education course and
any sexual behavior, be it intercourse, contraceptive use, or
pregnancy (Davis & Harris, 1982; Goldsmith et al., 1972; Reichelt
& Werley, 1976). The lack of relationships is not because education
is not important—indeed it does improve knowledge—but because
sexual behaviors are influenced by so many factors.

A second solution to the issues and problems of adolescent
sexual activity is to make birth control available to adolescents
throughout the country. The growth of family planning clinics
in the last decade has equalled, if not surpassed, the popularity of

sex education courses. The expansion was largely due to efforts on the federal level, through Title X funding, and legal rulings guaranteeing the rights of adolescents to confidential contraceptive services (Alan Guttmacher Institute, 1981; Paul & Pilpel, 1979).

Adolescents make up one-third of the client population in federally funded family planning clinics. While the accessibility of clinics varies greatly from one part of the country to another, between clinics and private physicians it is estimated that 56% of the sexually active adolescents who do not want to become pregnant are receiving contraceptive care, 1.5 million from clinics and 1.2 million from private physicians (Torres, Forrest, & Eisman, 1981).

These impressive figures make it hard to argue against the positive impact that family planning clinics have had on preventing adolescent pregnancies (though admittedly there are critics who have argued just this point). After a visit to a clinic, more than three-fourths of the adolescents use oral contraceptives or an IUD, whereas at first intercourse most did not use any method of contraception or they used the less reliable methods of douching or withdrawal (Alan Guttmacher Institute, 1981). Indeed, it has been estimated that in 1979 family planning clinics were responsible for preventing 367,000 unwanted births to adolescent women and nearly this many abortions (Forrest, Hermalin, & Henshaw, 1981). Even with these contributions there are three areas that family-planning clinics are working to improve.

The first is to reach adolescents before they become sexually active. Surveys show that nearly nine in ten of the female clients are sexually active before they go to a clinic (Zabin & Clark, 1981). Moreover, the majority of the teenage clients have been active for more than a year (Akpom, Akpom, & Davis, 1976; Settlage, Baroff, & Cooper, 1973). The importance of early visits for contraception is highlighted with the finding that half of the adolescents who become pregnant do so within the first six months of sexual activity (Zabin et al., 1979). In fact, at least one-third of the adolescent clients first go to a family planning clinic because they suspect they are pregnant (Zabin & Clark, 1981), and most of these young women are already expecting.

The major reason a large sample of adolescents gave for delaying their first visit to a family planning clinic is that they just "didn't get around to it" (Zabin & Clark, 1981). This is related to their reason for not using contraception; 36% of a national sample said they weren't planning on having intercourse (Zelnik & Kantner, 1979).

Even though adolescents procrastinate in seeking contraceptive care, when they do decide to go for help, an important reason in choosing a clinic is because their parents will not be told (Herold & Goodwin, 1979). Confidentiality is very important, even though over half of the clients have told a parent of their clinic visit (Torres, Forrest, & Eisman, 1980). Confiding in parents is especially common for younger teens. Many come to the clinic at their parents' suggestion or even with a parent (Bury, 1980). Other important reasons for choosing a family planning clinic are the adolescents' perceptions that clinics were a place for young people, their friends had come, or could come to the clinic, and a clinic was located close to them (Zabin & Clark, 1983).

For whatever reasons adolescents seek out a family planning clinic, getting them there is one step in the right direction. But keeping them enrolled for regular visits is a second troublesome step for many family-planning providers. Studies that look at clinic return rates show that after one year at least one-third of the clients will have stopped making regular visits (Ager et al., 1982; Cosgrove, Penn, & Chambers, 1978; Furstenberg, Masnick, & Ricketts, 1972; Shea, Herceg-Baron, & Furstenberg, 1983).

We don't really know why adolescents drop out of the clinics. Undoubtedly, some stop making appointments because they are no longer sexually active. Other young women switch to nonmedical methods of contraception and/or to private physicians. What is apt to be an important reason also is that regular supervised contraceptive care is too much trouble. For many adolescents, the family planning visit is their first experience with seeking medical care on their own. It takes a lot of initiative to schedule and meet regular visits. Indeed, one of the most successful programs, achieving more than a 90% return rate over a three-year period, was integrated into a high school setting (Edwards, Steinman, Arnold, & Hakanson, 1980). The adolescents were familiar with the nurses, they could drop in with questions, and they could easily be tracked down if they missed an appointment. In short, this unique program was adapted to fit the adolescents' social contexts.

Whatever their reasons are for dropping out, there is a need to help adolescents make regular visits. Timely visits are associated with better contraceptive use. In one study it was found that two-thirds of the adolescents who returned for scheduled appointments continued to be good contraceptive users over a 15-month period, compared to less than one-fourth of the adolescents who missed their first revisit (Shea, Herceg-Baron, & Furstenberg, 1983).

The third goal family planning providers have set for themselves is to be more appealing to male adolescents. Clinics are built to efficiently serve the client as an individual. This usually means excluding her partner or any one else the client might want to include. Moreover, the most effective methods of contraception are for women (Alan Guttmacher Institute, 1981), and there is a pervasive but unspoken assumption that contraception is a female's responsibility (Scales, 1977). Thus, developing services for males, or integrating them into existing programs will not be easy. There are some notable exceptions (see, for example, Scales & Beckstein, 1982), but trial programs for males have not been too successful (Johnson & Staples, 1979; Middleman, 1972). It will take a lot more effort and education to reverse some of the attitudes held by men and women and to provide men with quality sexual and contraceptive education.

Who uses contraception? Although this question has been addressed by professionals in numerous fields, few answers have been found. About the only thing that can be said with certainty is that the older an adolescent is when she initiates intercourse, the more likely she is to use contraception (Chilman, 1980; Cvetkovich, Grote, Lieberman, & Miller, 1978; Zelnik & Kantner, 1977). Sometimes race differences are observed for males and females. These generally show whites are more likely to use contraceptives than are blacks and hispanics (Chilman, 1980; Finkel & Finkel, 1978), though the differences are disappearing and blacks are more likely to use contraception at first intercourse.

Use of contraception tends to be better in urban than rural populations (Olson, 1980), probably because there is greater access to contraceptive services (Chamie, Eisman, Forrest, Orr, & Torres, 1982). Religious affiliation, frequency of attending religious services, and religious commitment are generally not related to contraceptive use (Chilman, 1979). Young women in one-parent households are more likely to go to a family planning clinic (Fox, 1981), but it appears that effective use of contraception is more prevalent by adolescents with employed and well-educated parents (Furstenberg, Herceg-Baron, Shea, & Webb, 1983).

Contraceptive use has also been related to a host of attributes, or characteristics, of the adolescent girls themselves. (Adolescent men have not been studied often enough to write about.) The more popular questions have focused on her attitudes about contraception and her aspirations for her adult life. (Refer to the Chilman [1979] reference for a comprehensive review.) In general, young women who believe in contraception—that it will work and that it will not be harmful—tend to be better users (Shea, Herceg-Baron, & Furstenberg, 1983). These supportive attitudes are not the same thing as knowledge about reproductive physiology or contraception. Indeed, as mentioned earlier, it is unclear if and how knowledge is related to behavior.

Birth control use has been associated with nontraditional views about female roles (Fox, 1977), and use is related to satisfaction with the particular method being used (Shea, Herceg-Baron, & Furstenberg, 1983). No amount of communication, support, or education is likely to be effective if the adolescent does not like the method she has chosen.

Educational and occupational aspirations have predicted use for some samples of adolescent girls. As one would expect, adolescents with clear-cut and high educational goals are more able (or willing) to use birth control effectively (Chilman, 1980). In general, a sense of "planfulness" predicts better use (Mindick & Oskamp, 1982). Overall, however, it is important to emphasize that no one individual attribute consistently distinguishes "good" contraceptive users from "bad" users or nonusers.

The failure to understand contraceptive use by looking at individual attributes has led clinicians and researchers to look to an adolescent's social network—her parents, her girlfriends, and her boyfriends—for increasing understanding. This line of inquiry has offered some interesting, but again inconclusive, possibilities.

Peer influences have historically been the most widely talked about. Peers are seen as instrumental in pulling the adolescent away from his or her family and pushing the adolescent into behaviors that he or she would not normally engage in. In fact, peers are consistently the most frequent source of information about sex-related topics (Bennett & Dickinson, 1980; Reichelt & Werley, 1976), and adolescents' attitudes about sex are more similar to those of their peers than those of their parents (Shah & Zelnik, 1981). But in reality we probably overstate peer influences (see Guerney & Arthur, Chapter 4). For example, most adolescents select friends with attitudes similar to their own and their parents' (Lerner, Karson, Meisels, & Knapp, 1975; Lerner & Knapp, 1975). When adolescents have to choose between advice from parents and advice from friends, they are apt to side with peers on immediate and inconsequential topics such as clothing and music but consult with parents on questions that have long term implications (Brittain, 1963). Moreover, young adults realize that much of the information about sex that they hear from their peers is incorrect (Dickinson, 1978; Shipman, 1968), and few see peers as the most important source of information (Bennett & Dickinson, 1980).

On the other hand, peers do sometimes oppose parents in supporting sexual activity (Jessor & Jessor, 1975; Lewis, 1973). What is often overlooked though is that peers also support effective contraceptive use (Jorgensen et al., 1980). Several researchers have found that peers were the most important influence in promoting family planning clinic attendance and stimulating the search for contraceptive advice (Akpom et al., 1976; Herold & Goodwin, 1979). Peers are especially useful in recruiting teens to clinics, and clinics using teens for outreach and as counselors in the clinic services have been very successful (Kar, Talbot, & Coan, 1982).

One interesting finding about peer influences shows that they operate in a very complex and indirect manner. A group of researchers found that adolescents' sexual behaviors and attitudes were more closely related to what they thought their friends were doing and thinking than to the more conservative behaviors and attitudes actually reported by their friends (Udry, Newcomer, Gilbert, & Bauman, 1980). Unfortunately, this may translate into a number of adolescents who feel like they are being encouraged to be sexually active when in fact they are not. But, it is also important to remember that it is these same peers who will, in all likelihood, support contraceptive use.

Dating partners can also influence adolescent women's contraceptive behaviors. It is within a heterosexual relationship that an adolescent will have the opportunity for sexual involvement. Adolescent males are frequently viewed as the "villians" who force, or at least persuade, their partners to have intercourse, using justifications such as "they need it" or "if you really love me. . . ." While we cannot discount the unequal distribution of power in many relationships, it is certainly unfair, and probably inaccurate, to view most adolescent men in this light. Even if these generalizations were true at one time, over the past few years males have been ascribing to less exploitive lines of reasoning (Jurich & Jurich, 1974). Also, we tend to overlook the point that until relatively recently male methods of contraception were the main choices available, especially to teenagers (Scales, 1977). Even though this is no longer the case, they remain the most popular choices at first intercourse (Alan Guttmacher Institute, 1981; Zelnik & Kantner, 1980).

Both males and females believe that they, themselves, should take the responsibility for using birth control rather than leaving it up to the partner (Shea, Jemail, Nathanson, & Baird, 1983). For males, though, this belief does not usually translate into taking the initiative. Few males have ever been to a family planning clinic, a perhaps understandable situation with such clinics' women-only orientation (Scales, Etelis, & Levitz, 1977). In addition, as mentioned earlier, even when male-oriented programs are developed, attendance tends to be quite low (Johnson & Staples, 1979; Middleman, 1971). Moreover, there is little discussion in adolescent couples about birth control, in part because young men work under the assumption that "she will use something." In fact, in one study of adolescent boys, fewer than two in ten had actually taken an active role in contraception by either using a condom or asking his partner if she were protected (Cohen, 1982). Indeed, with this seeming collusion between partners not to talk about contraception, what is perhaps most surprising is that so many young people do use birth control.

Overall, partner influences have been found to be stronger comparatively than parents and peers (Jorgensen et al., 1980; Thompson & Spanier, 1978). Birth control is most likely to be used in steady relationships of several months' duration, often with some commitment or at least some desire to marry (Furstenberg, 1971; Shea, Herceg-Baron, & Furstenberg, 1983). This finding can probably be explained by the fact that it is in these durable relationships that intercourse is more predictable and more legitimate. In any event, making regular visits to a family planning clinic, and thus using birth control effectively, is likely to be interrupted when a couple breaks up (Shea, Herceg-Baron, & Furstenberg, 1983). While this is understandable from the young woman's viewpoint, the unfortunate result is that she is often unprepared for her next sexual encounter.

Parental influences on contraceptive use are less clear-cut than those of partners and peers. Traditionally, parents have been responsible for the sexual socialization and education of their children (Fox, 1981; Spanier, 1977b). Though never an easy task, sex education was reinforced when institutions such as churches and schools could be counted on to uphold a mandate of abstinence until marriage (Hunt, 1976; Kenkel, 1960). The agreement in values and appropriate behaviors allowed earlier generations of parents to teach as they had been taught, through subtle, indirect communication.

Today, for a number of reasons, socialization about sexuality has become more problematic. First, it is hard for parents to know what should be taught in the home, as peers and schools have assumed a greater role in education (Hansson, Jones, & Chernovetz, 1979). Second, today's parents are perhaps the first generation of parents who must, if they are realistic, consider the need to teach alternatives to abstinence (Roberts, Kline, & Gagnon, 1978). Third, it is easier to minimize conflict and maintain smooth family functioning if conversations about sensitive, intimate topics are avoided (Chess et al., 1976). Fourth, parents have little and often inaccurate knowledge themselves, and thus it is difficult to speak to children knowledgeably (Herceg-Baron & Shea, 1982). Finally, parents are reluctant to "force" their values and attitudes upon anyone else, even their children.

In spite of these difficulties, parents are taking a more active role in the children's sexual education (although usually this is restricted to mothers and daughters). Daughters report learning more from their mothers now than adolescents did a decade ago (Dickinson, 1978; Gebhard, 1977; Thornburg, 1972), parents are getting involved in tasks such a developing school curricula (Orr, 1982), and throughout the country programs are springing up to equip parents with the knowledge, skills, and confidence to be better educators (Furstenberg, Herceg-Baron, Mann, & Shea, 1982). The value of these efforts is clear, assuming that they do increase communication, and, in fact, evaluations of several programs do document increased levels of communication (Herceg-Baron & Furstenberg, 1982; Philliber & Tatum, 1981). However, programs and policies are often based on the assumption that communication between parents and their adolescents about sex and contraception will in turn lead to better contraceptive use. While some authors have made similar conclusions (Lewis, 1973; Miller, 1976; Spanier, 1977a), *most* studies have not found this link (cf. Herceg-Baron & Furstenberg, 1982).

Why don't parents have a stronger impact on their adolescents' contraceptive behaviors? As suggested earlier it is partially because parents are communicating, often nonverbally, double messages (Thomson, 1982). While parents almost unanimously prefer that their adolescents delay intercourse at least until their late teens, in the event adolescents are sexually active most parents would also want them to use contraception (Coughlin & Perales, 1978; Herceg-Baron & Shea, 1982). The net effect of these conflicting messages is to create an atmosphere of ambivalence for both parents and teens. Parents, as socializers, and adolescents, as maturing young adults with ever-increasing sexual interests, must figure out how to best respond to the message "don't . . . , but if you do. . . ." Even parents who clearly say "don't" may unwittingly leave their child unprepared to use contraception in the event he or she does (and probably will) become sexually active, because it is these parents who omit instruction on contraception (Thomson, 1982). In sum, there is no easy answer for parents or any other adult who must assume the responsibility for educating and guiding adolescents. A workable strategy is to take an active role in socialization while remembering that it is unrealistic to expect that any one person or conversation will have a straightforward or lasting impact.

Summary. Thus far, some of the most important issues in adolescent sexuality have been reviewed. Sexual development and learning have been occurring since childhood, although physical maturation and new social experiences require that adolescents rewrite their sexual scripts. Most adolescents will have premarital intercourse by the age of nineteen, if not sooner. Initiating intercourse appears to be very situation specific—"it just happens"— and it is not easy to predict when it will happen nor to keep it from happening. Using birth control, whether at first intercourse, ever, or at most recent intercourse, is increasingly likely, but fewer than half of all sexually active adolescent females practice ongoing, preventive contraception.

There have been numerous attempts to improve contraceptive use. The most widespread ones are sex education and family planning clinics. Education has certainly improved knowledge. But, for the most part, we cannot see that it has had an effect on adolescents' behaviors. Family planning programs, on the other hand, have been very successful at helping thousands of teenagers avoid unwanted pregnancies. Still, many sexually active adolescents do not use contraception. The only consistent explanation is age at first intercourse. The older a female is, the greater the likelihood of using birth control. Other than age, sexual activity and contraceptive use *may* be related to individual attitudes, aspirations, and social influences. It is impossible to predict what will happen in any one situation, but there is every reason to think that with guidance and support adolescents can be successful in their attempts to avoid pregnancy.

Adolescent Pregnancy. Given the high levels of sexual activity and the less than perfect use of contraceptives, adolescent pregnancy is a common event. In 1978 there were 1.1 million pregnancies among women aged 19 and younger, and only 17% of these were conceived in marriage (Alan Guttmacher Institute, 1981). This represents a 13% increase in the numbers of adolescent pregnancies since 1973. However, the pregnancy rate among the sexually active has actually declined because so many more adolescents are having intercourse (Furstenberg et al., 1981).

The chances of becoming pregnant in the two years after initiating sexual activity are 33% for white adolescents and 43% for black adolescents (Koenig & Zelnik, 1982a). Moreover, for a sample of adolescent women interviewed in 1979, nearly half of the pregnancies were conceived in the first six months after initiating intercourse (Zabin et al., 1979). Clearly, the chances of a pregnancy are high. In 1978 it was estimated that four out of every ten 14-year-old women would become pregnant at least once by the age of 19 if the levels of sexual activity remained the same and contraceptive use did not improve (Tietze, 1978). In fact, these figures probably underestimate the true likelihood of pregnancy since the prevalence of sexual activity continues to increase and fewer adolescents are using the most effective methods of contraception (Zelnik & Kantner, 1980).

Early and consistent use of contraception makes a big impact on pregnancy. According to a 1979 survey of metropolitan teen-aged women, among women who never used contraception, 50% became pregnant within two years, whereas the pregnancy rate for women who always used contraception was only 12% (Koenig & Zelnik, 1982a). Similarly, 41% of the adolescents who were sexually active before the age of 15 became pregnant, but only 27% of the women who postponed intercourse until their late teens conceived premaritally (Koenig & Zelnik, 1982a).

The outcomes of these premarital pregnancies shifted over the last decade. Rushing to marry before the birth of the baby is no longer the preferred solution for whites (and it never was for blacks). Only 10% of all adolescents pregnant in 1978 chose this option. Rather, nearly four in ten received abortions, and 22% had out-of-wedlock births. One in ten gave up their children for adoption or care by someone else, and almost all selecting this option were white. Overall, women 19 and younger make up only 18% of the population able to bear children, but they contribute 31% of the abortions and 46% of the out-of-wedlock births (Alan Guttmacher Institute, 1981).

Little is known about how adolescents reach their decisions about pregnancy outcomes. Among two samples of adolescent couples, most of whom chose to deliver and keep the child, few reported difficulties or disagreements in making the decisions and most claimed it was a joint decision (Shea & Freeman, 1983; Shea, Jemail, Nathanson, & Baird, 1983). In fact, decision may be too strong a term; few alternatives were discussed by the couples even if one or the other person thought about other options. However, in another study of pregnant adolescent women, half of whom delivered and half of whom chose abortion, the authors report that very few of the adolescents were decisive: more than half of the young women changed their mind at least once (Klerman, Bracken, Jekel, & Bracken, 1982).

The outcome of a pregnancy may be related to the closeness of the young woman's relationships with her partner and parents. In one study, adolescent women who delivered were more apt to discuss the pregnancy with their parents, friends, and partners than the women choosing abortion. They were all happier about the pregnancy, less likely to have ever used birth control, and they perceived more support for their decision (Klerman et al., 1982). Over half of a younger sample of adolescents also reported that their mothers and boyfriends were influential in their decision-making process once the pregnancy was confirmed (Rosen, 1980). Prior to this time, when they suspected they were pregnant but did not know for sure, few turned to their parents for advice.

Because of the consequences of choosing to deliver a child, the decision-making process is one area in need of greater study. This is not to say that abortion is without its problems nor that it should be used as a substitute for pregnancy prevention. Indeed, the potential psychological trauma for women (Walter, 1970) and men (Rothstein, 1977; Shostak, 1979) cannot be ignored, especially given the evidence that it is more difficult to decide on abortion than on delivery (Klerman et al., 1982). But, comparatively, the health risks are smaller for a first trimester abortion than a delivery (Klerman et al., 1982), the chances of a second pregnancy are reduced (Koenig & Zelnik, 1982b), use of contraception is better following an abortion (Evans, Selstad, & Welcher, 1976), and women who choose to abort are certainly more able to continue with their educational and occupational plans.

Consequences of Teenage Childbearing

The scope of the problems that have been discussed as consequences of adolescent childbearing is almost unending. On almost any dimension one cares to look at, those who became parents as teenagers are at a disadvantage compared to those who were able to remain childless. Though the stigma of teenage childbearing has lessened, other problems remain (Alan Guttmacher Institute, 1976, 1981; Bolton, 1980; Furstenberg, 1976; McKenry, Walters, &

Johnson, 1979; Stuart & Wells, 1982). The most severe include the following:

- Adolescents have the highest rates of infant mortality and infants born to adolescent mothers often suffer from low birth weight.
- Adolescent mothers are susceptible to toxemia, anemia, and other pregnancy related problems.
- Adolescent mothers who marry have high rates of divorce.
- Adolescent mothers are often forced to truncate their education because they lack adequate childcare facilities.
- Adolescent mothers, especially those who marry, are likely to experience repeat pregnancies. Over a lifetime they have more children than women who postpone childbearing until later in life.
- Adolescent mothers lack skills and training to hold good jobs, if they are able to find work at all. Consequently, many are forced to rely on parental and public support.
- Children of adolescent mothers are somewhat more likely to fall behind their peers with older parents in social and cognitive skills.
- Some studies suggest that children of adolescents are more likely themselves to become parents as adolescents.

The list could go on but the point is clear. Adolescent parenthood is not a desirable position. Moreover, the problems associated with adolescent childbearing are not limited to the adolescent mothers and their children. The adolescent's family must also find ways to cope. Quite often they are central in providing: a place for the mother and child to live, child care, and financial support (Furstenberg, 1976; Presser, 1980). In fact, the single most significant factor contributing to an adolescent mother's well-being is support from her family. Many problems are eliminated if she is allowed to continue her education and thus eventually hold a job.

It is important to recognize also that parenthood can be problematic for adolescent fathers. Over the long term they also experience higher divorce rates and lower job prestige (Card & Wise, 1978). Even earlier, although some do conform to the stereotype of the "disappearing father," the majority are genuinely concerned about their responsibilities (Barret & Robinson, 1982;

Hendricks, Howard, & Caesar, 1981; Shea & Freeman, 1983). Unfortunately, they, too, are sadly lacking in skills and knowledge to be supportive fathers. The problems are compounded as more often than not they are excluded from special programs designed to help adolescent parents.

To balance this negative picture, we need to consider the following. First of all, the majority of adolescent women do not get pregnant. This, in itself, is quite amazing given the high levels of sexual activity and the low levels of contraceptive use. Moreover, of those that do become pregnant, most are happy about the pregnancy (Furstenberg, 1976; Ryan & Sweeney, 1980), although, at most, one in five wanted to become pregnant (Alan Guttmacher Institute, 1981). This is not to say that they were happy when they first found out they were pregnant; but in the following months they go through a process of assimilating and looking forward, however unrealistically, to becoming a parent. This process of adjustment has been observed for adolescent women (Furstenberg, 1976, 1981), adolescent men (Shea & Freeman, 1983), and parents of adolescent mothers (Furstenberg, 1981). Clearly, an unplanned pregnancy does not mean an unwanted one.

Finally, it is important to realize that careful analyses of the consequences of adolescent pregnancy are beginning to show that many of the earlier publications have exaggerated the negative effects (Chilman, 1980). The so-called problems are not observed for many samples of adolescent parents. Moreover, when adolescent parents do show deficits, they are most often due to broader social and economic problems that would have existed even without a pregnancy. Nevertheless, adolescent pregnancy does not enhance life opportunities. As Furstenberg noted: "it is quite likely that if teenagers had to take a pill to become pregnant, early childbearing would quickly vanish as a major social problem." (Furstenberg et al., 1981, p. 11)

SOURCES OF HELP

There are no easy answers to combat the problems associated with adolescent sexual activity. This is especially so if one sees the problem as one of sexual activity. Surveys of teenagers across the country give us no reason to believe that the numbers having intercourse will decline. In fact, if current trends continue it is only reasonable to expect that more adolescents will become sexually active and that they will do so at younger ages. Encouraging abstinence may help but discussing sexual activity as a choice and a responsibility will probably make a bigger impact on preventing unwanted pregnancies.

Nevertheless, the situation is not hopeless. There are probably more resources designed to address the problems associated with sexual activity than any other facet of adolescent development. Two of the most visible have already been discussed: sex education and family planning clinics. Regarding sex education, it is disappointing that the gains in knowledge do not have a more obvious impact on behaviors. The following changes could increase the chances of making a positive impact. They are also relevant for parents who are interested in improving communication with their children.

- Revise the content of discussions to make them more relevant. It is important to include information on contraception—where to get it, how to use it—in addition to the more common, and more easily discussed, physiological facts.
- Address attitudes as well as knowledge. Knowing all about birth control is not likely to be useful if one also believes things such as "making love without contraception is a way of showing love" or "birth control is harmful."
- Realize the diverging knowledge and interest of males and females and search for ways to make adolescent males more responsive to and responsible for contraception.
- Correct prevalent myths such as "You can't get pregnant the first time."
- Make sex education an ongoing part of an adolescent's learning—as opposed to a few-hours segment—that begins before an adolescent is sexually active.
- Be aware of the changing interests and vocabularies of adolescents as they mature.
- Don't be put off by an adolescent who claims he or she already knows it. Chances are at least some of the information is incorrect.
- Don't wait for the adolescent to ask all of the questions. He or she is probably just as uncomfortable as you are, and

silence shouldn't be misinterpreted as knowledge or lack of interest.

Admittedly, these suggestions are not easy to implement, especially within a school setting. Sexuality can be difficult for adults to talk about, just as it is for adolescents. Also, within a school one may have to contend with the seemingly endless restrictions placed by concerned parents, school boards, administrators, and community groups. In combination with the practical limitations of time and resources, upgrading curricula may seem like an impossible task. But it can be done, especially when parents who do favor sex education get involved to support the educators.

Family-planning programs serve the obvious role of making prescription and nonprescription contraceptives available to adolescents. Planned Parenthood affiliates are perhaps the most visible family-planning providers, but services are also available through health departments, hospitals, and neighborhood health centers as well as private physicians (Chamie et al., 1982). If an agency cannot easily be located, directory assistance, school counselors and sex education instructors, and leaders of youth groups such as YMCA's, Girl Scouts, and Boy Scouts can be very helpful in tracking down the facility nearest to you. Many communities also have a hotline that provides referrals for appropriate services (e.g., VD testing, pregnancy testing, counseling) and may even offer counseling over the phone.

Family-planning providers who receive federal funds (and most do) guarantee the adolescent's right to confidential services. While this is understandably upsetting to some patients, it should be reassuring to know the following:

- The services include high quality and closely monitored medical services. An adolescent is given a thorough medical exam before she receives a prescription for contraceptives, and regular check-ups are required for ongoing prescriptions.
- The adolescent receives counseling and education to help her examine her options. This means that she is given information about every kind of birth control and that she is not pushed or persuaded into accepting one kind.

- Many family planning counselors encourage an adolescent to talk to her parents about her decisions. Even though not every adolescent will choose to confide in her parents before she becomes sexually active or before she seeks contraceptive care, most will talk with someone in their family in the following months.

What family planning programs also provide that is often overlooked are a host of educational and counseling services for adolescents and adults. Many have libraries where books, pamphlets, and filmstrips can be borrowed or purchased. Clinical personnel are frequently available to talk to individuals about their concerns and questions and more and more clinics are offering training sessions for parents and educators to help them be more comfortable in their role as sex educators (Furstenberg et al., 1982). "Rap sessions" for mothers and daughters are very popular, and many programs are designing groups to include fathers and sons. Some clinics offer parents the opportunity to work on advisory boards or planning committees. Also, family-planning providers are underutilized as links between parents and other groups or organizations. Given the demanding schedules of parents, it may be too difficult to make the time commitment necessary for participating in special clinic programs. However, family-planning professionals are available to come to where groups of parents are already gathered, such as schools or churches.

In addition to these professional resources, it is important to realize that some of the best resources are right in your own neighborhood. Most parents find that talking to adolescents about sexuality is a touchy issue that brings out anxieties and insecurities for everyone. Gathering with neighbors and relatives to share experiences and concerns can provide ideas and insights to make the task easier. A parent can readily see that he or she is not alone. Moreover, since these friends will usually be acquainted with one's own children, they can help clarify the troublesome issues. People who know one well can also offer support for teaching personal values that they are likely to share, something professionals may not be able to do. In short, neighborhood discussion groups give support and encouragement that enable parents to better face their responsibilities of educating and guiding their children.

ANNOTATED REFERENCES

Alan Guttmacher Institute. *Teenage Pregnancy: The Problem that Hasn't Gone Away.* New York: Alan Guttmacher Institute, 1981.

The benefit of this book is that it presents, in a very readable format, some of the most often quoted statistics about adolescent sexuality and pregnancy.

Bell, R., and co-authors. *Changing Bodies, Changing Lives: A Book for Teens on Sex and Relationships.* New York: Random House, 1980.

This is an excellent book for adolescents and parents. The authors (who also wrote *Our Bodies, Our Selves*) present technical physiological facts as well as raise more general issues of decision making, attitudes, and dating.

Chilman, C. S. *Adolescent Sexuality in a Changing American Society: Social and Psychological Perspectives.* Bethesda, MD. DHEW Public Health Service, National Institute of Health, No. (NIH) 79-1426, 1979.

This is the most comprehensive research review available about the causes and consequences of adolescent sexuality. The author reviews data collected over a period of several years and carefully points out where there are inconsistencies and contradictory findings.

Ooms, T. (Ed.). *Teenage Pregnancy in a Family Context.* Philadelphia: Temple University Press, 1981.

This edited volume came out of the Family Impact Seminar which called together experts in adolescent sexuality to discuss family involvement in services for adolescents. The authors make recommendations and discuss problems with current policies and programs.

Shea, J. A. *An Annotated Bibliography about Family Involvement and the Delivery of Family Planning Services.* Unpublished report, 1983. (Available from The Family Planning Council of Southeastern Pennsylvania, Suite 616, 2 Penn Center Plaza, Philadelphia, PA 19102).

Research about the impact of family members on adolescents' sexual decisions and behaviors is summarized in a nontechnical manner. The focus is on highlighting conclusions and suggesting strategies to involve parents in adolescents' decisions.

Stuart, I. R., & Wells, C. F. (Eds.). *Pregnancy in Adolescence: Needs, Problems, and Management.* New York: Van Nostrand Reinhold Company, 1982.

This edited volume, written for counselors and practitioners, gives summaries of some of the most current research projects designed to prevent adolescent pregnancy and help young mothers meet their parenting responsibilities. The discussions at the end of each chapter give some very practical suggestions.

REFERENCES

Adams, G. R., & Gullotta, T. *Adolescent Life Experiences.* Monterey, CA: Brooks/Cole, 1983.

Ager, J. W., Shea, F. P., & Agronow, S. J. "Method Discontinuance in Teenage Women: Implications for Teen Contraceptive Programs." In I. R. Stuart & C. F. Wells (Eds.), *Pregnancy in Adolescence: Needs, Problems, and Management.* New York: Van Nostrand Reinhold Company, 1982.

Akpom, C. A., Akpom, K. L., & Davis, M. "Prior Sexual Behavior of Teenagers Attending Rap Sessions for the First Time." *Family Planning Perspectives,* 1976, *9,* 203–206.

Alan Guttmacher Institute. *Eleven Million Teenagers: What Can Be Done about the Epidemic of Teenage Pregnancies in the United States?* New York: Alan Guttmacher Institute, 1976.

Alan Guttmacher Institute. *Teenage Pregnancy: The Problem That Hasn't Gone Away.* New York: Alan Guttmacher Institute, 1981.

Baizerman, M. "Can the First Pregnancy of a Teenager Be Prevented? A Question Which Must Be Answered." *Journal of Youth and Adolescence,* 1977, *6,* 343–351.

Barret, R. L., & Robinson, B. E. "Teenage Fathers: Neglected Too Long." *Social Work,* 1982, *28,* 484–488.

Bennett, S. M., & Dickinson, W. B. "Student-Parent Rapport and Parent Involvement in Sex, Birth Control, and Venereal Disease Education." *Journal of Sex Research,* 1980, *16,*114–130.

Bolton, F. G., Jr. *The Pregnant Adolescent: Problems of Premature Parenthood.* Beverly Hills: Sage Publications, 1980.

Brittain, C. V. "Adolescent Choices and Parent-Peer Cross Pressures." *American Sociological Review,* 1963, *28,* 385–391.

Bury, J. K. "Some Social Aspects of Providing Contraception for under 16-year-olds." *Fertility and Contraception,* 1980, *4,* 1–6.

Campbell, B. K., & Barnlund, D. C. "Communication Patterns and Problems of Pregnancy." *American Journal of Orthopsychiatry,* 1977, *47,* 134–139.

Card, J. J., & Wise, L. L. "Teenage Mothers and Teenage Fathers: The Impact of Early Childbearing on the Parents' Personal and Professional Lives." *Family Planning Perspectives,* 1978, *10,* 199–205.

Chamie, M., Eisman, S., Forrest, J. B., Orr, M. T., & Torres, A. "Factors

Affecting Adolescents' Use of Family Planning Clinics." *Family Planning Perspectives*, 1982, *14*, 126–139.

Chess, S., Thomas, A., & Cameron, M. "Sexual Attitudes and Behavior Patterns in a Middle Class Adolescent Population." *American Journal of Orthopsychiatry*, 1976, *46*, 689–701.

Chilman, C. S. *Adolescent Sexuality in a Changing American Society: Social and Psychological Perspectives.* Bethesda, MD: DHEW Public Health Service, National Institute of Health, No. (NIH), 79-1426, 1979.

Chilman, C. S. "Social and Psychological Research Concerning Adolescent Childbearing: 1970–1980." *Journal of Marriage and the Family*, 1980, *42*, 793–805.

Cohen, D. *Male Adolescent Psychosexual Development: The Influence of Significant Others on Contraceptive Behavior.* Unpublished doctoral dissertation, University of Pennsylvania, 1982.

Cosgrove, P. S., Penn, R. L., Jr., & Chambers, N. "Contraceptive Practice after Clinic Discontinuation." *Family Planning Perspectives*, 1978, *10*, 337–340.

Couch, G. B. "Youth Looks at Sex." *Adolescence*, 1967, *2*, 255–266.

Coughlin, D. J., & Perales, C. A. *Family Planning and the Teenager: A Service Delivery Assessment.* Report to the Secretary of HEW, New York: November 1978.

Cvetkovich, G., & Grote, B. "Psychosocial Maturity and Teenage Contraceptive Use: An Investigation of Decision-making and Communication Skills." *Population and Environment*, 1981, *4*, 211–226.

Cvetkovich, G., Grote, B., Lieberman, E. S., & Miller, W. "Sex Role Development and Teenage Fertility-related Behavior." *Adolescence*, 1978, *8*, 231–236.

Davis, S. M., & Harris, M. B. "Sexual Knowledge, Sexual Interests, and Sources of Sexual Information of Rural and Urban Adolescents from Three Cultures." *Adolescence*, 1982, *17*, 471–492.

Dickinson, G. "Adolescent Sex Information Sources, 1964–1974." *Adolescence*, 1978, *13*, 653–658.

Donovan, P. "Airing Contraceptive Commercials." *Family Planning Perspectives*, 1982, *14*, 321–324.

Dryfoos, J. G. "Contraceptive Use, Pregnancy Intentions and Pregnancy Outcomes among U.S. Women." *Family Planning Perspectives*, 1982, *14*, 81–94.

Dryfoos, J. G., & Heisler, T. "Contraceptive Services for Adolescents: An Overview." *Family Planning Perspectives*, 1978, *4*, 223–233.

Edwards, L. E., Steinman, M. E., Arnold, K. E., & Hakanson, E. Y. "Adolescent Contraceptive Use: Experience in 1762 Teenagers." *American Journal of Obstetrics and Gynecology*, 1980, *137*, 583–587.

Evans, J. R., Selstad, G., & Welcher, W. "Teenagers: Fertility Control Behavior and Attitudes before and after Abortion, Childbearing, or Negative Pregnancy Tests." *Family Planning Perspectives*, 1976, *8*, 192-200.

Finkel, M. L., & Finkel. D. J. "Sexual and Contraceptive Knowledge, Attitudes, and Behavior of Male Adolescents." *Family Planning Perspectives*, 1975, *7*, 256-260.

Finkel, M. L., & Finkel, D. J. "Male Adolescent Contraceptive Utilization." *Adolescence*, 1978, *13*, 443-451.

Forrest, J. D., Hermalin, A. I., & Henshaw, S. K. "The Impact of Family Planning Clinic Programs on Adolescent Pregnancy." *Family Planing Perspectives*, 1981, *13*, 109-116.

Fox , G. L. "Sex-role Attitudes as Predictors of Contraceptive Use among Unmarried University Students." *Sex Roles*, 1977, *3*, 265-283.

Fox, G. L. "The Family's Role in Adolescent Sexual Behavior." In T. Ooms (Ed.), *Teenage Pregnancy in a Family Context*. Philadelphia: Temple University Press, 1981.

Fox, G. L., & Inazu, J. K. "Mother-Daughter Communication about Sex." *Family Relations*, 1980, *29*, 347-352.

Freeman, E. W., Rickels, K., Huggins, M. R., Mudd, E. H., Garcia, C. R., & Dickens, H. O. "Adolescent Contraceptive Use: Comparisons of Male and Female Attitudes and Information." *American Journal of Public Health*, 1980, *70*, 790-797.

Furstenberg, F. F., Jr. "Birth Control Experience among Pregnant Adolescents: The Process of Unplanned Parenthood." *Social Problems*, 1971, *19*, 192-203.

Furstenberg, F. F., Jr. *Unplanned Parenthood: The Social Consequences of Teenage Childbearing*. New York: The Free Press, 1976.

Furstenberg, F. F., Jr. "Burdens and Benefits: The Impact of Early Childbearing on the Family." In T. Ooms (Ed.), *Teenage Childbearing in a Family Context*. Philadelphia: Temple University Press, 1981.

Furstenberg, F. F., Jr., Herceg-Baron, R., Mann, D., & Shea, J. "Parental Involvement: Selling Family Planning Clinics Short." *Family Planning Perspectives*, 1982, *14*, 140-144.

Furstenberg, F. F., Jr., Herceg-Baron, R., Shea, J., & Webb, D. *Family Communication and Contraceptive Use among Sexually Active Adolescents*. Paper presented at the annual meeting of the National Family Planning and Reproductive Health Association, Washington, D.C., April 1983.

Furstenberg, F. F., Jr., Lincoln, R., & Menken, J. *Teenage Pregnancy and Childbearing*. Philadelphia: University of Pennsylvania Press, 1981.

Furstenberg, F. F., Jr., Masnick, G. S., & Ricketts, S. How Can Family

Planning Programs Delay Repeat Teenage Pregnancies? *Family Planning Perspectives*, 1972, *4*, 54–60.

Furstenberg, F. F., Jr., Shea, J., Allison, P., Herceg-Baron, R., & Webb, D. "Contraceptive Continuation Among Adolescents Attending Family Planning Clinics." *Family Planning Perspectives*, 1983, *15*, 211–217.

Gagnon, J. H., & Simon, W. *Sexual Conduct: The Social Sources of Human Sexuality*. Chicago: Aldine, 1973.

Gallup, G. *Reflecting Epidemic of Teenage Pregnancies: Growing Number of Americans Favor Discussion of Sex in Classroom*. Gallup Poll, Princeton, NJ, January 23, 1978. (a)

Gallup, G. *Teens Claim Sex Education Classes Helpful*. Gallup Youth Survey, Princeton, NJ, October 4, 1978. (b)

Gebhard, P. H. "The Acquisition of Basic Sex Information." *Journal of Sex Research*, 1977, *13*, 148–169.

Goldsmith, S., Gabrielson, M. O., Gabrielson, I. W., Matthews, V., & Potts, L. "Teenagers, Sex, and Contraception." *Family Planning Perspectives*, 1972, *4*, 32–38.

Goodman, B., & Goodman, N. "Effects of Parent Orientation Meetings on Parent-Child Communication about Sexuality and Family Life." *Family Coordinator*, 1976, *25*, 285–290.

Hansson, R. O., Jones, W. H., & Chernovetz, M. E. "Contraceptive Knowledge: Antecedents and Implications." *Family Coordinator*, 1979, *28*, 29–34.

Hendricks, L. E., Howard, C. S., & Caesar, P. P. "Help-seeking Behavior among Select Populations of Black Unmarried Adolescent Fathers: Implications for Human Service Agencies." *American Journal of Public Health*, 1981, *71*, 733–735.

Herceg-Baron, R., & Furstenberg, F. F., Jr. "Adolescent Contraceptive Use: The Impact of Family Support Systems." In G. L. Fox (Ed.), *The Childbearing Decision: Fertility Attitudes and Behavior*. Beverly Hills, CA: Sage Publications, 1982.

Herceg-Baron, R., & Shea, J. *Sex Related Communication in Families with Adolescent Children: Implications for Family Planning Providers*. Final report to Bureau of Community Health Services, Office of Family Planning, December 1982.

Herold, E. S. "Contraceptive Embarrassment and Contraceptive Behavior among Young Single Women." *Journal of Youth and Adolescence*, 1981, *10*, 233–242.

Herold, E. S., & Goodwin, M. S. "Why Adolescents Go to Birth-Control Clinics Rather Than to Family Physicians." *Canadian Journal of Public Health*, 1979, *70*, 317–319.

Hunt, W. B., II. "Adolescent Fertility—Risks and Consequences." *Population Reports*, Series J, Number 10, July 1976.

Inazu, J. K., & Fox, G. L. "Maternal Influence on the Sexual Behavior of Teen-age Daughters." *Journal of Family Issues*, 1980, *1*, 81–102.

Jaffe, F. S., & Dryfoos, J. "Fertility Control Services for Adolescents: Access and Utilization." *Family Planning Perspectives*, 1976, *8*, 167–175.

Jessor, S. L., & Jessor, R. "Transition from Virginity to Nonvirginity among Youth: A Social Psychological Study over Time." *Developmental Psychology*, 1975, *11*, 473–484.

Johnson, L. D., & Staples, R. E. "Family Planning and the Young Minority Male: A Pilot Project." *Family Coordinator*, 1979, *28*, 535–543.

Jorgensen, S. R., King, S. L., & Torrey, B. A. "Dyadic and Social Network Influences on Adolescent Exposure to Pregnancy Risk." *Journal of Marriage and the Family*, 1980, *42*, 141–155.

Jurich, A., & Jurich, J. "The Effect of Cognitive Moral Development upon the Selection of Premarital Sexual Standards." *Journal of Marriage and the Family*, 1974, *36*, 736–741.

Kallen, D. J., & Stephenson, J. J. "Talking about Sex Revisited." *Journal of Youth and Adolescence*, 1982, *11*, 11–23.

Kar, S. B., Talbot, J. M., & Coan, C. E. *Impact of Peer Counseling on Teen Contraception in Los Angeles*. Paper presented at the annual meeting of the National Family Planning and Reproductive Health Association, Washington, D.C., April 1982.

Kenkel, W. F. *The Family in Perspective*. New York: Appleton-Century-Crofts, 1960.

Kirby, D. "The Effects of School Sex Education Programs: A Review of the Literature." *Journal of School Health*, 1980, *50*, 559–563.

Kirby, D., Peterson, L., & Brown, J. G. "A Joint Parent-Child Sex Education Program." *Child Welfare*, 1982, *69*, 105–114.

Klerman, L. V., Bracken, M. B., Jekel, J. F., & Bracken, M. "The Delivery-Abortion Decision among Adolescents." In I. R. Stuart & C. F. Wells (Eds.), *Pregnancy in Adolescence: Needs, Problems, and Management*. New York: Van Nostrand Reinhold Company, 1982.

Koenig, M. A., & Zelnik, M. "The Risk of Premarital First Pregnancy among Metropolitan-area Teenagers: 1976 and 1979." *Family Planning Perspectives*, 1982, *14*, 239–247. (a)

Koenig, M. A., & Zelnik, M. "Repeat Pregnancies among Metropolitan-area Teenagers: 1971–1979." *Family Planning Perspectives*, 1982, *14*, 341–44. (b)

Kuhnen, K. K., Chewning, B., Day, T., Bosworth, K., Gustafson, D., & Hawkins, R. *BARNY: A Computer Who Cares About Adolescents' Sex Education*. Paper presented at the annual meeting of the American Public Health Association, Montreal, 1982.

Laws, J. L., & Schwartz, P. *Sexual Scripts: The Social Construction of Female Sexuality*: Hinsdale, IL: The Dryden Press, 1977.

Lerner, R. M., Karson, M., Meisels, M., & Knapp, J. R. "Actual and Perceived Attitudes of Late Adolescents and Their Parents: The Phenomenon of the Generation Gap." *Journal of Genetic Psychology*, 1975, *126*, 195–207.

Lerner, R. M., & Knapp, J. R. "Actual and Perceived Intrafamilial Attitudes of Late Adolescents and Their Parents." *Journal of Youth and Adolescence*, 1975, *4*, 17–36.

Lewis, R. A. "Parents and Peers: Socialization Agents in the Coital Behavior of Young Adults." *Journal of Sex Education*, 1973, *9*, 156–170.

Luker, K. *Taking Chances: Abortion and the Decision Not to Contracept.* Berkeley: University of California Press, 1975.

McKenry, P. C., Walters, L. H., & Johnson, C. "Adolescent Pregnancy: A Review of the Literature." *Family Coordinator*, 1979, *28*, 17–28.

Middleman, R. "Services for Males in a Family Planning Program." *American Journal of Public Health*, 1972, *62*, 1451–1453.

Miller, P. Y., & Simon, W. "Adolescent Sexual Behavior: Context and Change." *Social Problems*, 1974, *22*, 58–75.

Miller, W. B. L. "Sexual and Contraceptive Behavior in Young Unmarried Women." *Primary Care*, 1976, *3*, 427–453.

Mindick, B., & Oskamp, S. "Individual Differences among Adolescent Contraceptors: Some Implications for Intervention." In I. R. Stuart & C. F. Wells (Eds.), *Pregnancy in Adolescence: Needs, Problems, and Management.* New York: Van Nostrand Reinhold Company, 1982.

Olson, L. "Social and Psychological Correlates of Pregnancy Resolution among Adolescent Women: A Review." *American Journal of Orthopsychiatry*, 1980, *50*, 432–445.

Orr, M. T. "Sex Education and Contraceptive Education in U.S. Public High Schools." *Family Planning Perspectives*, 1982, *14*, 304–313.

Paul, E. W., & Pilpel, H. F. "Teenagers and Pregnancy: The Law in 1979." *Family Planning Perspectives*, 1979, *11*, 297–302.

Philliber, S. G., & Tatum, M. L. N. "Sex Education in the Biology Classroom: An Evaluation by Parents and Faculty." *American Biology Teacher*, 1981, *43*, 141–147.

Presser, H. "Sally's Corner: Coping with Unmarried Motherhood." *Journal of Social Issues*, 1980, *36*, 107–129.

Rains, P. *Becoming an Unwed Mother.* Chicago: Aldine-Atherton, 1971.

Reichelt, P. A., & Werley, H. H. "Sex Knowledge of Teenagers and the Effect of an Educational Rap Session. *Journal of Research and Development in Education*, 1976, *10*, 13–22.

Reiss, I. L. *The Social Context of Premarital Sexual Permissiveness.* New York: Holt, Rinehart, & Winston, 1967.

Roberts, E. J., Kline, D., & Gagnon, J. *Family Life and Sexual Learning: A Study of the Role of Parents in the Sexual Learning of Children* (Vol. 1: A Summary Report). Cambridge, MA: Population Education Inc., 1978.

Rogel, M. J., Zuehlke, M. E., Petersen, A. C., Tobin-Richards, M., & Shelton, M. "Contraceptive Behavior in Adolescence: A Decision-making Perspective." *Journal of Youth and Adolescence,* 1980, *9,* 491-506.

Rosen, R. H. "Adolescent Pregnancy Decision-making: Are Parents Important?" *Adolescence,* 1980, *15,* 43-54.

Rothenburg, P. B. *Mother-child Communication about Sex and Birth Control.* Paper presented at the annual meeting of the Population Association of America, Altanta, 1978.

Rothstein, A. A. "Men's Reactions to Their Partners' Elective Abortions." *American Journal of Obstetrics and Gynecology,* 1977, *128,* 831-837.

Ryan, G. M., & Sweeney, P. J. "Attitudes of Adolescents toward Pregnancy and Contraception." *American Journal of Obstetrics and Gynecology,* 1980, *137,* 358-362.

Scales, P. "Males and Morals: Teenage Contraceptive Behavior amid the Double Standard." *Family Coordinator,* 1977, *26,* 211-222.

Scales, P., & Beckstein, D. "From Macho to Mutuality: Helping Young Men Make Effective Decisions about Sex, Contraception, and Pregnancy." In I. R. Stuart & C. F. Wells (Eds.), *Pregnancy in Adolescence: Needs, Problems, and Management.* New York: Van Nostrand Reinhold Company, 1982.

Scales, P., Etelis, R., & Levitz, N. "Male Involvement in Contraceptive Decision Making: The Role of Birth Control Counselors." *Journal of Community Health,* 1977, *3,* 54-60.

Schinke, S. P., & Gilchrist, L. D. "Adolescent Pregnancy: An Interpersonal Skill Training Approach to Prevention." *Social Work in Health Care,* 1977, *3,* 159-167.

Settlage, D. S. F., Baroff, S., & Cooper, D. "Sexual Experience of Younger Teenage Girls Seeking Contraceptive Assistance for the First Time." *Family Planning Perspectives,* 1973, *5,* 223-226.

Shah, F., & Zelnik, M. "Parent and Peer Influence on Sexual Behavior, Contraceptive Use, and Pregnancy Experience of Young Women." *Journal of Marriage and the Family,* 1981, *43,* 339-348.

Shah, F., Zelnik, M., & Kantner, J. F. "Unprotected Intercourse among Unwed Teenagers." *Family Planning Perspectives,* 1975, 7, 39-44.

Shea, J. A., & Freeman, E. W. *Young Men Involved in Teenage Pregnancies: Experiences and Needs.* Unpublished manuscript.

Shea, J. A., Herceg-Baron, R., & Furstenberg, F. *Clinic and Contraceptive Use of Adolescent Clients.* Paper presented at the annual meeting of the National Family Planning and Reproductive Health Association, Washington, D.C., April 1983.

Shea, J. A., Jemail, J. A., Nathanson, M., & Baird, A. *Prospective Fathers and Their Adolescent Partners.* Unpublished Paper.

Shipman, G. "The Psychodynamics of Sex Education." *Family Coordinator*, 1968, *17*, 3–12.

Shostak, A. B. "Abortion as Fatherhood Lost: Problems and Reforms." *Family Coordinator*, 1979, *28*, 569–574.

Smith, P. B., Nenney, S. W., Weinman, M. L., & Mumford, D. M. "Factors Affecting Perception of Pregnancy Risk in the Adolescent." *Journal of Youth and Adolescence*, 1982, *11*, 207–215.

Sorenson, R. C. *Adolescent Sexuality in Contemporary America: Personal Values and Sexual Behavior, Ages 13–19.* New York: World Publishing Co., 1973.

Spanier, G. B. "Formal and Informal Sex Education as Determinants of Premarital Sexual Behavior." *Archives of Sexual Behavior*, 1976, *5*, 39–67.

Spanier, G. B. "Sources of Sex Information and Premarital Sexual Behavior." *Journal of Sex Research*, 1977, *13*, 73–88. (a)

Spanier, G. B. "Sexual Socialization: A Conceptual Review." *International Journal of Sociology of the Family*, 1977, *7*, 87–106. (b)

Stuart, I. R., & Wells, C. F. (Eds.). *Pregnancy in Adolescence: Needs, Problems, and Management.* New York: Van Nostrand Reinhold Company, 1982.

Thompson, L., & Spanier, G. B. "Influence of Parents, Peers, and Partners on the Contraceptive Behavior of College Men and Women." *Journal of Marriage and the Family*, 1978, *40*, 481–492.

Thomson, E. "Socialization for Sexual and Contraceptive Behavior: Moral Absolutes versus Relative Consequences." *Youth and Society*, 1982, *14*, 103–128.

Thornburg, H. D. "A Comparative Study of Sex Information Sources. *Journal of School Health*, 1972, *42*, 88–91.

Tietze, C. "Teenage Pregnancies: Looking Ahead to 1984." *Family Planning Perspectives*, 1978, *10*, 205–207.

Torres, A., Forrest, J. D., & Eisman, S. "Telling Parents: Clinic Policies and Adolescents' Use of Family Planning and Abortion Services." *Family Planning Perspectives*, 1980, *12*, 284–292.

Torres, A., Forrest, J. D., & Eisman, S. "Family Planning Services in the United States, 1978–1979." *Family Planning Perspectives*, 1981, *13*, 132–141.

Udry, J., Bauman, K., & Morris, N. "Changes in Premarital Coital Experience of Recent Decade-of-Birth Cohorts of Urban America." *Journal of Marriage and the Family*, 1975, *37*, 783–787.

Udry, J. R., Newcomer, S., Gilbert, M., & Bauman, K. *Friends' Influence on Adolescent Sexual and Contraceptive Behavior.* Paper presented at the annual meeting of the American Psychological Association, Montreal, 1980.

Vener, A. M., & Stewart, C. S. "Adolescent Sexuality Behavior in Middle America Revisited: 1970–1973." *Journal of Marriage and the Family*, 1974, *36*, 728–735.

Walter, G. S. "Psychologic and Emotional Consequences of Elective Abortion." *Obstetrics and Gynecology*, 1970, *36*, 482–491.

Yankelovich, D. *The General Mills American Family Report, 1978–1979. Family Health in an Era of Stress.* Minneapolis, 1979.

Zabin, L. S., & Clark, S. D. "Why They Delay: A Study of Teenage Family Planning Clinic Patients." *Family Planning Perspectives*, 1981, *13*, 205–217.

Zabin, L. S., & Clark, S. D. "Institutional Factors Affecting Teenagers' Choice and Reasons for Delay in Attending a Family Planning Clinic." *Family Planning Perspectives*, 1983, *15*, 25–29.

Zabin, L. S., Kantner, J. F., & Zelnik, M. "The Risk of Pregnancy in the First Months of Intercourse." *Family Planning Perspectives*, 1979, *11*, 215–222.

Zelnik, M. "Sex Education and Knowledge of Pregnancy Risk among U.S. Teenage Women." *Family Planning Perspectives*, 1979, *6*, 355–357.

Zelnik, M., & Kantner, J. "Sexual and Contraceptive Experience of Young Unmarried Women in the U.S., 1976 and 1971." *Family Planning Perspectives*, 1977, *9*, 55–71.

Zelnik, M., & Kantner, J. "Reasons for Nonuse of Contraception by Sexually Active Women Aged 15–19." *Family Planning Perspectives*, 1979, *11*, 289–296.

Zelnik, M., & Kantner, J. F. "Sexual Activity, Contraceptive Use, and Pregnancy among Metropolitan-Area Teenagers: 1971–1979." *Family Planning Perspectives*, 1980, *12*, 230–237.

Zelnik, M., & Kim, Y. J. "Sex Education and Its Association with Teenage Sexual Activity, Pregnancy, and Contraception Use." *Family Planning Perspectives*, 1982, *14*, 117–125.

4. ADOLESCENT
SOCIAL RELATIONSHIPS

Louise Guerney and Joyce Arthur

In family and educational "folklore," adolescents are branded as the most difficult age group to relate to. Agencies attempting to place adolescent youngsters find few experienced foster parents willing to volunteer to take them. Foster parents list them as their least preferred age group (Guerney, 1976). Is this because these are *foster* children experiencing family and/or personal difficulties? Probably not. It would appear that it is a cultural expectation in many Western countries that adolescence is a time of great "storm and stress." (See Bandura, 1964; Lerner & Spanier, 1980, for discussions.) This view is reflected in the writings of teachers, parents, popular magazines and professional journals. Can all of this smoke exist if there is no fire creating it? Are we simply stereotyping? Can most adolescents be relating quite well to family and other significant adults and yet be categorized with a minority of those who *are* in trouble? Or is there really something about the characteristics of adolescents which commonly creates relationship difficulties with adults responsible for them?

The overriding relationship issue for normal adolescents is acceptance by their peers. Is it necessary that pleasing the peer group results in conflict with the parental generation? It would be very satisfying to the reader and the writers as well, if a clear-cut answer to the questions posed were presented in this chapter. The fact is that there is a great deal of confusion and controversy about what is inevitably a part of this period of development, and what is generated unnecessarily by the adult culture, the peer culture and the value and problem-solving style of the culture as a whole.

Some studies indicate that the adolescent period is far less problematic to adults in other cultures, and for the youngsters themselves, than it is in our culture (Kandel & Lesser, 1969). All cultures in one way or another recognize the special status of those living in this transitional period. Even when adult roles are assigned with the establishment of puberty, expectations and rules are different for at least those in the early teen years than for older members of the society. The recognition that lack of experience with adult roles makes a difference seems to be essentially universal. What differences in performance expectations and interpersonal behaviors should be sanctioned or tolerated is not at all clear. To what degree this transitional age should remain under the rules of relationship and expected performances of childhood is also not clear in our society.

Some anthropologists and sociologists believe that families and other community members can relate best to adolescents when social rituals are attached to the physiological establishment of puberty. These bring a different status and clear-cut role responsibilities and rights. In the North American culture, no prescribed pattern is identifiable for which children can prepare. Each family, even each family *member* (fathers and mothers are often quite different) must attempt to come to some terms with the new children who face them—the taller, stronger, more capable, more mature children that are suddenly theirs to deal with.

Many books have been written and, recently, parent and teacher training programs have been developed to try to help adults relate more effectively to adolescents. The bibliography section of this chapter gives these; however, the degree to which the adolescent years will be a time of strained and conflictual relationships between most teens and adults may never be reduced to zero. Some differences that arise may be developmental—i.e., a direct result of age and stage of the youngster's development. Or, they may have nothing or only a little to do with their own and adult responses to the anatomical and physiological changes going on. On the other hand, the differences could be a result of our failure as a culture to prepare teen-agers and others in their lives for their new status and to create a clear-cut set of role behaviors which would satisfy the developmental needs of the teens, yet limit the degree to which the behaviors of this transitional period would conflict with family, school, and neighborhood.

ADOLESCENTS AND THEIR FAMILIES

It is generally accepted that accompanying the incalculable number of maturational activities in the bodies and minds of adolescents come changes in the behaviors of the adolescents and changes in the response of others to them. Parents find themselves saying, "A kid as big as you ought to be able to. . . ." Thus changes in expectation and toleration of non-compliance also take place in those relating to teen-agers. Do most parents and teen-agers see these parental responses as fair and appropriate (Bigler, 1979; McCandless & Coop, 1979)?

More studies than parents with worrisome teen-agers probably would imagine indicate that most teens are reasonably content with their parents, their home life, and their parent-teen relationships. Active desire to please the parents is present in at least two-thirds of the youngsters. Most regard their parents as useful models for their own behavior. This, however, is to some degree at least, a function of how much the adolescents see their parents as having succeeded. Some Black youngsters, for example, whose parents have no or low-paying jobs and experience other consequences of poverty, are less likely to *wish* to model their parents (Himes, 1964). Whether in fact they do is a function of factors other than their feelings about their parents' status and accompanying behaviors.

So it is a first step in coping to recognize that it is age appropriate for teen-agers to need space away from the family, to prefer not to join all family activities, not to confide in parents (this is true of boys in particular), to have rapid mood changes (partly biological) reflecting success and failure in relating to others or meeting their personal goals. The latter may be particularly hard on parents because they are not aware of what the frustration or elation might mean to the adolescent. Since the youngster communicates these feelings to no one else or shares these concerns with only his peers, the parents really cannot know what prompts them. Some family specialists believe that the adolescents, at this point of individualizing for themselves, *need* to believe that no one else or at least no adult, could truly understand what they are interested in, concerned about, or believe.

Lerner (1975), based on studies he and co-workers conducted, came to the interesting conclusion that later teens (as well as older adolescents in the 20's, an age group we are not emphasizing in this chapter) perceive their parents as having attitudes that are more different than they really are from their own. In relation to attitudes, Lerner suggested, it would appear that the "generation gap" is more of a *projection* of difference, emanating originally from the adolescents. This would indicate that the values conflict between adolescents and their parents may be less real than is widely believed.

However, clinicians do know that it is at the adolescent stage that many serious relationship problems do become identified. Again, it is not a certainty whether these problems are generated at adolescence or whether they are perhaps the continuation of earlier conflict, which now becomes intolerable when youngsters become physically and mentally more mature and *egocentric* (that is, preoccupied with their own thoughts and feelings). Many acting-out adolescents have a history of such behaviors throughout the school years. Others are reported as adjusted to school and family expectations until adolescence. One well-known study (Kandel & Lesser, 1969) indicates that in Danish society, where children have greater demands on them as children and presumably therefore have learned to behave in ways that make them more responsible in the eyes of adults, adolescents are given more freedom from adult control. The adolescents express greater feelings of independence and are less problematic to parents. However, another important difference between Danish and American adolescents is that Danish families are significantly more democratic in handling their youngsters. Overwhelmingly, American families are authoritarian. (Authoritarian parental control allows little room for views other than the parents'; democratic control allows for input from children, but established parental standards are upheld.) The greater the involvement of teen-agers in decision-making and the greater the concern for helping them understand and not subjecting them to arbitrary rules, the less the conflict seems to be between teens and parents. Many of the current parent educators take this position and attempt to teach American parents to be less authoritarian (for example, see Gordon, 1970).

The reader should be clear in understanding that involving adolescents (sharing some power) in decisions relevant to them does not mean that the parents surrender final authority on family matters. It simply is a recognition of the reality of the youths' mental and physical abilities to understand, contribute, and have opinions. Such participation in decision making is critical to taking full responsibility for oneself as an adult. Some researchers in drug abuse prevention believe that practice in decision-making and having responsibility for one's own behavior, to the full extent possible for one's age, leads to more mature decisions about drugs and other potentially destructive activities.

However much the family power structure and emotional atmosphere contribute, these can be no more than background for the foreground task of the adolescent's shifting at least a certain degree of loyalty from the family to peers. This appears to be a necessary phase in the *individuation process*, that is, the manner in which a person becomes a unique, separate individual, with his or her own interests, values, personality, identity, etc. To develop a positive concept of self, the need for acceptance from peers rises with age, so that by the teen years it is the all-important area for acceptance and approval.

Nonetheless, experts suggest that there are limits for age-appropriate behaviors directed toward freeing oneself from parents and becoming a full member in the society of one's peers. It is not within the limits to abuse drugs, act out sexually, be in trouble with the law, be violent at home, or fail in school. While some adolescents may perceive some degree of the above named behaviors as "the modern way," parents should be alerted that trouble is brewing for their adolescents as well as themselves when such behaviors are evidenced. The peer group as a whole, not some subgroups of it, quickly rejects adolescents who go beyond the boundaries of age-appropriate nonconformity.

Larson (1972) introduced the notion of a difference in youngsters on a dimension of parent-versus-peer orientation. When the youth is going through the adolescent period and attempting to shift identity to the peer group, the extent of parent-orientation will determine whether he/she will side with his/her best friend or the parents. Those who are "peer-oriented" will opt for the way of the friend, and the "parent-oriented" will choose the parents' approach. Whether either orientation is superior for later adjustment is not known. Inability to resolve conflicts between the two can lead to alienation from one or the other group. Nonetheless, even when alienation or physical separation from the parents develops in the process of moving toward a new self-identity, adolescents sometimes try to relate to a different family unit, as opposed to a "crowd of peers." For example, such phenomena as joining religious communes which are organized as surrogate families, the designation of certain peer leaders in residential institutions to play parent roles for the other young residents, and the joy in being welcomed into the family of a beloved friend which appears to the adolescent to be a totally superior one to his or her own, suggest that the need for a family structure runs deep. The establishment of surrogate families appears to be one way to assist adolescents to resolve the conflicts they experience between an outgrown birth family identity and a fragile, newly emergent personal identity. Parents will be cheered to know that the ultimate resolution generally results in a young adult who is far more similar to the members of the birth family in values, attitudes, and the behavioral expressions thereof, than their oppositional adolescent's behavior might indicate. It would seem that once psychological emancipation from the family is perceived as complete by the adolescent and identity sufficiently established, adolescents can be more objective about their parents and families.

PEER RELATIONSHIPS

Overview

Experts in development view adolescent peer relationships as the foundation upon which the social skills necessary for a successful adulthood are developed. Peer relationships also serve as a mechanism through which earlier dependencies on parental guidance and support may be more easily loosened.

Many view the adolescent period as one in which the primary developmental task is the attainment of the interpersonal skills critical for success in intimate heterosexual adult relationships (Havighurst, 1951). Further, it is believed that preparation for successful *adult* friendships is also facilitated through adolescent peer activity. Adolescents learn to accept responsibility for others outside of the family sphere. In sum, peer relations provide a training ground for the incorporation of essential social skills as well as an outlet for the beginning expressions of individuality. Additionally, peer relationships play a critical role in adolescent personality development.

The Role of Peer Groups

The most powerful feature of the peer group is its ability to offer a sense of belonging at a time when conventional institutions and authorities are being questioned. It provides support and emotional security to adolescents who are unsure of themselves and their position in the grand scheme of things. Experts generally agree that peer opinion largely directs adolescent activity. It seems ironic that in the quest for identity, adolescents initially strive towards conformity. Research tends to support the importance of peer acceptance; psychological maladjustment among teens often has been attributed to a lack of significant peer attachments (Janes & Hesselbrock, 1978).

Day to day contact with friends offers the opportunity to discuss events and persons of interest and provides reassurance on pertinent issues like dating. Long telephone conversations provide much of the interaction between friends. Although both male and female adolescents engage in these activities, sex differences as well as age differences do exist in the nature of peer activities.

Sex and Age Differences in Peer Relationships

Not surprisingly, it appears that males are allowed more independence from parents at an earlier age than are females (Douvan & Adelson, 1966). Consequently, males initially demonstrate higher peer orientation than females. Early adolescent males spend a greater amount of time with peers and less with family. However, female early adolescents still tend to cling rather closely to parental authority.

Early friendships. Same sex friendships are strongest during the early adolescent period for both males and females. Neither sex has begun to view the other with any sense of significance. But the characters of the friendships are quite dissimilar. Males tend to cluster in larger groups than females and for an entirely different purpose. The early adolescent gang serves as a united effort against invasions of adult authority (Douvan & Adelson, 1966). Early adolescent females have fewer friends but closer relationships within those friendships. Also, females tend to openly confide personal information more readily than males do (Bigelow & LaGaipa, 1980).

Early adolescents of both sexes choose friends that are more similar than dissimilar in terms of social class and likes and dislikes. Friends are chosen more for compatibility with individual preferences than for unique internal qualities. Friendships center around activity rather than personalities for both sexes. Some believe that early adolescent friendships tend to incite fewer emotional, interpersonal conflicts because of the lack of committed emotional involvement.

Research indicates that friendships are less stable during the early adolescent years; stability of friendship increases with age (Gold & Douvan, 1969). It has also been reported that adolescent males tend to have more stable friendships than adolescent females.

Mid-adolescent friendships. As early adolescent girls mature, they also become less tied to the family and more concerned with the quality of friendship. Indeed, friendships become more of a mutual exchange for both sexes. Close and "best" friends are sought to share secrets and ideas with on topics of interest. Quite importantly, friends also serve as sources of information and feedback regarding the opposite sex. Additionally, as adolescents grow older, the emotional support needed in moments of inadequacy is aptly provided by peers.

Late adolescent friendships. The role of the peer group during late adolescence continues to be one of providing a context of support and encouragement in the realm of heterosexual relations. Social skills and knowledge of societal expectations are refined in this pre-adulthood stage of development. Dating relationships are important and serve as the major preparation for adult intimacy. Older adolescents tend to have fewer friends but are committed to more intense attachments to these select few (Douvan & Adelson,

1966). Further, an appreciation of friends' individuality has been fostered, and there is less need for conformity to peer expectations. Finally, there is a movement back to acceptance of parental input and its value in most decision-making situations.

Structure of Peer Groups

Dunphy (1963) made a classic study of the structure of adolescent peer groups, primarily in urban settings, through an examination of cliques and crowds. *Cliques* are associations of very close friends of similar ages, backgrounds and interests. Larger groups of cliques were identified as *crowds*. Crowds were usually distinguished along age lines, with the older group having higher status.

Stages of peer group development. Dunphy describes five stages of peer group development. In Stage 1, isolated single-sex cliques exist. The crowd has not yet emerged. Stage 1 typically characterizes early adolescent relationships. The crowd begins to develop in Stage 2. Although the sexes are still clique segregated, there is group-to-group interaction. Stage 3 of Dunphy's model reflects the transition that occurs in peer relations with the initiation of dating activity. Single-sex cliques begin to merge with each other, forming a heterosexual clique. In Stage 4, the crowd is fully developed and heterosexual cliques are tightly knit. However, by Stage 5 and late adolescence, the crowd begins to dissipate, and there is only a loose association of couples.

Nature of cliques and crowds. Dunphy suggests that cliques and crowds have definite boundaries. Admission to a clique may be largely a function of conforming to clique standards. Dunphy found that expulsion from the clique is most often due to failure to conform to group authority or failure to achieve expected dating standards. The predominant activity of the adolescent cliques studied was conversation; crowds primarily attended movies and sports events.

Dunphy's work serves as an appropriate springboard from which other aspects of the so-called adolescent peer subculture may be examined.

Impact of Peer Relationships upon Parents

Contrary to what may have been expected, it appears that adolescents are likely to choose peer groups with values and expectations quite similar to parental values and expectations. Indeed, when conflict occurs between adolescents and parents, it is usually related to the relatively insignificant matters already noted, such as choice of music or dress; furious disagreements regarding basic values are more the exception than the norm.

Research also reveals that parents play a much greater role in decisions with long-range implications than do peers. For example, in matters regarding future educational goals, parents probably are much more influential than the adolescent's closest friends. Peers may override parental input on issues such as dating activities, but parents retain the edge in long-range planning contexts (Brittain, 1963).

Peer-oriented individuals are more likely to exhibit much more anti-social behavior than those who have strong parent relationships. It may be the case that the extremely peer-influenced adolescent is that way due to a lack of parental interest and support. Parental failure to meet the needs of the adolescent and to structure a solid parent-adolescent relationship may cause an adolescent to be more favorably oriented toward those peers who espouse different values.

ADDITIONAL SOCIAL RELATIONSHIPS

Correctly so, most of the previous discussion has centered around parents and peers. However, alternative significant others can be found. After the home setting, adolescents spend the major portion of their time in school. Granted that teachers represent adult authority, the presumed antitheses to adolescent growth, many adolescents do maintain constructive relationships with some instructors. The most popular teachers chosen by adolescents are ones who exhibit a genuine warmth and caring attitude toward youth. Frequently, athletic coaches, camp counselors, and youth leaders are highly valued and serve as models. Those who respect youths as persons and as performers are favored.

Encounters with other adults may also occur in work settings for those adolescents who have begun to accept jobs. How helpful this exposure to external adult influence is to development is yet to be determined. The adolescent and work will be covered in Chapter 10, this volume, by Vondracek and Schulenberg.

DATING RELATIONSHIPS AND ROMANTIC LOVE

Dating, initially introduced in the early 1900s, is an almost exclusively American tradition. Most countries have no comparable counterpart to this activity in which American teen-agers participate as a rite of passage. The term is used to describe a variety of social interactions in which adolescents engage. However, a universally accepted definition of the concept does not exist. Group activities as well as single-couple experiences easily classify as dating behavior. For clearer understanding, perhaps the most useful perspective to adopt would be one which views *dating* as social activity that allows the opposite sexes to engage in social interactions with non-familial age-mates.

Dating, of course, occurs at ages beyond the adolescent years, but the tremendous significance of the activity at this period of the life span assures its uniqueness as a concept of adolesence. Further, the underlying dynamics and functions of dating during the adolescent years are quite different from the purposes of the date in later years.

Functions of Dating

Dating provides an additional means for adolescents to begin to achieve the necessary autonomy from adult figures. It is often the case that parents exert little meaningful influence over the adolescent's selection of a dating partner. Adolescent social dating also serves as a mechanism through which social skills in opposite-sex relationships are refined for application in adult relationships. Simply speaking, a foundation for the development of future intimate relationships is laid with the dating process.

Some specialists view the adolescent period as one of temporary freedom before having to assume adult responsibilities such as work. Therefore, one can appropriately utilize dating activity not only as a learning tool, but also as an outlet for social enjoyment, recreation, and entertainment.

In addition, heterosexual dating provides a means for the release of sexual tensions. An awakened sexuality comes forth during this period of development, and the touching or petting that occurs on dates may permit some sense of sexual gratification (see Shea, Chapter 3, this volume).

Social dating can be used to obtain a certain status level. Some partners are chosen because they enjoy high status among their peers. Popular and physically attractive partners are regarded favorably. Therefore, adolescents in such dating relationships are more easily accepted, whether or not a genuine interest actually exists between the couple.

Finally, dating was traditionally viewed as a form of courtship with marriage as the ultimate goal. The automatic association of dating as courtship has been largely dispelled over the years. Nevertheless, the activity continues to orient the adolescent towards issues of marriage and mate selection.

Kinds of Dating

Dating activity falls into several different levels. Steady, steadily, casual, group, and double-dating exemplify the wide range of adolescent dating behavior (Hurlock, 1967).

In casual dating, the adolescent partners are fairly formal with each other. Conversation is usually general and quite uninvolved. The major purpose of casual dating is one of providing acquaintance.

In steadily dating, which is different from steady dating, the relationship is secondary to individual personal satisfaction. Although the couple may frequently see one another, personal wants are more important than sustaining the relationship.

Steady dating reflects a need for companionship. The relationship is more emotionally charged than the casual dating relationship. The partners date each other exclusively, and the relationship moves toward one of equal authority. An increased intimacy may also develop. However, it should be noted that going steady means different things to different adolescents. Going steady may be more serious, even approaching engagement, for some adolescents, whereas with others it simply means an exclusive arrangement for dating between the two. Group and double-dating are both done as frequently as single-dating. Most of these dates take place at movies or athletic events.

Variations in Dating Behavior

Early adolescence. Researchers of adolescent development have found that noticeable variations exist among adolescents of different ages and sex.

Early adolescence is the time at which "crushes" develop. The object of a crush is frequently a teacher or older schoolmate. The basis for the attraction may be some admired attribute which is lacking in the adolescent. Crushes arise primarily because adolescents need some outlet for affectionate expression other than parents or relatives (Hurlock, 1967). Females tend to have more crushes than males since they typically acknowledge romantic attraction much more readily. Crushes are intense while they last but are generally forgotten easily when interest in other opposite sex members is ignited.

Females are more likely to have "sweethearts." It is unimportant if the attraction is unreturned or, more likely, unknown by the male in question. Sweethearts exist for discussing boyfriends with other girls. Often the "boyfriend" has no idea that he has captured anyone's attention. Girls tend to choose older boyfriends, and boys select younger girlfriends.

Mid-adolescence. At approximately 14 to 15 years, the segregation of friendship choices decreases. Both males and females prefer to choose same-sex partners in most school settings, such as the cafeteria, but both groups would rather go to a movie or take a walk with an opposite sex partner (Douvan & Adelson, 1966).

There is an increased openness in communication, and each partner tends to know the other's feelings, unlike the earlier years when neither sex would inform the other of actual emotional interest. Continuing the earlier trend, males are still more inclined to choose younger female partners, and females consistently

choose older males. Members of both sexes often attest that they
have been in love at least once during the previous year (Broderick,
1966).

Older adolescence. At ages 16 and above most adolescents
have best friends among the opposite sex. Almost all have begun
to date. Data indicate that older adolescents date much more
frequently than those at younger ages (Jersild et al., 1978). In
addition, females continue to talk more about the dating relationship to parents and friends than do males.

At the older ages, the frequency of steady dating is much
higher. Usually these relationships are quite open and reciprocal
in nature. Also, late adolescent dating activities tend to be much
less supervised by parents and other adults.

Conclusions About Dating

For the most part, as in same-sex relationships, adolescents
tend to choose partners who are most similar in terms of social
class and personal interests. If asked to describe an ideal dating
partner, the majority of adolescents would cite popularity and
physical attractiveness as critical factors. Intelligence or academic
excellence are not necessarily viewed by adolescents as highly
important attributes in the selection of a dating partner. As adolescents mature, they tend to regard qualities of personality such as
dependability and considerateness as the important characteristics
they want their partners to possess.

Typically, adolescent dating reflects a wide range of activity
(parties, movies, sports). Most dates involve some physical contact
such as hand-holding or light petting. Interestingly enough, it
appears that petting has increased significantly among younger
daters in recent years. This and other trends in adolescent sexuality
are discussed in Chapter 3, of this volume.

Most adolescents date because they want to, although the
importance of peer conformity cannot be ignored in the making
of such decisions. It is generally agreed that dating has its value in
preparation of the adolescent for adulthood. However, no great
consensus supports a specific age as being more appropriate than
another for initiation of dating activity. Needless to say, early
dating may facilitate growth in social skills and heterosexual

interpersonal communication. Adolescents who begin to date at approximately 13 to 14 typically have several years experience in dealing with the opposite sex before the entry into adulthood. It is possible that an expanded range of skills in heterosexual relations is encouraged by early dating activity. Alternatively, it may be that early dating can lead too soon to an intimacy that neither partner is ready for and before a clear understanding of an identity is established. Late daters may be more comfortable with themselves as individuals but lack the social graces and expertise cultivated through direct contact with the opposite sex. It is possible that this lack of sophistication may hinder smooth adjustment into adult heterosexual relations.

Since dating occupies a certain status position with the peer group, a lack of dating among adolescents may lead to reduced acceptance by peers. Poor self-esteem may emerge if the teen-ager associates personal worth with dating success.

In balance, it would appear that the advantages of early adolescent dating experience more than outweigh possible advantages to not dating. However, the reader should realize that because of the wide variations possible from community to community, and across subgroups within communities, and from individual to individual, recommendations about dating activities in specific instances cannot be given. Whatever the benefits, this method of relating to the opposite sex is firmly entrenched in our culture as a way of getting through the task of separation from family and moving toward the ultimate task of establishing adult heterosexual relationships.

It must be acknowledged that the data base which supports the preceding discussion on dating behavior draws primarily from research conducted with white middle-class adolescents. It is possible that variations may exist across class and racial lines (Hill, 1972; Scott & McHenry, 1977).

Romantic Love

Due to the general nature of the period, adolescence is probably the most opportune time for romantic love to surface. Experts often assert that teens are drawn toward idealization and committed beliefs. The adolescent's search for, and finding of, the "perfect" mate can be considered an extension of those tendencies. Even though teen-age love has been comically downplayed by many adults, some believe that the intensity of the emotions and the usefulness of the state cannot be denied.

In a sense, romantic love further facilitates the adolescent's identity growth. A love relationship implies a reasonable amount of mutual acceptance and respect. An adolescent who is easily accepted by an important other may more easily accept himself or herself as a worthwhile person. As a result, a stronger awareness of individuality is nurtured and contentment with that identity is anchored.

It is not very difficult to substantiate the commonality of the experience of romantic love in the adolescent years. The assumption that teens fall in love on several different occasions before reaching adulthood is usually supported when research with adolescents is conducted. Indeed, a number of youths report being in love as many as six different times. However, there are some scientists who argue that external factors, such as poor parent or school relations or a great need for emotional security, are much more important in directing the strength of the love relationship than the individual alone.

TEEN-AGE MARRIAGE

The great majority of adolescents devote the teen years to fulfilling self-development tasks of which deep same- and opposite-sexed relationships are an important part. Opposite-sexed relationships, in particular, serve to reinforce the adolescent's separateness from family, potential for adult behaviors, and sense of self-worth. For most teens, opposite-sex relationship issues take their place among the other age-appropriate relationship issues—the establishment of modified roles within the birth families, strengthened peer relationships, modified relationships with school and other institutional authorities, and perhaps involvement in some work relationships. However, a substantial number of teens take on the responsibility of a marital relationship and assume the role of husband or wife.

Fewer youths are entering their 20's married than was the case in recent decades. However, those who do are still more than likely to do so because of the impending birth of a child. Since the marriage of teen-agers under 17 is most frequently associated with pregnancy, it can be expected that marriage for this group will usually bring two new roles to manage rather than one. These adult roles must be acquired, in most instances, before the tasks of adolescence have been completed. Teens opting for marriage (which pregnancy facilitates) frequently express the belief that the love relationship and the establishment of a new family are, in fact, a means of resolving problems they have with emancipation from the birth family and/or esteem from peers.

In discussing teen marriage, we will address primarily marriages which involve two teen-agers, as opposed to marriages of a young woman in the late teens to a man 20 or more years of age. Until the marriage age began rising in the 1970s, this pattern of a young woman 19–20 marrying a young man 21–22 was relatively common, and even today cannot be viewed as unusual. However, the success of marriages in which at least one partner is 20 or under is likely to be low. A rule of thumb when it comes to marriage is that the older the partners, the more likely the marriage will be stable.

Why should this be so? It is not that teens are incapable of deep, enduring, intimate relationships with a chosen partner. Indeed they are. It seems to be less the choice of a "wrong" partner that contributes to the high dissolution rate than two other sets of factors, discussed in the following sections.

1. Reasons for Marriage

Adolescents who are estranged from their families and peers appear to be the ones who are likely to become very attached to a member of the opposite sex. This relationship appears to be used to supply a great deal of emotional support for the teens involved, support which would be more available to others from families and friends. In addition, there is an inverse relationship between success in school and early marriage. Another source of role satisfaction—that of achieving as a student—is missing for many of these teens. They look to romantic love to supply or substitute for the lack of fulfillment of needs to feel loved and capable. For a time, romance and very frequently its sexual expression appear to be the answer.

2. Group Identity Problems

Since relatively few teens are married in most communities, the young man of, say, 17 and his wife of 16 are likely to find themselves isolated from others of their age group. Since they still may be in school, they are likely to find that the life style of other students does not bend to include a husband and wife. Alternately, few more mature, married adults will welcome them as peers into their groups. While carrying the roles of older adults, they will be consigned, nonetheless, to a lower status than most older marrieds enjoy. If they have few financial resources, they will find that this further alienates them from sharing fully in the life of any group. In fact, most teen marriages are financially dependent on some outside source—family and/or public assistance. This type of resource limitation can lead to complex interpersonal patterns of power and dependence, involving also their parents in some cases, which can be destructive to individuals and their relationships. These factors, added to the unrealistic base for marriage, appear to be the major deterrents to success.

The divorce rate for teen-aged marriages is very high. Estimates range from a 60% divorce rate in six years to 50% in four years when both mates are 18 or under. In addition to the problems noted above for teen-aged marriages, other difficulties seem to involve the idealization of marriage to a degree unlikely to be possible for partners of any age. This is inevitably followed by frustration as reality sets in, and finally by disillusionment or disenchantment with each other and the marriage. Evidence is not clear as to whether living with in-laws or independently is more likely to lead to divorce. Finally, the failure to have completed the individual developmental tasks of adolescence and fully participate in the adolescent subculture before plunging into marital roles, and most likely parenthood as well, would seem to be still another powerful factor in the high rate of marriage failure among teens.

PARENTHOOD

Many couples are faced nearly simultaneously or within a short time with parenthood. For some young people who appear to have few other opportunities to demonstrate their worth, having a child may serve as evidence that they are capable of filling the role of man or woman. However, since the ability to succeed and enjoy parenting, unfortunately, is not related to the production of children, parenting problems can be severe and place further strain on the individuals and their marriage. Knowledge of child-rearing and care among adolescent parents has been found to be minimal and frequently unrealistic. Lack of awareness of developmental norms, e.g., the normal time for babies to be able to learn "to listen to their parents" can lead to extreme frustration for the young parents expecting better responses from their babies. Adolescent parents are at risk for child abuse and neglect. Researchers and practitioners have noted that infants of teen-aged mothers have disproportionately high numbers of developmental problems, which could be due to low verbal interaction with the mother as much as to problems in prenatal development.

In addition to the problems experienced in parenting, per se, early parenthood nearly always results in enduring socioeconomic problems for the young parents. The majority of girls drop out of high school during pregnancy never to return again. Fortunately, many school districts are now attempting to administer special programs for pregnant and new mothers, even offering nursery care for the babies in some instances. Such programs offer some potential for closing the destructive education gap these young mothers experience. However, early parenthood still does limit the degree to which the young parents can participate in other societal roles (Russell, 1980).

Relationship of Young Parents to Grandparents

After the birth of their babies, young wives in one study indicated that in-law problems increased, although many husbands did not share this view (deLissovoy, 1973). In instances where the baby's parents have not married and the mother is alone at home with her parents, problems still are created by the young mother's situation. Whether the mother has married and divorced and/or lived elsewhere, living with her parents appears often to create a "triangle of enmeshment" in which the young mother and her parents (usually her mother only) form a triangle of the baby, the mother, and the grandparent(s), making it impossible for the child to know who his/her parents are and denying the role of mother to the young mother. Being young and dependent upon her parents, the mother is unable to free herself from the role of daughter and fully participate in the parent role as an emancipated adult would have the capacity to do much more effectively.

Grandparents are the single most common source of baby-sitting, some grandmothers even giving up their jobs to care for their grandchildren. The pleasant picture of grandparenthood usually anticipated is hardly possible when the grandparents are functioning virtually as parents. One researcher examined the effect of the early parenthood of their daughters on grandparents (Smith, 1975). She found that few grandmothers expected or wanted to become a grandmother when it meant assuming at least partial responsibility for a grandchild and a daughter. The grandmothers frequently expressed concern for themselves because they were just entering a period of their lives when they might be able to satisfy some of their own needs—take jobs, etc. Commonly, when hearing of the daughter's pregnancy they reacted with shock, anger, sorrow for their pregnant daughter and self-questioning about what they had done wrong. Smith (1975) points out that despite a view among professionals that minority families accept teen-age pregnancies and welcome the baby, she found that they are just as concerned as non-minority families with the financial and other problems an additional child means to an already overburdened family. Furstenberg (1980) found the same thing; among his sample of teen-agers of whom 91% were Black, only 3% of the grandparents reacted favorably to the pregnancy.

Aside from the intergenerational conflict about responsibility and authority over the baby, grandmothers express the view that their daughters should stay home and care for their babies and not date. Their fears center largely on the possibility of another pregnancy. Grandmothers are concerned that their daughters' opportunities for marriage will be limited because of their parent status. Statistics invariably have shown over the years that the future life of the unwed or divorced teen-aged mother is very limited as far as the range of outcomes. With a poor education, few job skills, and one or more young children, the chances of finding desirable husbands are enormously reduced. This becomes an intergenerational problem also, as grandparents are turned to in crises of separation, desertion, and abuse (Dell & Appelbaum, 1977).

In addition to the other responsibilities, the parents of young parents typically provide financial help, whether there is a marriage or not. In the case of single mothers, one study of Black families showed that 51% of the parents were helping their daughters two years after the birth of their babies (Smith, 1975).

Readers should remember that young fathers are required by law to contribute to the support of their children, whether married or not. In fact, at two years after the baby's birth, 44% of young Black fathers were found to be doing so (Nye & Lamberts, 1980). Even this is rather remarkable, since few of the young men had regular or well-paying employment and many were not yet 20 years old.

ALTERNATIVE FAMILY EXPERIENCES FOR ADOLESCENTS

Adolescent youngsters frequently live in families which currently experience, or in earlier years experienced, divorce, resulting in their living with a single parent (usually the mother) or stepparents. A minority of youth never had a father in the home, but a great number live with a stepparent who may have children of his or her own. Thus, these adolescents live in blended or reconstituted families, as they are sometimes called. The experience of living with siblings and parents who are not part of the birth family during the adolescent years undoubtedly has significant effects on adolescents. How profound these influences are and to what degree they alter the ability of the affected teen-agers in dealing with emancipation from parents and forming new identities is not clear.

Some research indicates that boys, in particular, are more likely to act out in and/or out of the family when divorce has taken place in the years immediately prior to adolescence. One well-known researcher (Hetherington, 1979) has established that adolescent girls living with their divorced mothers are more precocious sexually and more mature in social development than girls living in father-present families. Adolescents who have experienced divorce during the teen years and have been interviewed about it report that, while they would have preferred that their parents not divorce, they generally regarded the action as sensible (Reinhard, 1977). They perceived themselves as having to take greater responsibilities than youths from intact homes and to have to mature faster. They did not see themselves as suffering socially from the experience.

Some clinicians' studies suggest that there is a delay of a few years in the response of young teens to the loss of a parent through divorce or to the acquisition of a stepparent. At that point, rage against the family finally surfaces and much acting out behavior is expressed. It is well established that adolescents are at risk for abuse and neglect in single-parent and stepparent living arrangements. Also, violence against parents by teen-agers is sometimes reported in broken and step families. Burgess, in Chapter 5, discusses the issue of family violence during adolescence.

Although the effects are not yet known, there are suggestions in clinical reports that adolescents who find themselves in reconstituted families with siblings who are older, younger, or even the same age as themselves where previously they dealt with siblings of different ages, experience a great deal of difficulty in learning how to relate to these new family constellations. Younger children, not yet old enough to have acquired sibling roles, would not experience the same problems (Bachrach, 1982; Camara et al., 1979).

While the picture is far from clear, there is a preponderance of evidence from the research indicating that when parents have succeeded in keeping the family functional, by cooperating with each other and building on consideration for children's feelings and life styles throughout the divorce and ensuing adjustments, the impact of the divorce is far less destructive. Here again, it would seem that democratic family styles would be of value in offering a structure for input from the youngsters involved in the marriage dissolution and/or remarriage. Working out visiting arrangements with non-custodial parents and opportunities to stay in contact with grandparents and significant other family members should interfere less with the normal course of adolescent development (Kelly & Wallerstein, 1977).

Although their numbers are few, adolescents in foster care experience a complexity of social relationships that deserve comment. Foster care involves children and youths living in homes other than those of their birth families, with substitute parents. These parents, at least temporarily, function on a daily basis in the place of birth parents. When the youngsters' own parents are still in the picture, there are two sets of parents for the young person to relate to. Usually social agencies also are involved, which introduces still other adults who attempt to influence the youths. Differences in goals for the youngster can create confusion and loyalty conflicts.

Foster care for adolescents has been increasing in recent years. It is considered preferable to non-family environments when life with the birth family must be disrupted (Stone, 1977). Some placement programs are considered supportive for adolescent development (e.g., Lanier & Coffey, 1981). Relating to several parents and their children undoubtedly complicates the tasks of adolescence for youngsters who become involved in the foster care system during this critical period. Support programs for birth parents and foster parents are considered essential and are increasingly available (e.g., Stone, 1977).

Concluding Remarks

Social role changes that necessarily take place in adolescence impact on everybody in the adolescent's social environment. Unlike growing 10 inches, which is essentially an individual and personal experience (albeit a boon to jeans and sneaker manufacturers), shifts in social roles of the adolescent require others to change also. For example, adults must learn how to share power with the newly maturing young person. Fortunately, the struggle to achieve maturity generally is followed by a positive, relatively quiet state which all adults in the adolescents' social system may enjoy.

SOURCES OF HELP

Most of the following organizations offer direct services to parents and/or adolescents who may be experiencing temporary or long-term difficulties. Local chapters or headquarters usually can be found across the country.

American Institute of Family Relations
5287 Sunset Boulevard
Los Angeles, CA 90027

Professional staff at the Institute counsel adolescents and engaged and married couples. Typically, referrals are made to local member counselors. Also, literature on family relations can be requested.

Big Brothers/Big Sisters of America
2220 Suburban Station Building
Philadelphia, PA 19103

Big Brothers/Big Sisters operate within over 400 agencies across the country. Professional social workers match mature adult volunteers with youths from single-parent homes. The organization's objective is to aid the social and emotional development of these young people who may not have access to sufficient adult guidance.

Family Service Association of America
44 East 23rd Street
New York, NY 10010
(212) 674-6100

The Family Service Association of America is a federation of approximately 300 local agencies which provide family counseling services and other programs to help families with parent-child, marital, and other common problems of family living. Over 200 communities have member affiliations.

Help
638 South Street
Philadelphia, PA 19147
(215) 546-7766

Help organizations operate a telephone counseling and referral service for youths who seek legal, medical and psychological advice. Youths command the phone lines, but professional consultation and supervision is utilized.

International Youth Council
7910 Woodmont Avenue
Suite 1000
Washington, D.C. 20014

The International Youth Council is a youth subgroup of the Parents Without Partners organization. Teens are given guidelines on how to successfully contend with the common problems or concerns possibly generated by a single-parent family structure.

National Alliance Concerned with School-Age Parents
7315 Wisconsin Avenue
Suite 211-W
Washington, D.C. 20014

The Alliance offers technical assistance to young parents and to those professionals who might work most closely with school-age parents. Also, assistance is given to parents, community groups and agencies that are interested in developing programs to combat adolescent pregnancies.

National Runaway Switchboard
2210 North Halsted
Chicago, IL 60614
(800)621-4000
(800)972-6004 (Illinois)

The Switchboard is a toll free referral service for runaway youths throughout the nation. Information and assistance for youths in problem situations is provided.

Parents Anonymous
2810 Artesia Boulevard
Redondo Beach, CA 90278
(213)371-3501

Parents Anonymous attempts to help prevent damaging relationships between parents and their children through referrals for proper treatment. In addition, group participation helps parents improve their self-image, thereby increasing the quality of family relationships.

Parents Without Partners
7910 Woodmont Avenue
Suite 1000
Bethesda, MD 20014

The major objective of PWP is to further the interests of the single parents and their children. Activities are highly politically oriented.

Step Family Foundation, Inc.
333 West End Avenue
New York, NY 10023

The Foundation organizes workshops, lectures, training programs, and counseling services for individuals and family units in step-family situations. Clients outside of New York are assisted through long distance telephone counseling and special workshops.

Young Men's Christian Association of America
291 Broadway
New york, NY 10007
(212)374-2000

The YMCA provides programs designed to encourage positive educational, physical, and social development for both male and female youths.

Young Women's Christian Association of America
National Board
600 Lexington Avenue
New York, NY 10022
(212)753-4700

Programs supported by the YWCA are aimed at fostering social and physical growth in female youth members.

In addition to the organizations previously described, youth and family services and programs are coordinated by state and county welfare departments. Moreover, parental skills training may be sponsored by various community agencies. See also *Parent Effectiveness Training* (Gordon, 1970), and *Assertive Discipline* (Canton, 1979).

Sources of Indirect Assistance

The sources detailed below distribute information concerning youth organizations at local, state and national levels.

Coalition for Children and Youth
815 1st Street, N.W.
Suite 600
Washington, D.C. 20005
(202)347-9380
The Coalition strives to serve as a focal organization for the receipt of information pertinent to public policy as it relates to children and youths. CCY frequently conducts research on issues of concern to children and youths and publishes a number of national periodicals.

National Commission on Resources for Youth, Inc.
36 West 44th Street
New York, NY 10036
(212) 682-3339
The Commission records youth participation programs that permit the young to assume responsible societal roles. For example, an organization that provides an opportunity for teens to run a museum or publish a magazine will most likely be listed in the Commission's files. Films, guides, and newsletters are published.

Mediation Associates, Inc. (National Headquarters)
8018 Warfield Road
Gaithersburg, MD 20879
Mediation Associates, Inc. is an organization of experienced family law attorneys trained in mediation and conflict resolution. Members work toward cooperative settlement of separation, divorce and post divorce disputes. Teen and pre-teen children old enough to participate in family issues related to them may be included in the mediation. Referrals to local mediators can be obtained.

ANNOTATED REFERENCES

The following sources may provide further insights into the nature of the adolescent's social world and are intended to assist parents, teens and professionals in successfully coping with pertinent issues that may arise. In addition, several information guides for organizations that specifically serve youth and their families are given.

Parents

Buntman, P., & Saris, E. *How to Live with Your Teenager: A Survivor's Handbook for Parents.* Palo Alto, CA: Birch Free Press, 1979.

The authors discuss ways in which to facilitate harmonious parent-teen relationships during the sometimes tension-filled adolescent years. Guidelines are given on such topics as how to help teens become more cooperative and to increase parent-teen communications.

Ginott, H. *Between Parent and Teenager.* New York: Avon, 1972.

Ginott offers suggestions for parents on how to avoid common parent-adolescent conflicts. A number of examples describe types of effective parent behaviors in dealing with problems that may occur.

Visher, E., & Visher, J. *Step-families: A Guide to Working with Step-parents and Step-children.* New York: Brunner/Mazel, 1979.

An overview of the step-family as a whole is provided along with an examination of the adults as individuals and as a couple. The special needs of the step-children are also considered.

Teens

Gnagey, T. *How to Put up with Parents: A Guide for Teenagers.* Champaign, IL: Research Press, 1976.

The author helps teens to understand and empathize with parents. Gnagey also provides guidelines for teens to follow to enhance their lives and their relationships with parents.

Larkin, D., & Schneider, A. *The Sweet Dreams Love Book: Understanding Your Feelings.* Toronto: Bantam, 1983.

Romantic love at adolescence is described. The authors attempt to help teens understand the stirring emotions that many feel toward an opposite-sex mate.

Richards, A., & Willis, I. *How to Get It Together When Your Parents Are Falling Apart.* New York: Bantam Book, 1976.

Richards and Willis list alternative sources of assistance to teens who cannot expect sufficient parental guidance and support when personal concerns arise.

Witt, A. *TA for Teens (and Other Important People).* Rolling Hills Estate, CA: Jalmar Press, 1981.

Teens are given an easy-to-understand version of transactional analysis, a tool sometimes used by psychologists to improve clients' communication skills. The book provides a fun way for youths to use the ideas to encourage closer relationships with parents and others.

Zerafa, J. *Go for It.* New York: Workman Publishing Col., 1982.

Teen-agers are supplied instructions on how to become popular, successfully deal with parents and foster close relationships with others. The book is primarily aimed at increasing the self-confidence of the uncertain adolescent.

Professionals

Cantor, L., & Cantor, M. *Assertive Discipline.* Los Angeles, CA: Cantor & Associates, Inc., 1976.

The authors provide methods in which classroom teachers can successfully assert themselves with students and retain control of classroom activities. Limit-setting and other tools found to be effective are discussed.

Ginott, H. *Between Teacher and Child.* New York: Avon, 1972.

Ginott alerts teachers to some of the classroom issues that may impact upon the nature of the teacher-child relationship. Although presented in a light-hearted manner, many useful, constructive suggestions can be found.

Goldstein, A., Sprafkin, R., Gershaw, N., & Klein, P. *Skill-streaming the Adolescent.* Champaign, IL: Research Press, 1980.

A structured learning approach to teaching pro-social skills to adolescents is detailed. Instructions on how to reduce disruptive behavior in the classroom in a manner beneficial to both teacher and student are described.

National Children's Directory. Edited by M. L. Bundy & R. G. Wholey. College Park, MD: Urban Information Interpreters, Inc., 1977.

This reference tool identifies organizations, commissions, and councils that are engaged in some activity to improve unfavorable conditions faced by young children and youth. Organizations such as the Child Welfare League and Children's Defense Fund are listed.

National Directory of Children and Youth Services. Compiled by editors of Child Protection Reports.

State, county (and some city) agencies across 48 states that serve families and youth are provided along with the names of individual contact persons. Also included are federal children and youth programs and clearinghouse information resources.

Youth-Serving Organizations Directory. Edited by A. Brewster. Detroit: Gale Research Co., 1980.

Organizations that are directly or indirectly concerned with the well-being of youth, 12–20, constitute the bulk of this volume. However, child development research centers are also included.

REFERENCES

Bachrach, C. "Children in Families: Characteristics of Biological, Step, and Adopted Children." *Journal of Marriage and the Family*, 1983, *45*(1), 171–179.

Bandura, A. "The Stormy Decade: Fact or Fiction?" *Psychology in the Schools*, 1964, *1*, 224–231.

Bigelow, B., & LaGaipa, J. "The Development of Friendship Values and Choice." In H. C. Foot, A. J. Chapman, & J. R. Smith (Eds.), *Friendships and Social Relations in Children*. New York: Wiley, 1980.

Bigler, J. *Parent-child Relations.* New York: Macmillan Publishing Co., 1979.

Brittain, C. V. "Adolescent Choices and Parent-Peer Cross Pressures." *American Sociological Review*, 1963, *28*, 385–391.

Broderick, C. "Socio-sexual Development in a Suburban Community." *Journal of Sex Research*, 1966, *2*, 1–24.

Brownstone, J., & Willis, R. "Conformity in Early and Late Adolescence." *Developmental Psychology*, 1971, *4*, 334–337.

Camara, K., Baker, O., & Dayton, C. *The Impact of Separation, Divorce, and Remarriage on Youth and Families: A Literature Review.* Palo Alto, CA: American Institute for Research, 1979.

Coopersmith, S. *Antecedents of Self-esteem.* San Francisco: W. H. Freeman and Co., 1967.

deLissovoy, V. "High-school Marriages: A Longitudinal Study." *Journal of Marriage and the Family*, 1973, 245–255.

Dell, P., & Appelbaum, A. "Trigenerational Enmeshment: Unsolved Ties of Single-parents to Family of Origin." *American Journal of Orthopsychiatry*, 1977, *47*, 52–59.

Douvan, E., & Adelson, J. *The Adolescent Experience.* New York: Wiley & Sons, 1966.

Dunphy, D. "The Social Structure of Urban Adolescent Peer Groups." *Sociometry*, 1963, *26*, 230–246.

Erikson, E. *Identity, Youth and Crisis.* New York: Norton, 1968.

Furstenberg, F. "Burdens and Benefits: The Impact of Early Childbearing on the Family." *Journal of Social Issues*, 1980, *36*, 64–87.

Gold, M., & Douvan, E. *Adolescent Development: Readings in Research and Theory.* Boston: Allyn & Bacon, 1969.

Gordon, T. *Parent Effectiveness Training.* New York: Plenum Publishing Co., 1975.

Guerney, L. *The Foster Parent Skills Training Programs, Part I.* University Park, PA: Institute of Human Development, 1976.

Havighurst, R. *Developmental Tasks and Education.* New York: Longman, Green, 1951.

Hetherington, M. "Effects of Father Absence on Personality Development in Adolescent Daughters." *Developmental Psychology*, 1972, *7*, 313–326.

Hill, R. *The Strength of Black Families.* New York: Emerson Hall, 1972.

Himes, J. "Some Work-related Cultural Deprivations in Lower-class Youth." *Journal of Marriage and the Family*, 1964, *26*, 447–451.

Hurlock, E. *Adolescent Development.* New York: McGraw-Hill, 1967.

Janes, C., & Hesselbrock, V. "Problem Children's Adult Adjustment Predicted from Teacher's Ratings. *American Journal of Orthopsychiatry*, 1978, *48*, 300–309.

Jersild, A., Brooks, J., & Brooks, D. *The Psychology of Adolescence.* New York: Macmillan, 1978.

Kandel, D., & Lesser, G. "Parent-adolescent Relationships and Adolescent Independence in the United States and Denmark." *Journal of Marriage and the Family*, 1969, *31*, 348–358.

Kelly, J., & Wallerstein, J. "Part-time Parent, Part-time Child: Visiting after Divorce." *Journal of Clinical Psychology*, 1981, *10*, 48–50.

Lanier, J., & Coffey, J. "Therapeutic Homes: An Alternative to Foster Care." *Journal of Clinical Child Psychology*, 1981, *10*, 48–50.

Larson, L. E. "The Influence of Parents and Peers during Adolescence: The Situation Hypothesis Revisited." *Journal of Marriage and the Family*, 1972, *34*, 67–74.

Lerner, R. "Showdown at Generation Gap: Attitudes of Adolescents and Their Parents toward Contemporary Issues." In J. Thornburg (Ed.), *Contemporary Adolescence: Readings.* Monterey, CA: Brooks-Cole Publishing Co., 1975.

Lerner, R., & Spanier, G. *Adolescent Development: A Life-span Perspective.* New York: McGraw-Hill, 1980.

McCandless, B., & Coop, R. *Adolescents.* New York: Holt, Rinehart and Winston, 1979.

Nye, F., & Lamberts, M. *School-age Parenthood: Consequences for Babies, Mothers, Fathers, Grandparents and Others.* Pullman, WA: Washington State University, Extension Bulletin 0667, entire issue.

Reinhard, D. "The Reaction of Adolescent Boys and Girls to the Divorce of Their Parents." *Journal of Clinical Child Psychology,* 1977, *6,* 21–23.

Russell, C. "Transition to 'Parent' for Teen-agers." *Journal of Social Issues,* 1980, *36,* 45–63.

Scott, P., & McHenry, P. "Some Suggestions for Teaching about Black Adolescents." *The Family Coordinator,* 1977, *26,* 47–57.

Sebald, H., & White, R. "Teenager's Divided Reference Groups: Uneven Alignment with Parents and Peers." *Adolescence,* 1980, 979–985.

Smith, E. "The Role of the Grandmother in Adolescent Pregnancy and Parenting." *Journal of School Health,* 1975, *45,* 5.

Stone, H. *With a Little Help from Our Friends: A Collection of Readings for Parenting an Adolescent.* New York: Child Welfare League of America, 1977.

5. CHILD ABUSE DURING ADOLESCENCE

Robert L. Burgess and Rhonda A. Richardson

We all trace our roots to what sociologists call the family of orientation, which consists of our brothers and sisters, if we have any, our parents, their siblings, our grandparents, greatgrand-parents, great aunts and so forth. The family is certainly the oldest and perhaps the most significant social institution in our lives and is often a source of solace and support when problems beset us. Nonetheless, as a result of careful and objective documentation by behavioral and social scientists, we have become increasingly aware that things can go awry and the family may become a battlefield (Straus, Gelles, & Steinmetz, 1980). In this chapter, we begin by discussing the origination of the concept of adolescence and why that age period may pose special problems for families. We then take up such issues as the definition and incidence of adolescent maltreatment, its possible causes, and some promising solutions.

THE DISCOVERY OF ADOLESCENCE

Virtually every human society practices some form of social differentiation based on chronological age. A person's age is commonly used as a basis for the expectations others have of that person. We expect different things from a "baby" than we do from an "old man." Thus, the social roles of children, adults, and the aged are usually quite different. Moreover, in almost every case, these role differences have involved differences in power, prestige and privilege. The ultimate basis for these distinctions lies in human biology; children are both physically and intellectually less developed than adults. The environment also plays a role; having had fewer opportunities to acquire experience and information, children are at a competitive disadvantage.

Even though age differentiation is found in all societies (as is sex differentiation), there are, nonetheless, differences across societies. They differ in terms of the number of age gradations, the transition points for moving from one grade to another, the ceremonies or rites of passage associated with transitions, and the particular expectations held by others for those in specific age grades (Linton, 1942). In most societies, there have been only four recognized age stages: infancy, childhood, adulthood, and old age. Adolescence, which is the interim status between childhood and adulthood, has, in fact, been recognized only relatively recently as a distinct age grade.

In a book titled *Centuries of Childhood* Philippe Aries (1962) noted that through the 17th century the French language distinguished only three major age gradations: childhood, youth, and old age. "Youth" referred to the prime of life. The common term for referring to children from birth through their teens was *enfant*. The French did not distinguish between infancy and the rest of childhood until later in the 19th century. Medieval books did, however, sometimes refer to an age category called adolescence, but it encompassed a period that began with puberty and extended into the middle thirties.

After careful historical study, Aries concluded that the identification of the age status, adolescence, resulted from several changes in French society, including the prolongation of the life span and the rise of militarism. With the increased martial spirit, great emphasis was placed on preparing boys for a military life. Consequently, in the beginning, there was a tendency to reserve the term "adolescence" for boys and for the well-bred and disciplined boys of the middle and aristocratic classes, at that.

In contrast to Aries' views, other scholars have emphasized the role of industrialization in the growing acceptance of adolescence as a distinct and unique age status. For example, Bakan, in "Adolescence in America: From Idea to Social Fact" (1971), attributes the recognition of adolescence as a stage of life to three major and interrelated social movements in the last two decades of the 18th century. These social changes were aimed at: compulsory education, child labor legislation and the establishment of the juvenile court. In earlier, non-industrial, agrarian societies, children were incorporated into the adult world of work at the earliest possible age. While quite young, they were given a variety of chores suitable to their abilities. As the children grew older, they were given more difficult and more responsible jobs until, in their early or middle teens, they assumed full adult responsibilities. Only a tiny fraction of the children would still be in school at this age.

Under this kind of system, young people were quickly absorbed into the adult community. With industrialization, however, there was a growing need for skilled labor that led to the development of compulsory education. To accomplish this, children had to be removed from the labor force. In industrial societies, therefore, opportunities for employment are severely restricted for teenagers which, as we shall see later, creates certain problems, especially for boys. Law and custom, then, compel adolescents to remain in school—a world made up almost exclusively of other youngsters. The only adults present are a handful of teachers, administrators, and janitors, none of whom is particularly important to the informal social world of young people.

Not surprisingly, these new social communities gradually developed distinctive subcultures of their own. This is a phenomenon that happens whenever groups of people with common concerns are brought into frequent contact with one another. While the specific focus of these juvenile subcultures varies from one group or cohort to another, they do have certain characteristics in common that may set the stage for conflict between them and older generations. First, adolescent groups are characterized by a succession of fads and fashions. These run the gamut from styles of grooming and dress to music and speech. The more rapidly these fads change, the more difficult it is for adults to keep up with them. This, in turn, provides the youth with a criterion by which to judge otherwise dominant adults as inferior, making it hard for adults to dominate or influence the youths. In this way, these constantly changing fads and styles function to maintain the boundary between adolescents and the adult community.

A second characteristic of adolescent groups is their rejection of adult values and authority. There is often even a tendency to flout the standards of the adult community (see Guerney & Arthur,

Chapter 4, this volume). Related to this is a third characteristic of adolescents: intolerance of nonconformity. Deviations or departures from peer norms or standards are often punished severely and frequently by ridicule, physical force and ostracism. Parents of teenagers are often keenly aware of the great concern that their sons and daughters display when it seems the adolescents are about to break one of these precious rules. It appears as if this harsh treatment is necessary because many adolescents feel ambivalent; they are often torn between their earlier-formed respect for and commitment to the values of their parents and the larger adult community and their desire to be accepted and liked by their friends. Discipline within their own ranks, then, serves to hold their ambivalent members in line and legitimize the existence of their subculture and its claim to a degree of autonomy within the larger culture.

ADOLESCENCE AND SOCIALIZATION

All societies and cultures have the need to socialize their members. Consequently, socialization is one of the most ubiquitous social processes. It is the means whereby behaviors are developed to allow an individual to function effectively within an established on-going group. Technically, socialization is defined as an interactional process wherein an individual's behavior is modified to conform to the rules or standards of the groups to which he or she belongs (Burgess & Bushell, 1969). All groups socialize new members. Immigrants are socialized into their adopted societies, recruits into the army, junior executives into the firm, freshmen into the campus community, and "new kids" into the neighborhood.

Thus, just as parents socialize their children, so, too, do adolescent peer groups socialize their members (Sherif & Sherif, 1964). But, adolescents do eventually become adults. Consequently, the separation between adolescent and adult groups is often a source of serious difficulties because many of the decisions that are crucial to a person in adulthood are made while he or she is still a member of the adolescent community and subject to its values and norms. Given the conflict between these two communities, many decisions that are made, consistent with youth values, prove unsound later. This is one reason why parents are often so concerned about who their sons' or daughters' friends are and why they commonly complain that their teenager spends too much time with friends.

Before the age status of adolescence was recognized, older adults were concerned with the recalcitrance of young people and their youthful misbehavior. There has even been an age-old tendency to see this problem as being worse than ever before. "Youth is disintegrating. The youngsters of the land have a disrespect for their elders and a contempt for authority in every form. Vandalism is rife and crime of all kinds is rampant among our young people. The nation is in peril." Those words were uttered almost 4000 years ago by a seemingly despondent Egyptian priest. Similarly, the ancient Greek philosopher, Socrates, put it this way: "Children today love luxury. They have bad manners, a contempt for authority, a disrespect for their elders, and they like to talk instead of work. They contradict parents, chatter before company, gobble up the best of the table, and tyrannize over their teachers."

Perhaps because of this inherent conflict, there have been strict codes and serious penalties in history past. According to the Code of Hammurabi (2270 B.C.), "If a son strikes his father, one shall cut off his hands." The Bible, too, provides us with examples of the seriousness of all this. In the Book of Exodus, it is written that children who strike or curse their parents should be put to death. In the Book of Deuteronomy it is decreed that any child guilty of disobedience or rebellion should be stoned to death (Kocourek & Wigmore, 1951).

This view of the incorrigibility of youth continues today. For example, the President's Commission on Law Enforcement and Administration of Justice (1967) concluded that: (1) "enormous numbers of young people appear to be involved in delinquent acts"; (2) "youth is responsible for a substantial and disproportionate part of the national crime problem"; and (3) "America's best hope for reducing crime is to reduce juvenile delinquency and youth crime" (pp. 169–170). The message is that adolescents, in general, and delinquents, in particular, are felt to be deficient in self-control and in their ability to resist temptation and delay gratification and they are not motivated to work for the common good.

But, whose rules or standards should we apply? As we noted

earlier, we are subjected to socializing pressures from all the groups to which we belong. When a child is young, parents may have high reward (or, reinforcing) value because they provide the child with affection, material benefits, help, companionship and recreation. Such a condition is conducive to the child's being strongly attached to his or her parents (Gewirtz, 1972). Moreover, the more positive consequences a parent has to provide contingently upon the child's behavior, the greater the parent's influence as a socializing agent for the child, e.g., as a model and teacher (Bandura, 1965). In other words, the more rewarding the parent is to the child, the easier it is for the parent to motivate the child to change his or her behavior in directions desired by the parent, and the easier it is to foster commitment to and compliance with the parent's norms and values. To put it in a slightly different way, the more dependent the child is on his or her parents for positive outcomes, the more power and influence the parents have over the child (Bandura, Ross, & Ross, 1963). This is not to say, of course, that the child has no influence over the parent's behavior. It is just that effective or successful socialization implies an imbalance in power with one person's behavior being changed more than the other's. Indeed, it is this greater state of dependency that provides the motivation for the child to comply with parental wishes.

But this is the rub. With increasing age, children typically spend less time in direct contact with their parents and more time with other adults, e.g., teachers, and, especially, more time with their age-mates or peers, at school and on the block. As a young person spends more and more time interacting with peers, the value of the rewards controlled by those peers can be expected to increase (Burgess & Akers, 1966). And, as the youngsters become increasingly dependent on each other, they become less dependent on their parents, and with this decrease in their dependency on their parents there is a concomitant decrease in parental power and influence. As parental influence wanes, the parents begin to worry about their teenager's relationship with his or her friends. The particular youth subculture to which an adolescent belongs may have norms and values similar to or quite different from those held by parents and the larger adult community. In either case, the young person may experience considerable pressure to conform to peer-group standards, and his or her parents may find their own loss of control quite distressing.

Associated with this change in the balance of power in a family as a child reaches adolescence is increasing role ambiguity. Parents are often unsure whether they should respond to their child as a "child" or as an adult. Inconsistency, in turn, breeds unpredictability and subsequent misunderstanding as well as disaffection. The normal conflicts of interest that occur in any family may already be magnified because of the greater demands on family resources being made by this child-adult. There is the use or misuse of the family car, the demand for a larger clothing allowance, the need for expensive orthodonture and stereo equipment. And, on top of all this, the balance of power is becoming more equal and role ambiguity increases.

From the perspective of many adolescents, most of their problems stem from the fact that their parents "treat them like children." In short, they feel that their parents refuse to adjust to the fact that they are no longer children. It is quite possible that the common teenager complaint that he or she has nothing to do may not necessarily be a complaint about the lack of amusements but instead a complaint about the lack of opportunities to perform responsible adult tasks. One of the reasons that girls seem to survive adolescence with fewer antisocial behavior problems than boys may stem from the fact that a girl's contributions to the family, especially in terms of domestic chores, are utilized, acknowledged and appreciated at a much earlier age. The girl may be a victim of sex discrimination, but it is the boy who probably suffers the most. Partly because they are deprived of useful activities to perform, boys contribute disproportionately to school problems, delinquency, automobile accidents and family strife.

The touchstone of parent-adolescent conflict seems to be the waning of parental influence. It is an insensitive parent who is unaware of the increasing influence of his or her teenager's friends. Adolescents are rarely alone, and they seem most at ease when they are with their friends. It is when they are together with their friends that they feel most free of parental pressure. As we indicated earlier, the peer group does have its own rules and regulations stipulating, for example, what to wear and when to wear it, what to say and how to say it. And the group may enforce these rules unmercifully and in concert. But, for several reasons, it is often easier for young people to conform to their peer-group norms than to adult norms. First, peer group rules are often simple and few in number. Second, they are more likely to specify behaviors that require less effort and have immediately reinforcing consequences. It is much easier to comply with a rule that says "Thou shalt spend time rapping with thy friends" than a rule that decrees "Thou shalt study hard and earn good grades." A common complaint by parents is that their teenager spends too much time with friends rather than "doing something more worthwhile." Third, compliance with peer-group norms is followed by a great deal of attention and acceptance and little punishment. In contrast, parents typically focus on a wide-range of the teenager's behaviors and are quick to resort to reprimands, threats and nagging for rule violations. Fourth, even if the adolescent must obey his peer group norms, he may also enforce them! Finally, compliance to those rules helps to establish his independence *vis à vis* his parents. Thus, the stage is set for battle. Indeed, matters may become so serious that events get out of hand and actual violence may erupt. Therefore, we shall now turn our attention to a description and explanation of the abuse or maltreatment of adolescents by their parents.

THE DEFINITION OF ADOLESCENT ABUSE

Before we can look at the incidence and causes of adolescent abuse we must have a clear idea of what we mean by "abuse." In trying to develop a definition of abuse, there are several troublesome issues that have plagued this area of research for over a decade. One is the question of intentionality; that is, must a parent's harmful behavior toward an adolescent be intentional in order to be considered abusive? Most would argue that it must. But answering in the affirmative leaves us with the problem of proving intentionality. Suppose, for example, that a father and his teen-age son are arguing during dinner about the son's 11:00 curfew. The argument becomes loud and angry; the father loses his temper and throws his hot coffee at his son; and the boy's face is scalded. Clearly, the father meant to throw the hot liquid, but did he intend for it to harm his son? Aside from simply asking him, is there any way to prove whether or not this was an accident?

Along with this issue of intentionality, a definition of abuse must also deal with the question of injurious outcome. That is, must a parent's behavior result in injury to the adolescent in order to be considered abusive? In the example above, does the mere fact that the son was harmed mean that the father's action, whether intentional or not, was abusive? Suppose that instead of hot coffee the father had thrown iced tea; now, even if he intended to harm his son, he failed to do so. Is the father's behavior in this instance an example of abuse?

The definition of abuse is complicated further by the fact that abusive parental behavior must be placed along a larger continuum of parent-adolescent relations, of adolescent "treatment" (Burgess, 1979). At one extreme along that continuum is behavior of a parent toward an adolescent that is so destructive that the adolescent's life is threatened. Further along the continuum are behaviors that are less easy to classify as abuse but that represent harsh childrearing styles relying heavily on physical punishment, extreme emotional humiliation, and the like. At the other end of the scale are the range of parental behaviors considered to be socially appropriate, effective childrearing practices. At what point along this entire continuum do we make a distinction between abusive and nonabusive parental behavior?

Finally, in defining adolescent abuse, four major types of parental behavior need to be considered. Perhaps the most commonly recognized and most frequently studied type is physical abuse. Such physically harmful acts range from pushing, slapping or spanking, to choking, punching, cutting or burning the adolescent. A second type is sexual abuse, which is the exploitation of the adolescent for the sexual gratification of an adult and includes exhibitionism, fondling of the genitals, incest, and rape.

Parental neglect represents the third major type of abuse in that it involves the harming of an adolescent through lack of care or supervision. It is a condition in which the parent permits the adolescent to experience avoidable suffering or fails to provide one or more of the ingredients necessary for physical, intellectual and emotional development (Polansky, Hally, & Polansky, 1975). Thus, we can distinguish between physical neglect, educational neglect, and emotional neglect (Burgdorff, 1982).

Along with physical and sexual abuse and the neglect of adolescents, we should also consider a fourth type of abuse, namely emotional abuse. This type of abuse provides a common thread linking the other three types. That is, physical and sexual abuse and neglect are of concern not only because of the physical injuries that result, but also because they threaten an adolescent's emotional well-being. Emotional abuse refers to parental behavior that jeopardizes an adolescent's interpersonal skills, patience, ability to set reasonable personal goals, or self-esteem (Garbarino, 1980). Examples of this form of abuse include refusing to care for the adolescent, punishing normal pro-social behaviors, or placing the adolescent in a consistently negative light.

Obviously, most cases of neglect and physical and sexual abuse also contain an element of emotional abuse. Furthermore, the first three types are not always independent of one another. In many cases of sexual abuse, for example, there is also physical abuse going on in the home. Although for purposes of identifying abusive parents it is useful to recognize four categories of abuse, we must keep in mind that the four are not distinct and that a given parent may fall into more than one group. Therefore, instead of talking about physical abuse, sexual abuse, neglect, and emotional abuse separately we find it useful to put all four under the single heading of adolescent abuse or maltreatment. We can then define adolescent maltreatment as "nonaccidental physical and psychological injury to a child between 11 and 18 years of age which occurs as a result of physical, sexual, or emotional acts of omission or commission perpetrated by a parent or caretaker and which threatens a child's developing competence" (Burgess & Richardson, 1984).

Incidence of Adolescent Abuse

Having established what we mean by abuse, we can now turn to a consideration of the number of adolescents experiencing such maltreatment. We must note, however, that just as there are problems in developing a precise definition of abuse, so too are there difficulties in getting an accurate estimate of its incidence. Throughout most of history, family matters have been treated as "private" affairs, immune from public or governmental intrusion.

Family members were free to behave as they saw fit in the privacy of their homes. It was not until the 1960s that child abuse became a subject of public attention. By 1968 all fifty states had passed legislation mandating the reporting of child abuse and neglect. According to these laws, members of the medical, educational, social service, law enforcement, and child care professions are required to report suspected cases of abuse or neglect to Child Protective Services authorities.

Despite these advances in the detection of parental maltreatment, there remains a continual problem of underreporting. Indeed, a summary of the National Analysis of Official Child Neglect and Abuse Reporting prepared by the American Humane Association (1981) indicates that in 1979 only 21%, or less than one-fourth, of all recognized cases of child abuse and neglect were reported to authorities. Several factors may contribute to this underreporting. One is the reluctance of professionals who come in contact with potential abuse victims to label parents as abusive without definite proof. That is, there is a fear of reporting "false positives" or cases that look like abuse but turn out not to be. Second is the difficulty of defining abuse, as we discussed above. Without a precise definition of abuse, marginal cases, in particular, may go unreported.

Finally, there is the problem of disproportionate reporting of abuse among various groups. That is, some cases of maltreatment are more likely to come to the attention of authorities than are others. Families on public welfare, for example, have ongoing contact with social service workers, which makes detection of abuse in these families easier than in middle-class families whose financial independence enables them to avoid professional scrutiny. Another example of disproportionate reporting is particularly relevant to our discussion of adolescent abuse. This is the fact that cases of abuse involving young children are more likely to be recognized and reported than are those involving adolescents.

Why is underreporting especially evident for this older age group? Part of the reason may be that abused adolescents often show up as delinquents, truants, runaways, or suicide attempts. Thus, they are mis-labeled as incorrigible or anti-social—i.e., as the recalcitrant youth we discussed earlier in this chapter. The issue of parental maltreatment in such cases is overlooked. The disproportionate underreporting of adolescent abuse may also be partly due to society's greater tolerance of strict discipline for adolescents than for young children. As we pointed out earlier, adolescence is a period when youngsters become less dependent on their parents and begin to adopt the norms and values of their peer group. Because these new standards of behavior frequently conflict with parents' own expectations for their adolescents, the parents, and adults in general, may believe that it is in the best interest of society to induce conformity to adult norms and values. Strict discipline, which may in some cases border on abuse, becomes an acceptable means of achieving this conformity and is therefore overlooked as an instance of parental maltreatment.

Lastly, underreporting of adolescent abuse may also stem from our tendency not to see youths as victims. Many believe that since teen-age boys are physically bigger and stronger than young children, they should be able to defend themselves against abuse. Similarly, the developing sexuality of teenage girls leads some adults to conclude that sexual abuse is a result of the adolescent's sexual promiscuity. Clearly, members of our society harbor many misconceptions about the intentions of seemingly misbehaving youth; misconceptions which lead to a severe underreporting of adolescent abuse. We must keep this in mind as we examine reported rates of child abuse in general and adolescent abuse in particular.

In spite of the problems encountered in defining and detecting cases of abuse, there is substantial evidence that we are dealing with a serious national problem. Furthermore, reports indicate that a large portion of the victims of parental abuse are adolescents. Findings from the National Study of the Incidence and Severity of Child Abuse and Neglect (Burgdorff, 1982) suggest that 47%, or nearly one-half, of reported cases of maltreatment involve adolescents between the ages of 12 and 17.

In their National Analysis of Official Child Neglect and Abuse Reporting, the American Humane Association (1981) reported over one million substantiated cases of child abuse and neglect, which represented a 71% increase between 1976 and 1979. The reasons for this increase are unclear and undoubtedly complex. Much of the increase, however, is probably due to our increased sensitivity to the problem, an expansion of our definition of what constitutes abuse and neglect and greater compliance to reporting laws. It is also possible, of course, that some of the increase is due to an increased frequency of abusive and neglectful behavior. The most prevalent forms of parental maltreatment were deprivation of necessities (i.e., neglect), minor physical injuries, and multiple maltreatment. In addition, the investigators concluded that the problem of abuse and neglect is not limited to young children. A full 36% of all children involved in substantiated reports of maltreatment were between the ages of 10 and 17.

This latter figure is consistent with that of Straus, Gelles, and Steinmetz (1980). In a nationwide survey of 2,143 families, these family violence researchers found that 73%, or nearly three-fourths, of all parents had used violence against their children at some time. This high rate is not simply due to the fact that they included physical punishment (i.e., slapping or spanking) in their definition of violence. Nearly one-half of the parents reported that they had pushed or shoved their children, while one-fifth of them also said they had hit their children with an object. Even more disturbing is the fact that four out of every 100 parents had engaged in severe violence (including kicking, biting, punching, beating, or using a knife or gun) against their children. Although, according to Straus and his colleagues, younger children are more likely to be abused than are older children, teenagers do experience a wide range of parental violence. In fact 54% of the 10–14 year olds and 36% of the 15–17 year olds in this study had experienced some form of maltreatment.

We saw earlier that the parent-adolescent relationship contains many potential sources of conflict. Moreover, we indicated that this conflict may erupt into violence. Such is not always the case, however. Our review of the incidence of adolescent maltreatment suggests that while many teen-agers are victims of abuse or neglect, many others are not. This brings us to a discussion of the reasons for adolescent abuse.

Reasons for Adolescent Abuse

Adolescent abuse may take one of three patterns (Lourie, 1979). First, it may represent the continuation of abuse from earlier childhood. In Protective Service settings the number of reported instances of this type may be lower than expected because it becomes manifest only in those cases where the adolescent is no longer willing to tolerate it. Rather than reporting it, however, the more common response by the adolescent may be in the form of other problems that divert the attention of authorities such as truancy, delinquency, drug abuse, adolescent pregnancy, etc. The second pattern is where there is a rather sudden or marked change in the intensity of parental punitiveness and control as the child enters adolescence. As Lourie (1979) put it "open-handed slaps or spankings become blows delivered with closed fists and greater force" (p. 969). The third pattern is one where the onset of abuse begins during adolescence. In these cases, calm, positive parent-child relations become stormy and violent. It is quite possible that the determinants of abuse may vary in some respects across these three patterns as Lourie (1979) has suggested. We will consider this possibility as we examine four categories of factors that may place a parent at risk for mistreating his or her adolescent. These are: personal characteristics of the parent, personal characteristics of the adolescent, structural features of the family, and social characteristics. Let us consider each group of risk factors.

Personal characteristics of the parent. In early attempts to understand and explain the occurrence of child maltreatment, parents were seen as the source of the problem. Research focused on identifying characteristics of the individual that distinguish abusive from nonabusive mothers and fathers. Thus, personal characteristics that place a parent at risk for adolescent maltreatment include emotional disturbances (Elmer, 1967), difficulty in dealing with aggressive impulses (Wasserman, 1967), a rigid and domineering personality (Johnson & Morse, 1968), and low self-esteem (Spinetta & Rigler, 1972). Other parent characteristics linked to child and adolescent maltreatment include alcoholism (Blumberg, 1974) and a history of having been abused or neglected as a child (Steele & Pollock, 1974). In addition, more recent research suggests that a high level of life stress is associated with the incidence of child or adolescent maltreatment (Conger, Burgess & Barrett, 1979; Straus, 1980). It has been suggested that those parents who continue their abusive behavior toward their children on into adolescence tend, especially, to be very disorganized and generally overwhelmed by their life circumstances (Lourie, 1979).

Although very little research has looked exclusively at the problem of adolescent maltreatment, we can speculate about personal characteristics of parents that may be especially important as risk factors during the teenage years. As their children move into their teens, most parents are entering middle age. During this mid-life phase, adults may begin to recognize their own mortality and to wish that they were younger. Parents who resent the youth of their teenage children may be at risk for behaving abusively. Indeed, recent research has found that women who want to be younger than they are report greater difficulty rearing adolescent children than women who accept their age (Rossi, 1980). Aside from this age factor there are other parental characteristics that may lead to abuse when children enter their teens. We discussed earlier the increasing independence and the role ambiguity that arise during adolescence. A parent who is unable or unwilling to take the perspective of the adolescent may be setting the stage for conflict. This is probably particularly true for parents who have had a tendency to be very rigid, controlling, and punitive all along. These parents may become especially frustrated by their teenager's growing independence and unwillingness to respond to discipline. These are the conditions that Lourie (1979) suggests are most likely to lead to the pattern of abuse identified by a quality change in the intensity of a parent's punitiveness as a child makes the transition to adolescence. Such a parent, in an attempt to maintain control, may resort to inappropriate use of physical punishment. Although the use of physical punishment is nearly universal (a study by H. Erlanger [1974] found that 85-97% of all parents have used physical punishment at some point in their child's life), we should be especially concerned when it is administered to adolescents. Not only might the punishment be applied with excessive force in order to counteract the youth's physical strength, but it may be emotionally damaging as well in that it relays a message of parental dominance and threatens the adolescent's self-esteem.

Characteristics of the adolescent. Looking only at the parents as the source of the problem may be a one-sided view. Research indicates that certain children may actually elicit maltreatment from their parents. An adolescent with a physical or mental handicap, for example, may be at risk for abuse or neglect (Sandgrund, Gaines & Green, 1974). Furthermore, displaying annoying behavior or being manipulative of one's parents may lead to maltreatment (Patterson, 1979). The increased need for independence and the shifting balance of power between parent and adolescent may also precipitate abuse. Finally, two other fundamental characteristics of the adolescent require consideration. The sex of the adolescent influences the likelihood of maltreatment. According to the National Incidence Study mentioned earlier (Burgdorff, 1982), rates of physical, sexual, and emotional abuse are up to three times greater for girls than for boys. Boys, on the other hand, are more likely to experience emotional neglect, perhaps because physical size and strength are not an issue with this form of maltreatment; any parent can give a son the "silent treatment" regardless of his size. In addition to gender, the age of the child may also determine the likelihood of receiving abusive treatment. As we discussed earlier, younger children are more likely to be victims of abuse (Straus et al., 1980). This may be partly due to the above-mentioned size and strength issue. Other research has shown, however, that when compared to their younger brothers and sisters, older children in abusive families receive less attention, both positive and negative, from their parents (Richardson, Burgess, & Burgess, 1984). By simply interacting less often with their parents, adolescents may avoid maltreatment but they may also be deprived of positive attention.

Structural features of the family. In addition to characteristics of the parent and adolescent, certain structural features of the family can also be predictive of parental abuse. Research indicates, for example, that family size, or the number of children in the family, is related to the likelihood of maltreatment (Gil, 1970; Straus et al., 1980). It seems that the larger the family, the greater the risk of abuse. Parents in these larger families must divide their economic resources, as well as their time, patience, and energy among more children (Richardson et al., 1984). Brothers and sisters may find themselves competing for attention. Trying to meet the diverse needs of their children may place a great deal of stress on the parents, and this stress may lead to abusive actions. These family size effects are less severe if the children are spaced further apart in age (Richardson et al., 1984). This wider spacing creates more "breathing room" in the family. This may be particularly important during adolescence. Dealing, for example, with an adolescent's increased demands on the family's material resources (e.g., use of the car, clothing allowance) will be easier when all of the other children in the family are either much younger or have already passed through adolescence, and therefore are not making similar demands. That is, it can be easier on parents if they only have to cope with one adolescent at a time.

Family size and spacing are important to consider not only because of their influence on the amount and type of stress that *parents* are experiencing, but also because of their influence on brothers' and sisters' actions toward one another. When there are more children in the family, there is more competition for family resources. Everything from living space, to parental time, to food must be shared among more people. Anyone who grew up with brothers and sisters can vouch for the fact that such sharing does not always come about without conflict. Who among us cannot recall fighting over the last piece of cake or who's next in the bathroom?! Indeed, although rarely the subject of research, sibling violence is the most prevalent form of family violence (Straus et al., 1980). In their nationwide survey, Straus and his colleagues discovered that while only three out of every 100 youths had ever been kicked, bitten or punched by a parent, an incredible 42%, or nearly one-half, had experienced such violence at the hand of a brother or sister! When she included hitting and slapping in her definition of violence, Steinmetz (1977) found that 70% of the families she interviewed had siblings who engaged in violent acts.

The problem of sibling violence is critical to a thorough understanding of adolescent abuse. Adolescence is a period of high sibling confrontation, with 76% of all 10–14 year olds and 64% of 15–17 year olds engaging in physical violence with their brothers and sisters. Moreover, such violent interchanges occur on the average of 19 times per year (Straus et al., 1980). As one might expect, boys are more violent toward their siblings than are girls, and the highest level of sibling violence appears when a boy has only brothers. In fact, by the time children reach their teens the rate of sibling violence in all-boy families is double the rate in families with all girls (Straus et al., 1980). Clearly, sibling violence represents yet another form of adolescent abuse. But it also brings us back to the problems of parents, for it illustrates still another way in which family size and spacing may place stress on parents and precipitate adolescent maltreatment.

Other structural features of the family also contribute to abusive behavior. Single parent households are heavily implicated in cases of abuse (Friedman, 1976). Indeed, households headed by a single female account for approximately 42% of reported cases of maltreatment. This relationship is probably due in part to the economic and psychological stress that accompanies divorce and single parenthood. Moreover, single parents may have to place more demands on their children for sharing in household responsibilities (e.g., cooking, cleaning, caring for younger siblings). While this may lead to greater maturity for some adolescents, for others it will interfere with efforts to achieve independence. Hence, once again parent-adolescent conflict will occur, to which the single parent may respond with abusive behavior.

In addition to single parents, stepparents are disproportionately represented in cases of abuse (Burgess, Anderson, Schellenbach, & Conger, 1981). The reasons for this have not been adequately investigated by researchers, but what we know about remarriage and stepfamily formation offers some clues. We know, for instance, that when asked about the difficulties of their family arrangements many stepfathers cite financial concerns stemming from their need to support not only the stepchildren but also their own children from a previous marriage (Albrecht, 1979). Again, we have the situation of competition for limited family resources and the accompanying potential for conflict. Stepfamily members also must deal with new family roles that have no clear behavioral expectations attached (Visher & Visher, 1978). For example, to what extent should a stepfather be responsible for disciplining his wife's children from a former marriage? And even if he does attempt discipline, to what extent are the stepchildren expected to follow his instructions? Adolescents in such situations may find themselves choosing between not just two, but three competing sets of norms and values—those of the peer group, those of the natural parent, and those of the new stepparent. Hence there is even greater potential for conflict.

The issue of how much a stepparent should treat his stepchildren as his own brings us to yet another example of adolescent maltreatment. Sexual abuse, or incest, occurs most frequently between fathers and daughters, particularly within stepfamilies (Finkelhor, 1979). The developing sexuality of the teenage girl makes this form of abuse especially likely during adolescence. Stepdaughters may be particularly vulnerable because their step-fathers may believe that the incest taboo prohibits sexual contact between blood relatives and thus does not extend to stepfamily members.

Social characteristics. Aside from personal characteristics of parents or children and structural features of the family, there are social characteristics that have received attention as predictors of child or adolescent maltreatment. Although the problem is by no means restricted to lower class families, low socioeconomic status (e.g., low income, high rate of unemployment, lack of education), perhaps again due in part to the stress it places on parents, results in a higher probability of child and adolescent abuse (Garbarino, 1977). Research also suggests that abusive families tend to be socially isolated (Garbarino, 1980). That is, they do not belong to many clubs or organizations, they have few friends, they rarely see their neighbors; in short, they do not spend much time with other people. Parents in these isolated families are often cut off from potentially helpful neighborhood and community resources. They may not have anyone to discuss problems with, to leave their children with in an emergency, to get advice from. In addition, because they have so little contact with people outside the family, these parents end up spending most of their time with their children. This means that there are more opportunities for con-flicts to arise and fewer opportunities to escape when tension begins mounting. Surely we can all recall at least one time in our past when, perhaps due to bad weather, we were stuck indoors with our families for an entire day and our children or our brothers and sisters began to "get on our nerves." With no chance to leave the house for awhile, persons are bound to argue and fight; and this pattern, begun in childhood, is likely to continue after the child has become an adolescent.

Thus, we have seen that numerous factors may account for the occurrence of adolescent abuse. Yet, even summarizing risk factors in this way does not really explain the phenomenon of adolescent maltreatment. For example, while single parents may be more likely than married parents to abuse their youngsters, not *all* single parents do so. Similarly, not all low income parents are abusive, nor are all abusive parents poor. Furthermore, even in those cases where the factors we have discussed *do* result in abuse, the process by which this happens remains unclear. We have mentioned repeatedly that some of these personal characteristics may place stress on the parent or lead to family conflict. But does this stress or conflict always lead to violence? Obviously, the answer is "no." Clearly, many of us are able to resolve family disagreements peacefully. In order to complete our understanding of the reasons for adolescent maltreatment, then, we need to look at the process by which stress and conflict erupt into actual abusive incidents. The key lies in studying the dynamics of family interaction.

Family interaction. In a carefully designed study involving detailed observations of families interacting with each other in their own home, it was found that abusive and neglectful families relate to each other differently on a day-to-day basis than do families with no known history of abuse (Burgess et al., 1981). In brief, families with a history of maltreatment dispay a style of interaction that undoubtedly sets the stage for overstepping the boundaries of acceptable discipline and treatment. Five characteristics of their interactional style stand out. First, they simply pay less attention to each other and they talk with and touch each other less often than do members of more normal families. Second, this lower level of activity was especially true for acts of positive regard. Members of abusive families were significantly less likely to hug or kiss each other or to praise or compliment one another. On the other hand, they also tended to exhibit higher than normal frequencies of negative behavior. They complained about things more often. Threats were common. Mutual disparagement of personal qualities occurred more often, and family members were more likely to strike one another. Fourth, these families have a tendency, literally, to command each other to do things. It was not, "Could you find time to wash the car today?" but, instead, "Are you deaf as well as dumb? I told you to wash the car. Now wash it!" Finally, these investigators discovered that such families have a pattern of reciprocating one another's disagreeable and harsh behaviors rather than their pleasant behavior, which is, instead, the pattern displayed by well-functioning families. To paraphrase the lyrics from an old song, abusive and neglectful families tend to accentuate the negative, eliminate the positive, and they mess around a lot with Mr. In-Between. Under these conditions, it becomes easier to understand how the natural tensions between parent and adolescent can escalate to the degree that physical force, humiliation, and exploitation become the rule rather than the exception.

But, how do families come to behave this way? Unfortunately, it is easier to describe an on-going process and to document its effects than it is to trace its development. Nonetheless, we are making some headway, and we shall try to describe what, so far, seems to occur. Research suggests that the development of a pattern of coercion, whereby family members treat each other as adversaries in their efforts to resolve conflicts of interest and disagreements, is a gradual process made easier by the various precipitating factors that we described earlier (Burgess et al., 1981; Patterson, 1982).

As we have mentioned, as a child progresses into adolescence, it is normal for the balance of power to shift. Parents are no longer the powerful influences in the lives of their teenagers they once were. They may even feel they are running out of time in their efforts to exert their influence. Parents may feel that there is so much yet that the teenager has not learned that they try to fix everything at once, commenting about every mistake or every instance of misbehavior, real or not. This, of course, is often perceived by the adolescent as constant parental nagging. It seems as if there is little time left for providing positive rewards to the adolescent who, in turn, is keenly aware of the fact that he or she can get those rewards from friends.

Parents, themselves, often become aware of the growing disaffection between themselves and their adolescent children and periodically attempt to reverse the trend. Thus, the parents may provide rewards with no contingencies or requests from the teenager. This can have two effects. One, the parents may increasingly feel that they are sacrificing family and personal resources for the benefit of an insatiable and unappreciative adolescent and, hence, resentment sets in. Two, because these rewards are noncontingent and unpredictable and, perhaps, because they are provided in the context of "the sacrificing parent syndrome," the rewards lose their potency to function as positive reinforcers that can provide the incentives for the adolescent to comply with parental requests. As these "reinforcers" lose their effectiveness, parents may come to use them less and less in their effort to motivate their adolescents to behave in certain ways. This may account for the lower frequency of positive behavior found in the abusive and neglectful families studied by Burgess and his colleagues (Burgess et al., 1981). In any case, it certainly puts the parents at a disadvantage *vis à vis* their teenager's friends.

There will, of course, continue to be conflicts of interest and disagreements of various sorts that need to be resolved. With the best of intentions, parents may sit their teenager down so that they can "have a talk." Unfortunately, in the absence of effective rewards, threats are quickly voiced, voices are raised and, at the very least, the teenager gets "a good talking to." Given the increased sense of power experienced by the adolescent, he or she may respond in equally vociferous ways and matters escalate. This pattern of conflict wherein family members take an adversarial stance towards each other may itself become the norm. We humans, however, are very adaptable creatures and can grow accustomed to the most intolerable conditions. Thus, the harsh words and claims of disappointment that earlier led to tears, regret, and compliance may now fall on deaf ears.

In addition to general adaptation, two other circumstances can lead to an escalating cycle of coercive and punitive behavior. First, if children are exposed to a socialization history marked by inconsistent punishment, normal punishing stimuli, such as reprimands and the loss of privileges, lose their ability to discourage or terminate undesirable behavior (Parke, Deur, & Saivin, 1970). Consequently, parents who punish inconsistently may actually contribute to an increase in the very behavior, such as disrespect or "guff" from their teenager, they are trying to discourage. In fact, Patterson (1976) in his studies of families with unusually aggressive children has found that parental punishment actually seems to accelerate a child's on-going coercive behavior. He calls this the "punishment paradox" because the "punishment" does not, in fact, punish. In this way, a true cycle of coercion is established. The other condition that can lead to the ineffectiveness of punishment in suppressing or eliminating a behavior is the tendency to rely upon words rather than needs. Punishment loses its effectiveness if it consists of a large number of threats that are seldom backed up. This can happen easily. For example, the parent who threatens to punish her son if he ever swears again is, of course, in no position to fulfill that intention. For all of these reasons—i.e., adaptation, inconsistency, and hollow threats—an increasingly powerless and certainly frustrated parent may strike out verbally and even physically against the source of that frustration, the adolescent.

Single parenthood may present special problems of its own. It has been observed that single parent mothers issue twice as many commands as do parents in intact families (Burgess et al., 1981). This may be a common result of the stresses and strains experienced by single parent mothers. The problem is that whereas girls may accept this dictatorial atmosphere, boys are likely to resist until they and their mothers are virtually locked into a coercive cycle (Hetherington, Cox, & Cox, 1976).

Of course, not all parents who find themselves trapped in a cycle of coercion with their adolescent son or daughter go so far as to commit physical violence. Some parents may rely upon verbal degradation (emotional abuse) as a means of retaliation, while others may resort to ignoring the child completely (neglect). And, of course, sexual abuse has its own dynamics. To understand the occurrence of physical maltreatment as a response to a cycle of coercion, we need to recognize that violence is often impulsive, in that parental aggression is reflexive in nature, occurring in response to excessive physiological arousal (Vasta, 1982). Heightened arousal accounts for the escalation of coercion into physical abuse in two ways: it increases the intensity of the parental attack, and it interferes with the natural intellectual process that would otherwise presumably thwart such an attack.

In conclusion, according to the analysis we have presented, the personal characteristics of abusive parents and their adolescent children, the structural features of their families, and the social circumstances in which they find themselves place those parents at risk in that those conditions increase the likelihood of still other conditions that can come to ignite a cycle of coercion. There is another possibility, however, which is that this coercive cycle is important because it reflects an overall style of social behavior that is associated not only with poor parental functioning and adolescent or child abuse but also their various correlates such as personal stress, unemployment and social isolation (Burgess & Richardson, 1984).

In support of this suggestion is the research of Robert Wahler (1980a), whose work suggests that parents who commonly resort to coercive behavior with their children often display similar behavior toward spouses, friends, relatives and co-workers. When this happens, the parent experiences what Wahler (1980b) calls "general insularity," in that he or she finds little pleasure in most daily contacts with other people. As a result, these people tend to attribute negative qualities to themselves, to family members and to others outside the family. They also tend to be socially isolated, thereby cutting themselves off from opportunities for outside monitoring of, and feedback on, their actions as parents. Ironically, those parents who most need social support to help them deal with stresses and to alter their aversive styles of inter-action lack the social skills needed to obtain them. This cycle of coercion, as well as its various correlates, has implications for treatment and prevention strategies targeted at abusive parents.

SOLUTIONS TO THE PROBLEM OF ADOLESCENT ABUSE

Obviously, just understanding the reasons for adolescent abuse is not enough. Ultimately, we would like to see the maltreatment stopped. One problem that faces professionals in this area is, of course, the continual difficulty of identifying abused adolescents. Our earlier discussion of the problem of underreporting suggests that we do not yet have fully effective procedures for doing this. One way to improve our detection of abused adolescents is to increase public awareness. Each of us should realize the serious-ness of the problem and should report suspected cases to authori-ties. Such referrals can be made anonymously, by calling the toll-free child abuse hotline number that is listed in most yellow pages under "Hotlines."

When maltreated youth are identified, what are some of the steps that can be taken to stop the abuse? All suspected cases will be handed over to county protective service agencies. These agencies will investigate the report and, if it is verified, will arrange for proper services. According to the American Humane Association, the most common service provided in cases of maltreatment is casework counseling. Here, a social worker is assigned to provide counseling and other assistance to family members. In some cases, court action will be taken to remove the adolescent from the abusive family and place him/her in foster care.

Based on what we know about the "cycle of coercion," some professionals have developed behavioral parent training programs to teach parents how to deal more positively with their children. Parents may be taught, for example, how to reward their adolescent's good behavior and to punish undesirable behavior with techniques other than corporal punishment or hostile verbalizations. Results of these efforts indicate that parents can indeed improve their childrearing techniques (Burgess & Richardson, 1984).

In addition to these professional treatment programs, nonprofessional or lay help is also available for abusive parents. Parents Anonymous is a national organization which has established local chapters to assist abusive parents in overcoming their childrearing problems. Essentially, this is a social support program in which groups of abusive parents meet to share their problems and advice. Evidence suggests that parents who participate in Parents Anonymous in addition to receiving professional counseling are more likely to have their parenting problems resolved than are those who receive only counseling (Cohn, 1979).

Despite such promising attempts to solve the problem of adolescent maltreatment, there remain many parents for whom such training is ineffective. In fact, in one study of 1,724 parents, a full 30%, or nearly one-third, were reported to have seriously reabused or neglected their children *while they were in treatment* (Cohn, 1979). Even more discouraging is the fact that such reincidence is most likely among cases identified as "serious."

Clearly, once adolescent maltreatment has begun, it is difficult to stop. An ideal solution, of course, would be to prevent the abuse from ever happening. Professionals have put far too little time and effort into achieving this solution. Among other things, what is needed is education for parents whose children are entering adolescence, to prepare them for dealing with the changing behavior of their teenage children. Parents may need to be told that it is all right to give up some control over the adolescent, that youth do need to be respected and treated like young adults, that although discipline is still important, physical punishment and other forms of coercion are not appropriate techniques. In addition, parents of adolescents might benefit from informal sources of advice and support in rearing their teenagers. To be able to ask other parents how they deal with problems such as staying out past curfew, or simply to talk about the achievements of one's adolescent may ease some of the stress of parenting. The success of such organizations as Parents Without Partners in relieving some of the strains of single parenthood suggest that support groups for parents are indeed essential. Although few such groups have been established for non-troubled parents, a recent effort in Pittsburgh, Pennsylvania is a step in the right direction. The Parental Stress Center Inc. established a "Warmline" to encourage parents to call for help with their childrearing problems before resorting to child abuse. This service is intended for use by parents of young children, but a similar organization for parents of adolescents is certainly a possibility.

SOURCES OF HELP

The following organizations typically offer direct services to families. Local chapters can usually be found in the telephone yellow pages.

Big Brothers/Big Sisters of America
2220 Suburban Station Building
Philadelphia, PA 19103
This organization has over 400 agencies across the United States. Social workers match adult volunteers with children from single-parent families. The goal of this organization is to assist the single parent in offering guidance and support to young people.

Child Line
Pennsylvania Department of Public Welfare
Office of Children and Youth
Bureau of Child Welfare
(800) 932-0213 PA.

This organization, which has its equivalent in other states, provides a number where child abuse can be reported and where a person can find out where to get help or more information. A multilingual staff of telephone counselors and supervisors operates on a 24-hour, seven-day-a week basis.

Families in Stress
Consumer Information Center
Dept. 642 G
Pueblo, CO 81009

This agency provides information on handling crisis times with children and information about a variety of service organizations throughout the country that offer help to parents.

Family Service Association of America
44 East 23rd Street
New York, NY 10010

This association is a federation of around 300 separate agencies which offer services of various sorts for families experiencing difficulty.

National Committee for Prevention of Child Abuse
332 South Michigan, Suite 1250
Chicago, IL 60604

The Committee distributes and publishes educational materials that deal with a variety of topics pertaining to child abuse. The *NCPCA Catalog* is available free upon request. Written in a conversational style, the publications are excellent reading for professionals, lay persons, and students. Some NCPCA titles are:

Volunteers make it Happen/SuEllen Fried
The Significance of Cultural and Ethnic Facts in Preventing Child Abuse: An Exploration of Research Findings/Garbarino and Cohn
A Survey of Public Perceptions of Child Abuse: The State of the Economy, Risk of Involvement in Juvenile and Adult Crime, and What Individuals Can do to Prevent Abuse/Louis Harris & Associates
Relationship of Child Abuse to the Workplace: Employer-Based Strategies for Prevention/Peter Coolsen
An Introduction to the Children's Trust Fund/Thomas Birch
The NCPCA Chapter Network Profile

Child Abuse, Delinquency and Crime/Garbarino and Groninger
Incidence of Child Abuse Climbing/NCPCA Staff
What Have We Learned about Preventing Child Abuse? An Overview of the "Community and Minority Group Action to Prevent Child Abuse and Neglect" Program/Gray
Perinatal Intervention
Culture-Based Parent Education Programs/Gray
Public Awareness and Education Using the Creative Arts/Gray
Community-Wide Education Information and Referral Programs/Gray
Handbook for New Chapters/NCPCA Staff
Innovative Approaches to Preventing Child Abuse: Volunteers in Action Child Care and Family Functioning: A Review/Gray
NCPCA Policy Statement on Corporal Punishment in Schools and Custodial Settings

National Runaway Switchboard
2210 North Halsted
Chicago, IL 60614
(800) 621-4000
   This is a toll free referral service for runaway youth. Information and assistance for youth in trouble are provided.

Parents Anonymous
2810 Artesia Boulevard
Redondo Beach, CA 90276
   This organization, with over 450 chapters in 300 cities, offers assistance to parents who are experiencing difficulty relating to their children. The goal is to increase the quality of family relationships through group participation.

Resource Center on Child Abuse and Neglect
School of Social Work
The University of Texas at Austin
2609 University
Austin, TX 78712
   The Center has a variety of publications, developed by the National Center of Child Abuse and Neglect (NCCAN) available at no cost.

Step Family Foundation, Inc.
333 West End Avenue
New York, NY 10023
This Foundation organizes workshops, lectures, training programs, and counseling services for both individual and entire family units.

ANNOTATED BIBLIOGRAPHY

Burgess, R. L., & Richardson, R. A. "Coercive Interpersonal Contingencies as a Determinant of Child Maltreatment: Implications for Treatment and Prevention." In R. F. Dangel & R. A. Polster (Eds.), *Behavioral Parent Training: Issues in Research and Practice.* New York: Guilford Publications, Inc., 1984.

This chapter reviews what is known about the causes of child maltreatment and uses the "cycle of coercion" to describe how family conflict may escalate into abuse. Examples are used to explain the process in terms understandable to most readers. A description of actual treatment programs for abusive parents is included, as well as a discussion of prevention strategies. Other chapters in this book are also pertinent.

Cohn, A. H. *An Approach to Preventing Child Abuse.* National Committee for Prevention of Child Abuse, 1983 (55 pages). Available from NCPCA, Publishing Dept., 332 S. Michigan Avenue, Suite 1250, Chicago, IL 60604.

This is a very readable, informative booklet that describes services for preventing child abuse. Many of the programs described are also relevant to adolescent abuse. This booklet provides a good overview of current trends in child abuse prevention and would be especially valuable for teachers, club groups, and volunteers who are interested in working in the area of prevention.

Garbarino, J., & Gilliam, G. *Understanding Abusive Families.* Lexington, MA: Heath Publishing Co., 1980.

This is one of few books that deals with the problem of adolescent abuse. Written in a very readable and informative style, it provides a good understanding of physical, emotional, and sexual abuse of teenagers. Quotes from interviews with abused adolescents are used to highlight the problems these youth are facing. This is highly recommended reading for teachers and parents of adolescents, as well as adolescents themselves.

Patterson, G. R., & Forgatch, M. *Parents and Adolescents: Living Together.* Eugene, OR: Castalia Publishing Company, 1984.

This book reflects new data derived from the treatment of chronic delinquent adolescents and multi-level assessments of over one-hundred families with normal adolescent children. Particular emphasis has been placed on teaching the family procedures found to be important in the treatment of antisocial children. Case histories are used from a single-parent family and from a family with step-relations to illustrate throughout the book the problems that are often encountered by parents in implementing the recommended procedures.

Steinmetz, S. K. *The Cycle of Violence: Assertive, Aggressive, and Abusive Family Interaction.* New York: Praeger, 1977.

This book is based on a study of 57 two-parent families in Delaware. The research reported was designed to look at how members of American families typically resolve conflict with one another. In addition to looking at physical abuse, this study also discusses the use of verbal force in families. Comparisons are made between conflicts with children and conflicts with adolescents, and siblings as well as parents are included in the research.

Straus, M. A., Gelles, R. M., & Steinmetz, S. K. *Behind Closed Doors: Violence in the American Family.* Garden City, NY: Anchor Press, 1980.

This very readable book reports the findings of a nationwide survey of 2,174 families, designed to look at the problem of family violence. It describes the reasons for the study as well as the procedures used to collect the data. Most of the book is devoted to summarizing the findings of the study. There are separate chapters on violence between husbands and wives, parental violence toward children, and violence between brothers and sisters. The book contains many charts that summarize some of the important findings in an easily understandable form. A concluding chapter on solutions for family violence provides a good overview of the need for intervention.

REFERENCES

Albrecht, S. L. "Correlates of Marital Happiness among the Remarried." *Journal of Marriage and the Family,* 1979, *41,* 857–867.

American Humane Association. *The National Study on Child Neglect and Abuse Reporting.* Denver, CO: American Humane Assoication, 1981.

Aries, P. *Centuries of Childhood.* New York: Vintage Books, 1962.

Bakan, D. "Adolescence in America: From Idea to Social Fact." *Daedalus,* Fall, 1971, 979–995.

Bandura, A. "Influence of a Model's Reinforcement Contingencies on the Acquisition of Imitative Responses." *Journal of Personality and Social Psychology*, 1965, *1*, 589–595.

Bandura, A., Ross, D., & Ross, S. A. "A Comparative Test of the Status Envy, Social Power, and Secondary Reinforcement Theories of Identification Learning." *Journal of Abnormal and Social Psychology*, 1963, *67*, 527–534.

Blumberg, M. L. "Psychopathology of the Abusing Parent." *American Journal of Psychotherapy*, 1974, *28*, 21–29.

Burgdorff, K. *Recognition and Reporting of Child Maltreatment: Findings from the National Study of the Incidence and Severity of Child Abuse and Neglect.* Prepared for the National Center on Child Abuse and Neglect, Washington, D.C., December 1982.

Burgess, R. L. "Child Abuse: A Social Interactional Analysis." In B. B. Lahey & A. E. Kazdin (Eds.), *Advances in Clinical Child Psychology* (Vol. 2). New York: Plenum Press, 1979.

Burgess, R. L., & Akers, R. L. "A Differential Association-reinforcement Theory of Criminal Behavior." *Social Problems*, Fall, 1966, 138–157.

Burgess, R. L., Anderson, E. S., Schellenbach, C. J., & Conger, R. D. "A Social Interactional Approach to the Study of Abusive Families." In J. P. Vincent (Ed.), *Advances in Family Intervention, Assessment and Theory: An Annual Compilation of Research* (Vol. 2). Greenwich, CT: JAI Press, 1981.

Burgess, R. L., & Bushell, D., Jr. *Behavioral Sociology: The Experimental Analysis of Social Process.* New York: Columbia University Press, 1969.

Burgess, R. L., & Richardson, R. A. "Coercive Interpersonal Contingencies as a Determinant of Child Maltreatment: Implications for Treatment and Prevention." In R. F. Dangel & R. A. Polster (Eds.), *Behavioral Parent Training: Issues in Research and Practice.* New York: Guilford Publications, Inc., 1984.

Cohn, A. "Essential Elements of Successful Child Abuse and Neglect Treatment." *Child Abuse and Neglect*, 1979, *3*, 491–496.

Conger, R. D., Burgess, R. L., & Barrett, C. "Child Abuse Related to Life Change and Perceptions of Illness: Some Preliminary Findings." *The Family Coordinator*, 1979, *28*(1), 73–79.

Elmer, E. *Children in Jeopardy: A Study of Abused Minors and Their Families.* Pittsburgh, PA: University of Pittsburgh Press, 1967.

Erlanger, H. "Social Class and Corporal Punishment in Childrearing: A Reassessment." *American Sociological Review*, 1974, *39*, 68–85.

Finkelhor, D. *Sexually Victimized Children.* New York: Free Press, 1979.

Friedman, R. "Child Abuse: A Review of the Psychosocial Research." In Hefner & Company (Eds.), *Four Perspectives on the Status of Child Abuse and Neglect Research.* Washington, DC: National Center on Child Abuse and Neglect, 1976.

Garbarino, J. "The Human Ecology of Child Maltreatment: A Conceptual Model for Research." *Journal of Marriage and the Family*, 1977, *39*, 721–736.

Garbarino, J. "Defining Emotional Maltreatment: The Message is the Meaning." *Journal of Psychiatric Treatment and Evaluation*, 1980, *2*, 105–110.

Gewirtz, J. L. "Attachment, Dependence, and a Distinction in Terms of Stimulus Control." In J. L. Gewirtz (Ed.), *Attachment and Dependency*. New York: John Wiley and Sons, 1972.

Gil, D. G. *Violence against Children*. Cambridge, MA: Harvard University Press, 1970.

Hetherington, E. M., Cox, M., & Cox, R. "Divorced Fathers." *The Family Coordinator*, 1976, *10*, 417–428.

Johnson, B., & Morse, H. A. "Injured Children and Their Parents." *Children*, 1968, *15*, 147–152.

Kocourek, A., & Wigmore, J. H. *Sources of Ancient and Primitive Law: Select Readings on the Origin and Development of Legal Institutions*. Boston: Little, Brown, 1951.

Linton, R. "Age and Sex Categories." *American Sociological Review*, 1942, 7, 589–603.

Lourie, I. S. "Family Dynamics and the Abuse of Adolescents: A case for a Developmental Phase Specific Model of Child Abuse." *Child Abuse and Neglect*, 1979, *3*, 967–974.

Parke, R. D., Deur, J. L., & Saivin, M. "The Intermittent Punishment Effect in Humans: Conditioning or Adaptation." *Psychonomic Science*, 1970, *18*, 193–194.

Patterson, G. R. "The Aggressive Child: Victim and Architect of a Coercive System." In L. A. Hamerlynck, L. C. Handy, & E. J. Mash (Eds.), *Behavior Modification and Families. I: Theory and Research*. New York: Brunner/Mazel, 1976.

Patterson, G. R. "A Performance Theory for Coercive Family Interaction." In R. Cairns (Ed.), *Social Interaction: Methods, Issues, and Illustrations*. Hillsdale, N.J.: Lawrence Erlbaum Associates, 1979.

Patterson, G. R. *Coercive Family Process*. Eugene, Oregon: Castalia Publishing Company, 1982.

Polansky, N. A., Hally, C., & Polansky, N. F. *Profile of Neglect: A Survey of the State of Knowledge of Child Neglect*. Washington, DC: U. S. Department of Health, Education, and Welfare, 1975.

President's Commission on Law Enforcement and Administration of Justice. *The challenge of crime in a free society*. Washington, DC: U. S. Government Printing Office, 1967.

Richardson, R. A., Burgess, J. M., & Burgess, R. L. "Family Size and Age Structure and the Maltreatment of Children: A Social Interactional Analysis." Penn State, 1984.

Rossi, A. S. "Aging and Parenthood in the Middle Years." In P. B. Baltes (Ed.), *Life-span Development and Behavior* (Vol. 3). New York: Academic Press, 1980.

Sandgrund, A. K., Gaines, R., & Green, A. "Child Abuse and Mental Retardation: A Problem Cause and Effect." *American Journal of Mental Deficiency*, 1974, *79*, 327–330.

Sherif, M., & Sherif, C. *Reference Groups*. New York: Harper and Row, 1964.

Spinetta, J. J., & Rigler, D. "The Child-abusing Parent: A Psychological Review. *Psychological Bulletin*, 1972, 77, 296–304.

Steele, B. F., & Pollock, C. B. "A Psychiatric Study of Parents Who Abuse Infants and Small Children." In R. E. Helfer & C. H. Kempe (Eds.), *The Battered Child*. Chicago: University of Chicago Press, 1974.

Steinmetz, S. K. *The Cycle of Violence: Assertive, Aggressive, and Abusive Family Interaction*. New York: Praeger, 1977.

Straus, M. A. "Stress and Physical Child Abuse." *Child Abuse and Neglect*, 1980, *4*, 75–88.

Straus, M. A., Gelles, R. J., & Steinmetz, S. K. *Behind Closed Doors: Violence in the American Family*. Garden City, NY: Anchor Press, 1980.

Vasta, R. "Physical Child Abuse: A Dual-component Analysis." *Developmental Review*, 1982, *2*, 125–149.

Visher, E. B., & Visher, J. S. "Common Problems of Stepparents and Their Spouse." *American Journal of Orthopsychiatry*, 1978, 48, 252–262.

Wahler, R. G. "The Insular Mother: Her Problems in Parent-child Treatment." *Journal of Applied Behavior Analysis*, 1980, *13*, 207–219. (a)

Wahler, R. G. "The Multiply Entrapped Parent: Obstacles to Change in Parent-child Problems." In J. P. Vincent (Ed.), *Advances in family intervention, assessment, and theory* (Vol. I). Greenwich, CT: JAI Press, 1980. (b)

Wasserman, S. "The Abused Parent of the Abused Child." *Children*, 1967, *14*, 175–179.

6. ADOLESCENT DRUG AND ALCOHOL USE AND ABUSE

Judith R. Vicary

One of the problems of most concern to parents today is the potential for drug and alcohol (substance) use and abuse by their adolescents. Many parents, feeling particularly uninformed about this problem, lack knowledge about various drugs, patterns of and reasons for use, and prevention approaches. Often parents prefer not to know what's going on in their community regarding substance use and just hope their children are not involved because they do not know how to handle the problem. Parents also sometimes deny their child is using drugs for fear of being considered failures as parents.

However, parents can do something both before their children try drugs or alcohol and when they are at the ages at risk for beginning substance use. This chapter will present information on the extent of use by various age groups, patterns of initiation of use, reasons for or correlates of use behaviors, promising prevention and early intervention approaches, and resources available for a more extensive background on the subject. It is important to note here that all young people as they go through childhood and adolescence will be confronted with decisions about substance use and will have opportunities to try drugs. They will have to make choices repeatedly, and these decisions are now a normative aspect of growing up.

EXTENT OF DRUG AND ALCOHOL USE

The heading of this section is technically misleading because alcohol is also a drug, and in fact is the most widely used substance for all age levels. However, it is considered a socially accepted part of American life, for the majority of the population, and is conveniently, if not always legally, available. Most people separate it in their thinking from "drugs," which have a more ominous and illegal connotation. The government furthers this dichotomy by conducting prevention, treatment, and research programs under dual auspices: the National Institute on Drug Abuse (NIDA) and the National Institute on Alcoholism and Alcohol Abuse (NIAAA).

However, a first step in understanding substance use is acknowledging that alcohol is also a drug, potentially as dangerous as, or more dangerous than, other licit or illicit substances. This latter classification is also an important distinction. While media concern and law enforcement efforts often focus on heroin, cocaine, and marijuana—all legally restricted drugs—many other legal substances are used "illegally," that is, without proper restrictions (a prescription), or, abusively, at levels or in a manner exceeding recommended dosages. Tobacco is also considered a drug and is included in adolescent use data.

Beginning in the 1960s, the "drug problem" was seen as a new, major, and growing crisis in America. The hippie era, student unrest, Vietnam, and various social protest movements were all considered part of the drug scene through the early 1970s, and vigorous enforcement and scare-based drug education programs resulted. Psychedelic drugs (e.g., LSD); marijuana; and pills, both amphetamines and barbiturates, were of most concern for middle-class young people, while heroin was the drug of consequence in black urban areas. During the past decade, however, major changes have occurred in the drugs used, age of onset and rate of use, and the proportion of young people using various substances. It is important to know what is being used by adolescents, and to what extent, in order to understand, prevent and/or intervene in these behaviors.

The following data are taken from a NIDA-funded yearly project which measures the use of drugs by high school seniors in America. The summary for the years 1975-1981 (Johnston, Bachman, & O'Malley, 1981) is the source for this information:

1. In 1978, daily, or on 20 occasions in a 30-day period, use of marijuana had peaked, at nearly double the rate of 1975,

at 11 percent of all high school seniors. The use has since been receding, to seven percent in 1981, or the equivalent if one in every 14 seniors. This figure does not include, of course, those young people who have already dropped out of school and are often found to be using drugs at even higher rates.

2. Annual use of marijuana for seniors overall, combining all frequencies, is down to 46 percent, from 51 percent in 1979. There is also moderation in use being noted.

3. There has been a corresponding increase in seniors reporting "great risk" to smoking marijuana regularly, from 35 percent to 58 percent; and 75 percent believe their close friends would disapprove of regular use.

4. Another smoking behavior, that of cigarettes, is also continuing to decline in this age group. The proportion of seniors smoking half a pack a day or more has decreased from 19.4 percent in 1977 to 13.5 percent in 1981, a drop of nearly one-third. An overall increase in awareness of health concerns by young people is being credited with these cigarette and marijuana statistics.

5. The use levels of many illicit drugs has been declining from the peak levels of the 1970s. PCP, inhalants such as amyl and butyl nitrites, and tranquilizers all reflect this pattern.

6. Heroin, barbiturates, and LSD had been declining somewhat in use and now appear to be at a constant level. Other opiate use continues a steady pattern begun in 1975.

7. Cocaine use rose sharply from 1976 to 1979, from six percent to 12 percent of seniors using this substance, and remains steady although there are more extreme regional differences. (Use levels still appear to be rising in the west and northeast.)

8. The most widely used class of illicit drugs other than marijuana, amphetamines, increased in use for the previous three years, and one-third of 1981 seniors have tried them without medical supervision.

In summary, Johnston et al. note that the use of many illicit drugs has declined somewhat from the 1970's peak levels, and current use appears to reflect smaller quantities and reduced "highs" for many substances, although not for alcohol and tran-

quilizers. However, drug use is still extremely prevalent for teenagers in America, probably at the highest level of any industrialized nation in the world: among the 1981 high school graduates,
two-thirds acknowledged at least some illicit use of drugs, and
this is considered a conservatively low estimate. Figure 1 below,
from Johnston et al., 1981, summarizes use levels for high school
seniors in 1981.

There are two additional findings of interest, based on seventh
through twelfth grade students in Pennsylvania in 1982 (Swisher
& Figlin, 1983). These graphically reflect attitudes about alcohol
use among adolescents. The percentage of ninth graders who
indicated that they would use beer at a party or "anytime they had
a chance" is equal to the actual percentage of twelfth grade
students who report drinking beer monthly or more frequently.
The young people are in effect predicting or acknowledging their
own future use behaviors. In addition, slightly more than one-
third of high school seniors drink beer once or twice a week, or
more frequently, and just slightly less than one-third of the seniors
report being drunk *weekly or more often*. This statistic should be
of particular conern to parents, reflecting the serious abuse, rather
than the social nature, of teenagers' alcohol consumption—that
is, a pattern of regular drinking to get drunk.

Obviously, there are regional, sex, and socio-economic differences in all these figures. For instance, males drink more frequently than females, but this differential rate is narrowing considerably, as it is in tobacco use also. Whites have a higher
proportion of drinkers than blacks, and black teenagers drink
lesser amounts. The reader is referred to the Johnston, Bachman,
and O'Malley publications, available through NIDA, for a more
detailed summary of these findings. However, the overall use data
show the general extent and frequency of use of drugs and alcohol
by teenagers today. Parents, school personnel, and others working
with adolescents should be knowledgeable about these trends in
order to best help young people during these years of substance-
use decisions. Today it is an expected and normal developmental
task for adolescents to learn the place, if any, of drugs and alcohol
in their lives, and experimentation will occur for many, as will
abusive behavior for some.

FIGURE 1

Prevalence and Recency of Use
Eleven Types of Drugs, Class of 1981

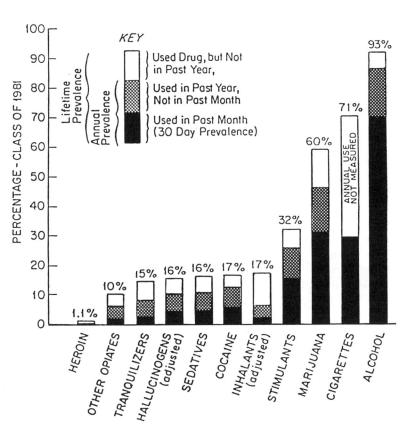

Figure 1. Prevalence and recency of use of eleven types of drugs, class of 1981.

REASONS FOR AND PATTERNS OF USING DRUGS AND ALCOHOL

Usually the next question adults ask is "Why?" What makes a 12 year old or a 15 year old, for example, decide to try various substances? With the age of first use occurring earlier now than ever before and the available number of drugs increasing as well, it is important to recognize some of the factors known to be associated with drug use. Adolescence is a time when a vast range of physiological and psychological changes occur, and many of these influence a variety of behaviors considered negative by adults. Often drug use does not occur in isolation, but is linked with other problem behaviors. There also appears to be a developmental pattern to the initiation of substance use, and the age of onset generally has been declining to include even very early adolescence. Four possible stages of drug use have been suggested (Kandel, 1981): (1) first, beer and wine; (2) followed by cigarettes and/or hard liquor; (3) then marijuana use; and (4) finally other illicit drugs. The sequence is generally the same for black and white youth, although the former are somewhat more likely to go from marijuana directly to heroin use without intervening experimentation with pills and psychedelics. There are also specific social and psychological factors associated with the beginning of a particular drug use stage. However, participation in one phase does not guarantee that a youngster will progress to additional substances, and most will not progress past levels 1, 2, or 3.

Several studies of use behaviors (Kandel, Treiman, Faust, & Single, 1976; Kandel, Kessler, & Margulies, 1978) have identified four kinds of influences on adolescents' decisions about and stages of substance use, including: (1) parental, (2) peer, (3) their own beliefs and values, and (4) involvement in certain activities. For example, these studies show that young people who have participated in a number of minor delinquent activities, who are very sociable with their peers, and who are exposed to both parents and peers who drink are likely to start drinking. Parental drinking patterns are a very important influence, and the earliest exposure to alcohol for most youth occurs at home on special occasions, under parental supervision. Later, more frequent and heavier use occurs in unsupervised settings with friends. Peer influence and conformity to group norms are major factors influencing smoking behavior, especially smoking by a best friend.

Conditions preceding marijuana use include: a favorable attitude toward marijuana in opposition to the position held by most adults, peers who use, and participation in other deviant behaviors similar to those prior to the use of hard liquor. Youngsters involved with other illegal drugs often have: poor relationships with their parents; family and friends who use a variety of legal, medicinal and illegal substances; a good friend who is an influence in the use of illicit drugs; psychological distress; and personal characteristics more deviant than those of the lower-level user. Over a period of time these activities and drug behaviors become intertwined, with more delinquency, for example, following initial use, thereby establishing a condition favorable to additional drug use.

Research suggests that the drug use behaviors of parents and peers generally are of more influence than are the beliefs and values which an adolescent holds. Modeling also plays an important role in the decision-making process. In addition, the less serious the drug, the more that situational factors influence use or non-use. In fact, user and non-user adolescents at the earliest stage of potential use don't differ in their values and beliefs. Those who drink liquor often get involved in other deviant behaviors as well, without an active decision or just as part of group sociability. Marijuana users change their beliefs and values before using the drug but do not seem to have greater personal or family problems than non-users. Finally, young people who use illicit drugs, other than marijuana, apparently do so with a conscious decision, as a way of dealing with personal/psychological factors.

Frequently parents question their role in their children's drug behavior choices. It is obvious that their own substance use, most often seen in alcohol or prescription and over-the-counter medication use, is of great importance. Drinking patterns are learned at home, as are attitudes about when, why, and how to use various substances. In addition, there is also a strong and active population of abstainers, who choose not to drink themselves and/or campaign to prevent or limit drinking by others on moral, religious, medical or other grounds. However, the American culture obviously accepts drinking as a normal adult behavior, at least for the majority, as evidenced by the fun/sophistication = drinking advertisements so common in all aspects of the media. "Anticipatory socialization" is a term used to describe playing an adult role or trying to be "grown up." Drinking, particularly, provides such an outlet for young people, and with like-minded peers many opportunities are found for unsupervised drinking. Jessor and Jessor (1972) state that drinking can be a "status transition involving, especially for young adolescents, a departure from the regulatory norms defining appropriate behavior for that age or stage in life."

Another aspect of the parents' role has to do with the parent-child relationship itself. Kandel et al. (1978) note that closeness to parents apparently shields adolescents from participation in more serious forms of drug use. Closeness and warmth are important, as are maternal and familial control. The traditional family structure, according to studies summarized by Fishman (1982), "serves to insulate the adolescent from drug use . . . [and] the greater the . . . control the less likely it is that the adolescent will use drugs." Blum et al. (1972) found a low incidence of drug use occurring in families which value achievement and have high expectations for their children; such families also participate in a number of activities together. Involved parents who monitor their children's activities and peers also seem to have lower levels of drug involvement among their children.

In one study of marijuana abusers and their families, Hendin and his colleagues (1981) report that the families of these adolescents had considered the child "difficult" long before drug use began, had family difficulties, or had exaggerated and unmet expectations for the child. In such situations the drug use served as: defiance against the parents or other authority, a self-destructive act, a modifier of negative emotions, as an enhancer of withdrawal and/or as a reinforcer of success fantasies.

A number of other personal factors have also been found to be associated with drug involvement at a particular time of measurement of use (Kandel, 1981). Among these are poor academic performance, low self-esteem, depressive mood, and rebelliousness. Several childhood characteristics appear to be predictive of later substance use, including aggressiveness, rebelliousness, and peer ratings of dependency and pessimism. A relationship exists between use and alienation from accepted social values, and between use and valuing independence from parental control over school achievement. At the junior high school level, motivation to achieve is associated with low use levels.

Long term studies have been conducted far less often but are of particular importance because of their predictive value. Most drug research has focused on factors measured at the same time that drug use is evident and measured. More complete understanding can result, however, from studies which record a variety of family, peer, psychological and social factors *prior* to the onset of substance use behavior. For example, Wingard, Huba and Bentler (1979) report a number of predisposing characteristics, including liberalism, non-abiding with the law, extraversion, and a lack of diligence and deliberateness. Kellam and his colleagues (1982) found that social-maladaptive problems such as aggressiveness seen as early as first grade were related to subsequent drug use. Vicary and Lerner (1983) report similar results, using adjustment scores at age five, and other early childhood factors, to predict later drug use. They found that children of one to six years of age who were seen by their parents as not complying with their rules and as being frequently dissatisfed were most likely to be early users of tobacco, beginning between ages 10 and 13. Coping difficulties noted by both parents and teachers and discipline problems reported by parents were related to high levels of alcohol use in early adulthood. In summary, all the conditions which lead to drug use by young people have not been fully studied, but there is strong evidence for a sequential pattern of use influenced by family, friendship, and personal and social factors. These then can be a basis for prevention, intervention, and treatment efforts.

PRIMARY, SECONDARY, AND TERTIARY PREVENTION

There are three levels of programmatic efforts available to deal with substance use. Each involves activity at a different point in the use sequence, and there is obviously an overlap or coordination possible in these efforts. The following outline, based on Swisher (1979), will be used here to delineate types of community, school, and family strategies.

Type of Prevention	Timing	Type of Activities
Primary	Before use/abuse	Information, Education, Alternatives, Personal and Social Growth programs
Secondary	During early stages of use/abuse	Intervention Counseling, Crisis Intervention, Early Diagnosis, Referral
Tertiary	During later, more frequent and higher quantity stages of use/abuse	Detoxification, Treatment Programs, Psychiatric help during therapy

The level of most interest, affecting the greatest numbers of young people initially, is that of primary prevention. On a classification continuum, four types of primary prevention activities have been suggested by the National Institute on Drug Abuse (1980), all for the purpose of "preventing, discouraging, or delaying usage" (Durell & Bukoski, 1982, p. 229) in order to limit or prevent dysfunctional behavior. They are part of a "constructive process designed to promote personal and social growth of the individual toward full human potential . . ." (NIDA, 1975, p. 16) and target the entire population, promoting "positive, intra- and interpersonal skills, attitudes and behaviors impacting upon the formulations of life styles which are likely to exclude substance dependency" (Pennsylvania Governor's Council on Drug and Alcohol Abuse, 1974, p. 24).

Based on a continuum by NIDA (1980), the four primary prevention categories are:

Information modalities. Approaches that involve the distribution of accurate and objective information about all types of drugs and their effects on human beings.

Education modalities. Approaches that focus on skill-building through the use of well-defined and structured affective learning processes intended to encourage personal growth and development.

Alternatives modalities. Approaches that provide experiences and activities through which individuals develop increased levels of confidence and self-reliance.

Intervention modalities (Note that this relates to the secondary level of prevention). Approaches that focus on the reduction, elimination, and/or delay of drug use, drug use-related dysfunctional behavior, and other problems prior to the onset of serious, chronic, debilitative behaviors.

These four modalities have traditionally been used as a framework from which to work with youth at the earliest stages of potential drug use. Bukoski (1981) has suggested the emergence of a fifth approach, a variation of intervention, entitled "community organization and resource coordination," which targets the community rather than the individual.

NIDA's perspective has been that the discouragement of nonmedical psychoactive drug use, thereby changing societal acceptance of use, can decrease the number who use drugs and the levels of use; NIDA believes that this will reduce the population at risk for subsequent dysfunctional use. Obviously, measuring the results of prevention activities can be very difficult, and these results are not always clear. Nevertheless, a great deal of effort has gone into prevention programs in the past ten years, with a gradually changing focus on types of activities. As was noted earlier, primary prevention efforts began with informational or drug education approaches based on scare tactics warning of the dire consequences of use. It was found that drug information alone will not affect a person's attitudes toward or usage of drugs (Swisher & Hoffman, 1975) and, in fact, could be counter-productive. However, an abundance of materials has been produced and purchased by school districts to educate young people about the dangers of drugs. More recent efforts have focused on affective or psychological reasons for use; and materials and programs, both school and community-based, stress personal development and skills as a prevention strategy. These follow the concept of promoting personal and social growth, the NIDA Education modalities mentioned previously, and include three dimensions (Vicary, 1977):

1. Intrapersonal level—including internal perceptions, self-awareness, knowledge and acceptance, e.g., self-esteem and personal skills, such as developing one's value system and decision-making.
2. Interpersonal level—including perceptions concerning others, such as awareness, knowledge and acceptance of

others, and skills like communications, teamwork, and
leadership.
3. Extrapersonal level—including perceptions of society,
perspectives on the individual and group in relation to
their environment and social institutions, and skills involving coping, contributing, and changing.

Personal and social growth for an individual, therefore, encompasses skills at self, interpersonal and societal levels, as appropriate for each age. These can be developed or enhanced through
many types of programs, and the following descriptions are only
representative examples of a variety of settings, personnel, and
strategies. All four types of prevention activities—information,
education, alternatives, and intervention—can be used to address
both the cognitive and psychological factors related to substance
use.

Primary Prevention

Schools are the most obvious location in which to reach
youth, and curricula have been developed for kindergarten through
college ages. Some of these include drug information combined
with personal growth strategies, while others are limited to just
one of these content areas. Because the current direction in prevention stresses an integrated affective-cognitive approach, no
drugs-only curriculum will be discussed here. However, excellent
substance-specific information materials are available, and pamphlets, posters and public service announcements can be coordinated with other programs. The *Sources of Help* section of this
chapter lists where these may be obtained as well as addresses
through which the following integrated education materials are
available. Alternatives activities have been developed under school
auspices too, as have many early intervention programs which are
now housed in, or work with, schools. Sources are also listed for
these prevention modalities.

Education. North Carolina was one of the first states in which
primary prevention was mandated by the state legislature, and an
excellent K-12 curriculum was produced for state-wide distribution through the Department of Public Instruction. Entitled *Life*

Skills for Health: Focus on Mental Health (Frye & Rockness, 1974), it incorporates a range of personal development concepts, including self-esteem, decision-making and interpersonal relations. Teacher training is also provided by the state, and a coordinated planning and implementation process has emphasized widespread, skilled implementation of the materials. Georgia has undertaken a similar process, introducing throughout that state *Life Skills for Mental Health* (Georgia Department of Human Resources, 1977), which includes an evaluation component. Another model curriculum for grades K-12, "Here's Looking At You," was developed in King and Pierce counties, Washington (Roberts, 1974), with NIAAA support. Cognitive and affective components are equally essential to the program. A curriculum guide and seven grade-level kits with teacher support materials are included, as is a four-day teacher training course. Facts about alcohol use are presented with information about decision making, values clarification, self-concept, and alternatives to abuse strategies. An important feature is a plan to integrate these activities into different subject areas.

Another notable program, available for use by any school district nationally, is the *Quest* prevention course (Kirschenbaum & Glaser, 1982). The project's rationale is that most teenagers who abuse drugs and alcohol, as well as those with other problems, e.g., delinquency, low achievement, and premarital pregnancy, suffer from low self-concept and poor communication skills. *Quest* is designed to be integrated into the curriculum for 14-18 year olds as an elective skills-for-living one or two semester course. The ten chapters in the student manual address subjects of vital importance in teenagers' personal development:

- "You Are Somebody Special"
- "You Are Your Feelings"
- "You and Your Attitudes"
- "You and Your Friends"
- "You and the People at Your House"
- "You and Those Great Big Beautiful Dollars"
- "You and the Person You May Marry"
- "You and What You Will Do"
- "You and Your Own Parenting"
- "You and Your Concept of the Universe"

Preliminary evaluations have found the project to have a very positive impact, and the Kellogg Foundation has provided financial support to set up demonstration models throughout the country. A junior high school program is expected to be available soon.

It is important to note that agencies other than schools also conduct affective drug education programs and have developed parallel materials. The national YMCA, for example, with a grant from NIAAA, produced a training model in alcohol education for elementary/middle school aged children and their parents. Values clarification and decision making are basic components. The Boys' Clubs of America (Jordon & Windsor, 1978) produced Project TEAM (Teens Explore Alcohol Moderation), and seven model programs have been implemented by local clubs. These include:

- Media—youth directed publicity and information projects, encouraging responsible drinking.
- Keystone Clubs—community service clubs for adolescents, which sponsor prevention workshops and activities.
- Cultural exploration—participants study the effects of culture on drinking, by interviews, field trips, speakers, etc.
- Peer consulting—trained members become peer counselors, talking to youth with a variety of problems.
- Peer leadership—specially trained members help youth groups conduct alcohol awareness sessions and develop prevention programs in schools and the community.
- Valuing process—discussion sessions of young people and parents were organized, using values clarification and communication strategies.
- Arts and crafts—participants use various creative projects to express ideas about alcohol use and abuse.

It is worth noting that the TEAM activities overlap information, education and alternative modalities, and have young people take a major responsibility for program initiation and implementation. The American Red Cross has also developed a program, the *Alcohol Information Module* (AIM), which is primarily an information packet for use with youth groups in schools or other community settings.

While insufficient evaluation of primary prevention has occurred, a number of studies have shown that several of these social

skills approaches result in delays in the onset of drug use, reduction of intentions to use drugs, and reductions in actual use
once it has begun (e.g., McAlister, Perry & Maccoby, 1979; Wodarski & Lenhart, 1981; Williams & Horan, 1981). Similar programs
which target smoking behaviors have also shown positive effects
in reducing adolescent smoking. For example, Project CLASP
(Counseling Leadership About Smoking Pressures) (Perry et al.,
1980) incorporates antismoking testimonials, role playing resistance strategies, and skill training in dealing with peer pressure.
Students who were included in the project later smoked less than
non-participants, and were also less involved with marijuana and
alcohol, a positive "carry-over" effect. Hurd and colleagues (1980)
found that a Minnesota-based seventh grade Anti-Smoking Project
produced a 50–67% reduction in the onset of cigarette smoking for
participants, as opposed to children who did not experience the
program. It appears that early prevention education efforts which
combine strong positive peer models and skills in resisting smoking
influences will be effective.

Alternatives Modalities. The next approach to be discussed,
alternatives, is described by Cohen (1973) as creating more positive
environments and activities for youth rather than directly addressing substance use. "Alternatives programs provide adolescents with opportunities for constructive peer and adult interactions while working together on meaningful tasks that meet a
school or community need and enhance youths' self-esteem and
sense of personal involvement" (Gordon & McAlister, 1982, p. 214).

The underlying rationale suggests that providing alternative
activities to drinking and drug use can reduce abuse, and at the
same time increase young people's feelings of self-worth and
interpersonal skills. Many emotional needs can be met, including
the needs to belong and interact with peers, to explore career
interests and options, and to find personal meaning through
giving and being involved in a cause. Several assumptions about
drug-using behavior are important in using an alternatives approach:

1. People use drugs voluntarily and receive an experience
   they (usually) consider worthwhile.
2. Often people use drugs for "positive" reasons, e.g., to
   enhance the senses while listening to music or to experience adventure.

3. Drugs can be used for "negative" reasons also, as a way of dealing with negative feelings or situations, e.g., to relieve boredom, anxiety, depression, or tension; to rebel; or to escape from feelings of loneliness or anxiety.
4. Whatever the reasons for drug use, the same effects can be achieved through alternative means that are preferable and more constructive.
5. Alternatives should not be only a substitute for drugs, but should lead to a long-term constructive activity, not just short term gratification (Based on Resnik, 1979, p. 36).

Obviously, a number of traditional youth activities could be viewed as alternatives. Scouts, teams, church groups, and Y's have always provided constructive experiences for teenagers. However, often "high risk" adolescents are not participants in these programs, and new kinds of offerings may be needed to attract more young people.

Channel One is only a single programmatic example of alternative activities, but it represents dozens of different possibilities, as developed by each participating community. The growth of the project and examples of the different programs will be discussed here to show the range of what is possible. Many of the Channel One sites represent the community organization and resource coordination approach to prevention as well as the alternatives technique.

The project originated in Massachusetts as the Gloucester Experiment in 1973 under a NIDA grant. Developing alternatives to drug abuse and other problem behaviors was a major goal. Equally important was the development of career and employment skills. After a long search for a suitable project, community leaders involved a large segment of youth in a Bicentennial-related restoration of a local burial ground. Three major requirements were met in this activity:

1. High community visibility, with the attention attracting media interest and growing local support.
2. Multidimensionality (or multiple approaches), necessitating learning a range of new skills and challenging participants to grow.
3. Appeal to a wide variety of young volunteers, both those with problems and those well adjusted but interested in participating also (Based on Resnik & Adams, 1981).

The scope of the project was enormous, involving, for example, legislative efforts, surveying, gardening, public relations, and reports. Other activities followed this project, and follow-up evaluations found that participants were constructively involved in college or employment. When other communities expressed interest, it became obvious that additional structure and support had to be found in order to replicate the model. At this point, Prudential Insurance Company of America agreed to participate and joined with NIDA to sponsor Channel One.

The major contribution from the private sector was the time, leadership, and organizational skills of corporate staff. Media products were also developed and disseminated. Initially, ten pilot sites were selected, and by the end of 1980, over 100 communities throughout the nation has replicated the process. Other private sector support was generated, including a commitment by Metropolitan Life Insurance Company. These additional sponsors facilitated over half of the new Channel One programs. Of major importance to the success of these alternative activities is the structured process developed to set up a site. Community needs and resources are identified; key local leaders are involved, representing a broad cross-section of the area, including youth representatives; public support and identity are developed; and action agendas are implemented. Among the type of strategies undertaken by participating adolescents are:

- Vocational skills development
- Alternatives activities providing personal fulfillment, e.g., drama, arts and crafts, hiking
- Social services and an opportunity to help others
- Education and both learning and teaching, such as peer tutoring
- Historic preservation
- Ecology, including protecting or restoring environmental sites.

Additional information is available from the Prevention Branch, National Institute on Drug Abuse (see the *Sources of Help* section) to help potential new sites be developed. Many other agencies and communities have also set up similar alternatives activities, under varied sponsorship. Channel One is highlighted here because of its broad replication and wide range of activities and sponsors, but it is only representative of what is possible in a community.

Community Organization and Resource Coordination Modality. As noted previously, in many sites Channel One has become a community-level prevention approach, going beyond simply alternatives. An additional example of this approach to primary prevention is the Charlotte, North Carolina, Drug Education Center. Although the Center was originally started as a volunteer-run walk-in counseling service for adolescents, the focus has evolved to a community-wide prevention orientation for all age groups. A Department of Justice grant and funding from the local Junior League underwrote the Center's first few years of prevention efforts. Multiple funding sources, including fee-for-services, then supported such activities as:

- Identification of high risk individuals
- A resource library
- Parent groups, e.g., support, counseling, and training
- School programs, including both drug education and affective education teacher training
- Community development programs, such as recreational activities for low income neighborhood residents
- Youth advocacy and consultant services within the judicial system
- Training programs for business and industry groups (Based on Resnik, 1979).

In fact, it has been suggested that "The Center has reached a stage of development where it is beginning to have an impact on almost every segment of community life" (Resnik, 1979, p. 53). This interactive effect—linking other social service agencies, schools, and the business sector—can bring about a more widespread and effective community effort for prevention, with a far greater impact on a range of problems, not just substance abuse.

Secondary Prevention or Intervention

In every community, despite the successes of primary prevention, there are still young people who become involved with drug and alcohol abuse. Secondary efforts focus on reducing or intervening in this abuse or dysfunctional behavior. A variety of services can be provided to accomplish that goal. For example, crisis hotlines or drop-in centers provide immediate assistance to someone who wants to talk about a problem, whether it is drug related or not. The mental health system, drug abuse agencies, and similar groups often staff these 24-hour services. Following initial contact, additional counseling or referral to more specialized agencies is available. It is important to note that either young people with problems or parents or other adults concerned about youngsters will make use of this intervention process.

Another effective type of intervention is conducted by, or in coordination with, the school system. One such project is the Alpha Center, cooperatively originated by a drug abuse service agency, the Door of Central Florida, and the Orange and Osceola County School Systems, and now replicated throughout that state. The center bases its model on the assumption that substance abuse is part of a larger grouping of maladaptive behaviors, all of which are extensions of early developmental problems. Therefore the staff work in elementary schools with students aged eight to twelve who are showing negative behaviors at home and school. Special classes are held in both social and academic skills; counselors help the parents; and in-service workshops train teachers in positive classroom management techniques and interpersonal communication skills (Pringle, Gregory, Ginkel, & Cheek, 1981). Unique to this intervention is working with children who have a range of personal problems before, or just as, they begin drug use.

The following example is a counseling project, funded by the county board of supervisors in Alameda, California. Their Youth Intervention Project (Y.I.P.) provides outreach counselors, based in community agencies, to work directly in the schools. Among the intervention goals for troubled youth needing services are reducing truancy and drop-out rates, increasing grades and high school graduation rates, and improving self-concepts. The counselor is seen as a catalyst for change and innovation, and can be an advocate for youth, as well as someone who works with parents and school personnel (Resnik, 1979).

Another locale for intervention services is the juvenile justice system. Often young people who are using drugs become involved with the law because of a range of problem and/or delinquent behaviors. Intervention services at this point can often reroute a youngster into more positive behaviors before incarceration or hospitalization is necessary. One such program, the Juvenile Intervention Project (JIP), works with 12 to 17 year olds with drug problems, through Law Enforcement Assistance Administration, Mental Health, United Way, and state drug agency funds in Toledo, Ohio. An adolescent can enter the program through self-referral or through contacts initiated by a school official, parent or justice official, although voluntary involvement is required—no juvenile is made to participate as a condition of sentencing or probation. Individual and group counseling sessions for the youths and their parents are provided. The goals are to improve family communication patterns, teenagers' self-esteem, and drug knowledge, so that the youths will be less likely, therefore, to continue to use or abuse substances (Iverson & Roberts, 1980).

In summary, secondary prevention or intervention targets early users, both during a crisis phase (overdose, parents' discovering a child's use, judicial contact) and as a result of a range of dysfunctional behaviors which are of concern to the young people themselves, or to their friends, parents, and school personnel. School and community-based services are available, often under the auspices of mental health or drug and alcohol agencies or of schools. The goals of these programs are similar to those of primary prevention services, but necessitate a more in-depth counseling/problem orientation rather than just promoting positive development.

Tertiary Prevention or Treatment

The need for treatment for substance abuse is limited to a smaller, but critical, percentage of adolescent abusers, and for those who reach this stage, extensive professional help is required. It is not within the scope of this chapter to provide that detail; however, various types of programs will be briefly described. Readers who question whether treatment is necessary for someone of concern to them are urged to immediately contact their local or regional mental health or drug and alcohol agencies for help. Often school counselors are also aware of successful area programs, and juvenile justice officials usually can be a referral help.

A national directory of treatment sources is available (see *Annotated Bibliography*), and many states provide similar publications. The earlier the help is provided, the more hopeful, in most cases, is the prognosis.

Detoxification can be the first step in the treatment process and is conducted under medical supervision, usually in a special hospital facility. It is intended to stop a physiological dependence on a drug by eliminating the substance entirely from the person's system. Sometimes medication is given to reduce the physical symptoms of withdrawal during this time. Heroin users and alcoholics most often go through this process. However, being physically drug free does not address the psychological dependence or addiction experienced by drug abusers, and follow-up treatment is essential.

One approach, used for heroin users, is methadone maintenance, which provides controlled daily dosages of this synthetic opiate. Rehabilitation counseling should accompany the physiological stabilization in order to help the client develop a positive life style. Clients often stay in maintenance programs for as long as a year, but elimination of the methadone and a drug-free lifestyle are the eventual goals.

Outpatient drug-free modalities are used for addiction to both opioid drugs (e.g., heroin) and nonopioid substances (tranquilizers, amphetamines, sedative-hypnotics, etc.). While there is a great variety in the services offered, clients are expected to remain drug free and live at home or independently. Highly structured programs provide total daytime therapeutic activities, including group and individual counseling, recreational programs, vocational training, and personal skills development. Obviously, personal motivation and voluntary participation are important to successful treatment. Self-help groups are another dimension of this approach. Alcoholics Anonymous and Narcotics Anonymous are familiar programs and are based on mutual support and help from other "recovering" alcoholics or addicts. Juvenile versions have developed in some communities.

For many individuals, outpatient programs and counseling are not sufficient, and they must spend time first in a therapeutic community (TC), a full-time, drug-free residential program. Usually patients spend at least two months in these centers and often

174 Experiencing Adolescents

a year or more. Juvenile facilities particularly emphasize the longer time needed to change negative behaviors and develop a positive way of life. Most TCs have highly structured programs, using confrontation, residential job responsibilities, peer support, and counseling to address the behaviors and problems which brought about the drug abuse lifestyle.

Odyssey House, Phoenix House, and Synanon are among the well-known therapeutic communities which evolved in the 1960's and 1970's in response to the growing number of drug abusers. Most programs of this sort today take a holistic approach to treatment, dealing with all aspects of an individual. The Door is one such example, serving New York City's adolescent population. The philosophy underlying its program is a total person and total problem approach, taking into account the juvenile's "physical, emotional, intellectual, interpersonal, creative, and development dynamics, and his or her family, legal, educational, vocational, and other life problems and needs" (National Institute on Drug Abuse, 1981, p. 3).

The causes of problems and their symptoms are addressed, and patients can use services as varied as nutrition or sex counseling, creative or vocational workshops in music or carpentry, prenatal and parenting classes, legal advice and representation, or psychiatric therapy. The mental health, drug and alcohol abuse treatment program includes four stages: (1) life stabilization, (2) confrontation and therapy, (3) reintegration and exploration of alternatives, and (4) autonomy. A follow-up phase also occurs after completion of the program. Many similar comprehensive facilities exist in every state, under public or private auspices. Judicial determinations, parental petitions, and voluntary admissions are all possible entry mechanisms, but in each instance a total therapeutic process is necessary for treatment and rehabilitation to succeed. Less attention has been paid here to treatment than to prevention, primarily because most young people will not need to enter the treatment phase. Providing information about primary prevention is the basic purpose of this chapter, and such prevention is designed to reach the majority of adolescents and their parents and teachers, those for whom substance abuse will *not* become a major dysfunctional part of life.

WHAT CAN I DO?

Since prevention is a possible and realistic goal, and since decisions about drug and alcohol use are a normal and frequent part of an adolescent's development, the obvious next question is: What can a parent or teacher or friend do to help in that process? The following ideas include some obvious parenting/teaching skills as well as substance-specific suggestions; they are not listed in any particular order or level of importance, but result from the conditions discussed earlier which are associated with drug and alcohol use.

1. Caring is important and should be coupled with limit setting and clearly discussed standards. Input from teenagers is important, and it should be an on-going, interactive process.

The relationship of the parent and child is an influential factor, but so too is the young person's *perception* of that relationship. An adolescent's perception of being loved is seen as the "single most influential factor on behavior" according to family researcher Dr. Fred Street (NIAAA, 1979). He suggests that "those youth who see their parents as being loving and controlling but giving some freedom are not prone to severe problems" (p. 1).

2. Adult support and interaction are a necessary part of development, and teachers are among the other significant adults who can influence a child's growth.

Street adds, for example, that peers become more important when they represent the only way to achieve value. "The adolescent who is denied positive recognition by adults and who is made to feel as a non-person, needs the peer group to restore his/her identity."

3. Seek and encourage communication between adolescents and parents—and other adults as well.

All parents can give multiple examples of their attempts to talk to their children, with only one-way conversations resulting. However, starting at early ages, providing time for dinner table conversations, and valuing a child's opinion or contributions are only a few ways to establish a climate for communications. Another critical skill for parents to learn is to *listen*, an essential feature of true communication. Talking about drugs and alcohol specifically should occur also, at home and in school, from early ages on, and not from a scare tactic perspective. Young people will test out a variety of positions in these discussions, and it is important that parents be informed about substances or willing to admit they need to find out more.

4. Adults should be aware of their own substance use behaviors, recognizing the modeling effect these have, and being sure their words and actions are consistent.

Alcohol, tobacco, over-the-counter drugs, and prescription medications are a major factor in our culture or life-style, and adults' use of these, particularly to cope with psychological stress or enhance social interactions, teaches young people more than any words. Using illegal drugs occurs at a later stage of adolescent drug behavior, and attitudes about substance use are developed well before that point. Media messages and community attitudes also significantly affect young people's perception of the place of drugs in their lives.

5. Parents should know who their children's friends are and should provide opportunities for interaction with them. Peer activities should be supervised when appropriate, or limits and standards should be clearly defined—again, with input from the young people.

Recognizing the importance of friendships to adolescent development, adults can help provide positive activities and alternative opportunities in which youth may participate. Schools and social service agencies welcome additional support and interest from adults, particularly those willing to give time and effort to provide leadership. What *are* the recreational, social, creative, and athletic opportunities available in your community? Are young people participating in these activities, and are they supervised?

6. Talk to and discuss these issues with other parents, using positive *adult* peer pressure to develop agreed-upon standards and interest in teenage activities.

The traditional argument, "But everyone's allowed to go except me!" is often deflated by one phone call, to another parent who has just heard the same statement. In many communities parents have joined together in concerned groups to campaign against apathy, denial, and ignorance regarding their children's negative behaviors, and to promote positive standards and activities. Find out what other groups have accomplished, and support each other (See **PRIDE** in the *Sources of Help* section).

    7. Work with other adults, educate yourself about the extent and type of substance abuse in your community. Work with local agencies and find out the help and services available. Meet with school officials to determine the problems they see and their means of handling them.

Is drug education a required part of your school district's curriculum? It is important also to know what procedures are followed when drug use is discovered by school or other officials. Learning about local agencies can help identify limitations in, or the absence of, necessary services and can assist in providing support and visibility for good resources. Again, input from young people is of great value, and they can often provide leadership in this process.

    8. Recognizing that some youngsters need more help, be willing to intervene or support intervention when a youth—or your child—is abusing drugs or is having other problems.

Problem behaviors even in early childhood should not be ignored. Early awareness and appropriate help can often help prevent later and more difficult problems. It is important for parents to be receptive to seeking help, rather than denying or feeling guilty when their child is having difficulties or when they are having trouble "parenting."

    In summary, it is possible to promote positive total development during adolescence, thus reducing the possibility of substance abuse. The use of drugs and alcohol does not occur in isolation but is part of a total decision-making process called "growing up." Adults can help enhance that maturation by providing strength and support, caring and sharing, and love and limits.

SOURCES OF HELP

Alateen, P.O. Box 182, Madison Square Station, New York, NY 10010, (212) 475-6100.

    Alateen allows teen-aged children of alcoholics to obtain a degree of fellowship with other youths struggling with the prob-

lem of an alcoholic parent. The primary objective of the organization is to help the teens to cope with their problems and not let the
parent's addiction govern all aspects of their lives.

American Red Cross, Youth Services, 17th and D Sts., N.W.,
   Washington, DC 20006, (202) 857-3330.
   The American Red Cross has developed the Alcohol Information Module (AIM) for use by adults working with various youth
groups. Contact the national office or a local Red Cross chapter for
additional information.

Boys' Clubs of America, 771 First Ave., New York, NY 10017,
   (212) 557-7755.
   The Boys' Clubs of America have materials to help concerned
individuals set up alcohol abuse prevention programs for youth
organizations. Project TEAM (Teens Explore Alcohol Moderation) includes media, service clubs, peer models, discussion groups,
and craft activities.

Center for Multicultural Awareness, 2924 Columbia Pike, Arlington, VA 22204, (703) 979-0100.
   Multicultural prevention materials and suggested additional
sources are available through this NIDA-funded project. Many
posters and pamphlets have been developed by the Center for use
with various minority groups.

Charlotte Drug Education Center, Inc. 1416 East Morehead St.,
   Charlotte, NC 28204, (704) 374-3211.
   This local organization, a pioneer in prevention programming,
can provide materials for parents and teachers.

The Cottage Program International, Inc. 736 S. 500 East, Salt
   Lake City, UT 84102, (800) 752-6102.
   A private, non-profit organization, it has a community education program which seeks to reduce the fear and stigma of
alcoholism through changing the cultural mores and family
systems that frequently prevent the alcoholic from seeking treatment. Volunteers are trained to meet with community groups to
discuss various aspects of alcoholism.

Distilled Spirits Council of the United States, Inc., 1300 Pennsylvania Building, Washington, DC 20004, (202) 628-3544.

This organization is funded by the liquor industry and offers publications to adult sponsors of youth-oriented prevention projects, emphasizing responsible decision making and use of alcohol.

Do It Now Foundation, P.O. Box 5115, Phoenix, AZ 85010, (602) 257-0797.

The non-profit Foundation supplies informative and accurate publications on all drugs. They are considered highly readable and fair by young people. Their *Catalog* lists the dozens of items available and prices, and should be a major source for those beginning a drug information center.

National Clearinghouse for Alcohol Information (NCALI), P.O. Box 2345, Rockville, MD 20852, (301) 468-2600.

The NCALI provides publication, information, and referral services on request, including literature searches on specific alcohol topics. It also has recommended prevention and intervention materials designed for teachers, parents, the general public, and teenagers.

National Clearinghouse for Drug Abuse Information (NCDAI), 5600 Fishers Lane, Room 10A-56, Rockville, MD 20857, (301) 443-6500.

The NCDAI distributes publications on all aspects of drug abuse and operates the DRACON system, an outreach service supporting drug information centers nationwide.

National Clearinghouse for Mental Health Information (NCMHI), Public Inquiries Section, Room 11A-21, 5600 Fishers Lane, Rockville, MD 20857, (301) 443-4515.

The NCMHI provides free information on mental health education and services, as well as pamphlets dealing with various mental health topics such as stress.

National Council on Alcoholism (NCA), Publications Department, 733 Third Ave., New York, NY, 10017 (212) 986-4433.

NCA is a private, non-profit organization which distributes a wide variety of publications on all aspects of alcohol use and abuse. It develops programs to help recovering alcoholics also.

National Highway Traffic Safety Administration (NHTSA), Distribution Office, U.S. Department of Transportation, Washington, DC 20590, (202) 426-0874.

The NHTSA provides information about community education on alcohol safety and various other topics concerning drinking and driving.

National Institute on Alcohol Abuse and Alcoholism (NIAAA), 5600 Fishers Lane, Rockville, MD 20857. Public Affairs Office, Room 1695, (301) 443-4883. Division of Prevention, Room 16C-10, (301) 443-4733.

The NIAAA provides extensive educational materials for alcohol programs on health, awareness, and youth. There is also information available in Spanish.

National Institute on Drug Abuse (NIDA), Prevention Branch, 5600 Fishers Lane, Room 11A-33, Rockville, MD 20857, (301) 443-2450.

The Prevention Branch directs inquirers to their appropriate state agencies and other resources for program development and technical assistance.

North Carolina Department of Public Instruction, Division of Health, Safety, and Physical Education, Raleigh, NC (919) 773-3906.

The curriculum, *Life Skills for Health*, is available through this office and includes books for each grade level from kindergarten through twelfth grade.

PRIDE, Georgia State University, University Plaza, Atlanta, GA 30303, (800) 241-9746.

This organization, Parent Resources and Information on Drug Education, provides training for parent groups and youth, and also has a referral service, and consultation for school systems.

Pryamid (East), 7101 Wisconsin Ave., Suite 1006, Bethesda, MD 20814, (301) 654-1194. *Pyramid (West)*, 3746 Mt. Diablo Blvd., Suite 200, Lafayette, CA 94549, (415) 284-5300, (800) 227-0438.

Pyramid, a project funded by the National Institute on Drug Abuse, supplies information and program support for primary prevention efforts. Curricula and media are collected and catalogued. Technical assistance is provided to schools and agencies nationwide. On-site consultation may be arranged through NIDA, Prevention Branch.

Quest, Inc., 4360 Maize Road, Columbus, OH 43224, (614) 267-6800.

This organization developed the *Quest* prevention program and provides teacher training and implementation help when the curriculum is adopted by a school district. A student manual, teacher's guide, and parent's book are available.

Tough Love, P.O. Box 7C, Sellersville, PA 18960, (215) 257-0421.

A private self-help organization, Tough Love provides program development assistance for parents and youth who are dealing with adolescent drug problems.

United States Brewers Association, Inc. 1750 K St., N.W., Washington, DC 20006, (202) 466-2400.

The Association, funded by beer companies, distributes pamphlets on drinking decisions as part of its alcohol awareness program. It also provides manuals for colleges.

United States Department of Justice, Drug Enforcement Administration, 1405 Eye St., N.W., Washington, DC 20537, (202) 633-2000.

The DEA's Preventive Programs Section has materials for use by educators in developing school policies and guidelines for handling substance abuse.

ANNOTATED BIBLIOGRAPHY
(Sources are listed in parentheses.)

For Use By Parents

Come Closer Around the Fire: Using Tribal Legends, Myths and Stories in Preventing Drug Abuse
Written primarily by Native American parents and teachers, this publication incorporates values, beliefs, and perspectives specific to this culture (NCDAI).

Drug Abuse: A Realistic Primer for Parents
The perspective here can be especially useful for parents and can help open communications between parents and teenagers about drug use. A Spanish edition is also available (Do It Now Foundation).

Drug Abuse Prevention for Your Community
Drug Abuse Prevention for Your Family

These two publications are part of a series which target various aspects of the problem and make suggestions for what each person can do to help at home, with friends, and in neighborhood settings (NCDAI).

A Family Response to the Drug Problem (FIND/Families Involved in Nurture and Development) and *Group Facilitator Guidelines and Participants' Handbook.*
Materials to help families work together in preventing or intervening in drug use (NCDAI).

It Starts With People: Experiences in Drug Abuse Prevention
A manual for parents, teachers, and others who want to become involved in helping young people live without drugs. The guidebook provides an overview of the problem and six prevention strategies: information, affective education, peer/cross-age tutoring and counseling, life career planning, alternatives, and parenting/family communication. Various programs are used to illustrate principles for setting up school-based, community, and minority group prevention models. Profiles of three programs are included (NCDAI).

Manual for Working with Parents of Adolescent Drug Users
The report is intended to assist in the development of self-help groups for parents of adolescents involved with drugs and alcohol. Improved family functioning and treatment support are among their goals (NCDAI).

National Directory of Drug Abuse and Alcoholism Treatment Programs
This document is the result of a 1979 joint survey by NIDA and NIAAA, and includes addresses of 9,100 substance abuse services. The referral and treatment programs are listed by state, and alphabetized by city and program name within cities. It will continue to be updated. (NCALI).

National Institute on Drug Abuse Publication for Parents
An annotated listing of NIDA publications, compiled to provide information to parents interested in drug abuse or as a resource to parents involved in prevention programs in their communities (NCDAI).

Ombudsman: A Classroom Community
This is one of several community-oriented publications available which can help parents and others develop local programs (Charlotte, NC, Drug Education Center).

Parents, Peers, and Pot
Both adults and young people find the perspective of this publication accurate and useful. It can be the basis of family discussions (NCDAI).

Prevention Resources at the Grassroots: Concerned Parents, Concerned Youth, Concerned People. Volume VI, Number 1.
This volume focuses on local prevention efforts and the collaboration of prevention professionals, parents, and young people. Parental prevention groups are spotlighted (NCDAI).

Since You Care
A curriculum which helps parents to examine their behaviors toward their children and to improve their parenting behaviors. The manual is designed so that it can be used by parent facilitators (NCDAI).

For Use By Teachers And Other Youth Leaders

Alcohol Abuse Prevention: A Comprehensive Guide for Youth Organizations
The manual, which describes how to set up an alcohol abuse prevention program in a youth organization, also includes managerial issues, funding sources, and program evaluation strategies (Boys' Clubs of America).

Alcohol Education—What It is and How to Do It
This publication is of particular interest to persons working with youth. It explains the different aspects of alcohol education and gives information on various ways it can be accomplished (NCA).

Alcohol-Specific Curricula: A Selected List, 1981
The 11 selected curricula cover alcohol education for grades K through 12, as well as units on high school driver education and fetal alcohol effects. Annotations, ordering information, and a list of alcohol resources for teachers are included (NCALI).

Dial A-L-C-O-H-O-L and Jackson Junior High Adult Group Leader's Guide
Although these materials are designed for use with an alcohol education film series, for grades 9 through 12, the group leader guide can be used independently. Included are role plays, topics for group discussion, basic alcohol information, and a resource list (NCA).

Guide to Alcohol Programs for Youth
The sourcebook provides the latest NIAAA research statistics on youth alcohol use and related problems and on trends in drinking behavior. Alcohol abuse prevention theories and approaches are explained, along with prevention strategies for communities and schools. Eight

profiles of outstanding youth prevention and treatment programs funded by NIAAA are highlighted (NCALI).

A Guidebook for Planning Alcohol Prevention Programs with Black Youth, 1981
   This publication deals with community action strategies directed toward the black youth (NCALI).

Life Skills for Health: Focus on Mental Health, K-12
   The North Carolina state curriculum was a pioneer in incorporating psychological and social aspects of primary prevention (North Carolina Department of Public Instruction).

A Manual for Managing Community Alcohol Safety Education Campaigns
   This publication describes a communications plan for conducting a community alcohol safety education campaign. Specific guidelines include how to define objectives, assess needs, identify target audiences, survey community attitudes, obtain community support, increase awareness of the drinking/driving problem, and work with media (National Highway Traffic Safety Administration).

National Institute on Drug Abuse Publications for Teachers
   An annotated listing of the National Institute on Drug Abuse (NIDA) publications was compiled to serve as a resource and instructional tool for teachers interested in drug abuse prevention. It is also an excellent reference source for students studying various drug topics (NCDAI).

Prevention X Three: Alcohol Education Models for Youth
   The booklet offers detailed descriptions of three programs, originated by NIAAA, that have been replicated at test sites. Ordering information for curricula, training materials, and evaluation instruments is included (NCALI).

Quest—Skills for Living Program
   As a prevention program for 14–18 year olds, this program is a one or two semester skills-for-living high school course. Student, parent, and teacher books are included (Quest, Inc.).

The Right Questions: Evaluation Tools for Youth Alcohol Abuse Prevention
   This resource list contains selected questionnaires and prevention program evaluation materials for use in gathering information about alcohol knowledge, attitudes, and drinking patterns among youth. The resources are useful for youth programs wishing to conduct needs assessments and to evaluate program effectiveness (NCALI).

Suggested Resources for Alcohol Education
This guide includes an annotated bibliography of major publications and a list of sources for alcohol information (Distilled Spirits Council of the United States, Inc.).

Teaching Tools for Primary Prevention: A Guide to Classroom Curricula
The curricula selected were recommended by teachers and Pyramid's educational consultants and staff. The guide includes criteria for selection, index by grade level and a list of major topics: Communications Skills, Decision-Making, Drugs/Alcohol, Peer Relations, Self-Concept/Image, and Values Clarification. Fourteen model curricula are described with information about each: description of materials, target group and setting, goals and objectives, sample exercises or activities, materials needed, time requirements, previous training or experience required, general strengths, limitations and cautions, and ordering instructions, with prices (Pyramid).

For Use By Teenagers

All the informational materials mentioned in the text and highlighted in the Parents and Teachers section of the Annotated Bibliography are also useful for young people. The same Resource organizations are suggested as well. The following selected references are only examples of those which primarily target youth audiences. It is important that teenagers be included in the review and selection of materials, and that the information be appropriate to the various developmental levels of the students.

Alcohol Pleasures and Problems
This is a booklet for use by students in grades 9 through 12 which gives factual materials on alcohol use and abuse (NCA).

Before You Take to the Open Road, Think Twice
A pamphlet about drinking and driving, including facts about blood alcohol levels and highway statistics (United States Brewers Association).

Cleaning Yourself Up: A Guide to Getting Out of the Chemical-World Doldrums for People Who Don't Think They Are Addicts.
This booklet provides ideas on how to live with many of life's problems without getting oneself saturated with drugs (Do It Now Foundation).

Drug Abuse Prevention for You and Your Friends
A publication addressing the role of peers in drug use decisions and prevention of substance abuse (NCDAI).

Drugs: A Primer for Young People
This is a basic introduction to drug information and the problems resulting from various substances (Do It Now Foundation).

Kids and Alcohol
A student handbook for grades 5 through 8 (NCA).

New Comix! Drugs—A Different World
Using a comic book format, the publication is very readable for grade school ages and up, and gets children's attention (NCDAI).

Self-Test on Drinking and Driving for Teenagers
A self-test designed for teenagers, to examine the probability of their driving while intoxicated or of being involved in alcohol-related accidents. The test focuses on risk-taking and peer pressure in such behavior. Teenagers can compare their scores with other youth who have previously taken the test. Suggestions are given on ways to avoid drunk driving (National Highway Traffic Safety Administration).

Think Twice . . . Will I Drink? If I Do, Will I Drink in Moderation?
This pamphlet discusses drinking decisions, how they are made, and what influences moderate alcohol behaviors (United States Brewers Association).

This Side Up: Making Decisions About Drugs
A booklet which contains basic drug information designed to appeal to youth. It discusses why people use drugs and take risks, how to resist peer pressure, and the importance of interpersonal communication and self-awareness. It is appropriate for use particularly at ages 12–14 (NCDAI).

REFERENCES

Blum, R. *Horatio-Alger's Children*. London: Jossey-Bass, Inc., 1973.

Bukoski, W. *A Review of Drug Abuse Prevention Research*. Rockville, MD: Prevention Branch, National Institute on Drug Abuse, 1981.

Cohen, A. *Alternatives to Drug Abuse: Steps Toward Prevention*. Rockville, MD: National Clearinghouse for Drug Abuse Information, 1973.

Durell, J., & Bukoski, W. "Issues in the Development of Effective Prevention Practices." In T. J. Coates, A. C. Petersen, & C. Perry (Eds.), *Promoting Adolescent Health: A Dialog on Research and Practice*. New York: Academic Press, 1982.

Fishman, H. "A Family Approach to Marijuana Use." In *Marijuana and Youth*. National Institute on Drug Abuse Workshop on Marijuana Abuse in Adolescence. Rockville, MD: National Institute on Drug Abuse, 1982.

Frye, R., & Rockness, P. *Life Skills for Health: Focus on Mental Heath.* Raleigh, NC: North Carolina Department of Public Instruction, 1974.

Georgia Department of Human Resources. *Life Skills for Mental Health.* Atlanta, GA: Georgia Department of Human Resources, Division of Mental Health and Mental Retardation Prevention Unit, 1977.

Gordon, N., & McAlister, A. "Adolescent Drinking: Issues and Research." In T. J. Coates, A. C. Petersen, & C. Perry (Eds.), *Promoting Adolescent Health: A Dialog on Research and Practice.* New York: Academic Press, 1982.

Hendin, H., Pollinger, A., Ulman, R., & Carr, A. *Adolescent Marijuana Abusers and Their Families.* NIDA Research Monograph 40. Rockville, MD: National Institute on Drug Abuse, 1981.

Horan, J., & Williams, J. "Longitudinal Study of Assertion Training as a Drug Abuse Prevention Strategy." *American Educational Research Journal,* 1982, *19,* 341–351.

Hurd, P., Johnson, C., Pechacek, T., Bast, L., Jacobs, D., & Leupka, R. "Prevention of Cigarette Smoking in Seventh Grade Students." Journal of Behavioral Medicine, 1980, *3,* 15–29.

Iverson, D., & Roberts, T. "The Juvenile Intervention Program: Results of the Process, Impact, and Outcome Evaluations." *Journal of Drug Education,* 1980, *10,* 289–300.

Jessor, R., & Jessor, S. "Adolescent Development and the Onset of Drinking: A Longitudinal Study." *Journal of Studies on Alcohol,* 1975, *36,* 27–51.

Johnston, L., Bachman, J., & O'Malley, P. *Student Drug Use in America 1975–1981.* Rockville, MD: National Institute on Drug Abuse, United States Department of Health and Human Services, 1981.

Jordon, D. K., & Windsor, B. K. *Project TEAM: Teens Explore Alcohol Moderation.* New York, NY: Boys' Clubs of America, 1978.

Kandel, D. "Drug Use by Youth: An Overview." *Drug abuse and the American Adolescent.* Rockville, MD: National Institute on Drug Abuse, Division of Research, 1981.

Kandel, D., Kessler, R., & Margulies, R. "Antecedents of Adolescent Initiation into Stages of Drug Use: A Developmental Analysis." *Journal of Youth and Adolescence,* 1978, 7, 13–40.

Kandel, D., Treiman, D., Faust, R., & Single, E. "Adolescent Involvement in Illicit Drug Use: A Multiple Classification Analysis." *Social Forces,* 1976, *55,* 438–458.

Kellam, S., Brown, C., & Fleming, J. "The Prevention of Teenage Substance Use: Longitudinal Research and Strategy." In T. J. Coates, A. C. Petersen, & C. Perry (Eds.), *Promoting Adolescent Health: A Dialog on Research and Practice.* New York: Academic Press, 1982.

Kirschenbaum, H., & Glaser, B. *Skills for Living Program*. Columbus, OH: Quest, 1982.

McAlister, A., Perry, C., & Maccoby, N. "Adolescent Smoking: Onset and Prevention." *Pediatrics*, 1979, *63*, 650–658.

National Institute on Drug Abuse. "State Drug Abuse Prevention Grant Program: Program Announcement and Guidelines." Rockville, MD: NIDA, 1980.

National Institute on Drug Abuse. *The Door: A Model Youth Center*. Rockville, MD: NIDA, 1981.

NIAAA Information and Feature Service. *Child's Perception May Determine Behavior*. NIAAA Information and Feature Service, 1979, IFS No. 62, 1.

NIDA. "Toward a National Strategy for Primary Drug Abuse Prevention." (Final Report Delphi II). Rockville, MD: National Institute on Drug Abuse, 1975.

Pennsylvania Governor's Council on Drug and Alcohol Abuse. *Impact*. Harrisburg, PA: The Governor's Council on Drug and Alcohol Abuse, 1974.

Perry, C., Killen, J., Telch, M., Slinkard, L., & Danaher, B. "Modifying Smoking Behavior of Teenagers: A School-based Intervention." *American Journal of Public Health*, 1980, *70*, 722–725.

Pringle, H., Gregory, J., Ginkel, K., & Cheek, C. "Alpha Centers: A Viable Prevention Model for Substance Abuse Agencies and Public Schools." In A. Schecter (Ed.), *Drug Dependence and Alcoholism, Volume 2*. New York: Plenum Press, 1981.

Resnik, H. *It Starts with People*. Rockville, MD: National Institute on Drug Abuse, 1979.

Resnik, H., & Adams, T. *Channel One: A Government/Private Sector Partnership for Drug Abuse Prevention*. Rockville, MD: National Institute on Drug Abuse, 1981.

Roberts, C. *Here's Looking at You*. Seattle, WA: Educational Service District #121, Department of Education, 1974.

Swisher, J. "Prevention Issues." In R. Dupont, A. Goldstein, & T. O'Donnell (Eds.), *Handbook on Drug Abuse*. Rockville, MD: National Institute on Drug Abuse, 1979.

Swisher, J., & Figlin, L. *Final Report: Drug and Alcohol Needs Assessment for 1981–82 and 1982–83 Academic Years for 29 Schools in Pennsylvania*. Research report to the State Department of Education, Harrisburg, PA. State College, PA: Data Base, 1983.

Swisher, J., & Hoffman, A. "Information: The Irrelevant Variable in Drug Education." In B. Corder, R. Smith, & J. Swisher (Eds.), *Drug Abuse Prevention: Perspectives and Approaches for Educators*. Dubuque, IA: William C. Brown Co., 1975.

Vicary, J. R. "Toward an Adaptive Developmental Education." In L. Rubin (Ed.), *Curriculum Handbook: The Disciplines, Current Movements, and Instructional Methodology*. Boston, MA: Allyn and Bacon, Inc., 1977.

Vicary, J. R., & Lerner, J. "Longitudinal Perspectives on Drug Abuse: Analyses from the New York Longitudinal Study." *Journal of Drug Education*, 1983, *13*, 257–267.

Wingard, J., Huba, G., & Bentler, P. "Longitudinal Analysis of the Role of Peer Support Adult Models, and Peer Subcultures in Beginning Adolescent Substance Use." *Multivariate Behavioral Research*, 1980, *15*, 259–279.

Wodarski, J., & Lenhart, J. *Comprehensive Treatment of Adolescents Who Abuse Alcohol*. Paper presented at the Conference on Advances in Clinical Behavior Therapy, Banff, Alberta, Canada, March, 1982.

7. HEALTH ISSUES IN ADOLESCENCE
Evan G. Pattishall, Jr.

To paraphrase Charles Dickens, "Adolescence is the best of times and the worst of times." It is the best because most adolescents are quite healthy, and while they may need to be reassured from time to time that most of their health concerns are normal, they are so full of energy, enthusiasm, and exploration that they should be an exciting asset and challenge to their parents and families.

It can also be the worst of times, especially if adolescents' health problems are severe or if their parents do not know what to expect or how to understand the differences between normal and abnormal health problems. In many instances, the concerned adolescent becomes even more concerned when pressed or nagged by the overconcerned parent. Or, being confronted with a health problem, adolescents and parents may lack the information or understanding of its implications. A relatively normal health problem can be exaggerated so that it becomes, or is feared to be, an abnormal health problem. This often leads the adolescent or the parent to perceive the problem as a major crisis.

This chapter will discuss the health concerns of the adolescent, the health problems seen by physicians, and the adolescent health concerns of parents. The goals will be to help adolescents, parents, teachers, and physicians understand health issues in adolescents and to develop guidelines and strategies for dealing with some of the more frequent and disturbing issues.

Epidemic or Myth

Most reports describe the period of adolescence as being relatively free of illnesses and with lower rates of illness and health care utilization than childhood or adulthood (Blum, 1982; DHEW,

1979; Kovar et al., 1979). Adolescents represent 40 million citizens (about 17% of the population), yet they account for:

- Over twice as many automobile accidents as adults,
- Twenty percent of all suicides (5,000–7,000 adolescent suicides per year,
- Over 600,000 unmarried pregnancies per year,
- Being the only age group for which the death rate is actually increasing,
- A 32 percent pregnancy rate among premarital sexually active teenagers,
- A prevalence of smoking at 12 percent.

The alarming fact is that both accidents and suicides are increasing in frequency among adolescents while they are decreasing for the general population. Also, adolescents and young adults presently have a higher death rate than they did 20 years ago, with 70 percent of all of the deaths of teenagers resulting from accidents or violence, and only 30 percent from disease and other causes (DHEW, 1979).

These figures and others suggest that the "healthy adolescent" may be a myth and that teenagers suffer from many more health problems than we recognize, due to underreporting, lack of attention from the health establishment, and the attitudes and apparent lack of concern by teenagers for their own health (Green and Horton, 1982).

Importance of Health Behaviors

A major conclusion from the 1979 Surgeon General's Report (DHEW, 1979) was that most of the causes of death among the adolescent age group are related to behavioral factors, particularly those behaviors associated with experimenting and risk taking tendencies found most frequently in this age group. The various behaviors that are involved in causing health problems may seem to be more difficult for parents and physicians to deal with than the usual type of health concerns of viruses, pneumonia, physical development, etc. However, this book contains several examples of how behavior in many situations or conditions in adolescence are learned, and therefore can be unlearned or relearned; learning or unlearning provide opportunities for change, resolution, and illness prevention.

A major difficulty which parents and physicians need to appreciate is that adolescents in general have considerable difficulty making the connection between their own high risk behavior and subsequent poor health. Their risk behavior is often characterized by a very positive attitude, with adolescents feeling that they are invincible and acting as though they expect to live forever. While this often adds a certain degree of excitement and optimism to their own and others' lifestyles, it may be a factor for which parents should attempt to compensate. This is not done by parents just increasing their worrying or attempting to suppress their adolescent's behavior, but by establishing an open dialogue and helping to offer and encourage those activities which have a lower risk or for which the teenager appears to have the most realistic view of risk and consequences.

Anne Petersen has provided a practical definition of adolescence that will help parents and physicians understand, work with, and prevent health problems in adolescence. Petersen defines adolescence as "a period between childhood and adulthood, with a biological beginning (puberty) and a social ending (the assumption of adult roles such as full-time employment or parenting)" (Petersen, 1982). Unfortunately, when adolescents begin to act like adults, they also are "at risk" for adopting many adult behaviors which seriously increase their present and future health risks; such behaviors are smoking, drinking, driving, drug use, and sexual activity.

Indeed, the death rate for adolescents decreased steadily from 1900–1960, but since 1960 the death rate has shown a steady increase. Furthermore, most of this increase (70%) can be attributed to some form of violence: accidents, homicide or suicide. Motor vehicle accidents alone account for 36 percent of adolescent deaths (DHEW, 1979; Irwin and Shafer, 1982).

Other health problems include drug use and abuse (including alcohol, cigarettes, prescription drugs, marijuana, and other mind altering drugs), sexual activity (including premarital pregnancy and sexually transmitted diseases), nutritional problems (including deficiencies, imbalances, or excesses/obesity), depression, school performance, infections, and developmental worries (including puberty, tallness/shortness, acne, or appearance).

How Adolescents View Health

Although there are a number of studies attempting to establish adolescent perspectives about their own health, illness, and medical services, there is general agreement that adolescents:

1. Do worry about their own health and illnesses. ("If I'm really sick then maybe I'm not as invincible as I want to be.")
2. Are concerned as to whether they are developing normally. ("Am I too short?" or "Sometimes I feel real strange in my head.")
3. Tend to blend medical and psychosocial issues. ("I feel lousy because I'm not doing well at school." or "The more I worry, the more my face breaks out.")

The result is that adolescents will list health items that appear to combine personal problems and physical problems. Thus, parents and physicians need to abandon the narrow focus of looking only at the physiological determinants of health and illness, and adopt a much broader perspective that considers and integrates biological, psychological, social, and situational information.

An extensive study by Korlath, et al., of Minneapolis-St. Paul teenagers, found their health problems and concerns to be: colds (70%), depression (48%), dental problems (43%), personal problems (42%), flu (40%), family problems (35%), acne (34%), eye trouble (31%), headaches (27%), weight problems (26%), nervousness (25%), and difficulty sleeping (25%). It was significant that socio-emotional problems were ranked highest by the adolescents, for example, depression, personal problems, family problems, nervousness, anxiety, feeling insecure, and difficulty sleeping. These areas were ranked higher than menstrual problems or sexual problems, such as birth control, urinary and vaginal infections, venereal disease, and pregnancy (Resnick, 1982).

The above study does not mean that sexually related problems are not important, but it does indicate that adolescents are less immediately concerned with these problems (perhaps much less than parents). Recognizing these perceptions and priorities of adolescents should help parents to reorient their concerns or attempts to be helpful and to direct attention to the issues that are worrying the adolescent the most. Other areas are still very important, but perhaps we can decrease the parent/adolescent communication gap by parents showing genuine concern for areas that the adolescent is thinking and worrying about the most.

Again, of particular importance is the consistent view of adolescents that combines both health and personal problems. This can be viewed as a major asset in working with adolescents. Again, parents, teachers, and physicians should be reminded that the health and medical problems of adolescents should be approached within the broader context of considering how each of the particular health problems is influenced by the psychological or social situation of the adolescent. We must understand that such health issues as acne or dental problems have both physical and psychosocial components. If adolescents fantasize that such conditions might somehow scar or mutilate them for life, it should be clear that both the psychological and the physical aspects must be addressed at the same time. To address one without the other will tend to convince adolescents that adults do not understand their condition or do not really care enough (Resnick, 1982).

HEALTH PROBLEMS AND HEALTH BEHAVIORS

Throughout this chapter we consider some of the major health care problems and the strategies and mechanisms for health behavior intervention. We turn here to the specific health and illness problems of adolescents.

Motor Vehicle Accidents

Physicians consider the increase in motor vehicle accidents (automobile and motorcycle) to be of epidemic proportions. While motor vehicle accidents account for about 36 percent of adolescent deaths, one must also remember that the morbidity is even more severe, in that for every death from accidents there are many more injuries; often requiring months of hospitalization or resulting in a chronic disability for the rest of their lives (DHEW, 1979).

This leading cause of death of adolescents is not only of concern to physicians and health care providers, but is a major concern and worry of parents. In our day of mobile teenagers and increased use of alcohol, what can parents do to reduce the risk of their own teenager becoming the victim of such an accident?

To anticipate some of the intervention strategies described later, parents should try to model the driving behavior they expect from their kids. Next, they should certainly insist that the teenager take advantage of all driver education instruction offered in the schools. Even advanced driver education is desirable if it can be secured locally or in a nearby community. Supervised experience is also very important, and teenagers can be allowed to drive parents on short and long trips to gain as much experience as possible. One caution: parental supervision might best be structured as a learning experience with plenty of positive compliments (not just negatives) with the teenager attempting to "Do it Dad's way," but also allowing the adolescent to teach Dad or Mom how and why the driver education teacher said it should be done. Sometimes, parents can even learn from their teenagers, and this can help promote sharing and mutual concern with safety.

It is important to recognize and to teach that becoming a driver is an important adult privilege and should not be confused with masculinity, prowess, or bravado. The automobile and motorcycle are powerful and dangerous machines. Even though they often represent access to power and freedom, they become even more dangerous when the driver is angry or emotional. Indeed, driving while angry is a major cause of adolescent traffic fatalities, second only to driving while drinking or drugged. While drunken driving is the major cause of motor vehicle fatalities at every age, it is an especially serious problem for adolescents. It is not just a coincidence that every state that has lowered the legal age for drinking, has had a concurrent increase in the number of adolescents involved in traffic accidents and fatalities (DHEW, 1979; Schowalter & Anyan, 1979).

If parents discover that their own teenager or one of their friends has abused the privilege of driving, it should be expected that parents will take away driving privileges for a period of driver and responsibility re-education, or in the case of an off-spring's friend, prohibit their adolescent from riding with him or her, except under agreed upon conditions. In any event, when an adolescent drives, everyone in the car should be required to wear seat belts (helmets for motorcycles). Wearing seat belts and driving at the legal speed limit should be a condition for the privilege of driving or using the family car. Communication between parents can also help confirm and reinforce driving safety standards in other families.

Parents will do well to consider each of the intervention strategies listed above in terms of how each strategy may be applied to reduce the risk of the adolescent driver's becoming involved in an accident.

Homicides

The American homicide rate is about 10 times greater than that of most other industrialized nations. For young adults (aged 15–24), it is the second leading cause of death. Of the 21,000 Americans who were victims of homicide in 1977, about 25 percent were aged 15–24, placing this group at greater risk than any other population group (DHEW, 1979).

Although there are many factors that are undoubtedly related and are involved in the high-risk/high-homicide rate, the most significant appear to be easy access to firearms, the careless use of firearms, and the abuse of alcohol. From 1960 to 1974, handgun sales quadrupled. During the same period the homicide rate for the overall population doubled, while for young people it tripled. Homicide is also more common among the poor, on weekends, at night, and among males, and most occur as the result of disagreements and conflict. Firearms are also the major means of suicide among adolescents (DHEW, 1979).

Of all the causes of adolescent morbidity and mortality, homicide appears to be the least studied and written about. There are, however, certain actions which parents can take to help protect their adolescent.

Since easy access is a factor, parents should not keep any firearms within easy access, and ammunition should not be kept in the same locality. Sometimes, the time interval between the mysterious disappearance of a firearm and the time it takes to secure some ammunition for it can provide parents an opportunity to inquire or investigate, before someone is seriously injured or killed. If anyone in the family is suicidal or has made suicide gestures, the risk may be so great that no firearm should be allowed in the house under any condition.

Modeling and education can be another protective intervention. In this case, teenagers should be taught that a firearm (like the automobile) is a powerful and dangerous instrument that should in no way be associated with macho, manliness, or an instrument of retaliation, the violence of television notwithstanding.

If the parents feel strongly that one should know how to use firearms, then they should provide the best and most thorough instruction so that the adolescent can learn, indeed overlearn, the proper and safe use of firearms. If the family is one that participates in hunting, then the instruction should be thorough and rigidly enforced, and the adolescent should not be allowed to hunt unless supervised by a skilled and responsible adult; he or she should never be alone with a group of other adolescents.

As we discussed previously, adolescents are maturing into adulthood. Also they are risk-takers and often lack necessary experience and accumulated skill; thus, they are more apt to misjudge or behave unwisely. Therefore, parents must take a more active and controlling role on health issues of greatest risk (Petersen, 1982).

The social peer group should also be scrutinized, and strong controls and restrictions should be placed against the adolescent's affiliating with others in the group that may be carrying or using firearms. This means providing explanations and providing other alternatives, since arbitrary restrictions are apt to be just as arbitrarily resisted.

Suicide

Suicide is the third leading cause of death among teenagers and young adults (ages 15–24). Furthermore, between 1960 and 1970, the suicide rate for young people increased by 70 percent and is continuing to increase, while the suicide rate for the general population has decreased. Some estimates place the actual suicide rate at three times the reported rate (DHEW, 1979; Schowalter & Anyan, 1979).

Also, it is interesting that three times as many adolescent girls attempt suicide as adolescent boys; however, three times as many adolescent boys as girls succeed. This is particularly true during late adolescence. Each year 5,000–7,000 adolescents commit suicide, but an even greater number (over 50,000) attempt suicide (Finkelstein, 1983).

Suicidal behavior in the adolescent is usually an impulsive act and not considered a true wish to die. It may be attempted: as a threat, as a result of depression, out of spite, to punish oneself, to punish someone else as self-pity, in search of peace, to achieve reunification with a loved one, or as a response to feeling uncared for (Schowalter & Anyan, 1979).

Most often a suicide threat is a cry for help. While some studies differentiate between suicide threats (usually verbal) and suicide attempts, all agree that both a threat and an attempt should be taken very seriously.

Suicide gestures or attempts are most often related to increased chronic and acute stress so that the adolescent has increasing difficulty attempting to accomplish the normal tasks of adolescence. It may come to the attention of the parent, physician, or teacher as a behavior problem, or as a psychosomatic concern, often with the parents and adolescent mutually resigning themselves to the problem and with no further attempt to communicate. In the final stage, the adolescent fails to develop techniques for coping with the increasing problems, and, since there is most often no one to turn to, a suicide attempt may ensue (Irwin & Shafer, 1982).

In suicidal adolescents, the most common denominator is depression, although it is often difficult to recognize and most adolescents will not readily admit to being depressed. At high risk are adolescents who have had a previous suicide attempt or a serious accident, teenagers with poor impulse control, those who are psychotic or have experienced drug-induced hallucinations, teenagers who believe themselves to be unwanted or who have failed their family and peers, and those who have a long history of stresses and a history of suicidal attempts in close relatives (Finkelstein, 1983; Irwin & Shafer, 1982).

Parents can use the above information to help them assess the risk for suicide and to know when to get professional help from a medical center, a mental health center, or a crisis center. Most experts agree that individuals at high risk for suicide should be sensitively, but straightforwardly, asked about it. Most often the person who has considered suicide will be relieved that someone else recognizes his or her feelings and that these feelings can be talked about. If the answer is yes, or if there is concern that the person may be covering up, professional help should be secured. If the adolescent has threatened or attempted suicide, he or she should not be left alone at any time until evaluated by a professional.

Experts also seem to agree that if adolescents have a person or a family member to whom they can turn when they are feeling depressed or hopeless, then they are most unlikely to attempt suicide. Those without such a relationship are at much increased risk (Irwin & Shafer, 1982).

Again, communication, caring, and knowing what to look for are very important components of parental intervention. Parents can also receive help from one of the agencies or centers listed in local telephone directories.

Smoking

Smoking is the greatest public health hazard today, yet it is the most preventable cause of death. The 1979 Surgeon General's Report *Healthy People* states that the World Health Organization has declared that the control of cigarette smoking could do more to improve health and prolong life in developed countries than any other single action in the whole field of preventive medicine (DHEW, 1979, p. 124).

Health statisticians have estimated that one's life is shortened by fourteen minutes for every cigarette smoked and inhaled (Schowalter & Anyan, 1979). A little bit of simple arithmetic will tell you that amounts to 4.6 hours per pack, and if one smokes only one pack each day, that is equivalent to losing 70 days, or 2½ months, per year off one's life. After forty years, 7.6 years will be lost. But most adolescents and adults will say they do not expect to smoke that long. Yet, if you are presently the parent of a teenager and you have been a regular smoker, you have probably already accumulated nearly 20 years of smoking. That is equivalent to 3.8 years already lost. But you say "statistics don't mean me." (That is a convenient rationalization also used by adolescents.) Or you may think smoking mainly harms health later in life, and there is plenty of time to quit. Besides, do not some studies show that if you stop smoking your risk of lung cancer drops to just a little above normal after 2 or 3 years? That may be true for lung cancer, but the fact is that health damage begins immediately and there are many other chronic health conditions that are caused and aggravated by smoking. This is particularly true for most cardiovascular and respiratory conditions. The earlier one starts smoking, the more the damage to the body; and when smoking is combined with the use of alcohol, the effect is even more severe. Furthermore, out of every three persons who try to stop smoking, only one is able to do so. Smoking is both physically and behaviorally addicting.

What does this mean for the adolescent? Evans and Raines, who have reviewed the control and prevention of smoking in adolescents, report smoking rates for 12–17-year-old teenagers to be 12 percent, but 26 percent for 17–18 age group (Evans & Raines, 1982). The Surgeon General reports that about one-third of all 18-year-olds are regular smokers (DHEW, 1979). While the smoking rates appear to be dropping somewhat for all teenagers, the older group may have only leveled off. It may also be significant that the age for beginning smoking is decreasing, with 60 percent of the female smokers beginning before they are 13 years of age (Evans & Raines, 1982).

The factors which have been found to place certain adolescents at higher risk are: being employed outside the home (especially girls, being more than twice as apt to smoke); parents who smoke (teenagers are more than twice as apt to smoke if both parents smoke, less if one parent smokes, and much less if neither parent smokes); peer pressure (if best friend smokes, or the greater the number of friends who smoke, the greater the risk of taking up the habit); adult role models who smoke (teachers, TV stars, adult friends); mass media designed to recruit teenagers into the ranks of smokers (TV, magazine ads, and billboards portraying smokers as attractive, having a positive image, and action oriented); and rebelliousness (anti-authority, noncompliance, dissatisfied with how family treats them, problem behaviors such as alcohol and drug use). Still other factors which place an adolescent at risk are: students who do not participate in organized school and community activities; low achievement in school; significant changes in lifestyle or stress (change in residence, absence of a parent, entering new school or college, injury in an accident); being in a lower socio-economic class; having an external focus of control (feeling lack of control over life or that external forces determine what happens to you); impatience to assume adult roles; high impulsivity; and strong peer orientation. Finally, it has also been suggested that smoking may play an important role in establishing a sense of identity, and may help compensate for a low self-esteem, low social confidence, and a higher degree of anxiety (Botvin, 1982; Evans & Raines, 1982).

As one can see from the above lists, smoking is a multidetermined behavior. In order to understand the process of acquiring smoking behavior, we can organize and explain most of the above risk factors from the perspective of the social influence model and the coping model (Botvin, 1982). The social influence model promotes adolescent smoking through the adolescent's imitating or modeling of the smoking behavior of high status role models (parents, peers and media personalities, as well as persuasive advertising). The coping model would attribute great influence to the use of smoking as a means of coping with failure or expected failure (doing poorly in school or not achieving social status), coping with anxiety, stress, or inadequate self-image. Thus, it should be clear by now that any attempt of parents to prevent or stop teenage smoking would have to include strategies for dealing with both social pressure to smoke and specific individual characteristics that are apt to place an adolescent "at risk."

It is also clear from several large studies that attempting to frighten teenagers with the facts alone about the health horrors or death threats of smoking is not very effective. The facts and the scare tactic approach does not work well for smoking, drinking, sexual activities, drugs, venereal disease, or any of the unsanctioned or unhealthy behaviors we sometimes deplore in teenagers (and adults).

Now that it has been well demonstrated that knowledge (education) alone will not change behavior, a number of innovations have occurred. Newer programs focus more on the psychosocial factors that promote smoking behavior. They attempt to make teenagers familiar with the specific social and psychological pressures to smoke and to teach them specific techniques and behavioral skills for dealing with these pressures, particularly those pressures coming from peers, other models, and intrapersonal factors.

The other component is to recognize that behavior change is basically an individual phenomenon, so that the unique characteristics of each individual in each situation (environment) must be identified and translated in terms of how that particular individual can be affected or reached. This usually means that a combination of psychological, social, physiological and environmental factors need to be combined at the same time. For example, you may need to develop your intervention strategy on the basis of some very basic motivation; the teenager may know that his favorite uncle died from lung cancer after 20 years of heavy smoking (factual knowledge), but his own low self-esteem (psychological symptoms) is getting worse so that he now has trouble keeping up (physical) when he jogs with his best friend (peer influence) who does not smoke. Even though this example is grossly oversimplified, any attempt to intervene must be based on: determining causes for the low self-esteem (with the idea of improving it); knowing his relationship to the peer group (what needs do they fulfill and can it be fulfilled by a better group? etc.); the cough symptom which may reflect illness or physiological changes (but which might be used to help him see that he had better take charge of his own health); difficulty keeping up (again, a physical symptom which could help him accept what is happening to him); jogging (which at least is a positive health activity); and his best friend who does not smoke and might be used as a counterforce to draw him away from the "bad group" so that he spends more time with and is influenced by the "good guy."

Again to anticipate our later discussion, various intervention strategies could be highly relevant here, particularly in terms of: using parent-adolescent communication mechanisms; identifying and encouraging a better model and imitating or associating with it; linking knowledge about physical factors in smoking to what is happening to him physiologically, and socially in terms of his need for an "accepting" peer group; supporting his association with his jogging friend; limiting his association with the old peer group; and perhaps working with his jogging friend's parents to encourage/provide activities that would include more time and association with non-smoking kids.

Alcohol and Drug Use and Misuse

We shall consider alcohol and drug use and abuse separately, although alcohol is a drug as much as marijuana or cocaine. In effect they are all mind-altering drugs, but because of the social and legal approval placed on alcohol in certain situations in our culture, it represents a different problem, particularly in terms of access and acceptable adult usage. It is thought by many physicians that the biological and psychosocial damage of alcohol is so great that if it were "discovered" today, it would probably not be released by the Federal Drug Agency for human consumption.

The use of alcohol has been increasing greatly among young people. About 80 percent of teenagers (12–17-year-olds) report having had a drink of alcohol in the past; more than half report that they drink at least once a month; more than one-third drink once or twice a week, and nearly three percent report that they drink alcohol each day. The number of high school students who report that they become intoxicated at least once a month has more than doubled since 1966 (from 10 to over 20 percent of this age group). Among male high school seniors, nearly 80 percent report that they drink at least once a month, and more than six percent drink daily. It is also reported that young people tend to consume larger quantities of alcohol and are more likely to become intoxicated than are older people (DHEW, 1979; Vicary, Chapter 6).

It should be understood, then, why alcohol-related accidents are the leading cause of death in the 15 to 24 age group and why 60 percent of all alcohol-related highway traffic fatalities are among young people. Total accident data for 1981 show that the proportion of drivers with measurable blood alcohol concentration has steadily increased. The percentage of 16- to 19-year-old drivers with positive blood alcohol levels rose from 20 percent in

1977 to 28 percent in 1981, which was an 8 percent increase (Medical News, 1983).

Cirrhosis of the liver is largely attributable to alcohol consumption and ranks among the 10 leading causes of death. Cancer of the liver, esophagus, and mouth is also associated with alcohol use, with liver cancer being almost exclusively attributed to alcohol use. It is also known that excessive drinking during pregnancy can produce infants with severe abnormalities, including mental retardation. The increase in alcohol consumption in the U.S. has been generally attributed to the lowering of the legal drinking age in many states and the increased consumption of alcohol by women (DHEW, 1979).

As for drug use and abuse, it should be recalled that drug abuse (other than alcohol) was virtually unknown among young people in 1950. However, by 1977, 30 percent of the 12- to 17-year-olds had tried marijuana, 60 percent of the 18- to 25-year-olds had tried marijuana, and about 20 percent had tried stronger drugs such as cocaine and hallucinogens.

As Chapter 6 has indicated, there is some evidence that illicit drug use among adolescents may be declining. However, drug use is still prevalent for teenagers, even though only one percent of high school students report daily use of drugs other than alcohol, tobacco, or marijuana. Stimulants, such as amphetamines, are another category of drugs for which young people report frequent use. Even though the actual prevalence of drug misuse is hard to obtain, it is clear that drug misuse is a major problem in our society today. Among high school seniors, about 10 percent report daily use of marijuana (46% report annual use), and the relationship of marijuana to automobile accidents, especially in combination with alcohol, is a serious medical and social issue (DHEW, 1979). With the great increase in drug use and misuse, particularly marijuana and other psycho-active drugs, there is much concern by health care providers that many of our adolescents will never reach their full potential, and others will exhibit a severe reduction in motivation and performance, followed by chronic health problems which will affect them for the rest of their lives. As health problems, hallucinogens are especially dangerous, because they distort the perception of reality and because of their biochemical makeup. They can cause potentially fatal toxic reactions with unpredictable psychic effects that may result in irreversible mental and physical damage.

Parents are especially concerned and often express helplessness about teenage alcohol and other drug use for many reasons. Often they feel out of touch with what is going on, and adolescents are prone to promote this through lack of communication. Parents also may lack knowledge about various drugs, how and why they are used, and at what developmental stages or under what psychological or social situations their teenager is most at risk. There is also a fear of the stigma of failure as a parent if the teenager becomes involved with alcohol or illicit drugs.

It is important that parents recognize and deal with the above dimensions of drug use and abuse, especially if they are to develop an aggressive prevention or intervention program for their own family or the community. For example, the teenage pattern of drinking alcohol (usually beer) to become drunk is a serious abuse and requires a different intervention than an occasional beer that might be smuggled into a teenage party or gathering.

In Chapter 6, Vicary has already provided an excellent review of reasons for, and patterns of, using drugs and alcohol, as well as specific strategies and details for intervention or prevention action by parents, teachers, and teenagers. Caring with limit setting and good communication are two very important influences on adolescent health behavior. They may seem obvious, but they are also the most difficult to accomplish in a situation that is often volatile and one-sided. Modeling is equally difficult for parents and teachers (and adolescents). Most of us prefer to be seen and judged as we would like to be rather than as what we are, but as the old adage says "What you do speaks louder than what you say." Knowing who their adolescent's friends are and providing some positive peer activities can help parents and teachers communicate with their teenagers and can provide an opportunity to work with other parents and teachers.

As Vicary (Chapter 6) points out, the use of drugs and alcohol does not occur in isolation, but comes about as a part of a total decision-making process called growing up. Teenagers (and adults) should be taught that they do have a choice and that they have the power to decide not to use drugs or alcohol. Understanding that one has the power to decide "yes" or "no" is often the beginning of taking charge of, and responsibility for, one's own life and health.

Sexual Activity

Several aspects of sexual activity must be explored in order to deal with the health problems originating from adolescent sexual activity. One concerns the relationship of sexual activity to growth and development. Another concerns the relationship of adolescent pre-marital intercourse to the major health and social problems of adolescent pregnancy, sexually transmitted diseases, and other sex-related health disorders (Lerner & Hultsch, 1983).

Shea (Chapter 3) presents the important findings of several studies on adolescent sexuality. She points out that sexual development and learning about sex have been occurring since childhood, so that they do not just appear suddenly in adolescence. Petersen and Boxer (1982) also point out that the onset of puberty is only one of several factors that make adolescents become sexually active; there are other biological, social, and psychological factors, and the interactions among them (Lerner & Hultsch, 1983; Petersen & Boxer, 1982). Petersen and Boxer (1982) stress also two aspects of our society that have recently had an impact on the sexual behavior of adolescent females, namely the women's movement and the social sanction of, and permission for, sexual experiences, approvals granted in our families, via societal attitudes, and in the media. (Remember that adolescents are in the process of developing identities and that they look to the media and other sources in order to learn and find models for behavior.)

There have been a number of studies of sexual activity among adolescents, most among urban groups, and some with rather conflicting results. From a parental point of view, it is not all bad everywhere, and adolescents are not completely abandoning the relationships between sex, marriage, morals, and love. They are, however, adopting more liberal sexual norms. Shea finds that a majority of adolescents will have pre-marital intercourse by the age of 19. As to when it will happen, it appears to be "situation specific"; that is, it is not easy to predict when it will happen. Nor is it easy to keep it from happening. It is also important to recognize that the major shift in adolescent sexual activity has occurred among adolescent girls, rather than adolescent boys (Petersen & Boxer, 1982). While sexual activity among adolescents is increasing, they are not promiscuous: the majority have only had one sex partner, and sex is infrequent (Shea, Chapter 3).

Unmarried teenage pregnancy, a major health problem for adolescents, parents, and society, has been increasing rapidly, especially among the 10–14-year-olds (Blum, 1982). While Blum postulates more influence to the lowering of the age at menarche (from age 16 to 12 over the past half century) rather than to a revolution in sexual standards, most authors consider it to be a combination of multiple biopsychosocial factors. The recognition of multiple factors is important because it will allow for a broader pattern of intervention strategies.

While adolescent girls may appear to be strong and active, there is much evidence to show that the earlier the age at which one becomes pregnant the greater the health risk for the teenage mother and baby. For example, pregnancy in an early adolescent is more likely to result in toxemia of pregnancy, iron-deficiency anemia, and difficult delivery for the mother, and also result in the delivery of an underweight or premature baby with mental retardation or physical deformities. For example, if the pregnancy occurs within two years after menarche, the risk of having an underweight baby of less than 5½ pounds is almost doubled (Schowalter & Anyan, 1979).

Some of the above health risks can be reduced or prevented with comprehensive prenatal care, but the impact of an adolescent's pregnancy on social, psychological, and educational areas in her life is even more difficult to assess and assist. Shea (Chapter 3) provides much information on adolescent pregnancy and various strategies for prevention or helping the pregnant adolescent.

Parents are not usually the "first to know," so a close relationship with a physician or health care provider can encourage adolescents to seek help through information as well as medical examination. Recognize, however, that adolescents usually want complete confidentiality, until they decide who, if anyone, should be told. Recognize also that much of the literature that parents (and adolescents) read paints a very bleak picture of adolescent pregnancy. However, as Shea states "the situation is not hopeless." There are many resources, from sex education to family planning clinics or from adolescent clinics to physicians in adolescent medicine, who can provide help. There are also special clinics for anyone with an unwanted pregnancy, but one must be very cautious to select only those sources of help which will provide a truly comprehensive review and consultation about the alternatives available and the impact of each alternative on the lives involved. An abortion is not an innocuous psychological or medical procedure, nor is a birth and the raising of a child. There are also economic, social, family, education, psychological, and religious factors to consider for the present and for the future. So get the best counseling and help available. One has a choice. Just as one should try to stress the early assurance that one has a choice as to whether to engage in sexual activity, or become pregnant, or use a contraceptive, one also has a choice as to whether to terminate a pregnancy or continue a pregnancy to full term. Family and professional support will make a big difference.

Sexually Transmitted Diseases

Seventy-five percent of the 8 to 12 million cases of sexually transmitted diseases occur among young people ages 15–24. Even though the incidence of gonorrhea and syphilis has decreased somewhat over the past four years, both diseases have continued to increase among adolescents. Also on the increase in all groups is genital herpes and nonspecific urethritis, which have become major public health problems (DHEW, 1979).

Gonorrhea is a sexually transmitted infection due to *Neisseria gonorrhoeae*. Symptoms, usually appearing within one week after exposure, are: a purulent (pus) foul-smelling vaginal discharge in women; a burning on urination and purulent penile discharge in men. However, 75 percent of infected women and 25 percent of infected men do not have symptoms. An important complication includes pelvic inflammatory disease (PID) in about 6 percent of untreated women and can lead to sterility. Gonorrhea can be diagnosed by a physician or local health department, and without parental consent. It can be successfully treated by the proper antibiotic. Both partners must be treated, or the disease will continue to be transmitted (Blum, 1982).

Syphilis is less common, but is also on the increase. It is a sexually transmitted infection of *Treponema pallidum.* The first lesion usually appears at the site of direct contact with a carrier about three weeks after contact. The lesion is called a chancre, is about half an inch in diameter, is reddened, raised, firm, non-painful and moist and usually develops on the penis or scrotum of a male or on the external genitalia of a female, although it can occur inside the vagina or on the cervix. If this first stage is not treated, the chancre appears to heal, but after about six weeks the more widespread and systemic stage begins, often accompanied by fever, headache, fatigue, skin rash, and swelling of lymph nodes throughout the body. A physician or local health department can diagnose and treat syphilis. If it is untreated, it can progress to a very serious chronic illness with severe neurological damage (Schowalter & Anyan, 1979).

Herpes simplex (type II, genital) virus infection occurs through sexual contact. Ninety percent of the genital herpes infections are herpes simplex type II, and about 10 percent are herpes simplex type I (oral). The infection manifests itself as small blisters (similar to cold sores or fever blisters) appearing along the labia or introitus in the female or on the penis in the male. There is often initial itching followed by severe pain when the blisters rupture. The lesions are self-limiting, lasting 7 to 10 days, but recurring at variable intervals from months to years. Recurrence is often associated with ultraviolet light, friction, fever, gastrointestinal upset, and emotional stress. Genital herpes can cause serious neurological damage in about 50 percent of infants delivered vaginally by infected mothers. There is no treatment at the present time, except for a topical anesthetic for pain relief (Blum, 1982; DHEW, 1979).

Strategies for intervention consist of antibiotic treatment for gonorrhea and syphilis, but, again, there is no present cure for genital herpes. Guilt feelings or shame often interfere with adolescents' (and adults') seeking medical care, and occasionally, health professionals find it difficult to be nonjudgmental. Prevention is difficult because the best prevention is no sexual activity or the male's use of condoms. However, other intervention strategies include education of adolescents so that they understand early signs of the disease, screening high-risk groups, immediate treatment of all infected cases and identification and treatment of sexual contacts (Blum, 1982; DHEW, 1979).

Nutrition and Health

The evidence is now overwhelming that nutrition, dietary habits, and eating behaviors are directly linked to major health problems in all age groups; problems are as diverse as heart disease, tooth decay, obesity, and some kinds of cancer, to mention only a few (DHEW, 1979). Parents are especially aware that good nutrition is a major contributor to the health and development of infants and children, and yet adolescence appears to be a very difficult time for parents to promote and monitor healthy eating patterns in order to protect their adolescent's health for the rest of their lives.

Nutritional problems are generally categorized to include deficiencies, imbalances, or excesses. Fortunately, diet deficiency diseases which were very prevalent during the early 1900s are now rarely seen. However, iron deficiency in children and women of child bearing age remains a public health concern. Other deficiencies common in adolescence are Vitamin A and calcium. It is estimated that about one percent of the American population is undernourished, especially among lower socio-economic groups, but most of today's nutrition problems are more apt to be associated with eating too much and with imbalance in the kinds of foods that are eaten (Blum, 1982; DHEW, 1979; Rudolph, 1982).

It is very important to provide an ample and balanced diet. It should be remembered that adolescence is a period of rapid growth and that the greatest nutrient needs occur at the time of peak growth. And yet, adolescents probably have the least desirable food habits and the most compromised nutritional intake of all age groups. The adolescent is erratic in food intake, frequently misses family meals, relies on snacks of high sugar and salt and fat content, is apt to use vending machines for junk foods and for the senseless calories found in soft drinks, and indulges heavily in fast foods.

Many of the above eating habits, in combination, lead to obesity problems. We now know that obesity contributes to premature death and is associated with cardiovascular disease, hypertension, hyperlipidemia, orthopedic problems, peripheral vascular problems, diabetes, and gallbladder disease. In adolescents, obesity can have especially serious social consequences for a young person attempting to grow up in a society which places special value on slimness and athletic ability. It has been said that there is no health problem, disease, or condition that is not aggravated or made worse by obesity (Blum, 1982; DHEW, 1979; Rassin, 1983).

Most studies find that between 12 to 15 percent of American teenagers are obese. Obesity also seems to be more common among girls than boys. There is also an inverse relationship between socio-economic status and obesity, with more than twice as many girls from the lower socio-economic class being obese as girls in the upper socio-economic class. Boys from the lower socio-economic class are also more than twice as apt to be obese (Blum, 1982).

Cardiovascular disease, atherosclerosis, and hypertension are directly related to nutrition and food intake. Of special concern is the role of high intake of cholesterol and saturated fat, usually of animal origin, associated with atherosclerosis and cardiovascular diseases. Americans who habitually eat less fat-rich diets have less heart disease than other Americans. An increasing number of studies show that cardiovascular health can be favorably influenced by a lean body weight, regular vigorous exercise, smoking avoidance, and a diet with relatively more vegetables, fish, and white meats rather than red meats (DHEW, 1979). Adolescence is a particularly important time for establishing good eating and activity habits.

High blood pressure has also been significantly linked to high dietary salt, particularly in susceptible or genetically predisposed individuals. Studies also show that when hypertension is present, controlling salt intake can help control it.

Diet and cancer relationships are more tenuous, but are increasing. Populations with different dietary patterns do appear to have differing cancer rates. Most frequently implicated are: the high consumption of animal protein and the low consumption of fiber from plant sources; and the high consumption of fats, both saturated and unsaturated, may be linked to colon cancer and to hormone-related cancers of the ovary and prostate. All of these possibilities need further investigation (DHEW, 1979).

Intervention in nutrition and eating habits is very difficult to prescribe. It is important that an adolescent have an ample and balanced diet to support rapid growth and increased activity. Pregnant teenagers also have needs for special nutrition and should be carefully monitored for the sake of both the mother and the infant. The major approach is to make nutritious foods available when the adolescent is hungry. This includes fruits, cheese, and sandwich materials, rather than nutrition-poor snacks. Many nutritionists recommend that nutrition-poor snacks not be available in the house at all.

Breakfast is still considered to be a very important meal for adolescents, and parents should set a good example with children from an early age period. It is also important to watch for inappropriate dieting, and when adolescents begin to diet, they should omit foods, such as potato chips, candy, crackers, that contain little in the way of nutrition, and include foods that are balanced with the basic nutrients. Girls beginning to menstruate will also have an added need for iron (Rassin, 1983).

The Surgeon General's Report on health promotion and disease prevention states that Americans would probably be healthier if they consumed: only the sufficient calories to meet body needs and maintain desirable weight (fewer calories if overweight); less saturated fat and cholesterol; less salt; less sugar; relatively more complex carbohydrates such as whole grains, cereals, fruits, and vegetables; and relatively more fish, poultry, legumes (for example, beans, peas, peanuts), and less red meat, as well as less processed foods (DHEW, 1979).

Nutrition education is very important, but eating habits are more controlled by behavioral patterns than by knowledge. Therefore, parents should try to integrate skills in decision-making, coping, and assertiveness into any attempt to modify the eating behaviors of adolescents. Often parents can utilize the help of therapists from the nutritional, medical, psychological, behavioral, and educational fields. Parents should also attempt to observe the eating environment, identify health-risk eating behaviors, seek out the most promising targets, and evolve the best strategies to reduce the damaging effects of certain eating behaviors on adolescent health (Brownell & Stunkard, 1983; Frank et al., 1982).

Intervening in the obesity of adolescents deserves special mention. In terms of modeling (and perhaps some genetics), if no close family member is obese, the adolescent has little risk of becoming obese. However, if one parent, brother, or sister is obese, the adolescent has a moderate risk of developing obesity, and if both parents are obese, the adolescent has a greatly increased risk.

The basic way in which an individual becomes obese is that more calories are taken in and absorbed than are spent or are necessary to meet day-to-day requirements for activity and growth. That is why exercise and activity are considered to be of equal importance to food intake, and the most successful programs to reduce obesity will combine reduced calorie intake, increased activity, and the use of behavioral change strategies in an integrated approach. Keeping growth charts, food logs, and weight charts are all recommended for an adolescent attempting to lose weight over weeks and months. (Crash diets can be harmful.) This means that there must be a plan developed for changing eating behaviors and patterns, changes in food allowance, changes in activity, and long-term (as well as short-term) goals should be set and monitored (Schowalter & Anyan, 1979). Weight loss should be no more than one to two pounds a week, which means that it may take several months or perhaps a year to achieve ideal body weight.

Much emphasis today is put on the success of inducing changes in behavior, attitude, and lifestyle, rather than dieting alone. Adolescents can be helped to alter specific features of their personal, social, and physical environments in order to successfully alter their eating and exercise behaviors. Specific techniques include such factors as: eating more slowly; leaving food on the plate; eating only at specific times and in specific places; using methods other than eating to deal with emotional stress, boredom, or fatigue; providing a system of rewards for changing eating behavior and weight loss; keeping a diary of all food and activity;

setting contractual agreements with one's self or with others; trying to cut in half or eating only a fraction of undesirable foods (instead of total abstinence); involving the family in the treatment plan; providing support, reinforcement, and encouragement at all times; and, particularly, encouraging the adolescent to take responsibility for the management of his or her own treatment plan (Blum, 1982).

The ultimate aim should be prevention, which can establish a lifestyle and behavioral pattern that will reduce the chance of a lifelong battle with obesity, with poor nutrition habits, and with the concomitant physical health and psychological health problems related to nutrition.

Additional Health Problems

Other health concerns of adolescents include physical problems such as: shortness/tallness, menstrual irregularity, sexual immaturity, skin problems, juvenile diabetes mellitus, cardiovascular problems, and sports injuries. It is impossible to cover adequately each of these health problems in any one chapter, so they will only be reviewed briefly to alert parents to some of the more basic dimensions of each problem. More in-depth exploration of each health problem can be found in the references at the end of this chapter.

The major changes during *puberty* have already been discussed in Chapter 2. Since there is considerable variation in the growth patterns of different adolescents, it seems to parents that adolescents seldom stay the same for more than a few weeks or months. While this is occurring, the teenager often wonders whether he or she is growing enough or growing normally. Height and weight growth charts are easy to maintain and will help reassure (or alert) both parents and adolescents. There are as many short adolescents as there are tall ones, but most of the short and tall are within the range of normal. Family history is important, both in terms of physical size and rate of growth and maturation. However, growth can also be influenced by severe diseases in childhood, so that a boy or girl may reach adolescence with less height or weight than other adolescents. During preadolescence, most girls and boys can be expected to grow between 1½ to 2¾ inches per year and gain 3¼ to 9¾ pounds per year. Thus, if the growth rate falls below this range, it could be a signal that a health problem may be interfering with normal growth; thus, a physician's evaluation should be secured (Brooks-Gunn & Petersen, 1983; Lauton & Freese, 1981; Schowalter & Anyan, 1979).

Sexual maturity is highly variable; the link between age and maturation is never precise. As mentioned above, an adolescent may mature more slowly if other family members have matured relatively late, if there was a major or chronic illness in childhood, or if growth during childhood was normal but slow. In girls, the first sign of sexual maturation is the development of a small amount of breast tissue beneath the areolae, but sometimes this does not occur until the age of 13 or 13½. These initial signs are often followed by the development of pubic and underarm hair. In boys, the first sign is usually an accelerated growth of the testes, again which may not begin until 13½ to 14 years of age. In general, one should not be overly concerned about late sexual maturation if the adolescent has been growing normally, with no abnormal physical symptoms, and not older than the above ages. In addition to teenagers' worrying whether they are developing normally, however, the situation is made even worse by the fact that adults and other teenagers tend to treat sexually immature adolescents as if they were considerably younger than they actually are (Schowalter & Anyan, 1979).

With regard to delayed menarche, it should be pointed out that even though the average age for menarche is 12 to 13, it can actually occur anytime between the ages of 10 and 15. After the menstrual period begins normally, it can still vary considerably, missing a month or two during the first few years. Factors which can interrupt menstrual periods are: changing place of residence; going to camp or traveling; emotional stress; illness; rapid weight loss; or extensive and rigorous physical activity. If the teenager is sexually active and does not use contraceptives, menstrual interruption is one of the earliest signs of pregnancy. If more of the above signs are present, then a physician should check for other possibilities. Similarly, if heavy or prolonged menstrual periods cannot be explained by a longer than usual interval between menstrual periods, it is best to have the situation monitored medically, particularly since heavy bleeding is very worrisome to an adolescent. Symptoms of crampy lower abdominal and pelvic pain at the beginning of the menstrual period or during the first two days can sometimes be treated medically. Mid-cycle dull ache pain in the lower abdomen is usually caused by the ovary releasing the ovum, and generally needs no treatment (Schowalter & Anyan, 1979).

Skin problems in adolescence are numerous and varied. One of the most frequent and worrisome skin disorders is acne. It appears in a skin pore from which barely visible hair is growing. A sebaceous gland in the pore produces oily material which combines with bacteria (*Propionibacterium acnes* and *staphylococcus epidermidis*) and shedding skin to create an acne lesion and plug which are called blackheads and whiteheads. If the wall of the follicle ruptures, the material runs out into the surrounding tissues, redness and swelling develop, and a pimple is formed. These can leave scars when they heal, so the combination of red pimples and scars can seriously threaten the self-image of a growing adolescent. Mild acne can usually be helped with a daily application of benzoyl peroxide or tretimoin. Physicians can also prescribe such medication as retinoic acid, antibiotics, steroids, or extract the plugs. Major scarring can also be removed with dermabrasion (Lauton & Freese, 1981; McGuire, 1983).

Juvenile diabetes mellitus is the most common endocrine disorder of childhood and adolescence. Cells in the pancreas that produce insulin begin to produce less and less, and the body is less and less able to transfer glucose (sugar) from the bloodstream into cells for their use; the level of glucose in the blood increases, and some of the glucose is excreted in the urine. In order to get energy, the body begins to use fat which is not used completely, so the bloodstream accumulates ketones, which also appear in the urine. The appetite increases, urine production is increased, followed by thirst and water consumption, weight loss and feeling ill. The diagnosis of diabetes can be made at this point by testing the blood and urine. But if nothing is done, symptoms get worse; there are extreme fatigue, heavy breathing, lethargy, sleepiness, and abdominal pain. Diabetes at this point can be life threatening to an adolescent unless an insulin injection is given (Schowalter & Anyan, 1979).

Acute rheumatic fever is less frequent today, but it can still cause serious disability if allowed to develop. It may appear several weeks after a teenager has had an untreated or only partially treated infection of *betahemolytic streptococci* (Group A) bacteria. The acute rheumatic fever comes from a reaction to the strep infection (which usually could have been treated by antibiotics), a sore throat with fever, pain, swelling, and tenderness in various joints, often migrating from one joint to another, and often a fine skin rash on the chest or back. The most dangerous aspect of rheumatic fever is its effect on the heart, with inflammation of the heart, fatigue, chest pain, shortness of breath, and need for several pillows in order to breathe and sleep at night. It can be prevented by adequate treatment of the initial strep infection, which can be identified by a throat culture and treated with antibiotics (Lauton & Freese, 1981; Schowalter & Anyan, 1979).

Sports injuries are rather frequent in adolescence, but many can be prevented or treated with appropriate precautions and care. Interest in competitive sports develops gradually and reaches its peak in the teen years. Sports often offer many benefits to the adolescent, but they all pose some risk of injury. Parents, teachers, and physicians have a responsibility to recognize the risks of competitive sports and take precautions and action to enforce the best management, training, protection, and treatment. Sports enthusiasts are not always the best judges of risk or treatment. The four common and potentially serious injuries are: cerebral concussion, lumbar spine injuries, knee injuries, and sprained ankle. The long term consequences of neglect or ignorance can handicap a teenager over a lifetime. From the standpoint of health in the future, high activity (exercise) and less competition (alone or in partnership), less vigorous contact (less risk of injury), and maximum protection should be the long-range goals of all sports. The habit of exercising throughout life is a necessary component of good health (Blum, 1982; DHEW, 1979; Gross, 1981; Schowalter & Anyan, 1979).

There are many health problems of adolescence that cannot be covered in one chapter. They include special problems and vulnerability to respiratory diseases, gastrointestinal disorders, certain types of cancer, urinary infections, anemia, chronic conditions acquired in childhood, etc. Additional reading of some of the references should be helpful.

Healthy adults are derived from healthy adolescents and healthy children. If we are to prevent disease and promote health over the entire life span, we must begin at the beginning to develop the health behaviors that will insure a healthy old age. Adolescents are forming life-long habits and learning to practice lifestyles that will determine their own well-being and health as adults. Parents, teachers, physicians, and others whom they use as models can help them to reach their full potential as adolescents and as adults.

The health problems discussed in this chapter are all of concern to adolescents, and to parents, teachers, and physicians who are trying to help teenagers "get through" adolescence. It is a sobering responsibility, but as stated in the beginning of this chapter, adolescence can indeed be the best of times. The emphasis in this chapter has been on trying to combine the health problems with the behavioral requirements needed to prevent the problems or to intervene once they are present.

Even though behavior is not easy to change, we must learn as much about it as possible, since becoming a healthy teenager (or adult) is going to be as much related to developing healthy behaviors and lifestyles as it is related to medical intervention. Adolescents are at-risk, but so are parents at-risk. We should be able to work at it together.

SOURCES OF HELP

A reality of adolescent health issues concerns when to get help for health problems. Resnick reports extensive studies by Hedin et al. (1977, 1980), and by Resnick et al. (1980), which confirm many of the perceptions reported earlier about how adolescents perceive their health but also help us understand that adolescents really do not like to admit that they are ill or need help (Resnick, 1982). In general, they are extremely reluctant to seek health care help. They must either be in pain or in a crisis before admitting that they need help (are sick) or seek help. Their own concept of being healthy is closely linked to their own energetic activities, positive self-regard, appearance, and relationships with other people in their lives, especially family, peers, and teachers. Adolescents see all of these dimensions as putting severe pressure on them, and when one dimension begins to crumble, other dimensions seem to be threatened and thus play a major role in their admitting to illness. Not being healthy, or being ill, is represented by a severe disruption in any or all of the above dimensions.

A second major health issue identified in the studies was the excessive concern for use of alcohol and drugs. Adolescents expressed concern that balance and moderation of use was important for health and all areas of life, such as physical activity, stress, eating, substance use, and sexual behavior.

Sexual activity was also considered to be a third major area of health concern, especially as it related to unwanted pregnancy and venereal disease. Additional concerns were with depression and nutrition. Depression, rather than mood swings, appeared to be more severe and constant among the adolescents.

It is perhaps significant (and alarming to parents) that adolescents do not report, nor recognize, that the morbidity and mortality of automobile accidents and violence is of epidemic proportions among teenagers. Thus, it is important that parents, teachers, and physicians recognize both the perceptions and concerns of adolescents, as well as the reality of major morbidity and mortality data.

Where To Go for Help

In general, health care providers have done a very poor job of recognizing and providing for the health care of adolescents. In 1968, the Society for Adolescent Medicine was organized by physicians concerned with providing adequate and appropriate health care for adolescents. Recognizing the unique health needs of the growing individual between childhood and adulthood, adolescent medicine is committed to maximum physical and psychological growth and development. It is thus directed toward detecting and treating acute and chronic diseases experienced during adolescence and helping adolescents develop proper health habits and concerns which will result in optimal health and well-being as adults. These proper health habits can prevent many of the subsequent chronic illnesses of adulthood that are direct or indirect consequences of unhealthy behavior practices and habits often initiated during adolescence.

The development of adolescent medicine has been to a large extent the result of health problems and health concerns as seen by adolescents themselves. As mentioned above, adolescents are extremely reluctant to seek health care services, and there have been a number of studies attempting to identify the most appropriate health care services for teenagers. The most important aspects of providing health care appear to be staffing, setting cost, and confidentiality. As one might expect, the willingness of adolescents to utilize health care services is dependent on these dimensions (Resnick, 1982).

In adolescents' deciding where to go for help, the quality and style of staff members is very important, particularly with regard to caring and concern, including a willingness to listen, to explain, and to regard the adolescent as an intelligent, feeling individual fully capable of participating in the medical encounter. It is also important that the setting not include small children and mothers, who tend to create a sense of self-consciousness within the adolescent. Cost is also a major factor, particularly considering the adolescent's own lack of financial resources. Confidentiality is probably the most important component of the health provider-adolescent interaction and should be discussed with both the adolescent and the parents; the adolescent should be assured of confidentiality, and the parent should be assured that parental responsibilities will not be violated. Confidentiality is also a means of protecting the adolescent's own self-concept. It is important for parents and physicians to recognize the concerns teenagers have for their own reputations and the need for confidential health care and advice when they have sensitive and personal concerns, particularly problems involving potential venereal disease, chemical dependency, or pregnancy-related diagnosis and treatment (Finkelstein, 1983; Resnick, 1982). Confidentiality, caring, concern, cost, and continuity are major components of any health care system for adolescents. Parents can be of great help by assisting adolescents in the screening and selecting of a physician or other health care provider. Assuring these major components will not only help the adolescent assess the appropriateness of the service, but will encourage earlier entry into the health care system.

What Can Parents Do?

No parent expects his or her adolescent to be afflicted with any of the above health problems, but the fact is that most parents will find themselves confronted with several of them during the child's teenage years. The ideal, of course, is to be able to act to prevent the problems, and most of the emphasis and the goal of this chapter, and of this book, is to inform parents about adolescence, so that they can take positive preventive action as well as understand general issues and problems of adolescence. Thus, they will be able to fulfill their own major goals and responsibilities of promoting optimal growth and development.

There are many excellent intervention and action suggestions made in other chapters of this volume, most of which can be applied to health problems. I will only summarize some of the general strategies and tactics which are most applicable to specific types of health problems.

1. *Parent and Adolescent Communication.* Communication between parents and adolescents is one of the most important but difficult aspects of any prevention or assistance effort. Somehow, society or "small talk" communication between parents themselves has convinced many parents and teenagers that communication between an adolescent and a parent is almost impossible. However, there are many parents who are able to keep their channels of communication open, and we should be watching what they do and what they say. Of course, communication involves listening as well as talking and should start at the earliest age, but it can begin later with a "new start." Just be prepared to start again, and again, and again. Providing time for conversations at the dinner table, while driving, at bedtime, during music, sports, or other events, etc., can help. Anytime you find that you are together, you can talk with them (not at them) about drugs, driving, alcohol, peers, school, worries, thoughts, feelings, wishes, wants, etc. They need to know most of all that you care, but they

also need to share some of their (and your) thoughts, to test out ideas and feelings, especially to be able to find out if "I'm OK."

2. *Imitation and Modeling.* Imitation and modeling are very strong determinants of health behavior intervention. This is difficult for parents to accept, perhaps because of our ideal that we want our children to be better than ourselves. However, children first learn most of their behaviors by imitating adults and peers, then modifying their behaviors to serve individual needs, wants, and situations. It is important to ask ourselves whether we smoke, drive over the speed limit, enjoy relating to other people, use alcohol, set limits and standards for ourselves, show love and affection, use seat belts, admit to making mistakes and take corrective action, eat and like healthy foods. The list could go on and on. Admittedly, there may be times when you may feel that teenagers should "Do as I say, not as I do," but you must remember that they are children trying to become adults and that you and other adults are their best models, even though they should also learn that you are not perfect either.

3. *Knowledge, Education, and Experience.* Health behaviors are learned. Therefore, knowledge, education, and experience are important to any intervention plan. How much knowledge do you have about various health problems, about treatments, and about the results you can expect? Have you insisted that your physician tell you as much as possible about a particular illness or condition? Have you read about it? This volume provides much useful information about adolescence. You should now be in a position to begin to apply it and make that most important bridge between knowledge and action, thus gaining experience, skills and confidence in working with your own adolescent.

One reminder: Knowledge does not necessarily result in a change of behavior. It is just as important to learn how to use knowledge, as to acquire it. Therefore, remember that it will not be sufficient to provide a teenager with information alone about the hazards of driving, or drugs, or pregnancies, or malnutrition. Someone has to be able to translate that information into behavioral change, into positive experiences and rewards (for example, the administration of positive reinforcement).

4. *Peer Group and Peer Culture.* Parents must not only know who their adolescent's friends and associates are, they must take them into account when considering potential and existing health

problems. As you may learn from other chapters in this book, puberty is a very personal growth and development phenomenon, but it is also a social phenomenon; similarly, sexuality, drug and alcohol use, and being tall or short, etc., are social phenomena as well. Teenagers live and behave, are sick or well, happy or depressed within the context of themselves and their family, but they also influence and are influenced by their peers (Lerner & Hultsch, 1983). If the peer group cares about health, driving safety, not abusing their bodies, or their appearance, your job as parent will be much easier and successful. Considering the importance of peer influence, Vicary (Chapter 6) has given the excellent advice that parents should help provide positive activities and alternative opportunities for their teenagers and their peers. This is one of the best ways of promoting adolescent health: knowing who their friends are and what they are doing, and also setting a good example.

5. *Control and Support.* The intelligent, sympathetic, and understanding monitoring and controlling of adolescent behavior is very difficult to accomplish. There must be a balance between love, caring, standards, and flexibility. As stated above, having good communication with your own teenager, knowing his or her friends, what they are talking about, and what they are doing is very important. The ideal, of course, would be to have teenagers who are knowledgeable, mature, and experienced. Yet, we know that they cannot be expected to know enough, be mature enough, or have had enough experience to practice the best health behaviors to prevent future illness. The task is to learn how we can provide them with the best knowledge about health issues, the behavioral skills to prevent illness, and the experiences that will reinforce positive health behavior. Perhaps we can then achieve the goal of the mature adolescent/adult taking responsibility for his/her own health.

There are many ways that parents can exercise appropriate support and control of positive health behavior. Altering or controlling the environment, setting limits and standards on use or enjoyment of the environment, or providing opportunities for positive health activities and alternatives are appropriate and reasonable options to help parents safeguard health. For example, using the seat belt can be a condition for using the family car, or calling home and reporting one's whereabouts may be a responsible alternative to coming home late and being "grounded." Vicary summarizes it beautifully in Chapter 6 when she says that "Parents can help enhance that maturation by providing strength and support, caring and sharing, and love and limits."

6. *Consulting Other Parents.* One important way to intervene without feeling as though you are the only unreasonable and mean parent in the world is to talk frequently and openly with the parents of your adolescent's friends. You will learn more about their own teenagers, what kinds of values and standards they have and are transmitting to their children, and how you and other parents can work together to provide and insure the most positive health behavior and activities. The often heard proclamations—that everyone is allowed to take the family car, or smoke marijuana, or drink beer, or come home after 11:00 p.m.—can be easily countered by parents talking with each other. The information you learn about other teenagers and their parents can often help you to identify (but not tattle on) individuals and behaviors or activities which you may wish to talk more about to your own teenager in the future. You will also be able to relate to more health issues and risk behaviors that are of more immediate concern to your own adolescent.

Again, the peer group and the adolescent's best friends are terribly important determinants of future behavior. It may be of some comfort to you for your teenager to discuss openly with you that "I'm the only one in the group who doesn't smoke pot" or "I think most of them are having sex, but Susie (or Johnny) and I are not." However, knowing the tremendous pressure that can be exerted by the behavior of peers, the chances are that your "comfort" will not be long lasting. If they are best friends with individuals or groups who drive recklessly, smoke pot, have sex, have low achievement in school, hang around with anti-social or delinquent kids, eat nothing but junk foods, or do not plan to go to college, you know that they will have a greatly increased risk of adopting similar behaviors and, eventually, similar values.

ANNOTATED REFERENCES

Aten, M. J., and McAnarney, E. R. *A Behavioral Approach to the Care of Adolescents.* St. Louis: C. V. Mosby, 1981.

Several portions of this book may prove useful. It is well written, but brief, and the health topics are of interest. Special health topics are: adolescent accident statistics, physical growth, menstruation, pregnancy, chronic illnesses, somatic symptoms and suicidal behavior.

Baum, A., and Singer, J. *Handbook of Psychology and Health. Volume II: Issues in Child Health and Adolescent Health.* Hillsdale, NJ: Lawrence Erlbaum, 1982.

A helpful and clearly written explanation of such health issues as: hypertension, type A behavior patterns, the significance of menarche, managing diabetes, and modifying health related behaviors such as smoking.

Blum, R. W. *Adolescent Health Care. Clinical Issues.* New York: Academic Press, 1982.

Deals with adolescent health issues of concern to physicians, but also of help to parents in understanding and dealing with many health problems. Particularly relevant topics include: overview of normal and abnormal adolescent growth and development, nutrition requirements and problems, a comprehensive coverage of obesity, disturbed body images and social pressures, special nutritional requirements for athletes, injuries related to sports, adolescent pregnancy and contraception, and sexually transmitted diseases.

Coates, T. J., Petersen, A. C., & Perry, C. *Promoting Adolescent Health: A Dialogue on Research and Practice.* New York: Academic Press, 1982.

A comprehensive volume dealing with much more than research and practice, offering both information and understanding related to: health promotion, incidence rates for health problems, high risk behaviors, how adolescents make health decisions, goals of education in adolescent health training, stress and heart disease, good nutritional and dietary habits, anorexia nervosa and bulimia, chronic illnesses, and many issues in research on adolescent health promotion.

Gersh, M. J. *The Handbook of Adolescence: A Medical Guide for Parents and Teenagers.* New York: Stein and Day, 1983.

This reference should be helpful for parents and teenagers with special emphasis on such issues as: breast and pubic hair development, bodily changes and problems, shortness and tallness, obesity and how to lose weight, abdominal pain related to dysmenorrhea and amenorrhea, developmental issues of males vs. females, management of asthma, hepatitis, thyroid disorders, immunization, skin care, athletics, bed wetting, substance use and abuse, and depression and suicide.

Gross, L. H. *The Parent's Guide to Teenagers*. New York: Macmillan, 1981.

A very interesting collection of responses of "experts" to frequently asked questions about adolescent development, this covers almost every dimension of concern about growth, development, illnesses, social relationships, psychological stresses, diseases, and parental relationships. The responses are generally very brief and explicit.

Lauton, B., and Freese, A. S. *The Healthy Adolescent: A Parent's Manual*. New York: Scribner's, 1981.

This is well written in a conversational style and offers parents general advice on a variety of topics, including: height, immunization, sports, eye problems, orthodontics, allergies, mononucleosis, pneumonia, and recognizing the disturbed adolescent.

Lerner, R. M., and Hultsch, D. F. *Human Development: A Life-Span Prospective*. New York: McGraw-Hill Book Co., 1983.

An excellent textbook on human development. While it covers the entire life-span, the section on adolescence is particularly well done. The volume provides much more information and detail than most parents may wish, but it is an excellent volume to study in-depth the entire process of adolescence and how it relates to the entire life-span.

McGrath, P. J., and Firestone, P. *Pediatric and Adolescent Behavioral Medicine: Issues in Treatment*. New York: Springer, 1983.

A good reference source for information on specific conditions. Chapters are detailed and include incidence rates, etiology, treatments, and research evidence. Topics of special interest to parents and physicians are: recurrent abdominal pain syndrome, asthma, elevated blood pressure, obesity, eating habits and activity levels, and how parents can become involved to change behavior and restructure the environment.

Narramore, B. *Adolescence Is Not an Illness: A Book for Parents*. Old Tappan, NJ: Fleming H. Revell Co., 1980.

This book deals with issues related to adolescence in general, rather than dealing with specific health problems. It is written in a very conversational style, with a number of anecdotes, and takes a decidedly moralistic view toward the understanding of problems and recommendations for a religious resolution to them.

Pasnau, R. O. *Psychosocial Aspects of Medical Practice: Children and Adolescents*. Menlo Park, CA: Addison-Wesley, 1982.

This volume is a collection of chapters intended for pediatricians, but useful for others desiring depth. Topics of special interest are: treating cancer in adolescents, adolescent drug abusers, psychogenic bases of various diseases, advice on referring adolescents for psychiatric treatment; it addresses some of the concerns parents and teenagers have about contraception, pregnancy, childbirth, and abortion.

Schowalter, J. E., and Anyan, W. R. *The Family Handbook of Adolescence.* New York: Knopf, 1981.

A useful book with sections on physical and psychological problems, dealing with such issues as: shortness and tallness, common skeletal disorders, hair growth, skin infections and problems, endocrinological disorders, respiratory diseases, cardiovascular disorders, anemia, cosmetic problems; it includes a good description of normal vs. abnormal levels of anxiety and depression, mental illness, and suicide.

Winick, M. *Growing Up Healthy: A Parent's Guide to Good Nutrition.* New York: Berley, 1982.

This reference contains a good chapter devoted specifically to adolescents, their nutritional needs, and related topics. It also discusses growth spurts, maturational sex differences, calorie and protein intake, snacking, fast foods, vegetarianism, restrictive diets, alcohol consumption, soft drinks, and nutritional needs in pregnancy.

REFERENCES

Aten, M. J., & McAnarney, E. R. *A Behavioral Approach to the Care of Adolescents.* St. Louis: C. V. Mosby, 1981.

Blum, R. W. *Adolescent Health Care: Clinical Issues.* New York: Academic Press, Inc., 1982.

Brooks-Gunn, J., & Petersen, A. C. (Eds.). *Girls at Puberty: Biological and Psychosocial Perspective.* New York: Plenum Press, 1983.

Brownell, K. D., & Stunkard, A. J. "Behavioral Treatment for Obese Children and Adolescents." In P. J. McGrath and P. Firestone (Eds.), *Pediatric and Adolescent Behavioral Medicine: Issues in Treatment.* New York: Springer Publishing Co., 1983.

Coates, T. J., Petersen, A. C., & Perry, C. (Eds.). *Promoting Adolescent Health.* New York: Academic Press, Inc., 1982.

Daeschner, C. W., Jr. *Pediatrics: An Approach to Independent Learning.* New York: Wiley, 1983.

Finkelstein, J. W. "Common Health Problems in Adolescence." In C. W. Daeschner, Jr., (Ed.), *Pediatrics: An Approach to Independent Learning.* New York: Wiley, 1983.

Gersh, M. J. *The Handbook of Adolescence.* New York: Stein and Day Publishing, 1971.

Green, L. W., & Horton, D. "Adolescent Health: Issues and Challengers." In T. J. Coates, A. C. Petersen, & C. Perry (Eds.), *Promoting Adolescent Health: A Dialogue on Research and Practice.* New York: Academic Press, Inc., 1982.

Gross, L. H. *The Parent's Guide to Teenagers.* New York: Macmillan, Inc., 1981.

Hayes, C. D., & Kamerman, S. B. (Eds.). *Children of Working Parents: Experiences and Outcomes.* Washington: National Academy Press, 1983.

Irwin, C. E., Jr. "Approach to the Adolescent Patient: Health Maintenance." In A. M. Rudolph (Ed.), *Pediatrics.* Norwalk, CT: Appleton-Century-Crofts, 1982.

Irwin, C. E., Jr., & Shafer, M. A. "Suicide in Children and Adolescents." In A. M. Rudolph (Ed.), *Pediatrics.* Norwalk, CT: Appleton-Century-Crofts, 1982.

Lerner, R. M., & Hultsch, D. F. *Human Development: A Life-Span Perspective.* New York: McGraw-Hill Book Co., 1983.

Mahoney, M. J. *Self-Change: Strategies for Solving Personal Problems.* New York: Norton, 1979.

McGrath, P. J., & Firestone, P. *Pediatric and Adolescent Behavioral Medicine: Issues in Treatment.* New York: Springer Publishing Co., 1983.

McGuire, J. "Other Diseases of the Skin." In A. M. Rudolph (Ed.), *Pediatrics.* Norwalk, CT: Appleton-Century-Crofts, 1982.

Medical News. *Alcohol Use and Teenage Drivers, Fatal Accidents— United States.* JAMA, Vol. 250, No. 5, August 5, 1983, p. 585.

Narramore, B. *Adolescence Is Not an Illness.* Old Tappan, NJ: Fleming H. Revell Co., 1980.

Pasnau, R. O. *Psychosocial Aspects of Medical Practice: Children and Adolescents.* Menlo Park, CA: Addison-Wesley, 1982.

Petersen, A. C. "Developmental Issues in Adolescent Health." In T. J. Coates, A. C. Petersen, & C. Perry (Eds.), *Promoting Adolescent Health: A Dialogue on Research and Practice.* New York: Academic Press, 1982.

Petersen, A. C., & Boxer, A. "Adolescent Sexuality." In T. J. Coates, A. C. Petersen, & C. Perry (Eds.), *Promoting Adolescent Health.* New York: Academic Press, 1982.

Resnick, M. "Health Concerns of Youth: Multiple Perspectives." In R. W. Blum (Ed.), *Adolescent Health Care: Clinical Issues.* New York: Academic Press, 1982.

Rinzler, C. E. *Your Adolescent: An Owner's Manual.* New York: Atheneum Press, 1981.

Rudolph, A. M. *Pediatrics* (17th Ed.). Norwalk, CT: Appleton-Century-Crofts, 1982.

Schowalter, J. E., & Anyan, W. R. *The Family Handbook of Adolescence.* New York: Knopf, 1979.

U. S. Department of Health, Education and Welfare. *Healthy People: The Surgeon General's Report on Health Promotion and Disease Prevention.* Washington: DHEW (PH5), Pub. No. 79-55071, 1979.

8. MORAL REASONING AND BEHAVIOR

Cheryl R. Kaus, Edward Lonky, and Paul Roodin

INTRODUCTION

Psychologists have viewed moral development as a key dimension marking the adolescent's adjustment to the tasks and demands of adulthood. Popular and historical accounts of the turmoil and storm and stress of the adolescent experience can often make us wonder how adolescents ever survive the period and make a successful transition to adulthood. An examination of the characteristics and changes in moral and religious orientation experienced by adolescents can provide some clues to the adjustment most adolescents make to the tasks and demands of society and adulthood. Similarly, some insights can be provided for those adolescents who are not successful in making this adjustment (e.g., delinquent youth).

For Erikson (1968), moral and religious values are most often considered as central to the notion of adolescent ideological commitment. The development of a consistent moral and religious ideology (a philosophy of life if you will) is a most important component of one's identity. Understanding the moral and religious development of adolescents will aid, then, in our understanding of how teenagers deal with this primary task of adolescence, the resolution of the identity crisis.

Most parents and teachers are critical of adolescents' emergent moral sense, which they may find far too limited in scope, too peer-oriented, and devoid of long-term outlook. Yet, such criticisms are likely to undermine the vast progress in morality made by adolescents in their journey from early childhood. Most young children are rather dependent on the moral standards of parents and other adults who provide guidance, direction, and control of their moral responses. Young children need such external forces to ensure that they will do and say the right thing at the right time and place. Adolescents within the brief span of 5 or 6 years appear to develop an *internal* moral sense which enables them to make independent judgments of right and wrong or good and bad in guiding their decisions. This moral sensitivity, however, is incomplete and at times faulty when held up against the standards of adult morality. Our two major concerns are to help you to understand how the transitions from childhood to adolescent morality come about and to help you to understand exactly what makes the morality of adolescents somewhat different in character from that of adults.

We begin our consideration of adolescent morality with an overview of the major theoretical orientations which have served to guide and direct the psychological investigation of moral development. This discussion sets the stage for our treatment of the role of parents and peers as agents of adolescent moral socialization. We next pay special attention to key features distinguishing adolescent moral reasoning from that of children and adults. This focus describes how adolescents think about morality, and the role their reasoning may play in influencing moral behavior. We examine three areas of adolescent moral behavior: academic cheating, juvenile delinquency, and student activism. Specifically, we explore the influence of individual, family, and situational factors on these behaviors.

What role can our schools play in attempting to influence moral development? In exploring answers to this question, we present overviews of two current approaches to moral education: values clarification and the cognitive-developmental approach. We conclude with a consideration of adolescent religious orientation, examining the role of religion in the lives of adolescents and as one component of a moral value system.

FRAMEWORKS TO UNDERSTAND MORALITY

In order to address these topics, we need to see how psychologists view moral development. There are three major frameworks, each of which expresses a rather different kind of moral concern:

moral feelings-emotions, moral behaviors-actions, and moral thinking-evaluations. Each of these has been examined within three vastly different theoretical frameworks: the *psychoanalytic* view developed by Freud, the *social learning* view developed by Bandura, and the *cognitive-developmental* view most recently developed by Kohlberg. Let us briefly examine these different views.

The Psychoanalytic View

The *psychoanalytic* view builds a model of moral feelings by centering on the special relationship that a child develops with parents. The process is sometimes called the formation of conscience, or super-ego, and is based on the concept of identification found in the personality theory of Freud. To avoid feelings of guilt, children, without awareness or conscious intent, adopt parental moral standards and try to abide by them. The essence of these early feelings, then, is that they are largely unconscious. The adolescent who also experiences uncomfortable feelings of guilt when parental or societal standards are violated continues to show the healthy signs of personality development, e.g., the presence of a well-developed conscience.

Individuals who do not develop properly and who fail to *identify* with their parents are rare in our society; we call such people psychopaths or sociopaths and indicate with such labels an inability to experience guilt in any form. Fortunately for most of us, appropriate identification with parental moral standards ensures a lifetime of guilt reactions following misdeeds.

In particular, with adolescents we find a great willingness to express guilt after a transgression and a great reliance on techniques designed to remove guilt—such as confession, remorse, and self-punishment, all reactions which are rare in the behavior of younger children. Additionally, adolescents seem to try to avoid situations which make them feel guilty, and they may try to exert additional personal control over their own impulses—techniques which do not always work. The ability to control the negative feelings of guilt (both consciously and unconsciously) is the result of the adolescent's increasingly mature ego or self development. Advances in this area of adolescent personality give rise to greater control of negative impulses and greater awareness of self. In the psychoanalytic view, moral development is initiated through the process of identification with parents and is increasingly marked by the capacity to recognize and control guilt as the adolescent gains maturity in coping with feelings.

The Social Learning View

A second view, providing a different perspective on the development of adolescent morality, is the *social learning* framework. Moral behaviors are *learned*, e.g., by example, by direct teaching, and indirectly through observation of others in the social environment. In this framework, moral responses rather than emotions or feelings are the focus of concern. Moral behaviors are shaped and molded in both children and adolescents by significant people in the environment, including, but not limited to, one's parents. Adolescents have acquired moral responses which mirror what others have shown them. Through direct observation, imitation, modeling, and seeing what happens when people behave or fail to behave morally, the adolescents' moral responses are shaped and developed.

Of course, within the family brothers and sisters, parents, and other concerned relatives directly reward appropriate moral behaviors and punish those which are inappropriate. As the child grows, we find a wider sphere of social influences beginning to have an impact. Through the very same learning processes, adolescents acquire moral responses displayed by valued friends, coaches, teachers, or popular television, movie, or singing stars. Through rewards and punishments, direct observation, imitation and modeling, adolescents are seen as creating a set of unique moral behaviors representative of their growing sense of identity. While the psychoanalytic framework assigns special importance to the child's relationship with parents, the social learning view provides a considerably broader base in explaining the acquisition of moral behaviors.

Social learning theorists, such as Albert Bandura, are interested in the description and prediction of when, where, and how adolescents act or fail to act in a morally acceptable way. Also of interest are the effects of various social influences on moral behavior. For adolescents, it apears that when peers and parents are in conflict over moral behaviors a common strategy is to take a "middle-of-the-road" position and not side with one or the other (Bandura, Grusec, & Menlove, 1966). While such "averaging" is understandable, we must not lose sight of the fact that often peers and parents are in agreement. Under conditions of consensus, adolescents will readily adopt the moral responses they see in both parents and peers.

Imitative moral behaviors will most likely be acquired when there are numerous models who show the same responses. As a basic principle of moral behavior, we note that models are most likely to have an impact on adolescents when both the behavioral responses and expressed moral values are widely shared. As most parents can readily attest, adolescents, like younger children, are quick to follow by example the moral behaviors of their parents; that is, they imitate what parents *do* rather than what they say! Parents are encouraged not only to behave morally but to express moral values which are in keeping with their actions. Having additional reinforcement from the world of the adolescent—peers, school, church, and popular media figures who *both* espouse and follow these moral principles—also serves to further the moral behaviors of the adolescent.

The Cognitive Developmental View

By far the most extensive framework yet developed to explain the development of child and adolescent morality is the *cognitive-developmental* view. Here the focus is on moral evaluations —moral thinking. Do adolescents conceptualize and comprehend moral issues like adults or children? As the framework suggests, moral thinking and moral evaluations are rather directly linked to the adolescent's general cognitive-intellectual development.

Lawrence Kohlberg's work focuses on the development of the adolescent's moral judgments. He is primarily interested in the *process* of evaluating moral problems and the way in which individuals at different ages go about weighing alternatives and placing emphasis on particular salient issues. In Kohlberg's view, even kindergarten children have moral values; however, the important change in development is not in the content of these values but in the way in which various rights, privileges, and moral obligations emerge in the moral evaluation process. In other words, *what* people conclude about a moral issue (the ends) has less developmental significance than *how* they reason about it (the means).

Using a set of complex moral dilemmas which have no absolutely correct solution, Kohlberg (1969) has identified the typical pathway which marks the cognitive-developmental transitions from child to adolescent to adult morality. These transitions are said to follow a stage sequence. That is, for individuals in our Western society, we find that: (1) the stages follow a uniform and invariant sequence; (2) each of the stages represents a complete reorganization or re-structuring of moral thinking; (3) the stages become hierarchically integrated so that less mature forms of moral thought are integrated within more advanced stages; (4) each stage represents a qualitatively different way of thinking, conceptualizing, and evaluating moral problems (e.g., two adolescents may both refuse to tell lies but have vastly different reasons for upholding this value); (5) the rate of progression through the stages is determined primarily by social experience; and (6) a necessary component for adolescent transitions in moral evaluations is the attainment of formal, logical, abstract reasoning. Therefore, experience alone is not sufficient to promote change in moral evaluation (Kohlberg, 1969).

The concept of universal human developmental stages is always a source of controversy in psychology, let alone in the area of morality, and Kohlberg's ideas have been the target of frequent debate. Yet, his basic views remain reasonably supported in the research literature. Within his cognitive-developmental framework, we find a series of major changes in the process of moral evaluation. We note in advance that chronological age alone cannot identify an adolescent's or adult's level of moral reasoning; it is not a guarantee that a particular set of stages has been already achieved. We will look only globally at the three major developmental levels of moral judgment identified by Kohlberg.

Level I (Preconventional Morality). The most primitive form of moral evaluation is marked by choices which are based on fear of punishment, the consequences of disobedience, and the unlimited power and control which adults have over young children. In a somewhat more mature form, preconventional morality may also be articulated by the principles of equity and individual rights to freedom (individualism): if you can do something, then others should also be permitted the freedom to do it. Rules are desirable if they bring about immediate positive results which are concrete and personally rewarding.

Level II (Conventional Morality). The intermediary level at which we find some adolescents is marked by the desire to be positively evaluated in the eyes of others in society. It is also characterized by a general adherence to the Golden Rule and a recognition that positive relationships between people are based on what you do and how you act toward others. In a somewhat more mature form, we find that adolescents choose to maintain the social order at any cost. The logic employed under this form of morality is typically "what if everyone did it."

Level III (Post-Conventional Morality). This is the most mature form of morality for Kohlberg and is, in fact, an attainment that is rare even among mature adults. Post-conventional principles suggest that, although we all accept a society with certain rights, privileges, and guarantees, the social contract which we jointly hold may in fact be superseded if *basic* individual rights are being denied. For example, the social contract may be discarded if individuals are systematically denied their right to live or are systematically denied their constitutional freedoms. A cardinal belief is that there are universal moral principles, and that adults have a special duty to see that these principles are followed and supported as a matter of individual conscience. Such recognition and personal commitment are indeed rare among adults (Kohlberg, 1976).

An Example of the Use of Kohlberg's Approach. To illustrate how these levels might be applied to a moral dilemma, consider the following example:

Heinz and the Drug

In Europe a woman was near death from a special kind of cancer. There was one drug that the doctors thought might save her. It was a form of radium that a druggist in the same town had recently discovered. The drug was expensive to

> make, but the druggist was charging ten times what the drug
> cost him to make. He paid $200 for the radium and charged
> $2000 for a small dose of the drug. The sick woman's hus-
> band, Heinz, went to everyone he knew to borrow the money,
> but he could only get together $1000 which is half of what it
> cost. He told the druggist that his wife was dying, and asked
> him to sell it cheaper or let him pay later. But the druggist
> said "No I discovered the drug, and I am going to make
> money from it." So Heinz got desperate, and broke into the
> man's store to steal the drug for his wife.

We find that across the three levels, children, adolescents, and
adults might all find that it is important to preserve life; yet, upon
closer analysis we could separate their answers by examining
their explanation of the reasons underlying this principle.

A *pre-conventional* moral understanding would be likely to
focus on an explanation indicating that everyone has the right to
live; while property can be easily replaced, a human life cannot.

A *conventional* moral explanation of the problem would
focus on the importance that people place on the duties of a
husband to "cherish, love, and honor" his wife. Failure to meet
this social contract would make the husband appear not to love
his wife and would result in negative social sanctions.

The *post-conventional* moral evaluation of this problem suggests that with conflicting justifiable claims, of the druggist (to
property) and the wife (to life), individuals within society must
side with the latter. All of us may have to violate rules of social
convention in cases of imminent death. All people have a right to
live, and we have a right to bring about this goal (Kohlberg, 1976,
p. 42).

In this example we may see that *preconventional* moral evaluations most typically arise from the child. Judgments are focused
on what will happen to the person. Preconventional judgment is
highly individualistic and concrete; there are no general social
obligations recognized. *Conventional* moral judgments reflect an
identification with the larger society. Individuals cannot just act
as they please but must preserve order and the social structure.
Finally, *post-conventional* moral reasoning demonstrates a concern for universal principles which may be expected to emerge
across societies. That is, individuals (and there are very few) have

a reciprocal commitment to preserve and protect each other's basic rights. Adolescents appear initially to be struggling with the transition from pre-conventional to conventional moral thought.

How do cognitive-developmental views explain the process of transition from one level to another? In particular, it is important to recognize the importance of three general factors: (1) perceived conflict or dissatisfaction with one's current level of moral explanation/understanding, (2) social role taking, understanding that others are like you and, vice versa, and (3) formal logical abstract intellectual ability. In adolescence, an increased social sphere and participation in a peer group free from the control of parents helps to foster a greater understanding of the social environment. The comparative and evaluation processes, which adolescents employ to understand their own roots, values, and moral ideology as well as those of their friends, help to further their moral judgments. They take the role of their friends, imagine a world of idealistic possibilities (free from the concrete morality of the childhood era), and become somewhat dissatisfied with their own limited world view and limited social experience. It is social experience coupled with the abstract logical abilities necessary to process and produce developmental change which become paramount in the cognitive-developmental framework; these are the mechanisms of change and growth in moral judgment.

THE IMPACT OF PARENTS

The three basic frameworks developed by psychologists to explain morality place decidedly different emphases on the role or importance of parents in the way that they influence moral development. It appears that Freud places greatest impact on the role of parents in moral development. Bandura and the social learning theorists view parental impact as important but not as strongly as Freud, and Kohlberg and other cognitive-developmentalists imply that the role of the parent is relatively minimal (Windmiller, 1980).

The process of parental influence has already been briefly presented in both the psychoanalytic and social learning frameworks earlier in the chapter. Let us look at the impact of parents as seen through the eyes of the cognitive-developmental tradition. Kohlberg suggests that parents minimally influence their children's or adolescents' level of moral development since the parents' own moral reasoning is typically quite different qualitatively from that of their offspring. Adolescents, for example, are in the process of moving from Level I to Level II mode of moral reasoning. They develop dissatisfaction with their immature modes of reasoning, become increasingly aware of their abstract, logical thought processes, and create greater opportunities for peer interactions which promote social experiences, such as role taking, empathy, and joint construction of rules.

Social experiences may be more important in contrast to the impact of parents. In one study, more than 30% of individuals 21 years of age and older, had moral evaluative abilities which were at levels *higher* than their own parents (Haan et al., 1976). For Kohlberg, moral judgmental abilities are influenced indirectly by parents who provide greater opportunities throughout development for their children to participate openly and freely in the total environment (Windmiller, 1980). Certainly one of the major consequences of a generally open atmosphere is to ensure roletaking and social participation for adolescents. A second consequence is the attainment of more advanced intellectual skills (also a prerequisite for moral advances) since research has documented that enriched experiences facilitate intellectual development. Parents initially create the conditions for a positive environment conducive to the child's intellectual and moral growth and facilitate participation in the wider social context with peers, teachers, relatives, and community institutions. They indirectly foster development of advanced levels of thought and moral judgmental skills.

We may find, of course, that in some areas parents' morality contributes more directly to adolescent moral development. Holstein (1968), for instance, reported that parents at the postconventional level of moral judgment appeared to offer more freedom to their offspring to engage in moral discussion and evaluate moral resolutions. With opportunities for discussion and sharing of perspectives, moral developmental progress was more rapid compared to children with parents who failed to provide such opportunities. Clearly it is not just the parents' own moral developmental level which is important but their willingness to provide opportunities for their offspring's direct participation in the larger social environment.

INFLUENCE OF PARENTING STYLE ON MORALITY

There have been many attempts to study the specific impact of parents on their children's developing moral orientation. This is one of the few areas where results tend to be characterized by consensus, regardless of whether children's moral feelings, behaviors, or cognitive-developmental judgments are examined. In other words, the basic results apply across all three domains.

One of the more important advances in helping us to understand the process by which parents influence their children's moral development has been provided by Hoffman (1977). He suggests that it is the mother's disciplinary style which seems to underlie the specific influence of parents on their children's moral development. Mothers' basic styles of discipline fall into one of three types according to Hoffman (1977): power assertion, love withdrawal, and induction.

Power assertion includes techniques which rely on physical punishment, deprivation of resources, privileges, or family rights, verbal threats, or other methods which are based on the differential power and control separating parent from child.

Love withdrawal includes methods of expressing anger directly or disapproval of specific actions without using physical methods. Hoffman (1977) cites examples of mother simply turning her back on her child, refusing to listen or speak to the child, or expressing dislike for the child. Love withdrawal also includes techniques of social isolation (e.g., "Go to your room").

Induction is based on verbal reasoning with children in order to persuade (both emotionally and logically) them to change behaviors so that they are in keeping with family-based norms of acceptable behavior. The child is aware of these standards and has met them previously; thus, mother may appeal to the child's pride, may give an explanation for what will happen if negative behaviors continue (e.g., to the child and/or to others) and may also include a rationale and discussion of the implications of the child's behavior for others.

While few mothers or fathers fit entirely within one of these categories, it is easy to characterize a predominant category, that is, the one chosen most typically. Note that each of the three styles of discipline works by rather different processes. Power assertive techniques of discipline instill a fear of parental punishment. On the other hand, love withdrawal consists of a series of more intense and prolonged emotional threats, for example, the child's anxiety over possible abandonment by the parent or isolation (Shaffer & Brody, 1981). Induction seems to have its impact when the child can both empathize and comprehend the logical basis for complying with a particular parental request. It also demands a certain degree of internal control over impulses (Shaffer & Brody, 1981).

What is the influence of disciplinary style on children's moral orientation? Surprisingly, it appears that withdrawal of love is unrelated to moral development regardless of whether we assess moral feelings, behavior, or cognitive judgments. There is, however, a slight relationship between power assertiveness and children's moral behaviors, feelings, and judgments. The moral orientation that is created from this type of discipline is largely built on fear of punishment and fear of detection by authority figures (Hoffman, 1980).

The strongest link between discipline and morality emerges when induction is evaluated. Induction leads to significantly more advanced moral development both behaviorally and in the area of cognitive evaluative judgments. It also leads children to develop moderately high levels of guilt. These trends become even stronger in adolescence. Hoffman (1980) reports that for adolescents who continue to receive induction as the primary mode of discipline, two additional directions emerge. First, if mothers also show frequent variation in discipline, for example, if along with induction they also employ power assertion or love withdrawal, then the adolescent's moral orientation becomes "flexible-humanistic." That is, the adolescent internalizes the value of empathizing with others and maintains open tolerance of anti-moral/anti-social impulses (unless such impulses harm others). Second, if variation is absent and induction is strongly relied

upon, then adolescents appear to evolve an internal moral orientation which is labeled "rigid-conventional" (Hoffman, 1980). This
is a form of adolescent self-control which is based on anxiety and
the need to *control* strongly hostile feelings (Hoffman, 1980).

The specific effects of father's discipline on children and adolescents' moral development is disappointingly small. However, the
overall importance of having a father serve in some disciplinary
role (even if indirectly through his impact on mother's behavior)
has been found to be critical in the moral development of adolescents (Hoffman, 1980). Adolescent boys without fathers in the
home have been found to show less advanced moral development
than those who come from intact homes (Hoffman, 1963, 1971,
1980). As yet, *no* comparable results have been reported for girls.
The important influence of a male role model for boys is confirmed.

THE IMPACT OF PEERS ON MORALITY

It is common to view the impact that peers have on adolescents' moral orientation as sharply contrasting with the values,
attitudes, and behaviors supported by parents. However, this
difference is vastly overdramatized since peers tend to come from
similar homes, communities, and social classes; that is, friends
share similar kinds of socialization and family life experiences
within broadly defined limits. Peers and parents will have, as a
rule, far more similarity than dissimilarity in moral orientation.

Nevertheless, peers do play an increasingly greater role as
children mature into adolescents. Peers influence the morality of
adolescents in three ways: (1) they provide direct reinforcement
for some behaviors while ignoring and helping to extinguish
others; (2) they serve as appropriate models for behavior or for
curtailing behaviors which are inappropriate; and (3) they offer a
chance for group discussion to share and exchange ideology,
values, and personal insights (Shaffer & Brody, 1981). The first
form of influence can often serve to "push" adolescents into
mildly disobedient forms of behavior. Such acts as ringing door-
bells and running away and making phone calls and annoying
the persons answering by not talking are the type of misconduct

reinforced in the adolescent peer group. We find such pressures successful in coercing an adolescent to engage in more serious forms of misconduct such as acts of petty thievery, physical violence, or vandalism when the peer group takes the place of the family (that is, in gangs).

Not only are adolescents directly reinforced for some of the relatively minor deviant behaviors which we see, but such acts may arise spontaneously in the context of the peer group and become readily adopted by all members through contagion and imitative modeling. The sensitivity of adolescents to highly influential peers, such as leaders, is proof of the importance of modeling. Moreover, it lends additional support to parents to watch the company which their offspring keep. Bad company can often be responsible for the diminished sense of morality which we see among some adolescents. And, conversely, recall that if peers obey moral prescriptions, such prohibitions will likely be picked up by adolescents within the group through the very same processes of modeling and imitation.

Research suggests that with increasing age there is increasing susceptibility to social pressure and social influence (Shaffer & Brody, 1981). However, it is noteworthy that adolescents have the good sense to trust peers and follow their lead selectively, depending on the issue of concern. For instance, while peer influence dominates adolescent girls' choices of friends, parental influence is sought and dominates their decisions regarding future aspirations and school achievement (Brittain, 1963, as cited in Shaffer & Brody, 1981). Similarly, adolescents tend to agree with their parents on crucial moral issues but side with peers over contemporary concerns like hair length and style of dress (Kelley, 1972). It apears that personal identity (e.g., "Who am I?") is largely influenced by peers, while future identity (e.g., "Who am I to be?") is largely influenced by parents (Shaffer & Brody, 1981).

CHARACTERISTICS OF MORAL REASONING IN ADOLESCENCE

As we described earlier, psychological interest in adolescent morality has focused on three components of morality: moral feelings, behaviors, and judgments. While we would all agree that understanding morality in terms of the moral actions we engage in is probably the ultimate goal and objective in studying moral development, most psychologists agree that our moral behaviors are the result of a complex interplay between our moral feelings, judgments, questions, and decisions (Blasi, 1980). From a cognitive-developmental perspective, moral reasoning plays a central role in moral functioning. Perhaps, then, we could pay closer attention to the characteristics of adolescent moral reasoning, keeping in mind that its significance lies not only in its description of the kinds of knowledge adolescents have of rules, laws, social norms, and moral principles, but that this knowledge may serve as a bridge to moral behavior.

A good way to examine moral reasoning is from the perspective of new features of moral thought which emerge during adolescence. These characteristics include the growth of idealistic thinking, the capacity for social thought, the transcendence of the young child's punitive view of morality to an appreciation of moral rules and principles, and the development of a relativism in moral thinking. It is important to note again that these developing moral abilities are intrinsically related to more general cognitive developments in the logical and social domains. This is to say, the attainment of formal, abstract thought characterizing mature reasoning (Brainerd, 1979; Inhelder & Piaget, 1958), and the more sophisticated role taking abilities of the adolescent (Flavell, 1977; Selman, 1971) provide a strong foundation for these emerging adolescent moral capacities.

Idealistic Thinking

The development of mature cognition involves the ability to reason beyond concrete, actual issues to formal, abstract possibilities. A concrete reasoner deals only with reality and is limited to thinking in terms of actual objects and experiences. A formal reasoner sees reality as one of numerous possibilities and is able to deal hypothetically with the world. Piaget (Inhelder & Piaget, 1958; Piaget, 1932) claims that with the shift in logical thought from concrete to formal operations comes a corresponding shift in thinking about other people, relationships, and society. What Piaget calls the growth of idealistic thinking and envisioning of

utopian possibilities can be seem as a direct outgrowth of the
adolescent's newfound ability to think about abstract ideas that
have no concrete basis in the real world. Thinking about questions like: "What is possible?" "What is truth?" and "What is
just?" takes on new meaning with the advent of formal thought
and has distinct implications for the way one sees oneself, others,
family, society, and the world. With a new appreciation for possibilities, the adolescents can now see themselves, the world, friends,
and even love as they could possibly be, not only as they are. As
we ourselves have often experienced, many times there is quite a
gap between what could or should be and what is. For the adolescent, however, such "new" realizations of what could or should
be may mark a time of intense altruism and acute awareness of
injustice, and all our adult rationalizations and appeals to reality
do little to calm this idealism. The activism of youth, which we
will discuss later, can be seen as related to this cognitive awareness.

Similarly, adolescents may apply their newly acquired induc-
tive reasoning abilities to the construction of grand social systems
and theories. Typically, they are concerned with religion, justice,
morality, and ethics, and, although to the more "experienced"
adult eye these concerns may seem naive, unrealistic, and un-
sophisticated, they can be held to as dearly as scientists and
philosophers hold to their theories and world views.

Social Thought

Piaget and others (e.g., Selman, 1976; Selman & Byrne, 1974)
have also described a concurrent shift in adolescent thought from
an *egocentric* to a *sociocentric* perspective: Egocentrism involves
the inability of very young children to distinguish between their
own perspective (what they want), and the perspective of others
(what others want of them); egocentrism appears to undergo
rather distinct developmental progressions through middle childhood and adolescence. For example, it is not until early adolescence that it becomes possible to view oneself and others participating in an interaction in a relatively detached and objective
way, as if watching actors on a stage (Flavell, 1977). A sociocentric perspective involves social system role taking, the ability

to raise perspective taking beyond the dyadic interaction of individuals to the level of the social group or system. This ability appears around middle adolescence. Here for the first time, the perspective considered becomes that of the group rather than of the specific individuals involved. The consideration now becomes: What would *everybody* think about a certain action (Flavell, 1977)?

Undoubtedly, these developments in role-taking ability have important implications for the social and moral reflection of adolescents. In a broad sense these growing abilities to take the role of others and replace an egocentric with a sociocentric conception of society reveals a new ability to appreciate differing viewpoints and to understand the collective nature of social and moral problems. Further, with these more mature role taking perspectives in hand, the adolescent is capable of constructing moral judgments based on the concepts of reciprocity and natural rights.

More specifically, Kohlberg (1964) and Lickona (1976), have identified a number of dimensions on which adolescents' moral reasoning differs from children's as a result of these changes in logical and social thought. Adolescents are much less likely than children to maintain an absolute moral perspective in their determinations of right and wrong. The teenager is more likely, for example, to conceive of instances where stealing could be justified (e.g., in condoning a poor man's stealing a loaf of bread to feed his starving children). This flexibility of moral perspective extends to the consideration of rules as well. One of Piaget's (1932) earliest findings was that young children are inclined to be absolutist and almost authoritarian about questions of changing or breaking rules. A twelve or thirteen year old is likely to say that rules can be changed if all involved agree, demonstrating an understanding of the concept that rules rather than being engraved in stone, come about as the result of mutual agreement.

Other dimensions of difference between adolescent and childhood moral reasoning include the adolescent's consideration of: (1) the intentions of the actors in judging the seriousness of a transgression (young children being apt to base their judgments on the amount of physical damage done by the act), (2) equity and reciprocity in consideration of punishment for wrongdoing, and

(3) a conception of punishment as a social rather than a physical or natural phenomenon. In short, adolescents can be seen to employ the same sort of hypothetical-deductive and abstract role-taking abilities in reasoning about moral issues that they employ in logical and social thought. Rather than being tied to a concrete and egocentric view of narrow possibilities and perspectives, as is the younger child, the adolescent is capable of envisioning a much wider range of possibilities and interpretations in judging right and wrong, assigning blame, and considering appropriate punishment.

Reasoning about Law and Justice

As we have explained, Kohlberg (1969, 1976) has greatly expanded Piaget's work on moral reasoning, particularly with respect to the transformations that occur in moral reasoning through adolescence and even adulthood. In particular, we should pay attention to some of the characteristics of moral reasoning defined by Kohlberg's conventional and post-conventional morality outlined earlier.

By mid-adolescence most youngsters have attained the level of conventional morality. Entry into the conventional level marks the shift in perspective from the concrete individual to the standards of one's group or society (the sociocentric perspective we spoke of above). In point of fact, Kohlberg (1976) has defined *conventional* morality in terms of this member-of-society perspective. This new focus of motivation for morality has important implications for understanding the role of rules and law in reasoning about questions of right and wrong, for in making moral judgments it is not until adolescence that a concern for how our actions affect the social system becomes relevant. Note that this concern is a direct outgrowth of the mature role-taking ability of the adolescent. Most importantly, new values which emerge at the conventional level reflect a new emphasis on the moral order of the group and society.

Adolescent moral reasoning at the conventional level is characterized by two core values: (1) mutual trust and commitment, and (2) law (Hersch, Paolitto & Reimer, 1978). As a member of society the adolescent now realizes that we have certain moral obligations as a function of the social roles we acquire. These are commitments that we expect others to live up to and that others have a right to expect of us. Married persons have obligations to each other, doctors are responsible for curing, police for protecting, and so on. Anything that violates this trust and commitment is almost always wrong from the adolescent's viewpoint.

We can observe this strong "moral code" in action if we think about adolescents' understandings of the obligations they often feel toward their friends. How many teachers have come up against the situation of trying to convince high school or college students that helping their friends on a paper or take-home exam is still cheating? Most of these students feel quite strongly that they have a moral obligation to help their friends, and many will go through obvious contortions rationalizing their help: "I'm just teaching; isn't the function of school to learn?" Some even blame the teacher for having given that particular form of exam when they know full well how important friendships are. To break a commitment or violate a trust becomes, for adolescents, a cardinal wrong. Many will get quite angry at adults who, for example, ask them to "squeal" on their friends, regardless of the circumstances.

With this focus on how our actions affect others to whom we feel a moral commitment comes an appreciation for how our actions impact on society at large. In this context, law emerges as a central value for the adolescent (Hersch, Paolitto, & Reimer, 1979). Researchers have observed that with middle or late adolescence comes the appreciation that society is bound together by a system of rules and laws, and that actions that threaten these moral and social contracts are almost always wrong (e.g., Tapp & Kohlberg, 1971). It is important to note that what adolescents find appealing is any fixed system of laws or beliefs. To the extent that adolescents have adopted any ideological or theological blueprint, or even constructed a grand theory of their own, the key feature or thought which emerges is the consideration of the social or moral issue from the viewpoint of that system. Perhaps it is in this context that we can understand the moral outrage and even intolerance sometimes expressed by youth toward those who present views or systems opposed to their own.

In some, the fixed formula of moral obligations derived from the process of role-taking, and a system of social/legal contracts (i.e., conventional morality) is gradually replaced by a post-conventional or principled morality based on mutual agreement and principles of justice. This is a most controversial aspect of Kohlberg's theory, but it is important to explore insofar as it may define certain features of moral reasoning characteristic of older adolescents and young adults. Kohlberg (1973) has suggested that post-conventional morality is rarely attained before individuals reach their twenties. Nevertheless, we may in our interactions with youth discover appeals made to moral principle.

An understanding and appreciation of moral principles as distinct from the fixed obligations of roles and law provide the basis for post-conventional reasoning according to Kohlberg. It is an understanding which recognizes that the moral obligations associated with roles, rule, and law have at their base the pro-tection of basic human rights such as life and liberty. The appeal of such a rationale, then, is to the ethical principles which under-lie, and are prior to, the rules and laws of a particular social system. These ethical principles are, according to Kohlberg, principles of justice and fairness. Rather than try to summarize the complex argument Kohlberg makes with respect to prin-cipled morality, we suggest that interested readers consult his works directly (Kohlberg, 1971, 1973, 1976). Suffice it to say, that for some rare youth we encounter, the characteristics of post-conventional reasoning encompasses their moral perspective. For these individuals, it may be a principled understanding of justice which motivates their thinking abour right and wrong.

Relativistic Thinking

A characteristic of intellectual and ethical thought among older adolescents is the realization that we all view the world from individualized, subjective perspectives, and that there is no simple criterion of objectivity. No individual, social system, or culture may view or evaluate the same act in the same way; moreover, there may be no universal standard from which that action can be judged (Chandler, 1978; Flavell, 1977). The recognition of relativism might also provide the impetus for rejecting conventional morality in favor of post-conventional thought.

As we have just noted, Kohlberg has described the moral reasoning of the adolescent as predominantly conventional in nature. In appealing to the expectations of significant others, of social roles, and to a fixed system of rule and law, the adolescent most often possesses absolute ideas about what is wrong and right (Perry, 1968). While adolescents at this level may be aware of differing views and positions, only one can be granted the legitimate status of being correct; there can be only one right course, the one defined by the youth's own appeal to conventional moral standards. Given this rather rigid position, how can we account for the fact that adolescents seem to be particularly attracted to new and opposing views and acquire an appreciation for relativistic thinking?

The answer lies in the weaknesses and limits of such a dualistic black and white view of right and wrong. With such a view, how can one adequately deal with the diversity of a pluralistic society and world? In fact, from this conventional perspective, little validity can be granted views which differ from one's own. In their tolerance and often openness for differing views and in their exploration and experimentation with roles and behavioral standards, it should come as no surprise that some adolescents find no valid grounds for accepting any view as more moral than any other.

Developmental psychologists have observed that the rigid, dualistic view of the world begins to break down for many adolescents, particularly during the college years. During this time a dramatic new feature of ethical thought emerges, in large part as a function of the cognitive ability of *reflective abstraction,* or the ability to meditate on and think about one's own thought (Brainerd, 1979; Inhelder & Piaget, 1958). This ability to act as a critic of one's own thought (Perry, 1968) enables the adolescent to grant legitimacy to opposing social, moral, and even theological systems. The result is the emergence and development of a cognitive *relativism* in the social (Chandler, 1978) and moral (Kohlberg, 1973; Kohlberg & Gilligan, 1971) domains of reasoning. It is a characteristic of thought which has received a great deal of attention by psychologists studying cognitive development and has been viewed as a crucial transition point marking the emergence of mature reasoning in the intellectual and ethical domains.

Perry (1968) has traced the development of this feature of ethical thinking, and the interested reader is referred to his book for a thoughtful presentation of the issues and implications surrounding what he calls "intellectual and ethical development in the college years." The rejection of a dualistic view, Perry notes, is a gradual affair marked initially by exposure to, and awareness of, alternate views and positions. Still there is a hesitancy to leave the comfort of a black and white world for one in which there are no absolutes and no standards of objectivity. Michael Chandler (1978) makes note of some of the behavioral and affective implications of accepting such an awareness, reinterpreting many typically adolescent behaviors (e.g., the importance of peers and a youth culture, adolescent romance, and the attractiveness of cults and prepackaged world views) as attempts to provide stability and structure to a world which suddenly seems arbitrary and subjective.

In the moral domain, adoption of a relativism in reasoning results in the perspective that all morals are arbitrary and equally valid, and that no one has the right to impose values on anyone else. Both Perry and Kohlberg seem to agree that while relativism may characterize ethical thinking during late adolescence, there is a lack of stability to pure relativistic thinking. Kohlberg suggests that once young people enter positions of responsibility in society, most return to the comforts of conventional moral thinking. A minority may go on to construct a principled basis for their moral decisions. Perry, for example, describes a series of transformations which involve the relativistic thinker in a gradual rejection of pure relativism in favor of a commitment to personal choice and affirmation in life.

ADOLESCENT MORAL BEHAVIOR

As we stated at the outset of the section on adolescent moral reasoning, we believe that the ultimate goal and indeed test of the psychological study of moral development is an adolescent's actual behavior. We will now examine some of the ways psychologists have studied moral action by exploring three important aspects of adolescent moral behavior: cheating, juvenile delinquency, and political activism. Our intent is to focus on some of the personal and situational determinants of these behaviors, and to explore the possible role that moral judgment plays in influencing moral actions. This last issue, the relationship between moral judgment and moral behavior, is a complex and controversial one. Early optimism that moral reasoning might be the single best predictor of moral behavior (e.g., Fishkin, Keniston, & MacKinnon, 1973) and skepticism that moral reasoning can be used to justify and rationalize any kind of moral action (e.g., Mischel & Mischel, 1976) have given way to more studied accounts of the complex and often indirect relationship between thinking and action in the moral domain (e.g., Blasi, 1980). Again, the interested reader is referred to works by Blasi (1980) and Rothman (1980) for extended discussions of this issue.

Current thinking recognizes that moral reasoning is an important aspect of moral behavior, as it helps us define the moral meaning of situations and delimit the range of behaviors acceptable to our understanding. At the same time, the exact processes (e.g., motivation, self-concept, ego strength, situational specificity) that intervene between our moral judgments and actions have not been carefully studied or determined. In short, how people differ in their readiness to define situations as moral or not, and the factors which strengthen and/or weaken their desire to be consistent in judgments and actions need much further study. Where appropriate, we will present some evidence which bears on the reasoning-behavior relationship.

Cheating Behavior

Cheating in the classroom is an issue of very practical concern for teachers, administrators, parents, and students alike. Public reports of large scale cheating scandals among undergraduate, graduate, and medical students underscore the pervasiveness of the problem. Even our military academies have not been immune. Surveys of high school students (Mentor, 1971; Schab, 1972) reveal that anywhere from 70 percent to 96 percent of students in grades nine to twelve respond affirmatively when asked if they have ever cheated in school. Virtually all students agree that all students cheat sometimes. To add fuel to the fire, in the Mentor survey (1971), over 90 percent of the students did not consider cheating to be wrong.

This latter point raises an important issue with respect to the investigation of cheating behavior, namely, problems in defining cheating itself. Berzonsky has summarized this definitional problem with the following questions regarding cheating: "Is deliberate intent necessary? Is changing one answer the same as copying a term project verbatim? Does the copying of non-evaluated homework (or busywork) assignments constitute cheating?" (Berzonsky, 1981, p. 400). For some students, copying work that might not be graded may be cheating, but isn't necessarily wrong. Add to this the interaction with moral reasoning described earlier, where helping a good friend may be "more moral" than refusing, and we can begin to appreciate the difficulty of understanding what might appear at first blush to be a simple problem. The temptation to argue that cheating is cheating regardless does little to aid either psychological investigation of cheating behavior or our understanding of the variables influencing adolescent decision making.

Psychologists have researched a number of individual and environmental influences which may be determinants of cheating. At the individual level, IQ and academic ability tend to be negatively related to cheating (Barton, 1976; Krebs & Kohlberg, 1973). There is a generally held view among sociologists and psychologists that legitimate avenues to success will be exhausted before an individual will resort to illegitimate means such as cheating. (This applies to analyses of delinquency as well.) It may be that bright, academically achieving students have less need to cheat since they are already successful through legitimate means. Both the importance a student assigns to academic achievement and the likelihood of honest success are also relevant. Sheldon and Hill (1969) found that academically anxious students were more likely to cheat than their less anxious peers. Feedback about how well one has performed in comparison to peers also influences the incidence of cheating. When specific knowledge that one has not performed up to expectations of one's peer group is given, cheating is likely to increase, especially among more academically anxious students (Hill & Kochendorfer, 1969; Sheldon & Hill, 1969).

The likelihood of being detected is a situational variable influencing the frequency of cheating. When students feel a test is important and the probability of success low (e.g., a very difficult test), a low risk of detection leads to significantly more cheating than when there is a high chance of getting caught (Vitro & Schoer, 1972). In general, a low frequency of cheating occurs when conditions make the probability of getting caught high. Most psychologists agree that attempts to reduce cheating behavior should involve the kind of highly visible monitoring and surveillance procedures which make students aware of the high likelihood of getting caught.

Recognizing that setting up an authoritarian "police state" during exams is likely to be aversive to most teachers, Berzonsky (1981) suggests that a more authoritative atmosphere, where students are dealt with fairly and justly and are made aware of the rules, and where the rules are reasonable and administered consistently, may be a better supervising style. Fischer (1970) found that having students publicly affirm the value of not cheating on a test reduced cheating as much as explicit threats of punishment. This is not to say that value pronouncements of one's attitudes regarding cheating will be sufficient to influence one's behavior. Psychologists have long known that one's moral attitudes, values, and beliefs may bear little relationship to behavior (Lockwood, 1976). Fischer (1970), however, suggests a relationship if there is sufficient emphasis on public commitment. As we suggested earlier, moral reasoning may be a mechanism by which these attitudes, values, and beliefs could be made operational for given situations.

Research examining the relationship between moral reasoning and cheating behavior has not produced consistent findings (Blasi, 1980) and does not reveal a simple relationship between, for example, Kohlberg's stages of reasoning and cheating behavior. It may be that very few studies have been able to control the kinds of influencing variables we have discussed. A particularly well conducted study by Krebs and Kohlberg (1973) did find significantly less cheating among principled reasoners than conventional reasoners. They also found significantly less cheating among those conventional reasoners whose appeal is to rules and laws when compared to those students who reasoned at lower levels. Even so, the majority of these conventional reasoners did cheat (55 percent). It was only at the post-conventional level that a majority (80 percent) resisted temptations to cheat. Overall, the evidence suggests that it is at the post-conventional level of reasoning that we can expect greater consistency between judgment and behavior.

Juvenile Delinquency

There is no doubt that adolescent crime and juvenile delinquency are serious behavioral and social problems. Of all arrests reported to the FBI in 1979, 22.5 percent involved persons under the age of 18 (Federal Bureau of Investigation, 1979). The actual incidence of delinquency is even more extensive than is indicated by official arrest figures, because so many juvenile offenses go undetected. Estimates of undetected delinquency are derived from studies of self-reports. For instance, in one study of 522 teenagers, 80 percent reported committing delinquent acts, yet only 10 percent of the sample were ever arrested, and only for three percent of their total offenses (Haney & Gold, 1973).

Before examining delinquency as a moral transgression, it is important to understand the concept of juvenile delinquency and the problems associated with its study. The term "juvenile delinquency" refers to legally deviant behavior committed by people under the legal age, which is set somewhere between 16 and 21, depending on state of residence. There is a considerable range of delinquent acts, including not only all adult crimes but also status offenses such as alcohol consumption and truancy that would not be considered a crime except for one's age. Over three-fourths of American adolescents admit to having committed one or more delinquent acts. Most of these are relatively minor offenses such as drinking, smoking pot, petty theft, and vandalism. According to the self-report data of the National Survey of Youth, 1972 (Gold & Reimer, 1975), the frequency of such relatively minor acts accelerates from late childhood through middle adolescence, then begins to level off.

More serious delinquency, such as assault and breaking and entering, accelerates from early adolescence, peaks at middle adolescence, and then declines (Gold & Petronio, 1980). The gravity of delinquency seems to be greatest during middle adolescence, probably because these individuals are no longer under the social controls of "childhood" and are too young to identify with the emerging responsibilities of adult roles. Instead, they are somewhere in the middle, dealing with the desire for autonomy and peer acceptance and their search for identity. Middle adolescents, in this context, may be more vulnerable to forces that would permit and encourage deviant behavior.

The prevalence of juvenile delinquency has spurred many social scientists to study the characteristics of youthful offenders and the causes of their delinquency. This, however, is not an easy task. The behavioral study of delinquency is complicated because adolescents are not legally classified as "delinquent" until they have been arrested, taken to a juvenile court, and given the label. However, as we noted, much delinquent behavior goes undetected, and there are many more juvenile offenders than those who are caught. Because of accessibility, many studies examine only those adolescents who have already been identified and labeled. In several cases, these represent biased samples because the adolescents involved have been exposed to the court system and perhaps institutionalized. These ordeals could have affected individuals in such a way as to render any conclusions specific to them only, and not generalizable to the many offenders who are not identified. This point is particularly critical when we consider the influence of the environment on one's behaviors and attitudes. We will come back to the impact of environment on delinquent behavior when we discuss the relationship between moral thinking and moral action.

It is intuitive to believe that individuals who break the law might be deficient in moral character or at least might be reasoning at preconventional levels of morality. (Recall that laws and social contracts are central values for conventional moral reasons.) This speculation began to receive considerable attention in the 1950s, when it was proposed that antisocial conduct in children might relate to immaturities in moral reasoning (Anthony, 1956). Since then, numerous studies have examined the performance of delinquents on tasks specifically designed to assess the quality of their moral judgments (e.g., Kohlberg's dilemmas). However, in the course of critically examining this research, it becomes obvious that investigators have greatly underestimated both the complex nature of the moral judgment process and the multifaceted nature of juvenile delinquency. Therefore, in attempting to link moral immaturity to juvenile delinquency in a causal way, we must keep in mind the following points:

1. A relationship between two events does not necessarily imply that one causes the other. The fact that many delinquents come from broken homes does not mean that a broken home must always cause delinquent behavior. Similarly, if several delinquents display immature forms of moral reasoning, it does not follow that this immaturity is the cause of the behavior. As it turns out, juvenile delinquents display a considerable degree of variability in the maturity of their moral judgments (Jurkovic, 1980).
2. No single theory explains all delinquency. Patterns of delinquent behavior are different and vary among individuals. The reasons behind committing relatively mild status offenses, such as alcohol consumption, are not necessarily the same as explanations behind fighting, assault, and destructive violence.
3. It is difficult to isolate one single cause of crime or delinquency. Delinquent behavior may result from certain personality characteristics, low self-esteem, emotional disturbance, socioeconomic difficulties, family influences, inappropriate role models, peer pressure, conflicting values, societal breakdown, or some constellation of these forces.
4. As mentioned earlier, in examining causal explanations based on research with labeled offenders, we have the problem of separating causal forces from the impact of institutionalization and/or the administration of justice (arrest, courts, and prison).

Traditionally, most researchers have compared the moral reasoning of delinquents and nondelinquents by cognitive-developmental descriptions of moral judgments based on responses to hypothetical moral dilemmas. Blasi (1980) and Jurkovic (1980) have provided excellent reviews of these investigations. Many of the studies revealed delinquents reasoning at less mature moral levels than their nondelinquent counterparts. Delinquents were found to be preconventional, resolving dilemmas in order to produce optimal personal pleasure and avoid pain and punishment. Nondelinquents were conventional reasoners, resolving dilemmas by reference to conventional moral codes. However, other studies indicate variability in moral reasoning among the juvenile offenders, and although some youths appeared immature in their moral judgments, others evidenced reasoning beyond preconventional levels. In fact, Petronio (1973) studied 38 boys on probation and found that the 19 boys who were returned to court differed from those not returned only in their level of moral maturity. Counterintuitively, the recidivists were *higher* in their moral reasoning. Gold and Petronio (1980) offer one interpretation for this. It may be that delinquents who are capable of higher level reasoning rationalize their behavior by invoking "higher" socio-political standards that minimize their "badness" (e.g., "It is not so bad to steal from stores when stores are cheating people with high prices" or "It's OK to lie to get around laws and regulations since they are unnecessary anyway"). This is not to be confused with relativistic thinking. Relativism results in the perspective that no one has the right to impose values on anyone else. Rationalization, however, in this case, represents the use of cognition to justify behavior aimed toward personal gain.

In addition to variability in findings among studies of delinquency, it is important to remember, as with investigations of cheating behavior, that methods for controlling the variety of factors influencing moral behavior are imprecise. Researchers are just now beginning to take into account contextual influences on moral thinking and action. For instance, the consequences of being apprehended, adjudicated, and detained because of delinquent behavior have only recently been considered as contributions to the teenage offender's performance on tests of moral reasoning (Jurkovic, 1980). An institutional setting, such as a prison, may have a moral atmosphere that inhibits advanced moral behavior even though the individual possesses higher reasoning competence (Scharf, Hickey, & Moriarty, 1973).

Finally, attempts to examine the relation between moral reasoning and delinquency have neglected to consider the impact of psychosocial forces. Data exist concerning personality differences between delinquents and nondelinquents. However, keep in mind that the delinquents studied were probably those who were identified by the judicial system. Thus, there is a likelihood that these subjects might have been serious offenders rather than minor status offenders. In other words, the following findings should not necessarily be applied to those adolescents who are curfew breakers, drink underage, or occasionally engage in shoplifting. Legally speaking, these individuals are juvenile offenders as well, but they typically escape identification and are unrepresented in studies of juvenile delinquency.

In one study, Conger and Miller (1966) found that delinquents, in comparison to nondelinquents, were less well adjusted, displayed socially inappropriate behavior, got along less well with peers, were less responsible, and had poorer attitudes toward authority. As described earlier, delinquents generally tend to be characterized by low moral development and deviant values (Gold & Reimer, 1975). In addition, juvenile offenders tend to score high on measures of impulsiveness and low on self-control (Ahlstrom & Havighurst). Also, delinquents typically suffer from low self-esteem (Rosenberg & Rosenberg, 1978). As Atwater (1983) suggests, delinquency may be a way of coping with a poor self-image by serving to further the delinquents' personal identities in a recognizable way.

Many delinquents are victims of their environments. Delinquency is much more likely to occur in areas characterized by low income, low education, over-crowding, unemployment, racial and ethnic minorities, and broken homes (Atwater, 1983). Much of this is due to the fact that while our culture induces high aspirations and goals, legitimate means for attaining these goals are blocked in certain environments, perhaps because of inadequate academic and employment opportunities. This lack of opportunity may produce frustration which can lead individuals to strive for advancement through deviant means.

Delinquency continues to be a serious problem for economically deprived youth. However, delinquency is becoming more evenly distributed across all socioeconomic levels, and a marked rise has occurred among middle-class and affluent teenagers. Although some juvenile delinquents may have certain personality traits that predispose them to delinquent activity, one often witnesses or hears of delinquent behavior among seemingly well-adjusted, "nice kids." These offenders are less visible than lower class delinquents and are less likely to get caught. They, therefore, are the ones unrepresented in studies on officially reported delinquency.

One explanation for middle-class delinquency involves conformity to the expectations of the role of adolescent in the middle-class youth culture (Vaz, 1967). At this time of identity formation, adolescents are seeking to become autonomous from parents and look toward their peers for acceptance and status gain. The desire for popularity often encourages teenagers to engage in activities that would be applauded as exciting, risky, and novel among peers, but not condemned as overly vicious. In one study, adolescents indicated that fear of rejection and indirect peer pressure influenced their use of drugs and alcohol (Eisenthal & Udin, 1972). As an additional illustration of peer pressure, it is significant that most middle-class delinquency will not be committed alone but rather in small groups of three or less (Haney & Cold, 1973).

Association with delinquent friends has been found to be more related to delinquency for those adolescents who have weak parental support (Poole & Regoli, 1979). In fact, one of the best predictors of delinquency is the adolescent's relationship with his or her parents. Parental indifference, rejection, and weak affectional ties, in general, contribute to the problem.

Parental discipline is also a factor. Parents of delinquents tend to be either too strict, lax, or inconsistent in their disciplinary tactics (Martin, 1975). They also tend to use more physical punishment and less moral reasoning than parents of nondelinquents. Finally, family cohesiveness has been shown to be important in preventing delinquency. Although parental absence by death or divorce is automatically associated with non-cohesiveness, many intact families lack cohesiveness through dissension and hostility. What appears to be more important than homes broken by death and divorce is the adolescent-parent relationship and the emotional climate of the home (Atwater, 1983).

We have spent considerable time discussing juvenile delinquency, not only because of its relevance as a moral transgression, but also because of its significance as a major social problem that touches the lives of many who work and live with adolescents.

Political Activism

The late 1960s and early 1970s saw an upsurge in adolescent concern with questions of rights, liberties, war, and peace. More recent years have seen less vociferous yet no less committed youth express their feelings about the environment, nuclear power, disarmament, and draft registration. With an increase in political activity among youth came a corresponding increase in research investigating political involvement of adolescents.

Early accounts of activist youth tended to be extreme presentations. Either they were spoiled, irresponsible children, or they were the saviors of their generation and society. As is so often the case, the truth lay somewhere in between. Two recent reviews (Gallatin, 1980; Horn & Knott, 1971) present a picture of activists (defined by Block, Haan, & Smith, 1968 as politically involved youth fighting against the established system, including both radical dissenters and more moderate constructive adolescents) as independent youth with strong moral principles for which they were willing to take a stand. Although not outstanding students (a B-level grade average), they were willing to stand up and act in a way they felt would change governmental and educational institutions for the better. Additionally, parents of activists were described as warm and accepting, employing rational and consistent discipline methods. As Berzonsky points out, this authoritative style of parenting "would be expected to produce independent, formal reasoning youth with clear self theories and a set of moral standards to which they were personally and responsibly committed" (Berzonsky, 1981, p. 409). Such a picture suggests there may well be a relationship between moral reasoning and political activism. The work of Haan, Smith, and Block (1968) is particularly helpful in this regard.

Haan, Smith, and Block (1968) investigated moral reasoning, political attitudes, and political behavior among college students.

In terms of general political activity, they found that principled subjects belonged to more groups (political, service, and protest) and were more politically active and involved than non-principled students. Conventional students were relatively inactive politically and generally accepting of traditional American values. Also examined was the proportion of students at each stage of moral development who were arrested for participation in a sit-in demonstration. Results indicated that the highest proportion of students arrested were post-conventional reasoners. Sit-in participation was lowest at conventional levels of moral judgment. Surprisingly, quite a large number of preconventional reasoners (Kohlberg's lowest level of moral development) were also arrested.

Responses to an interview which included questions about participation in the sit-in provides some clues to the findings. Post-conventional students who were arrested were most concerned with the basic issues of civil rights and liberties surrounding the demonstration, and with the role of students as citizens in the college community. These concerns differed dramatically from those of the preconventional arrestees who were primarily concerned with their individual rights in the conflict over power, and thought the sit-in valuable because it resulted in the reforms they wanted. These students perceived the issues quite differently from the post-conventional students. Although their behaviors were the same, their motivations for moral action were not. Preconventional students were reacting out of anger at the college administration, while the post-conventional students were protesting a violation of basic rights.

The Haan, Smith, and Block study points out the importance of examining not only attitudes or behavior, but reasoning as well. Identical attitudes and behaviors can result from developmentally distinct forms of reasoning. Level of moral reasoning, then, can provide important information regarding our full understanding of adolescent moral behavior.

MORAL EDUCATION

With our emphasis on the developmental nature of moral reasoning and its relationship to moral behaviors, our presentation would be incomplete without some discussion of moral education. Although we recognize that training in moral attitudes, values, and beliefs is a byproduct of our socialization experiences (especially through parents and schools), our focus here will be to briefly introduce you to specific attempts to intervene with programs designed to optimize moral values, reasoning, and behavior. We should also recognize that our discussion of moral education comes at a time when the public increasingly seems to want schools to pay attention to values and moral education. In the 1976 Gallup poll of attitudes toward public education, 45 percent of parents felt that an increased emphasis on moral development would do the most to improve the quality of public education. Fully 79 percent of the parents responded that schools should take on a share of the responsibility for moral education. This is not to imply that the public is in agreement about the exact nature of the public school's role in moral education. We may be sensitized to the fact that increased attention needs to be paid to moral education, but the form of that education is still a source of a great deal of debate.

The question then becomes: What should teachers' roles be as moral educators? One response has been that teachers should act as moral indoctrinators. Value inculcation involves the teacher's telling the student which moral values are right and which are wrong. Through direct teaching, repetition, and reinforcement of correct responses, adolescents will learn to think and behave morally. From this perspective the teacher defines which behaviors are wrong and which are correct. As Scharf (1978) notes, the values usually chosen in indoctrination are defined in terms of virtues or culture-specific positive acts. The boy scout oath—A scout is trustworthy, loyal, helpful, friendly, courteous, kind, obedient, cheerful, thrifty, brave, clean, and reverent—defines just such a list of virtues. Schools in the nineteenth and early twentieth centuries adopted a similar indoctrination approach to further moral character development in school-age children. Today, this method of indoctrination is generally viewed as contrary to the goals of education in a democratic society.

Two current approaches to moral education are values clarification (Raths, Harmin, & Simon, 1966; Simon, Howe, & Kirschenbaum, 1972) and the cognitive-developmental approach based on Kohlberg's theory of moral development (Hersch, Paolitto, and Reimer, 1979; Kohlberg, 1975).

Values Clarification

A guiding principle of the values clarification approach is that moral values should not be taught directly. Past attempts in value instruction have not been successful, primarily because no agreement exists as to which values are the correct ones. The result has been confusion on the part of students due to confrontation with conflicting value positions expressed by their parents, teachers, friends, and the media. According to the clarification approach, teachers should not attempt to teach specific value positions, but should teach an approach to clarifying values through which students can arrive at their own personal values in a rational and clear way. This approach includes the following processes:

> *Prizing* one's beliefs and behaviors:
> 1. prizing and cherishing
> 2. publicly affirming when appropriate.
> *Choosing* one's beliefs and behaviors:
> 3. choosing from alternatives
> 4. choosing after consideration of consequences
> 5. choosing freely.
> *Acting* on one's beliefs:
> 6. acting
> 7. acting with a pattern consistency, and repetition.
> (Raths, Harmin, & Simon, 1966)

These processes define whether or not we can be said to possess a value. Values-clarification exercises are designed to bring our values into clear focus, and include ranking values, role playing, and making either-or choices among competing values. As the title of the approach suggests, the purpose of the program is to clarify one's values, and not subscribe to any one set of preexisting values.

Certain topics are considered more likely than others to provide a stimulus for value clarifying. These "value indicators" include attitudes (expressions of being for or against something), aspirations (statements of long range plans or goals), purposes (statements of short range goals or hopes), interests (expressions of likes), and activities (statements of how time is spent). According to Raths, Harmin, and Simon (1966), teachers need to sensitize themselves to their students' expressions of these value indicators, as they provide excellent raw material for value clarifying exercises.

Scharf (1978) summarizes the assumptions which underlie the values clarification approach by the definition and learning of values:

1. Values are, to a large extent, a matter of personal opinion. No person can tell another person what is right for him or her. While values in order to be considered as such must meet specific criteria, there exists the assumption that a particular value is neither right nor wrong. . . .
2. Learning, according to values-clarification theorists, is largely a matter of increasing awareness of self. Values clarification sees the child as developing his or her own values apart from others, rather than accepting society's values.
3. In values clarification, there is the implicit assumption that the moral norms of society have largely broken down and, further, that the moral pluralism of today's society forces individuals to define their own value commitments (Scharf, 1978, p. 27).

The values-clarification approach is probably the most widely practiced and accepted approach to moral education in American schools today. Its popularity is related to a number of factors. The approach is relatively easy to learn, and materials and a number of "how to" books are readily accessible to teachers. Second, it provides a method by which teachers can deal with important issues such as prejudice and life goals in an open and honest way. Most importantly for many teachers, these issues can be dealt with without the teacher imposing his or her own views on the students. Finally, teachers report that values clarification works, that students are stimulated and interested in the values-clarification process (Purpel and Ryan, 1976). Even strong critics of the approach report evidence of positive change in valuing and behavior (Lockwood, 1978). For a more detailed presentation of the values-clarification approach and accompanying criticism, interested readers are referred to Purpel and Ryan's (1976) collection of essays, *Moral Education . . . It Comes With the Territory.*

The Cognitive-developmental Approach to Moral Education

Based on Kohlberg's theory of moral development, the cognitive-developmental approach to moral education offers an alternative to, and extension of, the value-clarification approach. Kohlberg's intent is to get beyond the simple awareness of personal values to a stimulation of the development of more mature forms of moral reasoning. The goal, then, of this approach is to stimulate development toward a level of post-conventional morality. Kohlberg is quite explicit in stating that when educating people for citizenship in a democracy, a post-conventional morality represents the goal of moral education. He feels as well that this is not indoctrination, but that moral education from this perspective involves the stimulation of the natural developmental sequence revealed in his scientific studies of the development of moral reasoning.

Two concerns form the basis of Kohlberg's educational approach: (1) classroom discussion of moral issues with a focus on stimulating moral growth, and (2) restructuring the moral atmosphere of our schools to allow for democratic participation by students in the actual educational governing process. Kohlberg's concern for classroom curriculum derives from the work of Turiel (1966, 1974) and Blatt (Blatt & Kohlberg, 1975). First, Eliot Turiel demonstrated that by exposing students to moral arguments slightly more advanced than their own, a small upward movement in moral reasoning could be achieved. Blatt then followed this study with a more intensive curriculum of moral discussions over a longer period of time. During a 12-week period students met regularly to discuss moral issues and consider moral dilemmas. By the end of his project, Blatt reported that 63 percent of his class had gone up one full stage in moral reasoning.

Lockwood (1978) and Reihman (1978) review a number of moral discussion group experiments based on this approach, and have generally found them to be successful in stimulating the development of moral reasoning. Kohlberg's goal, however, is a curriculum for moral education which could be integrated into social studies, history, English, and sex education curricula. Hersch, Paolitto, and Reimer (1979) review a number of these attempts at curriculum design in the context of their book on moral education.

Kohlberg's second concern has involved an effort to "affect the social atmosphere and justice structure of the school" (Blatt & Kohlberg, 1975, p. 153). While Kohlberg believes that students' reasoning can be advanced through moral discussion, participating in real life moral decision-making is very important. Thus, restructuring the school to permit democratic participation by students in everything from rule making to disciplinary action is an important goal of the Kohlberg approach. This "just-community" approach to moral education has served as the basis for several attempts to create alternative high schools. Perhaps the best known is the Cambridge alternative school set up and run by professors and students from the Harvard Graduate School of Education. An extensive treatment of the history and design of the Cambridge school can be found in several works by Elsa Wasserman (1976, 1977). The sense one gets from reading her work and talking to both teachers and students who have taken part in "just-community" experiments is that the potential for positive influence on the lives of teachers and students alike is far greater than in individual discussion group curricula.

One final note: Kohlberg's discussion group and "just-community" approaches to moral education have been employed with some success with young adult prison inmates (Hickey, 1972; Kohlberg, Scharf, & Hickey, 1975). Their potential as interventions with delinquent youth should not be overlooked.

RELIGIOUS ORIENTATION

The development of values is a critical aspect of moral reasoning and behavior. We have just discussed how education can influence the awareness and development of values. Now, in this final section, we will consider religious beliefs as one component of a moral value system. Data indicate that organized religion continues to be an important moral, philosophical, and social institution for many American youth (Lerner & Spanier, 1980). However, there is also some indication that today's adolescents are placing more emphasis than previous generations on personal rather than institutionalized religion. According to Conger (1977), adolescents place greater stress on personal moral standards and relationships rather than on traditional forms of religion and rigid dogma. One reason may be that adolescents are becoming aware that institutionalized religion does not support their changing values. For instance, half of the teenagers in a national survey stated that churches are not trying to understand young people's ideas about sex and that adolescents are looking to God rather than to institutionalized religion for understanding attitudes about sex (Sorensen, 1973).

Adolescents maintain high levels of commitment to beliefs in God throughout their adolescent years and, according to Dacey (1979), are probably the most religiously devout of all age groups. However, as in the case of moral values in general, religious beliefs also reflect the adolescent's cognitive growth, greater commitment to relativism, and search for identity. As Lerner and Spanier (1980) point out, such developmental changes may influence the quality and meaning of adolescents' religious beliefs without affecting the level of overall commitment. As indicated at several points throughout the chapter, qualitatively different moral reasoning can underlie the same moral behavior. Similarly, the same belief in God could be associated with different meanings for the adolescent, depending on the level of maturation within the adolescent age-span.

What are the changes, then, that occur? Paralleling cognitive development, the young person's religious beliefs are likely to become more abstract between the ages of 12 and 18 (Kuhlen & Arnold, 1944; Wuthnow & Glock, 1973). God is seen more as an abstract power than as a fatherly human being (Conger, 1977). Religious views become more tolerant and less dogmatic, and the observance of religion changes from literal interpretations of institutionalized teachings to more personalized beliefs. In addition, during this time of searching for individual identity and values, the adolescent feels compelled to examine familial religious beliefs. While adolescents tend to adhere to deep family values, religious and otherwise, a time of questioning is certainly expected.

So far, it can be concluded that conventional religion remains important for many individuals throughout their adolescence. For others, especially older adolescents, commitment to an institutionalized dogma weakens, and individualized beliefs become stronger. This is not to say that personal religion and underlying principles of morality are being rejected, only the formalized rituals and theology.

For many youth in their late teens and early twenties, however, unconventional religious beliefs emerge. Some experience a religious awakening or "re-birth," and change their life-styles in accordance with fundamentalist views. Born-again Christians are representative of such fundamentalist groups. Recruitment is usually carried out by peers (Heirich, 1977), and as Gold and Petronio (1980) indicate, these groups are as much a social movement as they are a coming to God.

During the 1970s, another portion of older youth defected from conventional religion in favor of cults. A religious cult is a small group of individuals bound together by a common set of religious beliefs. Cults tend to be countercultural and based on the beliefs, teachings, and personality of one individual (Lerner & Spanier, 1980). Cults range from being informal and loosely structured to being totalitarian and authoritarian (Robbins & Anthony, 1978). Often, strict moral codes are enforced. One to three thousand cults exist in the United States (Slade, 1978), and the majority of the members are between 18 and 25 years of age (Shupe & Bromley, 1978). A few of the more common cults are the Unification Church of Reverend Sun Myung Moon, the Hare Krishna, and the Church of Scientology.

Adolescents join cults for many reasons. Some are disillusioned with their religion and society and search elsewhere for spiritualism and a meaning to life. Others may feel insecure in their own families, so the cohesive, tight-knit nature of cults appeals to them. They may try to find security in the rigid structure and philosophy of cults. (It would be interesting to examine these youths' level of moral reasoning. One might expect them to be conventional thinkers.) Still other adolescents may be seeking attention, status, or excitement (Doress & Porter, 1978). Often, cults attract those adolescents who are rootless, confused, or in some other way vulnerable.

Adolescents also leave cults for a variety of reasons. Perhaps the cult failed to live up to expectations. Some parents forcibly remove their children from cults and arrange for "deprogrammers" to undo the indoctrination used by some cults. Legal battles have surrounded parental "kidnapping" and deprogramming, the central issues being religious freedom and the right to choose one's own lifestyle.

Finally, one wonders about the effects of cults and deprogramming on youth. The influences are unclear, and the interested reader is referred to Singer (1979) for a detailed discussion.

SUMMARY

We have presented an overview of adolescents' moral development by initially examining the three dominant theoretical orientations: psychoanalytic, social learning, and cognitive developmental. In the struggle for a meaningful identity, adolescents begin to wrestle with many of the traditional problems faced by all adults—conflicts over moral beliefs, thoughts, and actions. The significant contributions to adolescent morality have been identified: parents, peers, and family attitudes. Careful attention was drawn to the special characteristics of adolescent thinking which influence moral evaluations: idealism, reasoning about law and justice, and relativism. Specific examples detailing adolescent moral orientations were cited in the area of academic cheating, juvenile delinquency, and student political activism. Finally, the burgeoning area of moral education was discussed along with adolescent religious orientations.

SOURCES OF HELP

National Resource Centers:

Harvard Center for Moral Education
322 Larson Hall
Appian Way
Harvard University Graduate School of Education
Cambridge, MA 02138

Sylvia Gray, Project Director
National Child Welfare Training Center
School of Social Work
University of Michigan
1015 E. Huron
Ann Arbor, MI 48104
(313) 763-4260

Hunter Hurst, Director
National Center for Juvenile Justice/Research Division
701 Forbes Ave.
Pittsburgh, PA 15219

Office of Juvenile Justice and Delinquency Prevention
Law Enforcement Assistance Administration
633 Indiana Ave., NW, 7th Floor
Washington, DC 20531

Joan Lipsitz, Director
Center for Early Adolescence
University of North Carolina at Chapel Hill, Suite 223
Carr Mill Mall
Carboro, NC 27510

Eugene A. Moore, Director
National Council of Juvenile and Family Court Judges
University of Nevada
P.O. Box 8000
Reno, NV 89507
(702) 784-6012

Stephen Rorke, Executive Director
National Network of Runaway and Youth Services, Inc.
1705 DeSales St., NW, 8th Floor
Washington, DC 20036

Carolina Craft, Director
Youth Services (HHS)
Division of Runaway Youth Programs
400 Sixth St. SW
Washington, DC 20201
(202) 755-8208

Local Resources

Potential guest speakers and resource persons are those local persons who have been personally or professionally involved in administering, offering, or reviewing services to adolescents and their families. The following are examples of such persons or organizations:

1. Directors of local youth centers
2. Social workers, supervisors, or administrators serving adolescents
3. Mental health centers
4. Hospitals
5. Hot-line information and referral services
6. Church-related adolescent discussion programs:
    a. Catholic Charities
    b. Catholic Youth Organization
    c. Protestant Youth Fellowship
    d. Jewish Family Services
7. Counselors and clergy
8. Family life education programs offered by high schools, colleges, and cooperative extension programs
9. Parent education programs offered by local and state Social Services and Social Welfare Departments
10. Parent support groups such as *Tough Love*
11. Salvation Army youth programs and outreach services
12. Adolescents currently receiving social services.

Films

Moral Judgment and Reasoning (CRM, 1978)
    The three basic orientations toward understanding morality are presented in this 17-minute color film. Clear discussion of these orientations helps in understanding the differences between psychologists' views of psychoanalytic, social learning, and cognitive-developmental approaches to the topic of morality.

Morality: The Process of Moral Development (Davidson Films, 1980)

The developmental processes underlying basic understanding of the legal system, justice, fairness, and sharing are presented in a 28-minute color film. Children from the age of four years up to adults are systematically explored to better chart their evolving knowledge.

Delinquency: The Process Begins; Delinquency: Street Violence; Delinquency: The Chronic Offender; Delinquency: Prevention and Treatment (MTI Teleprograms)

Four part film series dealing with the causes of delinquency and the institutions that influence and deal with it: the home, schools, police, the courts, corrections, parole and probation. The films are accompanied by a monograph, "Historical Overview and Critical Assessment of the Juvenile Justice System," by Paul Hong.

Innocent Criminal (Child Welfare League of American Library, New York)

The first half of tape examines the plight of the status offender, and the second half suggests an alternative method for dealing with status offenders, specifically a community-based program. A leader's guide is included.

The Young Convicts: Prison in the Streets (Xerox, 1973)

Movement toward community programs for the care and re-habilitation of the young offender. Focuses on programs in California and Massachusetts. (Published by ABC)

ANNOTATED REFERENCES

1. Moral Reasoning and Development

Hersch, R. H., Paolitto, D. P., & Reimer, J. *Promoting Moral Growth: From Piaget to Kohlberg.* New York: Longman, 1979.

Excellent introduction to the cognitive-developmental approach to moral development. Focuses on the implication of this approach for moral education with chapters on designing moral dilemmas for discussion groups, and leading moral discussions. Fine bibliography including programs and curricula designed around Kohlberg's approach to moral development.

Hoffman, M. L. "Moral Development in Adolescence." In J. Adelson (Ed.), *Handbook of Adolescent Psychology*. New York: Wiley, 1980.
Review of moral development in adolescence from various theoretical viewpoints including cognitive-developmental, psychoanalytic, and social learning. Also addresses the role of empathy as a motive for moral action.

Kohlberg, L. "Moral Stages and Moralization: The Cognitive-developmental Approach." In T. Lickona (Ed.), *Moral Development and Behavior: Theory Research and Social Issues*. New York: Holt, 1976.
Recent statement by Kohlberg on his approach to moral development.

Lockwood, A. L. "The Effects of Values Clarification and Moral Development Curricula on School Age Subjects: A Critical Review of Recent Research." *Review of Educational Research*, 1978, *48*, 325–364.
Critical analysis and review of moral education training programs. Do they really work?

Purpel, D., & Ryan, K. *Moral Education . . . It Comes with the Territory*. Berkeley, CA: McLutcham, 1976.
Collection of essays on moral education. Descriptions of major approaches to moral education in the United States with fine critical commentary.

Raths, L., Harmin, M., & Simon, S. B. *Values and Teaching*. Columbus, OH: Charles E. Merrill, 1966.
Basic statement of design and intent of values clarification by the designers of the program. Replete with examples for conducting values-clarification exercises. A classic introduction to this approach.

Rothman, G. R. "The Relationship between Moral Judgment and Moral Behavior." In M. Windmiller, N. Lambert, & E. Turiel (Eds.), *Moral Development and Socialization*. Boston: Allyn & Bacon, 1980.
Discussion of the relationship between moral reasoning and behavior.

2. Juvenile Delinquency

Advocating For Children in the Courts. Washington, DC: American Bar Association, 1980.
A manual to serve as a practical tool to help meet the needs of all those who advocate for children in the courts. Many pertinent areas of interest for the professional social worker: representation of the agency,

parent, child; judicial standards and criteria; representing the adolescent, etc.

deLang, J. M., Barton, J. A., & Lanham, S. L. "The WISER Way: A Cognitive-Behavioral Model for Group Social Skills Training with Juvenile Delinquents." *Social Work with Groups*, 1981, Vol. 4, p. 37–48.
Discusses a model of social skills training for juvenile delinquents. Combines behavioral training with a problem-solving process, called The WISER Way (representing the five steps: wait, identify, solve, evaluate, reinforce).

Jurkovic, G. J. "The Juvenile Delinquent as a Moral Philosopher: A Structural-Developmental Perspective." *Psychological Bulletin*, 1980, Vol. 88, p. 709–727.
Review of studies addressing the relationships between moral reasoning, moral behavior, and juvenile delinquency. Factors mediating these relationships are discussed.

Trojanowicz, R. C. *Juvenile Delinquency: Concepts and Controls.* Englewood Cliffs, NJ: Prentice-Hall, 1978.
A comprehensive text containing theories of delinquency causation, and emphasizing applied concerns. Extensive chapters on prevention programs and methods of treatment with examples of community-based treatment programs.

3. Religion and Cults

Doress, I., & Porter, J. N. "Kids In Cults." *Society*, 1978, Vol. 15, p. 69–71.
Discusses the reasons why young people join, stay with, and leave cults.

Robbins, T., & Anthony, D. "New Religions, Families, and Brainwashing." *Society*, 1978, Vol. 15, p. 77–83.
Examines brainwashing as a social weapon which provides a libertarian rationale for persecuting unpopular social movements and ideologies. Suggests that the brainwashing metaphor has amplified hostility between cults and their antagonists and, thus, often between parents and children.

Singer, M. T. "Coming Out of the Cults." *Psychology Today*, 1979, Vol. 12, p. 72–82.
Discusses how cults recruit members, what happens to persons while they are in cults, and how to understand and treat the problems presented by members when they leave cults.

REFERENCES

Ahlstrom, W. M., & Havighurst, R. J. *400 Losers*. San Francisco: Jossey-Bass, 1971.

Anthony, E. J. "The Significance of Jean Piaget for Child Psychiatry." *British Journal of Medical Psychology*, 1956, *29*, 20–34.

Atwater, E. *Adolescence*. Englewood Cliffs, NJ: Prentice-Hall, 1983.

Bandura, A., Grusec, J. E., & Menlove, F. L. "Observational Learning as a Function of Symbolization and Incentive Set." *Child Development*, 1966, *37*, 499–505.

Barton, R. U. "Honesty and Dishonesty." In T. Lickona (Ed.), *Moral Development and Behavior*. New York: Holt, Rinehart & Winston, 1976.

Berzonsky, M. D. *Adolescent Development*. New York: Macmillan, 1981.

Blasi, A. "Bridging Moral Cognition and Moral Action: A Critical Review of the Literature." *Psychological Bulletin*, 1980, *88*, 1–45.

Blatt, M., & Kohlberg, L. "The Effects of Classroom Moral Discussion on Children's Level of Moral Judgment." *Journal of Moral Education*, 1975, *4*, 147.

Block, J. H., Haan, N., & Smith, M. B. "Activism and Apathy in Contemporary Adolescents." In J. F. Adams (Ed.), *Understanding Adolescence: Current Developments in Adolescent Psychology*. Boston: Allyn & Bacon, 1968.

Brainerd, C. J. *Piaget's Theory of Intelligence*. Englewood Cliffs, NJ: Prentice-Hall, 1977.

Brittain, C. V. "Adolescent Choices and Parent-peer Cross-pressures." *American Sociological Review*, 1963, *28*, 385–391.

Broughton, J. M. "The Divided Self in Adolescence." *Human Development*, 1981, *24*, 13–32.

Chandler, M. J. "Relativism and the Problem of Epistemological Loneliness." *Human Development*, 1975, *18*, 171–175.

Conger, J. J. *Adolescence and Youth: Psychological Development in a Changing World*. New York: Harper & Row, 1977.

Conger, J. J., & Miller, W. C. *Personality, Social Class, and Delinquency*. New York: Wiley, 1966.

Dacey, J. S. *Adolescents Today*. Santa Monica, CA: Goodyear Publishing Co., Inc., 1979.

Doress, I., & Porter, J. N. "Kids in Cults." *Society*, 1978, *15*, 69–71.

Eisenthal, S., & Udin, H. "Psychological Factors Associated with Drug and Alcohol Usage among Neighborhood Youth Corps Enrollees." *Developmental Psychology*, 1972, *7*, 119–123.

Erikson, E. H. *Identity: Youth and Crisis*. New York: Norton, 1968.

Federal Bureau of Investigation. *Uniform Crime Reports for the United States*. Washington, DC: USGPO, 1979.

Fischer, C. T. "Levels of Cheating under Conditions of Informative Appeal to Honesty, Public Affirmation of Value, and Threats of Punishment." *Journal of Educational Research,* 1970, *64,* 12–16.

Fishkin, J., Keniston, K., & MacKinnon, C. "Moral Reasoning and Political Ideology." *Journal of Personality and Social Psychology,* 1973, *27,* 109–119.

Flavell, J. *Cognitive Development.* Englewood Cliffs, NJ: Prentice-Hall, 1977.

Gallatin, J. "Political Thinking in Adolescence." In J. Adelson (Ed.), *Handbook of Adolescent Psychology.* New York: John Wiley & Sons, 1980.

Gold, M., & Petronio, R. J. "Delinquent Behavior in Adolescence." In J. Adelson (Ed.), *Handbook of Adolescent Psychology.* New York: Wiley & Sons, 1980.

Gold, M., & Reimer, D. J. "Changing Patterns of Delinquent Behavior among Americans 13 through 16 Years Old, 1967–72." *Crime and Delinquency Literature,* 1975, 7, 483–517.

Haan, N., Langer, J., & Kohlberg, L. "Family Patterns of Moral Reasoning." *Child Development,* 1976, *47,* 1204–1206.

Haan, N., Smith, M. B., & Block, J. H. "Moral Reasoning of Young Adults: Political, Social Behavior, Family Background, and Personality Correlates." *Journal of Personality and Social Psychology,* 1968, *10,* 183–201.

Haney, B., & Gold, M. "The Juvenile Delinquent Nobody Knows." *Psychology Today,* 1973 (Sept.), *6,* 49–55.

Heirich, M. "Change of Heart: A Test of Some Widely Held Theories about Religious Conversion." *American Journal of Sociology,* 1977, *83,* 653–680.

Hersch, R. H., Paolitto, D. P., & Reimer, J. *Promoting Moral Growth: From Piaget to Kohlberg.* New York: Longman, 1979.

Hickey, J. E. "The Effects of Guided Moral Discussion Upon Youthful Offenders' Level of Moral Judgment." Doctoral dissertation, Boston University, School of Education, 1972.

Hill, J. P., & Kochendorfer, R. A. "Knowledge of Peer Success and Risk of Detection as Determinants of Cheating." *Developmental Psychology,* 1969, *1,* 231–238.

Hoffman, M. L. "Personality, Family Structure, and Social Class as Antecedents of Parental Power Assertion." *Child Development,* 1963, *34,* 869–884.

Hoffman, M. L. "Father Absence and Conscience Development." *Developmental Psychology,* 1971, *4,* 400–406.

Hoffman, M. L. "Moral Internalization: Current Theory and Research." In L. Berkowitz (Ed.), *Advances in Experimental Social Psychology,* Vol. 10, New York: Academic Press, 1977.

Hoffman, M. L. "Moral Development in Adolescence." In J. Adelson (Ed.), *Handbook of Adolescent Psychology*. New York: Wiley, 1980.

Holstein, C. "The Relation of Children's Moral Judgment to That of Their Parents and to Communication Patterns in the Family." In R. C. Smart & M. S. Smart (Eds.), *Readings in Child Development*. New York: Macmillan, 1972, 484–494.

Horn, J. L., & Knott, P. D. "Activist Youth of the 1960's: Summary and Prognosis." *Science*, 1971, *171*, 977–985.

Inhelder, B., & Piaget, J. *The Growth of Logical Thinking from Childhood to Adolescence*. London: Routledge & Kegan Paul, 1958.

Jurkovic, G. J. "The Juvenile Delinquent as Moral Philosopher: A Structural-Developmental Perspective." *Psychological Bulletin*, 1980, *88*, 709–727.

Kelley, P. K. "The Premarital Sexual Revolution: Comments on Research." *Family Coordinator*, 1972, *21*, 334–336.

Krebs, R., & Kohlberg, L. "Moral Judgment and Ego Controls as Determinants of Resistance to Cheating." Center for Moral Education, Cambridge, MA, 1977.

Kohlberg, L. "The Development of Moral Character and Moral Ideology." In M. L. Hoffman & L. W. Hoffman (Eds.), *Review of Child Development Research*, Vol. 1. New York: Russell Sage Foundation, 1964.

Kohlberg, L. "Stage and Sequence: The Cognitive-Developmental Approach to Socialization." In D. A. Goslin (Ed.), *Handbook of Socialization Theory and Research*. Chicago: Rand McNally, 1969.

Kohlberg, L. "Continuities in Childhood and Adult Moral Development Revisited." In P. B. Baltes & K. W. Schaie (Eds.), *Life Span Developmental Psychology: Personality and Socialization*. New York: Academic Press, 1973.

Kohlberg, L. "Moral Stages and Moralization: The Cognitive-Developmental Approach." In T. Lickona (Ed.), *Moral Development and Behavior: Theory, Research, and Social Issues*. New York: Holt, Rinehart, & Winston, 1976.

Kohlberg, L., & Gilligan, C. "The Adolescent as Philosopher: The Discovery of the Self in a Postconventional World." *Daedalus*, 1971, *100*, 1051–1086.

Kohlberg, L., Scharf, P., & Hickey, J. "The Justice Structure of the Prison: A Theory and an Intervention." *Prison Journal*, 1973, *51*, 3–14.

Kuhlen, R. G., & Arnold, M. "Age Differences in Religious Beliefs and Problems during Adolescence." *Journal of Genetic Psychology*, 1944, *65*, 291–300.

Lerner, R. M., & Spanier, G. B. *Adolescent Development. A Life-span Perspective*. New York: McGraw-Hill, 1980.

Lickona, T. (Ed.), *Moral Development and Behavior.* New York: Holt, Rinehart & Winston, 1976.

Lockwood, A. L. "Moral Reasoning and Public Policy Debate." In T. Lickona (Ed.), *Moral Development and Behavior.* New York: Holt, Rinehart & Winston, 1976.

Lockwood, A. L. "The Effects of Values Clarification and Moral Development Curricula on School-age Subjects: A Critical Review of Recent Research." *Review of Educational Research,* 1978, *48,* 325–364.

Martin, B. "Parent-child Relations." In F. D. Horowitz (Ed.), *Review of Child Development Research* (Vol. 4). Chicago: University of Chicago Press, 1975.

Perry, W. B. *Forms of Intellectual and Ethical Development in the College Years: A Scheme.* New York: Holt, Rinehart & Winston, 1970.

Petronio, R. "Self-esteem and Moral Attitudes as Factors of Recidivism in Juvenile Delinquent Boys." Unpublished manuscript, New School for Social Research, 1973.

Piaget, J. *The Moral Judgment of the Child.* New York: Harcourt, 1932.

Poole, E. D., & Pegoli, R. M. "Parental Support, Delinquent Friends, and Delinquency: A Test of Interaction Effects." *Journal of Criminal Law and Criminology,* 1979, *70,* 188–193.

Purpel, D., & Ryan, K. *Moral Education . . . It Comes with the Territory.* Berkeley, CA: McCutchan, 1976.

Raths, L., Harmin, M., & Simon, S. B. *Values and Teaching.* Columbus, OH: Charles E. Merrill, 1966.

Reihman, J. "Training in Political Development: A Cognitive-developmental Perspective." Unpublished doctoral dissertation, University of Wisconsin, Madison, 1978.

Robbins, T., & Anthony, D. "New Religions, Families, and Brainwashing." *Society,* 1978, *15,* 77–83.

Rosenberg, F. R., & Rosenberg, M. "Self-esteem and Delinquency." *Journal of Youth and Adolescence,* 1978, *7,* 279–291.

Rothman, G. R. "The Relationship between Moral Judgment and Moral Behavior." In M. Windmiller, N. Lambert, & E. Turiel (Eds.), *Moral Development and Socialization.* Boston: Allyn & Bacon, 1980.

Schab, F. "Cheating in High School: A Comparison of Behavior of Students in the College Prep and General Curriculum." *Journal of Youth and Adolescence,* 1972, *1,* 251–256.

Scharf, P. "Indoctrination, Values Clarification, and Developmental Moral Education as Educational Responses to Conflict and Change in Contemporary Society." In P. Scharf (Ed.), *Readings in Moral Education.* Minneapolis: Winston Press, 1978.

Scharf, P., Hickey, J. E., & Moriarty, T. "Moral Conflict and Change in Correctional Settings." *Personnel and Guidance Journal,* 1973, *51,* 660–663.

Selman, R. L. "Taking Another's Perspective: Role Taking Development in Early Childhood." *Child Development*, 1971, *42*, 1721-1734.

Selman, R. L. "Social-cognitive Understanding." In T. Lickona (Ed.), *Moral Development and Behavior*. New York: Holt, Rinehart & Winston, 1976.

Selman, R. L., & Byrne, D. F. "A Structural-developmental Analysis of Levels of Role Taking in Middle Childhood." *Child Development*, 1974, *45*, 803-806.

Shaffer, D. R., & Brody, G. H. "Parental and Peer Influences on Moral Development." In R. W. Henderson (Ed.), *Parent-Child Interaction: Theory, Research, and Prospects*, New York: Academic Press, 1981, 83-124.

Sheldon, J., & Hill, J. P. "Effects on Cheating of Achievement Anxiety and Knowledge of Peer Performance." *Developmental Psychology*, 1969, *1*, 449-455.

Shupe, A. D., & Bromley, D. G. "Witches, Moonies, and Evil." *Society*, 1978, *15*, 75-76.

Simon, S. B., Howe, L., & Kirschenbaum, H. *Values Clarification: A Handbook of Practical Strategies for Teachers and Students*. New York: Hart, 1972.

Singer, M. T. "Coming Out of the Cults." *Psychology Today*, 1979, *12*, 72-82.

Slade, M. "New Religious Groups: Membership and Legal Battles." *Psychology Today*, 1979, *12*, 81.

Sorensen, R. C. *Adolescent Sexuality in Contemporary America: Personal Values and Sexual Behavior Ages 13-19*. New York: Harry N. Abrams, Inc., 1973.

Tapp, J., & Kohlberg, L. "Developing Senses of Law and Legal Justice." *Journal of Social Issues*, 1971, *27*, 65-91.

Vaz, E. *Middle-class Juvenile Delinquency*. New York: Harper & Row, 1967.

Vitro, F. T., & Schoer, L. A. "The Effects of Probability of Test Success, Test Importance, and Risk of Detection of the Incidence of Cheating." *Journal of School Psychology*, 1972, *10*, 269-277.

Wasserman, E. R. "Implementing Kohlberg's Just Community Concept in an Alternative High-School." *Social Education*, 1976, *40*, 203-207.

Windmiller, M. "Introduction." In M. Windmiller, N. Lambert, & E. Turiel (Eds.), *Moral Development and Socialization*. Boston: Allyn & Bacon, 1980.

Wuthnow, R., & Glock, C. Y. "Religious Loyalty, Desertion, and Experimentation among College Youth." *Journal for the Scientific Study of Religion*, 1973, *12*, 157-180.

9. ADOLESCENCE AND EDUCATION
Nancy A. Busch-Rossnagel

Schools have become a fact of life for most adolescents today. In 1976 more than 23.7 million adolescents were enrolled in school, representing 97 percent of all youth ages 12 to 17 (Dearman & Plisko, 1979). Fifteen million, seven hundred thousand of those were enrolled in grades 9 through 12, grades which until a landmark court case, the Kalamazo decision of 1874, were not usually a part of the public education system. In 1900 one out of ten 14- to 17-year-olds were in school, while today nine out of ten of this age group are in school (National Center for Educational Statistics, 1980).

What are all these adolescents doing while attending school? In American society there are three major functions for schools (Busch-Rossnagel & Vance, 1982). The first function is literacy for the children of all social classes, not just the well-to-do. Until the Industrial Revolution, schools prepared the children of the upper class for the professions. Other children gained an education in an informal way through observation and imitation, much as infants learn to walk or talk today. Such an apprenticeship approach to education succeeded because the teachers, that is, the parents, knew what skills were necessary for survival in a world where social change was slow. However, with the Industrial Revolution, the skills of adults were rendered obsolete by rapid social change, which meant that parents no longer knew what skills and education would be needed by their children. The need for increasingly skilled labor helped to foster the movement toward compulsory education between the ages of eight and sixteen (Bakan, 1971). The purpose of this compulsory education was to teach the basic skills: reading, writing, and arithmetic. Such fundamental literacy skills are necessary for an industrialized society to be able to train workers rapidly, and this function of teaching literacy continues to dominate American education.

During the latter half of the nineteenth century, the rapid social change brought on by the Industrial Revolution and the huge number of immigrants created the feelings that parents were no longer capable of socializing their children, that is, enculturating their children with the values of the dominant society (Bakan, 1971). Therefore, compulsory education had, and continues to have, a second function of transmitting societal values. Under this function schools not only teach the "three R's," but also emphasize appropriate behavior such as self-discipline, social skills, and acceptance of group norms. In transmitting societal values, the prevailing mores of society predominate, so the schools have a decidedly middle-class bias.

If the second function of schools attempts to preserve the status quo, the third function attempts to change the status quo by improving society. The origins of compulsory education lie partly within this third function, curing society of the ills of the "immorality" of the growing cities, the "unAmerican" ideas of the immigrants and the crimes against property committed by juveniles (Bakan, 1971). We still continue to use the schools to reform society by compensating for racial and economic inequalities, correcting poor nutrition through school lunch programs, and overcoming ill-advised parenting (Sawhill, 1979). Society seems to have adopted the principle of residual functions in regard to schools; schools are assumed to have responsibility for any needs of children and society that are not satisfied by other institutions (Smith & Orlosky, 1974).

ISSUES AND FINDINGS

Each of these functions—of literacy, socialization, and cultural change—raises some issues about today's adolescents and their educational experience. For the function of literacy, the major issue is one of evaluating how well the nation's schools are performing the task of teaching the basic skills and then examining the factors which influence school achievement. For the function of socialization, the issues are evaluating the values and success of high school graduates, examining the behavior problems found in today's high schools, and exploring the reasons for, and plight of, today's high school dropouts. The issue for cultural change is to predict the future, by suggesting what changes are necessary to solve the problems of the educational system. These issues will serve as the organization of this chapter; along with the discussion of each issue, the findings of research which help to resolve the issue will be presented.

Teaching Basic Skills

Since fostering literacy is the primary function of education, the first issue which needs to be addressed is "How well are we doing teaching the basic skills?" Not so well, according to several major reports on the status of American education. The National Commission on Excellence in Education (1983) entitled its report "A Nation at Risk," and its conclusions branded American education as mediocre. The report's findings included some dire warnings:

1. American students scored lowest on seven out of nineteen academic tests and never were first or second when compared to students in other industrialized nations.
2. Only one year of math and one year of science are required for high school graduation in 70% of the states, but increasing these requirements will be difficult since there is a dire shortage of math and science teachers in all states.
3. Twenty-three million American adults, 13 percent of all 17-year-olds, and 40 percent of minority youth are functionally illiterate.
4. High school students are scoring lower on standardized tests than 25 years ago. Scores on the College Boards (SATs) have dropped 50 points for verbal content and 40 points for mathematics.

Such declines mean that our dream of progress from one generation to the next is being shattered. "For the first time in the history of our country, the educational skills of one generation will not surpass, will not even equal, will not even approach, those of their parents" (National Commission on Educational Excellence, 1983, p. 11).

The National Assessment of Education Progress

Obviously, such problems have not occurred overnight; they have been years in the making. Since the mid-1960's the National Assessment of Educational Progress (NAEP) has been charting what American youth are learning. Since this ongoing study can answer many of the questions about how well education is teaching the basic skills, it is necessary to describe the research in greater detail. NAEP uses periodic, census-like surveys to collect information about the knowledge and understanding of four age levels of Americans: 9-year-olds, 13-year-olds, 17-year-olds, and 26- to 35-year-olds. These levels correspond to the end of specific school periods: primary (grade 3), intermediate (grade 8), secondary (grade 12), and formal postsecondary education. The first assessment, in 1969, included the areas of writing, science, and citizenship (Ahman, 1982). Including that first assessment, the basic skill areas of reading, writing, and mathematics have each been assessed three times. During each of these assessments, between 15,000 and 30,000 9-, 13-, and 17-year-olds from varying geographical regions, from differing types of communities, from different races, and with varying levels of parental education were surveyed. Such an ongoing assessment provides information not only about educational achievement, but also about changes in that achievement. Information about those changes may be most crucial in improving the nation's educational system. (Refer to Tables 1 and 2 for a summary of the NAEP results.)

Reading. The reading skills of American youth were surveyed during the 1970–71, 1974–75, and 1979–80 school years (NAEP, 1981a). The assessment included three broad categories of reading achievement: (a) literal comprehension tested the student's ability to remember the exact meaning of material; (b) inferential comprehension required students to infer an idea that is not explicitly stated; and (c) reference skills tapped the student's ability to apply reading behavior to problem solving, for example, in finding an answer, correctly interpreting information, and organizing information for later use.

When information from the three assessments is compared, the results for the 9-year-olds are good. Their overall reading performance rose 3.9 percent from 1970 to 1980, while the overall

Table 1
Levels of Achievement of 17-Year-Olds
In the National Assessment of Educational Progress

	Percentage of Correct/Competent Responses		
	1st Survey	2nd Survey	3rd Survey
Reading[a]: all items	68.9	69.0	68.2
Literal comprehension	72.2	72.7	72.0
Inferential comprehension	64.2	63.3	62.1[3]
Reference	69.4	70.1	70.2
Writing[b]: overall	47.7	46.3	41.6
Expressive rhetoric	64.5	59.4[1]	74.8[2,3]
Persuasive rhetoric	not given	21.4	15.2[2]
Explanatory rhetoric	not given	46.5	46.7
Cohesion	80.4	78.2	86.4[2,3]
Mathematics[c]: all items	52	48[1]	
Knowledge	63	63	
Skills	55	50[1]	
Understanding	62	48[1]	
Application	33	29[1]	
Science[d]: all items	44.6	42.3[1]	39.9[2]
Biological	52.3	51.1[1]/53.3	52.2
Physical	42.9	39.3[1]/46.8	44.4[2]
Unclassified	35.6	32.1[1]/44.8	43.8

[a]Assessed in 1971, 1975, and 1980.

[b]Assessed in 1969, 1974, and 1979.

[c]Assessed in 1973 and 1978.

[d]Assessed in 1969, 1973, and 1977. In the 2nd survey, the first figure is based on items repeated from the 1st survey; the second is based on items repeated in the 3rd.

[1]Change from 1st survey to 2nd survey significant at .05 level or greater than two standard errors.

[2]Change from 2nd survey to 3rd survey significant at .05 level or greater than two standard errors.

[3]Change from 1st survey to 3rd survey significant at .05 level.

Table 2
Levels of Achievement of 13-Year-Olds
In the National Assessment of Educational Progress

	Percentage of Correct/Competent Responses		
	1st Survey	2nd Survey	3rd Survey
Reading[a]: all items	60.0	59.9	60.8
Literal comprehension	61.1	61.8	62.7[3]
Inferential comprehension	56.1	55.3	55.5
Reference	65.8	64.1[1]	66.7[2]
Writing[b]: overall	62.7	56.4[1]	54.7[3]
Expressive rhetoric	10.2	4.0[1]	6.2[3]
Persuasive rhetoric	not given	28.4	20.3[2]
Explanatory rhetoric	not given	not given	79.9
Cohesion	28.7	18.8[1]	20.5[3]
Mathematics[c]: all items	53	51[1]	
Knowledge	64	64	
Skills	51	49[1]	
Understanding	52	50	
Application	42	38[1]	
Science[d]: all items	63.3	61.4[1]	59.7[2]
Biological	60.9	59.6/61.1	62.0
Physical	59.7	57.1[1]/50.4	49.6
Unclassified	64.7	65.4/62.1	55.8[2]

[a]Assessed in 1970, 1974, and 1979.

[b]Assessed in 1969, 1973, and 1978.

[c]Assessed in 1973 and 1978.

[d]Assessed in 1969, 1972, and 1976. In the 2nd survey, the first figure is based on items repeated from the 1st survey; the second is based on items repeated in the 3rd.

[1]Change from 1st survey to 2nd survey significant at .05 level or greater than two standard errors.

[2]Change from 2nd survey to 3rd survey significant at .05 level or greater than two standard errors.

[3]Change from 1st survey to 3rd survey significant at .05 level.

performance of the 13- and 17-year-olds did not change significantly. However, the 13-year-olds did improve slightly (1.6%) in literal comprehension, while the 17-year-olds declined (−2.1%) in inferential comprehension.

Not all subgroups showed the same patterns of increase and decrease. Nine-year-olds, black students, students in the Southeast, and those from rural communities or from disadvantaged-urban communities showed the greatest gains. In the 13-year-old age group, black students showed a gain of 4.2 percent in overall performance. Thus, students from several groups narrowed the gap between their performance and the national average, although their levels were still below par.

Reading, thinking, and writing. In 1979–80 the NAEP added a new assessment that combined reading and literature and asked students not only to answer multiple-choice questions, but also to respond to open-ended questions (NAEP, 1981b). The findings from the study suggest that by age 17, students read a range of material appropriate for this age. However, they had difficulty examining the ideas in the reading. They could express their initial, often personal, reactions to the text, but they often did not explain these ideas. When explanations were given, they were superficial and did not use the passage as support; students seemed to lack strategies for increasing their understanding of reading material.

The authors (NAEP, 1981b) feel that these results reflect the current emphasis in teaching and testing. In the traditional recitation method of teaching, all students participate, but the comments of an individual student should be brief and discussion limited. While such recitation helps the class as a whole gain a conventional understanding of the passage, there is no opportunity for individuals to enrich their own interpretations. Testing of the multiple-choice or fill-in-the-blanks format also encourages short responses. The assessment showed that students could make accurate initial appraisals of passages in a multiple-choice/short answer format, but essay questions illuminated the limitations of their comprehension. When multiple-choice or short-answer formats "dominate standardized and teacher-developed tests [and] when doing well in most school contexts requires little beyond short responses, it is not surprising that students fail to develop more comprehensive thinking and analytic skills" (NAEP, 1981b, p. 2).

Writing. The NAEP assessments of writing were conducted during the 1969–1970, 1973–1974, and 1978–1979 school years (NAEP, 1980a, 1980b, 1980c). During each assessment, several writing tasks, such as narrative (Make up a story about a picture), expressive (How did you feel when you lost something or someone of importance?), persuasive (Write a speech supporting or opposing converting an old house into a recreation center for young people), descriptive (Describe something you know), and explanatory (Write a letter to order a poster calendar), were administered. The papers were evaluated for overall quality, rhetorical effectiveness, coherence, cohesion, syntactic fluency, and mechanical correctness. Students also provided information about their writing experiences and training.

Comparison of the three assessments provides a picture of writing achievement during the decade of the 70's. For 17-year-olds, rhetorical skill on narrative tasks declined between 1969 and 1974, but rose between 1974 and 1979. On a persuasive writing task, the percentage of 17-year-old students writing successful papers dropped from 21 percent to 15 percent between 1974 and 1979. About half of the 17-year-olds wrote successful papers on the explanatory writing task in 1974 and 1979. The cohesion of papers or of paragraphs in the descriptive essays increased during this decade. There was no substantial change in mechanical errors over the ten-year period, although punctuation errors, misspellings, and awkward sentences continued to cause problems for most 17-year-old students (NAEP, 1980a).

For 13-year-olds the overall quality of the descriptive essays declined between 1969 and 1973, and rhetorical skill in an expressive essay also declined over the decade. Between 1973 and 1978 the percentage of students who wrote a competent persuasive letter dropped from 28 percent to 20 percent. Only 29 percent of the papers showed good cohesion in 1969; by 1978 the percentage had dropped to 21 percent (NAEP, 1980b).

For 9-year-old students straightforward tasks caused fewer problems. About one-half of them wrote a successful letter to order material through the mail, but only one-sixth of them had letters containing good appeals for a persuasive task. Only one student in ten wrote an adequate narrative essay (NAEP, 1980c).

Comparison of the ages reveals that across the decade the expressive writing skills of 13- and 17-year-olds were stable or improving, while their persuasive and descriptive skills were declining. Most of the students at each age seemed to have some knowledge of the conventions of writing, but 10 to 25 percent have serious writing problems. Finally, neither 13- nor 17-year-olds were required to do much writing in school or receive much writing instruction. Very few of the 13-year-olds (3%) and 17-year-olds (7%) had experience with all of the techniques designed to improve writing: prewriting instruction, writing multiple drafts, written and oral feedback from teachers, and working to improve papers after they are returned.

The changes in performance of the various subgroups are slightly more positive than for all students. Black students ages 13 and 17 improved on almost all writing tasks, and 13-year-old blacks performed at the national average in rhetoric, in expressive writing, and in cohesion in descriptive writing. For the disadvantaged urban group, 17-year-olds made gains relative to the rest of their age group, but 13-year-old disadvantaged urban students stayed below the national norm or fell further behind.

Mathematics. The mathematics skills of American students were surveyed during 1972-73, 1977-78, and 1981-82 (Ahman, 1982). Mathematical achievement was examined in four cognitive-process levels: (a) mathematical knowledge included basic arithmetic facts and simple definitions; (b) mathematical skills required computation with whole numbers, fractions, decimals, and percents; (c) mathematical understanding asked for an explanation or illustration of mathematical knowledge or skill; and (d) mathematical application presented the task in the form of a word problem.

According to the 1978 results, American students had a good background in mathematical knowledge (NAEP, 1979). Most of the teenagers had no difficulty with basic addition, subtraction, multiplication, and division tasks. Around 70 percent of them knew measurement equivalents, such as number of quarts in a gallon, ounces in a pound, or feet in a yard. Knowledge of the metric system is improving, too, so that 80 percent of the 13-year-olds and 88 percent of the 17-year-olds knew that a centimeter is the most appropriate metric unit for measuring the length of a thumb.

This background in mathematical knowledge carried over into computational skills with whole numbers. More than 90 percent of the 17-year-olds could correctly add columns of two-digit numbers and subtract three-digit numbers using borrowing skills; three-quarters of them could correctly multiply three-digit numbers. Fractions, decimals, and percentages seemed to cause problems for teenagers. Fewer of them performed correct calculations with them, and they apparently did not understand the concepts. For example, only 39 percent of the 17-year-olds could correctly estimate the sum of 12/13 and 7/8. Many of the students added numerators and denominators and gave answers of 19 or 21. About one-third of the 17-year-olds did not realize that 5 percent represents 5 out of 100.

Mathematical understanding and applications are higher-order cognitive processes, and students had greater difficulty with exercises of these types. For example, given a classification/probability problem of picking a marble from a bag containing 8 red, 7 green, and 6 blue marbles, only 29 percent of the 13-year-olds and 40 percent of the 17-year-olds correctly understood that the marble picked is most likely not red. When solving word problems, one-quarter of the 13-year-olds had trouble distinguishing between relevant and extraneous information and multiplied all the numbers together. Students were able to do computational problems correctly, but were not able to solve a word problem with the same numbers. For example, 69 percent of the 13-year-olds could calculate the distance around a rectangle when it was pictured and the two dimensions given. But only 31 percent could determine the amount of fencing necessary to go around a rectangular garden when the garden was not pictured. (The same numbers were used in each problem.)

When the results of the 1973 and 1978 surveys are compared, the findings reveal that mathematical achievement declined over the five-year period. The decline was more substantial for 17-year-olds (4 percentage points) than for 13-year-olds (2 percentage points). Most of this drop can be attributed to decreases in problem solving ability. Some of the low-achieving subgroups improved their performance over the five-year period. While the average for black 13-year-olds was 21 percentage points below the national average in 1973, their average rose to 18 percentage points below the national average in 1978. The performance of 13-year-olds living in disadvantaged, urban areas also improved from 18 percentage points below the national level to 14 percentage points below.

Preliminary findings from the 1982 assessment somewhat change the dismal picture of decline (Ordovensky, 1983). The mathematical achievement of 13-year-olds rose four percentage points from 1978 to 1982, meaning that current achievement levels are two percentage points higher than in 1973. The drop in achievement skills of 17-year-olds has stopped, with performance levels being unchanged since 1978. However, the improvement was made in mathematical knowledge and skill. Students still had difficulty with problem solving ability—and they could not do simple problems in their heads; they needed pencils or calculators.

Science. Although not included in the literacy skills of reading, writing, and arithmetic, knowledge of the fundamentals of science should be considered a basic skill in a technological society. Indeed, such logic is behind the call for additional science courses for high school graduation requirements (National Commission on Excellence in Education, 1983). If science knowledge is indeed critical for a good education today, the National Assessments suggest that our educational system is failing (NAEP, 1978). Science achievement was surveyed in 1969-70, 1972-73, and 1976-77 and included both the biological and physical sciences. The surveys had three broad objectives for science education: (a) know the fundamental aspects of science; (b) apply fundamental knowledge to different problem situations; and (c) appreciate the processes, consequences and limitations of science and understand the personal and social relevance of science and technology in our society.

In biological sciences, 13-year-olds remained fairly stable across the three assessments. The performance of 17-year-olds declined between the first and the second and the second and third assessments. The achievement in the physical sciences was poorer. Both 13- and 17-year-olds declined across the three assessments with 17-year-olds showing the steepest drop.

The only good news from the science assessments is the performance of two subgroups. All ages of students from rural communities improved in science achievement from 1969 to 1977. While black students continue to perform below their white counterparts, 13-year-old black students improved in physical science achievement between 1972 and 1976.

Summary. What overall summary can be made of the three national assessments in each of the basic areas? Certainly, the achievement patterns show a general pattern of decline, especially for the 17-year-olds. The declines in math and science are especially a cause for concern as society continues to move toward greater technology. Some people suggested that math and science achievements were declining because of a new emphasis on the "whole child," with curriculums that included more humanities and fine arts. Unfortunately, achievement levels in art and music also declined in the 70's, suggesting that drops in math and science were not just trade-offs for improvements in other areas (Ahman, 1982).

However, there are some bright spots in the National Assessment surveys. First, the achievements of the 9-year-olds tended to show an increase rather than an overall decrease (Ahman, 1982). Since the decade of the seventies represented a period of increased commitment to elementary education, the results of NAEP suggest that the efforts paid off. Similar encouragement comes from the achievements of the various subgroups of students who performed below the national level. While in most cases these groups continue to score below their national peer group, they often showed gains over the three assessments while the performance of their peers declined (Ahman, 1982). This pattern was especially true for black students and those in disadvantaged urban areas. Once again the cause of these gains may be in the resources and commitment given to federally funded programs for disadvantaged youth. Thus, the gains in achievement for both 9-year-olds and low-achieving subgroups suggest that there are ways of rectifying the problems of American education.

Factors Related to Achievement

In looking for ways to improve school achievements, one approach may be to examine the factors which influence school achievement. Such factors may be found at many different levels of society from schools through peer groups and family influences to the individual variable of gender.

School factors. When considering the influence of schools on achievement, it is important to remember that children have had several years of experience in the educational system by the time they enter adolescence. This early experience with school exerts a profound influence on achievement during the junior high and high school years. Kifer (1975) has proposed that a history of academic success leads to positive personality characteristics while academic failure results in lower regard for the self and negative personality characteristics. In turn, the positive or negative personality characteristics lead to expectations for success or failure, and a pattern is established. Kifer has tested this model and found that indeed there are differences in self-esteem between successful and unsuccessful students in grades four through seven. The differences were the result of decreasing self-esteem among the unsuccessful students, since the self-esteem of the successful students was stable.

Most children enter school with an expectation of success (Entwisle & Hayduk, 1978), so their success or failure in the early school years is an important influence on achievement during adolescence. Several research studies have supported this idea. Zarb (1981) found that academic self-concept was the best predictor of GPA and suggested that a positive self-concept could be built through success. Similarly, Lloyd's (1978) results showed that ultimate success in school, that is, high school graduation, was predictable from course marks in reading, arithmetic, writing, spelling, and language in third grade.

Once students enter adolescence, the teachers within the schools can also influence student achievement. For students with high ability from affluent backgrounds, the best teachers seem to be ones with a fast pace, who challenge the students and who will not accept work that does not meet their high standards. On the other hand, the achievement of low-ability students from lower social classes is fostered by teachers who make the subject matter interesting, who adopt a friendly and accepting attitude, and, most of all, who offer encouragement rather than criticism to the students (Brophy, 1979).

When considering the school as a whole, it is not the school with the most money that has the most positive effect on student achievement. The important factor seems to be the value that is placed on school achievement by the students themselves (Coleman, 1961). If a letter in athletics is the symbol of status in a school, then students will devote their time and efforts toward athletic participation and neglect their studies. On the other hand, if scholastic achievement is valued, then students will strive for academic rewards. Part of the value placed on academics is the result of the emphasis placed on education by the parents.

Family influences. A generalization that can be drawn from the NAEP data is that students whose parents did not complete high school tend to achieve below the national average while the students whose parents had some post-secondary education performed about the national average (Ahman, 1982; NAEP, no date). Parental education also influences aspirations for further education, with parental advice being the major influence in the decision to attend college (Stahmann, Hanson & Whitlessey, 1973). Achievement is also influenced by identification with parents. For high achievers, this identification is with the parent of the same sex (Shaw & White, 1965); that is, high-achieving boys tended to identify more with their fathers than their mothers while high achieving girls identified with their mothers. Obviously, this relationship does not hold for every adolescent. There are students who succeed in spite of parental emphasis on other values, and there are students who fail when their parents expect (and perhaps pressure) them to succeed (Atwater, 1983).

Other familial variables also influence achievement. Morrow and Wilson (1961) found that underachieving boys came from families where there was a great deal of parental restriction and severe discipline. The parents often disagreed and expected either too much or too little from their sons. On the other hand, the families of high achieving boys were characterized by positive family morale, parental approval and trust, parental approval of peer activities, and the son's acceptance of parental standards. Similarly, Bledsoe and Wiggins (1974) found that students whose parents "understood" them had more favorable self-concepts of academic adequacy and higher desired academic aspirations, and expected to reach a higher academic level.

The influence of peers. Contrary to popular stereotypes, parental influence continues throughout adolescence and is greater than peer influence on long-term goals (see Guerney & Arthur, Chapter 4, this volume). The influence of peers is found more in day-to-day activities (Kandel & Lesser, 1969). The influence of peers on academic achievement is positive when these activities are school-related activities such as student government, athletics, or school clubs. Moderate levels of participation in extracurricular activities and some popularity with peers is associated with better school performance (Rigsby & McDill, 1972; Weatherford & Horrocks, 1967). However, if the activities with peers are more oriented toward the youth culture (outside of school), then the influence of peers on academic achievement may be negative. Grinder (1969) found that boys who started dating earlier, dated more frequently, and were out several nights per week showed poorer performance in school and had a higher level of absenteeism.

Part of the reason for the contradictory influence of peers on school achievement may lie in the different value systems of the schools (and school-related activities) and the youth culture. The school mirrors the society with an emphasis on conformity, the presence of middle-class values, and hierarchical structure modeled on the workplace (Bowles & Gintis, 1976). In contrast, the youth culture emphasizes the developmental tasks of adolescence, for example, independence, and fosters estrangement from, and questioning of, authority.

One classic study by James Coleman (1961) shows these discrepant values. Coleman asked high school students for which of three things they would like to be remembered. For boys the choices were brilliant student, athletic star, or most popular. For girls the choices were brilliant student, leader in activities, or most popular. Coleman also asked their parents how they would like their children to be remembered. Most boys wanted to be remembered as an athletic star, while girls wanted to be remembered as a leader in activities. The parents of both boys and girls, however, wanted their children to be remembered for their scholarship, not for their activities or athletics. Coleman proposed one reason for this discrepancy. Parents probably do value scholarship over "popularity or athletic skill. On the other hand, they may also want whatever is best for their children and may interpret this as being whatever would make the children happy in their own setting or successful in their own subculture. . . . Thus, the parents are unwittingly reinforcing values that are generated in the adolescent subculture" (McKinney, Fitzgerald, & Strommen, 1982, p. 194).

Gender differences. Many studies over a number of years have detailed gender-related differences in academic achievement. During the elementary years, these differences are in favor of girls, apparently because their conformity complies with the schools' expectations (Lee & Gropper, 1974). Thus, the higher grades of girls may reveal little about their competency and more about their socialization (Guttentag & Bray, 1976; Lightfoot, 1976). As socialization continues, girls tend to become underachievers. One study showed that girls who declined in intelligence were less active, less interested in controlling others, and more interested in social activities—all typically feminine traits—than the girls who did not decline (Campbell & McKain, 1975). This underachievement is often seen in mathematics where girls stop taking math when it is no longer required (Sells, 1978; Tavris & Offir, 1977). Even mathematically able girls prefer social activities and will turn down the opportunity to take accelerated math classes (Fox, 1975).

Perhaps the ultimate result of sex-role socialization is the fear of success in school that may occur more often in girls (Horner, 1972). Romer (1975) found that boys outgrow fear of success during high school while girls continue to have increasing levels during high school. Interaction with boys in an academic setting seems to accentuate girls' fear of success. Winchel, Fenner, and Shaver (1974) found that girls in co-educational high schools show greater fear of success than students at an all-girls school. Perhaps the contradiction between the expectations for competition and assertiveness toward males in classes and the stereotypes of passivity and "dumb blondes" in social interaction heightens the girls' awareness of the dilemma, and the result is greater anxiety over the possibility of alienating males because of academic success.

Transmitting Society's Values Through Socialization

Gender-related differences illustrate the overlap in the literacy and socializing functions of schools. Is fear of success an influence on academic achievement in the basic skill areas? Definitely, but it also represents the socializing aspect of the educational system, where the prevailing values (and gender-role stereotypes) of society are transmitted. To examine this function of the schools, this section will discuss three examples of socialization. First, we will look at the behavior problems found in today's high school. Next, the status and reasons for dropping out of high school will be explored. Finally, the aspirations and success of high school students will be discussed.

Discipline and Behavior in Schools

When examining the function of socializing children into the behavior acceptable in society, one source of information lies in the behavior of students in the schools. A recent government survey of high schools documented the existence of behavior problems in schools and the factors associated with them (Diprete, 1981). When asked to identify the behavior problems in schools, administrators estimated that there were fewer problems than the students identified, but students and administrators identified the same categories of problems. Physical conflicts were a minor problem in schools, and there were few instances of rape or possession of weapons. Criminal behavior was usually limited to robbery, theft, or vandalism. The major problems were with class-cutting, use of drugs and alcohol, and absenteeism, and in these areas administrators seemed to underestimate the scope of the problems when compared to student accounts.

Several factors were related to misbehavior in school. Students from middle class or blue collar families were better behaved than the children of the rich or the poor. Hispanic students misbehaved more than black or white students. White sophomores behaved better than black sophomores, but by the senior year, blacks were the better behaved. Students in Kentucky, Tennessee, Mississippi, and Alabama were the best behaved, while the West seemed to produce the most misbehavior in high school students.

Parents influenced the students' behavior in school. When parents were involved and monitoring their children's work, misbehavior declined. The attitudes and expectations of parents were also related to school behavior. If the parents had not found school useful for themselves, they were less likely to emphasize respect for it. Thus, the highest levels of misbehavior were found in children whose fathers had a college degree but earned less than $7,000 and those whose fathers did not graduate from high school but were financially very well-off.

Grades were related to misbehavior, but the direction of the cause-effect relationship was not clear. Poor grades may cause misbehavior, or, alternatively, misbehavior may cause poor grades. The relationship was probably not due to grades at all, but the influence of other factors. For example, students who were in the college preparatory curriculum behaved better, and schools that assigned more homework had fewer discipline problems.

Some of the discipline problems of high schools may actually represent student attempts to resolve the developmental tasks of adolescence. Jessor and Jessor (1975) have suggested that a pattern of eroding conventionality is found in those students who are striving for adult status. Since the developmental tasks of adolescence include achieving a unique identity and independence from authority figures, some of the discipline problems may represent a developmental progression toward adulthood. In one study, Everhart (1982) found that teachers and students viewed "goofing off" differently. Teachers perceived goofing off as random and purposeless, disruptive to their teaching, and counter-productive to the goals of education. Students, however, saw goofing off as an indicator of their place in the social structure of the school. The students with few friends rarely goofed off, while those in a particular group showed the most goofing off behavior. The goofing off was often an attempt to bug the teacher and thereby achieve some independence by defying authority. The author's conclusion is that goofing off encouraged group consensus and identification with that group—a necessary part of achieving identity. This study shows that the two functions of teaching basic skills and transmitting society's values through socialization are sometimes at cross-purposes. The goal of helping adolescents achieve independence may interfere with the goal of teaching reading, writing, and arithmetic.

High School Dropouts

Compared to three generations ago, when most students left school after eighth grade, the percentage of high school graduates today is large. For the past generation the percentage of all 18-year-olds who are high school graduates has remained steady at about 75 percent (Dearman & Plisko, 1980). Minnesota boasts the highest percentage of graduates at 85.6 percent, while Mississippi and Florida graduate only 60 percent of their 18-year-olds. The 25 percent who do not graduate represent more than one million teenagers each year who do not have what is considered the minimum educational credential. Most of these will not even take the high school equivalency examination (Dearman & Plisko, 1979).

There are a number of factors behind dropping out of high school, and some of them are related to the educational experience of dropouts. Cervantes (1965a) found that the following school-related problems were characteristic of dropouts:

1. Their course marks were below average, and their performance was two years below grade level in reading and arithmetic. Their overall performance was considered to be below their potential.
2. They have failed a grade; failure of grade one, two, eight, and nine was most common.
3. They displayed behavior problems which required discipline. They also show a pattern of irregular attendance and frequent tardiness.
4. They had changed schools frequently and had a feeling of not belonging. They did not participate in extracurricular activities.

Such a pattern of school problems begins early. Lloyd (1978) found that two-thirds of the future dropouts could be accurately classified on the basis of third grade data.

Not all dropouts show lower academic ability; many are capable of work at the average or above average level (Sewell, Palmo, & Manni, 1981). Dropouts with above average intelligence may find the requirements of high school stifling. These adolescents are not college-bound. They are uncertain about their vocational future and feel that school is not preparing them for "real" life (French & Carden, 1968). Interestingly, those dropouts with higher IQ's tend to drop out later, while those with lower IQ's form the bulk of the early dropouts (Voss, Wendling, & Elliott, 1966).

The isolation that many dropouts experience may be the result of poor social skill adjustment. Cervantes (1965a) found that school dropouts have friends who are not school-oriented; the friends are often much older or younger than the dropouts. The parents of the dropouts do not approve of these friends, perhaps because the peer group is rejecting not only the educational system, but all systems of authority (Stinchcombe, 1964).

Family relationships have also been implicated as a cause of dropping out. Children whose parents have lower levels of education and occupation are more likely to drop out, as are those from lower social classes. However, even when the socioeconomic status of the families is controlled, the dynamics of the dropouts' families are different from those who graduate. Cervantes (1965a; 1965b) concluded that the graduates' families were more characterized by primary relationships than the families of the dropouts. Specifically, four factors seem to be lacking in the homes of the dropouts. First, the members of the family do not accept one another as total persons; roles or status determine interactions rather than individuality. Second, there is a lack of communication within the family which results in inconsistent parental affection and discipline. Third, there is no personal satisfaction in each other's company. These family members do not share recreation or other pleasurable experiences. Finally, there is a low level of happiness in the home. These family dynamics are also related to the development of self-esteem, and it may be that self-esteem is the crucial factor for staying in school and for academic achievement.

The self-esteem of high school dropouts is lower than that of high school graduates (Cervantes, 1965a; Sewell, 1981), and there are other personality differences as well. According to research findings, male dropouts were lower in vocational maturity and more interested in skilled trades and labor (Combs & Cooley, 1968; Sewell, 1981). When compared to high school graduates of both sexes who did not go to college, the dropouts were more anxious and apathetic, while the graduates were more sociable, cultured, self-confident, and mature (Combs & Cooley, 1968). Dropouts tended to be resentful of authority, their ability to delay gratification was weak, and they suffered from feelings of inferiority (Cervantes, 1965a; Stinchcombe, 1964). All of this adds up to a personality profile inconsistent with many of the middle-class values of the school system, and this discrepancy may contribute to the decision to leave school.

What are the consequences of dropping out of high school? Certainly, the likelihood is that the dropout will have lower lifetime earnings than the high school graduate. They are also likely to have higher unemployment rates as more and more employers require a high school diploma. Finally, lower educational attainment is related to poverty, divorce, and early death (Lerner & Hultsch, 1983).

Aspirations and Success

Coleman's (1961) results suggest that the aspirations of most high school students were not for academic achievement, but for other definitions of success. These alternate paths to success show the socializing function of the schools. The findings of a recent study elaborate on Coleman's findings. Grabe (1981) found that athletic involvement was more characteristic of younger high school students, while older students were more concerned about academics. Even with the push for equality in sports, boys still participated more in sports while fine arts, clubs, and academics occupied the girls' time.

School size also affects socialization. While large schools usually have more courses, more services, and more extracurricular activities, student participation is greater in small schools. One study found that in a large high school 794 juniors were exposed to 189 activity settings which led to 3.5 performances per student. In a small school the 23 juniors were exposed to 48 activity settings which led to 8.6 performances per student (Gump, 1966). This greater involvement led to more cooperation with peers and a feeling of being important, which led to greater improvement in students' abilities. The negative side of small schools was that students who did not participate suffered great feelings of alienation. The great demand for participation in small schools led to loss of self-esteem in students who did not participate (Grabe, 1981). Because of the correlation between self-esteem and achievement, such socialization may also lead to lower academic achievement and lower future aspirations (Giffore & Parsons, 1983).

Aspirations can affect the long-term success of high school students by influencing what courses they take. Originally, the curriculum of the school was geared toward college preparation since about two-thirds of all high school graduates went on to college. Now, when the percentage of college-bound students has dropped to about 50 percent, different curricula are offered in most high schools (Atwater, 1982). The purpose of the *college preparatory curriculum* is to prepare students for success in college. This curriculum has become more specialized, with many high schools offering college-level courses and specialized courses in the social, physical, and biological sciences (Dearman & Plisko, 1979). Approximately one out of seven college-bound seniors has taken an honors course in math; the same percentage holds for English courses. The *vocational curriculum* prepares students to enter the labor force, often with on-the-job-training in fields such as automobile mechanics. These programs have been enhanced by the establishment of vocational/technical schools, some of which offer post-secondary education (Dearman & Plisko, 1979). The *general curriculum* is the "other" category for those students not preparing for college or a job. It attracts students with lower levels of academic ability and motivation and has the greatest proportion of dropouts (Combs & Cooley, 1968).

Nontraditional courses have proliferated in recent years, with two-thirds of the high schools offering consumer education and more than one-third offering career education and family living/sex education. The impact of these courses can be mixed. A seminar in career development can positively change the locus of control and enhance the career maturity of students (Gardner, Beatty & Bigelow, 1981). Similarly, a course in family life and sex education can enhance parent-adolescent communication (Blanco, Busch-Rossnagel & Martin, 1983). However, the growth of these courses has been blamed for the decline in student enrollment in traditional courses, a decline which is probably associated with the poor academic performance of today's high school students (National Commission on Excellence in Education, 1983). In effect, we need to examine the idea of residual functions for schools to see if the schools can in fact continue to do a good job of education when they are being asked to fulfill so many other needs.

For the students who select the college preparatory curriculum, the path to success is getting easier. As the number of outstanding high school students diminishes, colleges are recruiting them with a zeal once reserved for athletes. The number of colleges awarding scholarships solely on academic performance rather than financial need has more than doubled since 1976 (Zigli, 1983). And in spite of the high cost of college today, a college degree does pay off. According to the U.S. Census (O'Dell, 1983), the lifetime earnings of a male high school graduate will be about $861 thousand, while the earnings of a male college graduate will range between $1.19 million and $2.75 million. In spite of the inequality in lifetime pay between the sexes, college pays off for women, too; the female college graduate will earn between $520 thousand and $1.12 million compared to $381 thousand for the female high school graduate.

However, financial earnings are not the only measure of success. In adult community involvement, the socialization of the school is still an important factor. Hanks and Eckland (1978) found that greater involvement in the adult community (including voting behavior) at age 30 could be predicted from greater participation in extracurricular activities during high school. So there does seem to be life after high school.

Summary

The problems of declining academic achievement and school dropouts highlight the complexity of the problems facing schools today. Because schools are being asked to perform several roles in addition to teaching, they are in danger of not doing any of the jobs well. Because all of the roles are interdependent, the solutions to a problem in one area will affect every aspect of the school's functioning—and the results may not be positive. Thus, if we implement the suggestions aimed at raising the academic achievement in high schools, the result may be an increase in school dropouts. If we cater the schools' programs to the potential dropout, the result will probably be a continued decline in academic achievement. Instead of tackling problems as isolated occurrences, what may be needed is a re-evaluation of the goals of secondary education. Should our goal be an academically based high school diploma for everyone? Does that mean that in another generation the goal will be a bachelor's degree for all? Or do we seriously examine what individual differences there are in children and adolescents and design the educational programs to foster their development? Such an avenue means carefully considering and avoiding the pitfalls of "separate but equal" educational opportunities. John Dewey gave Americans such a challenge early in this century; it is time we met the challenge.

SOURCES OF HELP

The status of adolescents in today's educational system suggests that there are many problems in need of solution. Two such problems will be explored here along with possible solutions: How can we stem the tide of declining achievement in today's adolescents? And, how can dropping out of school be prevented? In proposing solutions to these problems, the third function of schools—changing society—is examined.

Combating Declining Achievement

With the release of several major reports on the condition of American education, there seems to be a consensus that the system is in need of reform. The search is on for solutions to the problems of declining achievements; two of the avenues that are being explored concern curricular reform and competency testing.

Curricular Reform

When the curricula of American high schools are examined, many people feel that the requirements for high school graduation are too lax. Most schools require only one year of science and of mathematics for the high school diploma (Dearman & Plisko, 1980). The National Commission on Excellence in Education (1983) would change the requirement to three years each of mathematics and science, as well as adding one-half year of computer science as a requirement. These courses would be in addition to four years of English and three years of social studies.

However, the number of years of study in a general area may not be the only problem. During the last several years, alternative ways of meeting the high school graduation requirements have increased (Dearman & Plisko, 1979). This means that working the lights in a school play or taking photographs for the yearbook may be counted toward the English requirement. Off-campus work, independent study, and correspondence courses are other alternate means to high school credit.

The plethora of alternate courses may mask the fact that some of our high schools do not offer the basic courses. In the science sphere, 5 percent of the high schools do not offer Biology I; 11 percent do not have Chemistry I; and Physics I is not available in 22 percent. Three percent of the high schools do not offer any algebra, and 3 percent do not offer any geometry. Only 25 percent of the schools offer computer courses (Dearman & Plisko, 1980). Thus, increasing the requirements for high school graduation will require new course offerings at a time when math and science teachers are scarce.

In addition to the number and type of courses, the content of the courses must be examined as well. Only one-third of today's adolescents think that the level of difficulty is about right in high school; 45 percent think that the work is "not hard enough" (Dearman & Plisko, 1979). One route to increasing the difficulty is to assign more homework and set up homework hotlines or tutoring programs to help the students complete the assignments. Another approach would be to recognize that ours is no longer an agricultural society that needs its children on the farms in the summers. Increasing the school year to eleven months (220 days) would be similar to the practices in most other industrialized countries. More homework and longer time in school have both been proposed as solutions by the National Commission on Excellence in Education (1983).

A third route to increasing the difficulty of courses is to examine the cognitive tasks that are required by the teaching methods used. In examining students' perceptions of course content, Walberg, House, and Steele (1973) found that the emphasis on lower-level cognitive processes, such as knowing the right answer and memorizing, increases in high school. The higher level cognitive processes, such as problem solving, putting methods and ideas to use, and discovering many solutions, have their

308 *Experiencing Adolescents*

greatest emphasis in *sixth grade*. Students and teachers also feel that athletics and maintaining order and quiet receive greater attention than academic achievement or transmission of cultural values but that the emphasis should be reversed (Johnston & Bachman, 1976). Unfortunately, the trend seems to be for alternatives to academic achievement and for student activities and the use of specialists, for example, psychologists, to be the preferred route for socialization (Dearman & Plisko, 1979).

In order to tap some of the higher mental processes and really get at the heart of the problems in achievement, a re-examination of the teaching methods used may be necessary. For example, the NAEP found that students' understanding of what they read may be limited by teaching and testing methods. Nix (1982) has proposed an alternate model for the teaching of reading comprehension which is termed LINKS. The model consists of developing an explicit system of links that are required for comprehension and can be taught step-by-step. Although the system was developed for reading instruction in elementary school, it has been used with a difficult college-level text being used by high school seniors. The results of the testing with LINKS indicate that it can foster comprehension in different areas of study and at different grade levels (Nix, in press).

Competency Testing

Another possible solution to the decline in achievement is the use of competency testing. Such testing has been proposed, in part, because of the increase in "social promotions." This is the term given to promotions of children even though they are not doing work at grade level, so that they will still be with their peers and not be stigmatized by repeating a grade. The evidence for the increase in social promotions comes from the changes in school enrollment. In 1950, 23.8 percent of the youth aged twelve to seventeen years were enrolled below modal grade, i.e. the grade in which most children of an age are enrolled. By 1976, the percentage of youth enrolled below modal grade had dropped to 9.3 percent (Dearman & Plisko, 1979).

Because such social promotions mean that a student can graduate from high school without the knowledge and skills assumed to be a part of secondary education, many people are calling for some type of competency testing. In fact 38 percent of the states have already instituted some form of minimum competency testing. Eighteen states use the tests to set standards for high school graduation, while three states use the testing to determine eligibility for grade promotion (Dearman & Plisko, 1980).

The public seems ready to support minimum competency testing. According to a Gallup poll on the public schools, 68 percent of American adults feel that children should not be promoted if they cannot pass an examination with minimal standards. However, only 14 percent feel the child should be required to repeat the entire year's work; most (81%) feel that special remedial classes are the key (Dearman & Plisko, 1979). Even half of the high school seniors support the requirement of passing some standardized national test, but one-third of the seniors do not support such an idea (Dearman & Plisko, 1980).

Preventing School Dropouts

Just as the factors associated with leaving school come from many different sources, there are many different approaches to the problems of dropout prevention. The best results are probably achieved when prevention programs begin early and involve the family. Cervantes' (1965a) suggestions of almost two decades ago are still valid today. He suggested that families should be asked early for a commitment to education. This commitment asks that parents do four things; (a) they require and monitor school attendance; (b) they require that their children study every day; (c) they visit the school; and (d) they review their children's report cards. Such early involvement on the part of the parents would not only help to prevent school dropouts, but would also foster academic achievement.

Once the students are into high school, many people ask what the schools can do to prevent dropouts. Unfortunately, what is often suggested is less classroom pressure for the potential dropouts (Abram & Cobb, 1978), and that goes against the current recommendations aimed at combating the decline in achievement.

While the suggestions of longer school years, more homework, and stiffer high school graduation requirements may be appropriate for the students in the academic curriculum, they may have a disastrous effect on the students in the vocational and general curricula. In these curricula we need what Cervantes suggested in 1965: different goals for the different curricula. To make these goals worthy, yet practical, there needs to be a recognition that many jobs which exist today did not exist a generation or even half a generation ago, and such changes will continue in the future. Schools need to be aware of, and tooled for, changes in the labor market, and this will require cooperation with labor and business (Cervantes, 1965a). Labor might consider examining apprenticeship programs and giving credit for vocational training. Business can open up to increased on-site visits to show students, teachers, and administrators the value of a high school diploma and the characteristics and skills which they expect to be fostered by high school.

With such suggestions it is important to realize that the problem of declining achievement deals with the first function of schools, while the problem of school dropouts may best be addressed by emphasizing the socializing function of schools. One program which was successful in using the socializing function of school to prevent dropouts was Project Intercept (Maurer, 1982). Project Intercept worked with potential dropouts, their parents, and their teachers. The potential dropouts went through a counseling course to develop their interpersonal skills and increase their self-knowledge. Teachers and students were taught about alternative academic skills. Parents were taught appropriate and effective discipline for use with adolescents. The results of Project Intercept was a decrease in the dropout rate, in the suspension rate, and in the absence rate.

Note on Sources of Help

Many levels of government are responsible for some part of the educational process in this country, so trying to find some help with a specific problem can be frustrating. For the problems discussed here, declining academic achievement and school dropouts, the responsibility for programs usually rests with the school district or state board of education. Contacting the district office in particular is the logical first step when looking for help with a school-related problem.

ANNOTATED REFERENCES

The Condition of Education. Washington, DC: U.S. Department of Education, National Center for Educational Statistics.

This series of annual reports compiles information about events in American education from a variety of sources and presents them in an easy-to-understand format. The statistics are limited to percentages, and the diagrams (graphs and pie charts) make them easy to interpret.

Herndon, E. B. *Your Child and Testing.* Washington, DC: U.S. Department of Education, National Institute of Education. (Available from Consumer Information Center, Pueblo, Colorado.)

With the attention given to declines in achievement test scores and minimum competency testing, this booklet should be required reading for all those involved in education. It outlines different types of tests, how they are used, and what the scores mean. Also included are sample items from tests and additional sources of information.

National Assessment of Educational Progress. Denver: Education Commission of the States.

The NAEP results and interpretations are available in several forms. An overview of the results and their implications in each survey area is presented in a leaflet. These contain concise summaries of the major points of the results in a manner that can be readily understood by those without a background in education or statistics. The leaflets for the learning areas in this paper are: "Three National Assessments of Reading: Changes in Performance, 1970–1980." No. 11-R-35; "Reading, Thinking, and Writing." No. 11-L-35; "Writing Achievement, 1969–1979." No. 10-W-35; "Mathematical Achievement." No. 09-M-35; "Three National Assessments of Science." No. 08-S-35. Leaflets are also available about art, career and occupational development, citizenship/social studies, music, energy, health, functional literacy, speaking and listening, consumer skills, Hispanic student achievement, and homework and TV.

For those who want to examine the findings in greater depth, there are research reports providing statistical analysis of the survey data and a discussion of their meaning for educators. (See Reference List for the research reports related to the areas in this chapter.) The NAEP also publishes a description of the objectives for each learning area and releases a portion of the exercises used in each survey. Contact NAEP (at the Education Commission of the States, 1860 Lincoln Street, Suite 700 PL, Denver, CO 80295) for a complete publication list.

Norris, C. A., Finley, M. J., and Wheeler, L. Utilizing community-based information to develop program recommendations and intervention materials for potential dropouts. (ERIC Document Reproduction Service No. ED 208 500 1980.)

These authors have developed a series of four brochures which describe the characteristics of dropouts and options for them in Phoenix. Based on data collected in the Phoenix area, they represent a means to get information to dropouts both before and after they leave school. The first pamphlet, "Check it out," is designed to facilitate counseling with dropouts before they leave school. "Dropouts who return" is the second in the series and gives reasons why dropouts return to school and the characteristics of those who return. "If I leave school, where can I get job training" reminds students that vocational and trade schools charge tuition and surveys the entrance requirements of these schools. The last brochure, "If I leave school, will I be able to find a job?" details the requirements for employment in major types of business and industry. The brochures are available through the Phoenix Union High School District, 2526 West Osborn Road, Phoenix, AZ 85017.

REFERENCES

Abram, M. J., & Cobb, R. A. *A Survey of Students Who Did not Graduate and Their Parents concerning Motivation for Leaving School and Students' Educational Plans for the Future.* Bowling Green, KY: PREPS Research Project, 1978. (ERIC Document Reproduction Service No. ED 206566.)

Ahman, J. S. "Educational Achievement Trends: A Mix of Gains and Losses." *Iowa Educational Research and Evaluation Association Bulletin,* October 1978, no. 2, 16–23.

Atwater, E. *Adolescence.* Englewood Cliffs, NJ: Prentice-Hall, 1983.

Bakan, D. "Adolescence in America: From Idea to Social Fact." *Daedalus,* 1971, *100* (no. 4), 979–995.

Blanco, K. A., Busch-Rossnagel, N. A., & Martin, D. H. "The Effect of Family Living Classes on Parent Adolescent Communication." Unpublished manuscript, 1983.

Bledsoe, J. C., & Wiggins, R. G. "Self-concepts and Academic Aspirations of 'Understood' and 'Misunderstood' Boys and Girls in Ninth Grade." *Psychological Reports*, 1974, *35*, 57–58.

Bowles, S., & Gintis, H. *Schooling in Capitalist America: Educational Reform and the Contradictions of Economic Life.* New York: McGraw-Hill, 1976.

Brophy, J. "Teacher Behavior and Its Effects." *Journal of Educational Psychology*, 1979, *71*, 733–750.

Busch-Rossnagel, N. A., & Vance, A. K. "The Impact of Schools on Social and Emotional Development." In B. Wolman (Ed.), *Handbook of Developmental Psychology.* Englewood Cliffs, NJ: Prentice-Hall, 1982.

Campbell, B. P., & McKain, A. E. "Intellectual Decline and Adolescent Women." Paper presented at American Education Research Association, Washington, DC, 1975.

Cervantes, L. F. *The Dropout: Causes and Cures.* Ann Arbor: University of Michigan Press, 1965a.

Cervantes, L. F. "Family Background, Primary Relationships, and the High School Dropout." *Journal of Marriage and the Family*, 1965b, *27*, 218–223.

Coleman, J. C. *The Adolescent Society.* New York: The Free Press, 1961.

Combs, J., & Cooley, W. W. "Dropouts in High School and After School." *American Educational Research Journal*, 1968, *5*, 343–363.

Dearman, N. B., & Plisko, V. W. (Eds.). *The Condition of Education: 1979 Edition.* Washington, DC: U.S. Department of Health, Education, and Welfare, National Center for Educational Statistics, 1979.

Dearman, N. B., & Plisko, V. W. (Eds.). *The Condition of Education: 1980 Edition.* Washington, DC: U.S. Department of Education, National Center for Educational Statistics, 1980.

DiPrete, T. A. *Discipline, Order and Student Behavior in American High Schools.* Washington, DC: U.S. Department of Education, 1981. (ERIC Document Reproduction Service No. ED 1.115:63.)

Entwisle, D. R., & Hayduk, L. A. *Too Great Expectations: The Academic Outlook of Young Children.* Baltimore: Johns Hopkins University Press, 1978.

Everhart, R. B. "The Nature of 'Goofing Off' among Junior High School Adolescents." *Adolescence*, 1982, *17*, 177–187.

Fox, L. J. *Career Interests and Mathematical Acceleration for Girls.* Paper presented at the meeting of the American Psychological Association, Chicago, 1975.

French, J. L., & Carden, B. W. "Characteristics of High Mental Ability Dropouts." *Vocational Guidance Quarterly*, 1968, *16*, 162–168.

Gardner, D. C., Beatty, G. J., & Bigelow, E. A. "Locus of Control and Career Maturity." *Adolescence*, 1981, *16*, 557–561.

Giffore, R. J., & Parsons, M. A. "Student Characteristics and Achievement in Desegregated Schools." *Urban Education*, 1983, *17*, 431–438.

Grabe, M. "School Size and Importance of School Activities." *Adolescence*, 1981, *16*, 21–31.

Greene, B. I. *Preventing Student Dropouts*. Englewood Cliffs, NJ: Prentice-Hall, 1966.

Grinder, R. E. "Distinctiveness and Thrust in the American Youth Culture." *Journal of Social Issues*, 1969, *25*, 7–18.

Gump, P. V. *Big Schools, Small Schools*. Moravia, NY: Chronical Guidance Publications, 1966.

Guttentag, M., & Bray, H. *Undoing Sex Stereotypes*. New York: McGraw-Hill, 1976.

Hanks, M., & Eckland, B. K. "Adult Voluntary Association and Adolescent Socialization." *Sociological Quarterly*, 1978, *19*, 481–490.

Herndon, E. B. *Your Child and Testing*. Washington, DC: U.S. Department of Education, National Institute of Education.

Horner, M. S. "Toward an Understanding of Achievement Related Conflicts in Women." *Journal of Social Issues*, 1972, *28*, 157–175.

Jessor, R., & Jessor, S. L. "Adolescent Development and the Onset of Drinking." *Journal of Studies on Alcohol*, 1975, *36*, 27–51.

Johnston, L. D., & Bachman, J. G. "Educational Institutions." In J. F. Adams (Ed.), *Understanding Adolescence* (3rd ed.). Boston: Allyn and Bacon, 1976.

Kandel, D. B., & Lesser, G. S. "Parental and Peer Influences on Educational Plans of Adolescents." *American Sociological Review*, 1969, *34*, 213–223.

Kifer, E. "Relationships between Academic Achievement and Personality Characteristics: A Quasi-longitudinal Study." *American Educational Research Journal*, 1975, *12*, 191–210.

Lee, P. C., & Gropper, N. B. "Sex-role Culture and Educational Practice." *Harvard Educational Review*, 1974, *42* (no. 3), 369–410.

Lerner, R. M., & Hultsch, D. F. *Human Development*. New York: McGraw-Hill, 1983.

Lightfoot, S. L. "Socialization and Education of Young Black Girls in School." *Teachers College Record*, 1976, *78*, 239–262.

Lloyd, D. M. "Prediction of School Failure from 3rd Grade Data." *Educational and Psychological Measurement*, 1978, *38*, 1193–2000.

Maurer, R. E. "Dropout Prevention: An Intervention Model for Today's High Schools." *Phi Delta Kappan*, 1982, *63*, 470–471.

McKinney, J. P., Fitzgerald, H. E., & Strommen, E. A. *Developmental Psychology. The Adolescent and Young Adult*. Homewood, IL: Dorsey Press, 1982.

Morrow, W. R., & Wilson, R. C. "Family Relations of Bright, High-achieving and Under-achieving High School Boys." *Child Development*, 1961, *32*, 501–510.

National Assessment of Educational Progress. *Three National Assessments of Science: Changes in Academic Achievement, 1969–79*. Denver: Education Commission of the States, 1978.

National Assessment of Educational Progress. *Changes in Mathematical Achievement, 1973–78*. Denver: Education Commission of the States, 1979.

National Assessment of Educational Progress. *Writing Achievement, 1969–79, Vol. I: 17-year-olds*. Denver: Education Commission of the States, 1980a.

National Assessment of Educational Progress. *Writing Achievement, 1969–79, Vol. II: 13-year-olds*. Denver: Education Commission of the States, 1980b.

National Assessment of Educational Progress. *Writing Achievement, 1969–79, Vol. III: 9-year-olds*. Denver: Education Commission of the States, 1980c.

National Assessment of Educational Progress. *Three National Assessments of Reading: Changes in Performance, 1979–80*. Denver: Education Commission of the States, 1981a.

National Assessment of Educational Progress. *Reading, Thinking, and Writing*. Denver: Education Commission of the States, 1981b.

National Center for Educational Statistics. *The American High School: A Statistical Overview*. Washington, DC: U.S. Department of Education, 1980.

National Commission on Educational Excellence. *A Nation at Risk*. Washington, DC: U. S. Department of Education, 1983.

Nix, D. "LINKS—A Teaching Approach to Developmental Progress in Children's Reading Comprehension and Meta-comprehension." In J. Fine and R. O. Freedle (Eds.), *New Direction in Discourse Processing*. Norwood, NJ: Erlbaum, 1982.

Nix, D. "Notes the Efficacy of Questioning." In A. C. Graesser and J. Black (Eds.), *The Psychology of Questions*. Hillsdale, NJ: Erlbaum, in press.

Norris, C. A., Finley, M. J., & Wheeler, L. "Utilizing Community-based Information to Develop Program Recommendations and Intervention Materials for Potential Dropouts." Paper presented at American Education Research Association, Los Angeles, 1980. (ERIC Document Reproduction Service No. ED 208 500.)

O'Dell, K. "Lifetime Pay for USA Men Is Twice Women's." *USA Today*, March 14, 1983.

Ordovensky, P. "USA Student Math Skills Adding Up." *USA Today*, May 5, 1983.

Rigsby, L. C., & McDill, E. L. "Adolescent Peer Influence Processes: Conceptual and Measurement." *Social Science Research*, 1972, *37*, 189–207.

Romer, N. "The Motive to Avoid Success and Its Effects on Performance in School Age Males and Females." *Developmental Psychology*, 1975, *11*, 689–699.

Sawhill, J. C. "Why Our Public Schools Don't Work." *Reader's Digest*, 1979, *115* (no. 69), 7–12.

Sells, L. "Math: A Critical Filter." *The Science Teacher*, 1978, *45*, 28–29.

Sewell, T. E., Palmo, A. J., & Manni, J. L. "High School Dropout: Psychological, Academic and Vocational Factors." *Urban Education*, 1981, *16*, 65–76.

Shaw, M. E., & White, D. L. "The Relationship between Child-parent Identification and Academic Underachievement." *Journal of Clinical Psychology*, 1965, *21*, 10–13.

Smith, B. O., & Orlosky, D. E. *Socialization and Schooling (Basics of Reform)*. Bloomington, IN: Phi Delta Kappa, 1975.

Stahmann, R. F., Hanson, G. R., & Whittlesey, R. R. "Parent and Student Perceptions of Influence on College Choice." *National Association of College Admissions Counselors Journal*, 1973, *16* (2), 21–22.

Stinchcombe, A. L. *Rebellion in a High School*. Chicago: Quadrangle Books, 1964.

Tavris, C., & Offir, C. *The Longest War*. New York: Harcourt, Brace and Jovanovich, 1977.

Voss, H. L., Wendling, A., and Elliott, D. "Some Types of High School Dropouts." *Journal of Educational Research*, 1966, *59*, 363–368.

Walberg, J. H., House, E. R., & Steele, J. M. "Grade Level, Cognition, and Affect: A Cross-section of Classroom Perceptions." *Journal of Educational Psychology*, 1973, *64*, 142–146.

Weatherford, R. R., and Horrocks, J. E. "Peer Acceptance and Under- and Over-Achievement in School." *Journal of Psychology*, 1967, *66*, 215–220.

Winchel, R., Fenner, D., & Shaver, D. "Impact of Coeducation on 'Fear of Success' Imagery Expressed by Male and Female High School Students." *Journal of Educational Psychology*, 1974, *66*, 726–730.

Zarb, J. M. "Nonacademic Predictors of Successful Academic Achievement in a Normal Adolescent Sample." *Adolescence*, 1981, *16*, 891–900.

Zigli, B. "Top Scholars Are Wooed Like Athletes." *USA Today*, April 28, 1983.

10. ADOLESCENCE AND CAREERS
Fred W. Vondracek and John E. Schulenberg

More than 20 years ago the popular television program "Candid Camera" presented a most enjoyable and entertaining film clip showing a traffic police officer directing city traffic. The film was set to music and showed the officer directing traffic as if conducting a Beethoven symphony, and obviously enjoying every minute of the action. Contrast this scene with the person who sees his/her work as a necessary evil, who watches the clock, and who apparently cannot wait to get away from the drudgery of work and to something enjoyable. The first example represents a situation where vocational development has led to a desirable outcome: satisfying and, therefore, successful adjustment to the world of work. The second example represents a failure in vocational development: more specifically, it represents a failure to produce a good match between the characteristics and needs of the individual, on the one hand, and the characteristics and features of his work role, on the other.

In this chapter we will examine how adolescents arrive at the divergent outcomes depicted above. A key feature of our discussion will focus on the understanding that people do not end up in one occupation or another because of a single good or bad decision, but that occupational or career choices represent no more than important crossroads in the vocational and career developmental course of the person—a course which begins in early childhood and continues, for many individuals, into old age.

Although it will thus be apparent that vocational and career development is a life-span phenomenon, we focus on adolescence in this chapter. This is not an inappropriate focus, for it is during adolescence and young adulthood that the process of vocational development occupies a central role in the individual's efforts to acquire a distinct self-definition, or identity. Furthermore, we shall see that a person's vocational identity influences not only his/her *self*-concept, but also that it significantly affects other aspects of the person's life and how other people see him or her. For instance, the answer to the common question "What do you do for a living?" usually tells us a great deal about the social status, the educational attainment, the financial position, and the life-style of the individual. Often, individuals choose their marital partners from within their own training or occupational settings: it is no accident that physicians frequently marry nurses and college students marry other college students. It is also increasingly recognized that some careers are generally more stressful than others and that they may significantly influence the health status and even life-expectancy of individuals.

Nonetheless, we would be overstating our case if we claimed that career development is a life or death matter. It would be hard to deny, however, that career development is a centrally important process in human development. In the following sections we will examine what is known about this process; we will examine different viewpoints and findings on the unfolding of vocational development, its leading to important occupational choices and decisions, and its resulting, if all goes well, in satisfying, rewarding, and challenging long-term careers.

One important determinant of the vocational and career decisions made by adolescents is their own, first-hand experience with the world of work. Consequently, in a subsequent section we will examine the role that adolescents play in the nation's workforce. Some of the issues to be covered include a look at how a variety of work experiences influence adolescents' attitudes toward work and how they may influence the vocational developmental process itself. Finally, we will comment on the impact of adolescents' exclusion from the workforce (i.e., extremely high youth unemployment) on their vocational and personal development.

ISSUES AND FINDINGS

In the most recent edition of his classic *Theories of Career Development*, Osipow (1983) lists half-a-dozen major theories of career development, as well as several less developed viewpoints put forth regarding various aspects of career development. Upon closer examination, one striking feature of all the theories presented is that, in spite of major differences, they have a number of features in common: (1) They agree that some important predispositions, preferences, interests, or personality features relevant to the career development process begin to take shape in childhood, long before the most important career choices are made; thus, they could all claim to incorporate some developmental features; (2) all agree that the context within which career development occurs exerts an important influence over it, with the family context recognized as the most important context for career development; and (3) all theories agree that it is the interactions between the person's individual characteristics (personality, interests, preferences, abilities, etc.) and the person's context (family, significant others, school, social and economic factors, etc.) which determine the ultimate course of an individual's career.

The relative importance assigned to each of these features by the various theories varies a great deal. Thus, sociologists (i.e., Blau & Duncan, 1967; Mortimer, 1974) tend to emphasize the role of social status, prestige, and family background as determinants of occupational choice. Psychologists, on the other hand, tend to focus on the individual characteristics of the person, such as personality (Holland, 1973; Roe, 1956) and self-concept (Super, 1953), in explaining the processes of career development.

More recently, Vondracek and his colleagues (Vondracek & Lerner, 1982; Vondracek, Lerner, & Schulenberg, 1983) have suggested a three-pronged emphasis in the study of career development. Specifically, they have urged the adoption of a conceptual framework which, at the same time, can take account of the *developmental*, the *contextual*, and the *relational* features of career development. To take a developmental perspective simply means that the person is studied not just as he/she appears currently, but in light of his/her past history and future aspirations: past, present, and future are seen as important in shaping the behaviors we can observe today. To take a contextual perspective means that particular attention is paid to the person's circumstances, and to take a relational perspective means that the developmental and contextual views are combined in order to arrive at the best possible explanations and descriptions of the vocational and career development process. It should be noted, however, that none of these perspectives are novel; as we have observed above, they appear to some extent in most theories. What *is* novel is the effort to simultaneously and (relatively) equally attend to all three. In the following section we will briefly review these emphases with particular reference to applicable contemporary theories of career development.

The Developmental Emphasis in Career Development

The most salient element of the developmental emphasis is the view that vocational and career decisions represent merely the culmination of a developmental process that reaches back into early childhood. Furthermore, the developmental perspective views career development as part and parcel of the broad stream of developmental processes which occur simultaneously in individuals as they pass through the landmarks of human development. Hence, concepts, explanatory principles, and methods useful in the study of human development are particularly useful in the study of career development. (See, for example, Beilen, 1955; Harris, 1972; Vondracek, Lerner, & Schulenberg, 1983.)

There are several theories which have pursued a developmental approach to career development. The first of these to be published was the theory of occupational choice formulated by Ginzberg, Ginsburg, Axelrad, and Herma (1951). Ginzberg et al. developed their theory on the basis of a series of interviews with adolescents. Most importantly, they systematically countered the prevailing notion that occupational choice is a one-decision event, usually taking place after the completion of mandatory education. They proposed, instead, that the individual engages in a series of choices which are irreversible in the sense that they impact on subsequent choices. In other words, choices made in childhood represent important antecedents of choices made in early adolescence, and choices made in adolescence serve as important antecedents of choices made in early adulthood. Finally, Ginzberg et al. further underscored the developmental nature of their theory by proposing three specific stages of occupational choice: the *Fantasy Period*, covering childhood up to about age 11; the *Tentative Period*, occurring between ages 11 and 18; and the *Realistic Period*, taking place between ages 18 and 24. During these periods, which are broken down into more specific stages, the individual is seen as moving from a play orientation to a work orientation, from an overriding emphasis on career interests to a concern with abilities and with the values that can be actualized by pursuing one career as opposed to another. Finally, during the Realistic Period, choices are narrowed and a crystallization and corresponding commitment to a final choice takes place.

Although Ginzberg (1972) later expanded his theory to reflect the growing awareness of career development as a life-span process, it was Donald Super (1953) who formulated what could well be called a life-span developmental theory of career development. Drawing from formulations of early life-span views of development (Bühler, 1933), he articulated his self-concept theory of vocational development (Super, 1953, 1957, 1963). Central to Super's theory is the notion that vocational development must be viewed within the framework of the entire life-span of the person. Remarkably, Super embraced this perspective long before it was rediscovered in developmental psychology (Charles, 1970), and he reinforced his commitment to a life-span perspective in more recent papers (Super, 1980, 1981).

Super postulated that along with the development of self-concept the individual develops a vocational concept of self: as the developing person formulates a view of him/herself separate from others, he/she also begins to formulate a self-view based on emerging ideas about what he/she favors or prefers to do—a vocation. Super proposed distinct stages in the development of this vocational self-concept: crystallization (ages 14-18), specification (ages 18-21), implementation (ages 21-24), and stabilization (ages 25-35). Obviously, the crystallization stage is most relevant in adolescent vocational development. It is during this period that adolescents develop their conceptualizations of, and preferences for, certain occupations, make relevant educational and training decisions, and engage in testing reality to determine whether, for example, their abilities and opportunities allow the pursuit of their favored occupation.

A review of the major formulations of a developmental emphasis in the field of career development should not conclude without a brief note on the theory elaborated by Tiedeman and his colleagues (Tiedeman, 1961; Tiedeman & O'Hara, 1963; Dudley & Tiedeman, 1977). Tiedeman's theory heavily emphasizes cognitive functioning in attempting to show that vocational development consists of the individual's making a succession of decisions in the Period of Anticipation and later in the Period of Implementation and Adjustment. During the Anticipation period, the individual progresses from merely exploring interests, capabilities, and opportunities to actually choosing a particular vocational role. During the Implementation and Adjustment period, the individual assumes a (career) position and adjusts to his/her context, including colleagues and superiors. Ultimately, successful vocational adjustment is achieved when an ever-changing balance, a "dynamic equilibrium," exists between the goals and vocational role behavior of the individual on the one hand and the interpersonal vocational context (colleagues and superiors), on the other.

The Contextual Emphasis in Career Development

The contextual emphasis focuses on the fact that individuals develop within specific social, cultural, and physical environments or contexts, and that these contexts materially affect individual development. Moreover, this perspective holds that the changing characteristics of the environment itself must be recognized. Most commonly this concern, especially with the social context (i.e., family, friends, society, culture, etc.), has been pursued by sociologists who, in turn, have rarely concerned themselves with the changing individual whose study is so important to developmentalists. Osipow (1983) has referred to this general approach as a "situational" approach, noting that it is "based on the notion that elements beyond the individual's control exert a major influence on the course of life, including educational and vocational decisions" (p. 225). What we call our *contextual* emphasis differs from Osipow's conception of a *situational* emphasis in that it (1) incorporates not only the social environment but also the cultural and physical environments, (2) tries to account for the ever-changing characteristics of the environment, and (3) views the individual as not just a passive subject on which the environment has an impact, but rather as being involved in a mutual relationship with the environment, capable of producing change in the environment as well.

Most of the relevant research pertaining to career development has, nevertheless, been of the "situational" type, concerned primarily with the identification of social environment variables that influence occupational choice. Thus, a substantial focus of research has been on determining the impact of social class on adolescents' academic and vocational aspirations and achievement (Blau & Duncan, 1967; Haller & Portes, 1973; Havighurst, 1964; Hollingshead, 1949). Hollingshead showed how, as social status increases, adolescents' vocational aspirations increase; Havighurst described the complex mechanisms, such as differential values and reward systems, operative in different social classes that produce the type of results reported by Hollingshead. Blau and Duncan, in a large-scale research project, looked at a multitude of social factors, including father's occupational level, family income, "intactness" of family (i.e., whether parents continue to be married and continue to provide a home for their under-age children), and others, and concluded that perhaps the most important feature of social factors is their capacity to open up or restrict career opportunities as well as opportunities for early education, training, and experience. Haller and Portes underscored the importance of this finding by concluding that the major impact of family socio-economic status on the individual's educational and occupational attainment "is due to its impact on the types of attainment-related personal influences that the person receives in his adolescence" (p. 64).

Although concerned with social status, Haller and Portes (1973) called special attention to the interpersonal environment as a key mediator between the individual and other environmental and cultural factors. Not surprisingly, Woelfel (1972) and Haller and Woelfel (1972) confirmed that, among significant others who influenced the individual's conception of him/herself in relation to occupational and educational roles, members of the nuclear family (e.g., mother, father) were most important, with peers rated a close second. Other researchers (e.g., Grandy & Stahmann, 1974; Mortimer, 1974) have confirmed the common notion that some degree of occupational inheritance exists for both males and females: children often follow in their parents' footsteps and "inherit" their occupation.

The ever-changing character of the social context and, therefore, the ever-changing impact it has on career development may be illustrated by the example of maternal employment. For a variety of reasons maternal employment has risen steadily so that 51 percent of women aged 18 to 34 were in the labor force in 1978 (U.S. Bureau of the Census, 1979). Huston-Stein and Higgins-Trenk (1978) have clearly documented a significant impact on the vocational aspirations and expectations of female adolescents who had "working mothers": specifically, such females had less stereotyped ideas regarding females' roles, and they were more willing to consider nontraditional roles, including those traditionally held by men. Thus, it is important to realize that recognition of the ever-changing nature of the context is necessary to adequately represent contextual features that impact on career development.

The Relational Emphasis in Career Development

The relational emphasis in career development focuses neither predominantly on the individual's characteristics nor predominantly on contextual features. Instead, it focuses on the interaction between individual and contextual factors. Thus, the ultimate concern centers on how well the developing person adapts to ever-changing environmental factors as they relate to a career; if the adaptation is optimal the individual obtains satisfaction and fulfillment from the career and is able to give high measures of productivity, creativity, and energy in return.

A number of career development theories have a strong relational emphasis. The most popular of these is the theory of vocational choice formulated by Holland (1973). His basic proposition is that there are six occupational or work environments which are matched by six corresponding modal personality orientations. If an individual has a dominant personality orientation, it will seek expression through the choice of the corresponding occupational environment. If the personality orientation is not well crystallized or if two orientations are equally strong, then the individual's choice of occupational environment is not nearly as clear-cut and indecision or vascillation may occur.

Holland's six personality orientations and occupational environments are described as follows (1973, pp. 14–18): The *Realistic* type possesses mechanical and athletic ability, lacks social skills, tends to value material things and power and gravitates toward occupations such as engineering, farming, and most blue collar jobs. The *Investigative* type is characterized by scientific ability, favors intellectual, analytical, methodological activities, and tends to choose careers in the natural sciences, mathematics, and computers. The *Artistic* type values aesthetic attributes, prefers to be expressive, intuitive, and nonconforming, and tends to select occupations such as artist, musician, or interior decorator. The *Social* type is socially competent and has the ability to teach, thus choosing teaching, ministry, or social service occupations. The *Enterprising* type possesses leadership and speaking skills, tends to be assertive, self-confident, sociable and popular, and tends to select business, law or public relations careers. Finally, the *Conventional* type is inclined to be orderly, conscientious, conforming, and inflexible, being attracted by clerical occupations, bookkeeping, and secretarial roles.

While this representation captures the essence of Holland's approach, it must be pointed out that it also represents an oversimplification (a limitation that also affects the necessarily brief presentation of other theories in this chapter). In his theory, Holland accounts for the differential abilities of individuals as well as differing self-evaluations which are viewed as a function of the individual's life history, social status, health, and level of education. Contrary to Holland's claims, however, his theory is not developmental in the sense of contributing to our understanding of how individuals acquire their personal styles and hence their preferences for certain occupational environments (Holland & Gottfredson, 1981). Finally, it should be observed that Holland's theory, in part because of its simplicity, has stimulated a great deal of research, as well as useful applications for counselors.

Another theory which focuses on the relation between individual and environmental characteristics is the Social Learning Theory of Career Decision Making, first formulated by Krumboltz and his associates (Krumboltz, 1979; Mitchell, Jones, & Krumboltz,

1979). By applying the principles of social learning described by Bandura (1969), Krumboltz has attempted to describe how individual characteristics, such as intellectual and motor abilities, race, and physical characteristics, interact with environmental (contextual) characteristics, features, and events, such as economic and social conditions, and job and training opportunities. Learning histories of individuals are considered important, along with the above inherited and contextual variables, in determining how people develop career interests, how they approach career-relevant situations, and how they make career decisions. More specifically, Krumboltz and his associates take the position that if an individual has been positively reinforced or rewarded for behaviors functional in the career development process, he/she will be more likely to exhibit those behaviors than would be the case if negative reinforcement or punishment had been administered following those same responses.

Needless to say, none of the above conceptualizations of career development has a monopoly on the "truth." The fact is that they, and others not represented here, all make a contribution to our understanding of how and why people end up being clerks or soldiers or doctors or laborers. The research evidence is accumulating that a developmental, contextual, *and* relational perspective is needed to account for the full complexity of the phenomena involved.

Optimizing Career Development in Adolescence

How children's conception of work changes over time provides some interesting insights into the background for the adolescent's more active pursuit of a career. Goldstein and Oldham (1979) reported that ". . . children's work and learning experiences (1) typically start in early childhood on a *very* small scale, (2) are extremely widespread, and (3) apparently are subject to age-related increments" (p. 169). Thus, contact with the world of work occurs earlier than is often assumed and results in increasing realism concerning the world of work as early as the elementary years. Moreover, by the time children are in fifth grade, they have relatively sophisticated comprehension of the world of occupations, and they feel positive about work as a means of making money. Goldstein and Oldham (1979) implore educators to not wait until junior high school or beyond to attempt to influence children's career development; they suggest the consideration of some form of institutionalized work program to ensure positive early work experiences for children.

This, then, represents the basis for our *first recommendation* to enhance career development in adolescence: *enable individuals to have a succession of positive work experiences from the time they enter elementary school all the way through adolescence.* In the next section we will discuss in more detail the current reality of adolescents in the labor force.

Our *second recommendation* to optimize career development in adolescence is to *encourage and foster career exploration through the provision of extensive, timely, and relevant career information.* The best decisions are well informed decisions. As we discussed earlier, children do acquire surprisingly sophisticated information about occupations at an early age. Nevertheless, the need to make increasingly finer differentiations about careers, as well as the ever-changing character of careers, requires adolescents to be up-to-date and well informed if they want to make career decisions that are optimal. In the last section of this chapter, we will provide references about some of the most useful sources of information about careers.

A pertinent question, however, has to do with the identification of factors that govern career exploration behaviors in adolescence. Super and his colleagues (Super, Starishevsky, Matlin, & Jordaan, 1963) described career exploratory behavior and pointed out its importance, particularly between the ages of 15–24 years. Jordaan's (1963) theoretical analysis of the concept of exploration in career development has resulted in the definition of a variety of dimensions of adolescent exploratory behavior. Career exploration, according to Jordaan, includes seeking information about careers and trying out career-relevant behaviors. He stressed, in particular, that the societal context for exploratory behavior, as well as personal characteristics, could exert significant influences upon how well career exploratory behaviors served their purpose. Thus, the person's willingness to consider information contradicting previously held beliefs is an important sign of that person's openness to new ideas and, hence, that person's personal and career growth. Society, on the other hand, influences career exploration behaviors via institutions and expectations which either inhibit or facilitate career exploration behavior in adolescents. Clearly, parents and teachers can have a most beneficial effect on the career development of adolescents by encouraging and facilitating career exploration behaviors.

The *third* and final *recommendation* regarding optimal career development in adolescence pertains to the decision-making process. In short, the recommendation is that *parents and teachers should facilitate circumstances which lead to good decisions without, however, unduly influencing either the timing or the direction of those decisions.* In line with our developmental perspective, we maintain that individuals mature at different rates; consistent with our contextual perspective we observe that individuals differ in both the timing and the content of their career-relevant experiences. Thus, as part of our commitment to a relational emphasis, we stress that as a result of the joint action of the person's developmental course as well as the person's experience and situational circumstances, important career decisions will be made when the person is ready—not sooner and not later. Simply, "facilitate but do not push" is the message.

Thus far, we have focused on employment as a future prospect for adolescents. In the following section, we will take a look at adolescents who currently work and the effects of their work upon them.

ADOLESCENTS AT WORK

It was just one of those ordinary spring-time Saturday afternoons and I was sitting on the front steps staring into space. I was fifteen and day-dreaming had become one of my favorite occupations. My father came out, and I quickly pretended that I wasn't day-dreaming, but rather studying the complexities of our front yard. But he caught on: "Day-dreaming again? Get a job—then you can start to make those dreams come true." I was struck by the sincerity in his voice and words. Usually, the old "get a job" discussion/argument seemed to be aimed at my laziness and inability to take care

of myself. But this was different—maybe he was right. I
could probably get a job at the car wash and maybe save up
enough money for a car or something. Just as I was about to
semi-agree with him, my mother yelled out the window:
"Leave the kid alone. Let him day-dream—he'll be working
all his life! Besides, he has enough work in school. You want
him to go to college, don't you?"

Should an adolescent work? If yes, then where can he or she
work? How much and what type of work can the adolescent do?
What are the costs and benefits of working? Of not working?
These questions are the concern of many parents, educators,
policy makers, researchers, theorists, and, of course, adolescents
themselves. The questions are important ones. With the high
unemployment rate, especially among the nation's youth (aged
16–24), it is important to consider the impact of this problem on
the individual and society. Though it has gone largely unnoticed,
there has been a steady rise of part-time employment of in-school
adolescents over the past few decades. This pattern and its effects
on adolescents and society also merit consideration.

The centrality of work in modern society cannot be denied. As
Wilensky (1964) stated, "in rich countries of the modern era,
work, whether it is becoming more or less central as a source of
personal identity and social solidarity, still remains a necessary
condition for drawing the individual into the mainstream of
social life" (p. 134). Clearly, in our society, working is deemed
"good" and not-working is "bad." However, when the individuals
in question are adolescents, the work issue becomes less clear. On
the one hand, working during adolescence is considered good. It
is generally assumed that for the adolescent, who is caught somewhere between adulthood and childhood roles depending on the
given situation, a job can move him or her a few steps closer to
adulthood. With a job, the adolescent can demonstrate responsibility, achieve some autonomy, and gain "real world" experience.
At the societal level, adolescent work provides a method of trans-
ferring appropriate work attitudes and competencies to tomorrow's adult workers, as well as a source of relatively cheap, usually
unskilled, and part-time labor. On the other hand, there are the
possible negative effects of working during adolescence. Specifically, what adolescents do, as well as what they learn, in the work-

place may not always be desirable. Furthermore as several authors have pointed out (e.g., Hamilton & Crouter, 1980; Steinberg, Greenberger, Garduque, Ruggiero, & Vaux, 1982), working during adolescence may take away from other experiences that are significant for the adolescent.

In this section we will explore issues of adolescent employment and youth unemployment. First, to set the stage, we will briefly discuss the historical progression and current context of adolescent employment. Secondly, the various types of adolescent employment, as well as the effects of such employment on adolescents, will be discussed. Then, the issues of youth unemployment will be considered. Finally, we will discuss the decision to work or not to work. From the start, it should be noted that the topic of work during adolescence has not received the research and theoretical attention that other topics of adolescence have received; hence, conclusions in this area remain tentative, and some issues can at this time be addressed only in terms of general trends. It is difficult, for example, to determine the effects of employment or unemployment on the various aspects of a specific adolescent's life. Nevertheless, we hope that an examination of the general trends will provide the reader with some insight into what may happen when the adolescent does or does not work.

Adolescent Employment in Perspective

Consider how you would view a 15-year-old adolescent who worked full-time and did not attend school. Most likely, this adolescent would be viewed negatively in today's society. However, up until the early part of this century, such an adolescent would have been viewed quite positively. In fact, it would have been unusual for a 15-year-old to be attending school and not working.

Several related factors contributed to the occurrence of child and youth labor in the past. First, it was simply expected— children worked as soon as they were able, and labor was a large part of the socialization process. Secondly, it was usually necessary for children and youths to work. The services they provided or the money they earned was often essential to their family's economic survival. In addition, work usually served to prepare them for their future occupation. It was quite common for children to follow in their parents' occupation, hence by working with their parents, they received "on the job training" (Greenleaf, 1979). Apprenticeships also served to train youths for their chosen vocations, and boys would often start apprenticeship training as early as twelve years of age (Kett, 1977). However, it should be noted that the "in-training" quality of youth employment began to diminish as capitalism arose and as the industrial revolution of the mid-1800's swept the country. During this time, the nation's youths filled the need for cheap, unskilled labor in the factories, and they became viewed as bona fide workers (Greenleaf, 1977).

Another contributing factor to child and adolescent labor was that formal education was optional and largely unnecessary for most occupations. In fact, until the end of the nineteenth century, when less than 10% of the nation's 14–17-year-olds were enrolled in school (U.S. Office of Education, 1973), extended schooling that interfered with work experience was often considered a detriment to future occupational success (Kaestle & Vinovskis, 1980). Finally, there were more than a sufficient number of employment opportunities for children and youths. This was especially true during the industrial revolution. In short, children and youths of the past worked to the exclusion of school because it was expected of them, because it was often economically necessary, because it was usually beneficial to their future occupational success, and because there were ample opportunities available.

Toward the end of the nineteenth century, the youth employment situation began to undergo major changes. A primary cause was the slow but steady rise of secondary education—the high school. For a variety of reasons, the high school was gaining acceptance. High school enrollment doubled each decade between 1870 and 1910 (Pounds & Bryner, 1973), and by 1930, 51% of the nation's 14–17-year-olds were in school (U.S. Office of Education, 1973). In effect, secondary education was releasing youths from employment. Laws to keep youths in school and limit their involvement with the workplace were vigorously enacted (even though they were not always as vigorously enforced) (Kaestle & Vinovskis, 1980). As the business sector began to support the educational system by offering college graduates greater occupa-

tional opportunities (Tyack, 1967), it became increasingly beneficial to complete school. Academic credentials were gaining a
certain pragmatic value. Another major factor that served to move
youth out of the workplace was the recognition of adolescence as
a distinct stage in life. Around the turn of the century, a host of
psychologists, social reformers, educators, and youth workers focused their attention on adolescence, and from their work adolescents became viewed as passive, vulnerable, and troubled (Kett,
1977). In other words, adolescents were now considered to be
different from adults, and not ready for adulthood roles and
responsibilities—including work.

The Great Depression of the 1930's, as well as improved industrial technology and automation, served to further diminish
the role of the adolescent in the nation's full-time labor force
(Havighurst & Neugarten, 1975). The Great Depression left the
majority of working adolescents jobless, and they were encouraged
to stay in school. As the depression subsided, adolescents did not
move back into the labor force. Automation decreased the need for
unskilled and semi-skilled labor, and hence the need for youth
workers. Meanwhile, technological advancements increased the
number of jobs requiring high school and college degrees, thus
increasing the incentive for adolescents to remain in school and
graduate. This pattern—school instead of work—received additional fuel from the affluent times following World War II—
simply, most adolescents no longer *had* to work full time.

Hence, the cultural expectations, economic necessities, long-
term benefits, and even the accessibility of full-time employment
for adolescents had been effectively diminished. In the course of
about fifty years, the adolescents' "place" was transformed from
the workplace to the school. Rarely were school and work combined. For example, in 1940, when 73% of the 14–17-year-olds were
in school (U.S. Office of Education, 1973), only 5% of the 16–17-
year-old males, and less than 2% of the same aged females combined school and work (U.S. Bureau of the Census, 1940).

Between 1940 and today, the situation has changed drastically.
As we have seen, the nation's youth moved from working exclusively to attending school exclusively. Since 1940, there has been a
rising trend for adolescents to combine school and part-time
work. For example, between 1950 and 1970 the percentage of

16–21-year-old *in-school* workers rose from 26.6% to 38.9% for males, and from 17.4% to 28.8% for females (U.S. Bureau of the Census, 1973). The most dramatic increase during this period occurred for white females, with the percentage of those 16 and 17-year-old in-school workers almost doubling. During the 1970's this rising trend continued. Between 1975 and 1979, the percentage of *16–24* year olds who combined school and work rose from 38.3% to 41.8% for males and from 36.9% to 41.9% for females (Young, 1976, 1980). During the same period, the percentage of 16–19-year-olds combining school and work rose from 33.9% to 38.2%. As can be seen, the employment rate of the in-school females matches that of males in 1979. However, it should be noted that there was a slight downward trend for employment of in-school youth, especially those aged 16–17, starting in 1978 and continuing into the 1980's (Young, 1982). Nonetheless, there were over 4.7 million (approximately 42% of the population) 16 to 19-year-old students who were employed in 1981 (Young, 1982).

When viewing work among in-school adolescents, it is important to realize that the above employment figures may not clearly depict the employment situation. As Steinberg and Greenberger (1980) state, "the proportion of high school students who have any paid work experience before graduating is, naturally, much greater, since many teenagers move in and out of the labor market frequently" (p. 160). Steinberg et al. (1982) estimate that almost 80% of the in-school adolescents will have had formal work experience by the time they graduate from high school.

Given this high rate of part-time employment of in-school adolescents, it is useful to consider a few of the factors that contributed to and currently maintain the high rate of adolescent part-time employment. First, there is that old "working is good" cultural assumption that we mentioned before. Specifically, it is held by many that a little "real" employment experience will help the adolescent in his or her transition into the full-time labor force. A second and related factor concerns the upsurge of interest in youth employment issues starting in the 1960's and continuing through the 1970's. This interest took many forms, most significantly government legislation and educational practices. During the Johnson and Carter administrations, such acts as the 1964 Economic Opportunity Act, the Comprehensive Employment and Training Act of 1973 (CETA), and the Youth Employment and Demonstration Act of 1977 (YEDPA) were passed. These acts provided billions of dollars for the development of various youth employment programs (e.g., Job Corp, the Summer Program for Economically Disadvantaged Youth [SPEDY], Youth Incentive Entitlement Pilot Projects [YIEPP]) (Sherraden, 1980). For the most part, these programs were aimed at improving the future employment prospects of disadvantaged youths by providing jobs, training, and sometimes educational incentives and job placement. In terms of educational practices, the 1970's witnessed a strong drive toward the integration of the school and the workplace. Various government panels (e.g., Panel on Youth, 1974; Work-Education Consortium, 1978) stressed the virtues of work for young people and recommended that efforts be made to combine education and work experience. Parenthetically, as Hamilton and Crouter (1980) noted, the conclusions drawn by the various government panels about the efficacy of adolescent employment were not based on hard evidence. In any event, the career education movement gained momentum during the 1970's, and programs aimed at bringing students and the workplace together were instituted.

Another factor that has contributed to the increasing rate of adolescent part-time employment has been the rise of the service sector of the economy (i.e., the distribution of goods and services as opposed to the production of goods). According to Ginzberg (1979), "almost the entire growth in post-World War II employment has been in the service sector" (p. 14). Much of this growth has occurred in the retail trade and service industries (e.g., restaurants, clothing stores), where employment is characterized by part-time work, low wages, and few benefits (Ginzberg, 1977). As Steinberg and Greenberger (1980) suggest, such businesses are fertile grounds for in-school, parent-supported adolescents looking for jobs.

Thus far, in discussing possible reasons for the high rate of part-time employment among in-school adolescents, we have pointed toward cultural assumptions, institutional (government and educational) support, and conducive economic conditions. These reasons represent broad societal factors that can directly influence the adolescent's decision to work; however, since it is the individual adolescent who is working, we must not lose sight of his or her reason(s) for working, be it money, experience, "something to do," or even enjoyment. We address adolescents' motivations to work in the next section.

Given the high part-time employment rate of in-school adolescents, as well as the fact that the times and conditions seem so conducive for such employment, one might reasonably wonder what the current uproar about the massive youth unemployment problem is all about. It is essential to recognize that part-time employment of in-school adolescents and youth unemployment constitute two different issues and usually two different populations. The youth unemployment issue generally refers to out-of-school youths aged 16–24 seeking full-time employment. Part-time employment is not sufficient for this population. Since they are likely to be supporting themselves, they cannot survive on part-time work characterized by short hours, low wages, and few fringe benefits. Ironically, as the adolescent part-time employment rate has sharply increased in recent decades, so has the youth unemployment rate. From 1969 to 1975, the unemployment rate for 16–24-year-olds rose from 10% to 15%. While the rate dropped to 10.8% in 1978 (Young, 1979), it rose to almost 14% in 1980 (U.S. Bureau of the Census, 1981) and almost 15% in 1981 (Young, 1982). As we shall discuss in a later section, youth unemployment is an acute problem for 16–19-year-olds, minorities, and high school drop-outs.

Adolescents Who Work

Adolescents work in a variety of settings, ranging from family-owned businesses to fast-food restaurants, from community volunteer programs to construction businesses. Also, length of employment and the number of hours worked per week vary widely. In addition, adolescents work for a variety of reasons. Some may work for the money, for spending or for saving purposes. Others work to gain "groundwork" experience in a field they find attractive, and others may work simply because they are bored or done with school and are ready to move on to "bigger and better things." With these points in mind, there is little reason to believe that all adolescents are similarly affected by work. How working influences an adolescent depends, to a large extent, on where, how much, and why he or she works. Below, we will take a look at the characteristics of those adolescents who work, the type of work they do, and the effects of working upon them.

In the spring of 1980, Lewin-Epstein (1981) conducted a nationwide survey of 58,728 high school sophomores and seniors. The focus of this study was on youth employment during high school. Due to the manner in which the students were chosen to participate (i.e., stratified probability sampling procedure), it is possible to generalize the findings from this study to the national population of high school sophomores and seniors.

Before reporting some of the specific findings of the study, it may be useful to distinguish between the labor force participation, employment/unemployment, and non-employment rates. The labor force participation rate refers to the percentage of those working or actively seeking work. The employment and unemployment rates refer respectively to the percentage of those in the labor force that are working and of those who are seeking but cannot find work. The non-employment rate denotes the percentage of those neither working nor seeking work. In this study, employment status was defined as work-related activity the week prior to the survey (e.g., those categorized as employed worked sometime during the previous week). It is important to note that Lewin-Epstein discussed the employment percentages of the entire group (i.e., both those participating and not participating in the labor force)—the employment/population ratio, rather than just the percentages of those who were in the labor force and working.

Almost 52% of the students were employed, with roughly 54% of the males, 50% of the females, 62% of the seniors, and 42% of the sophomores being employed. Table 1 illustrates the labor force participation, employment population, and unemployment rates of students according to grade, race, and sex. As can be seen in Table 1, seniors had higher labor force participation and employment/population rates and lower unemployment rates than sophomores. This would be expected since status and responsibility come with age and experience, specifically in a socio-cultural, legal, and individual sense. Also, as Lewin-Epstein indicates, seniors have a greater chance of being involved in work-study programs.

As Table 1 also shows, employment/population rates varied widely according to race (with the White students having the highest, Hispanic students having the second highest, and Black students having the lowest employment population rates). However, the labor force participation rates did not vary to such a large degree. In other words, while similar proportions of White, Hispanic and Black students were looking for jobs, the White students tended to have more success in finding a job. This racial gap represents one of the most burning problems among the employment issues. Whether the cause lies in discriminatory practices, discouragement, or lack of opportunities, the fact re-

Table 1
Labor Force Participation, Employment/Population and Unemployment Rates of High School Sophomores and Seniors According to Race and Sex

	Sophomores			Seniors		
	Labor Force Partici. Rate	Employ-ment/ Popul. Rate	Unemploy-ment Rate	Labor Force Partici. Rate	Employ-ment/ Popul. Rate	Unemploy-ment Rate
Total	58.6%	42.1%	28.1%	76.2%	63.2%	17.1%
Males	62.0	44.3	28.6	78.3	65.5	16.3
Females	55.3	40.0	27.5	74.3	61.1	17.8
Blacks	53.8	28.5	47.1	70.3	48.7	30.7
Males	58.6	33.1	43.5	74.0	53.7	27.4
Females	49.4	24.5	50.4	67.4	44.8	33.5
Hispanics	56.6	35.5	37.3	75.1	59.8	20.4
Males	64.9	43.4	33.1	78.7	63.5	19.3
Females	48.3	27.8	42.4	71.5	56.1	21.5
White*	59.0	44.4	24.8	76.7	65.2	15.0
Males	61.4	45.1	26.6	78.4	67.0	14.6
Females	56.7	33.7	23.0	75.3	63.7	15.4

*Includes White, non-Black, and non-Hispanic students. From *Youth Employment During High School*, N. Lewin-Epstein, Washington, D.C.: National Center for Education Statistics, 1981.

mains that it is a problem. As Lewin-Epstein (1981) stated: "the lack of work experience associated with lower employment ratios among Blacks is blamed for their greater difficulties in transition to adulthood" (p. 21). We will discuss the high rate of unemployment among minorities in a later section.

Finally, as Table 1 shows, females had lower labor force participation and employment/population rates than males across grade level and race. However, the gender differences in labor force participation rates are less in the senior than in the sophomore years. This would suggest that females tend to not enter the labor force as early as the male students (Lewin-Epstein, 1981).

Just as adult employment rates vary according to place of residence, so do adolescent employment/population rates. For example, Lewin-Epstein found that among the sophomore students, the employment/population rate in the Northeastern region was 49.1% compared to 32.0% in the East South Central region (Kentucky, Tennessee, Alabama, and Mississippi). Employment/population rates also varied according to the type of community in which the adolescents lived, specifically, urban, suburban, or rural residence. In both the sophomore and senior grade levels, employment/population rates are highest in the suburbs and lowest in the urban areas. In terms of unemployment, Black students residing in the urban areas have the highest unemployment rates (51.6% in the sophomore year and 33.7% in the senior year).

The chances of an adolescent's being in the labor force or being employed also vary according to certain characteristics of his or her family. For the most part, Lewin-Epstein found that labor force participation and employment/population rates were somewhat *higher* when the family's income is higher. Both rates tend to be highest in the family income bracket of $20,000 to $38,000 (middle-income families). This is not to say that money per se increases the adolescents' chances for work, rather there are probably intervening factors. One such factor includes socialization practices. According to Rees and Gray (1982) "much education takes place in the home so that youths who have well-educated parents and who have been exposed to books and to serious discussions while growing up may have advantages in finding and holding jobs over other youths with the same amount of formal schooling" (p. 454).

Lewin-Epstein (1981) suggests that another reason for the higher employment/population rates among adolescents of middle-income families is that parents and other family members may have better and more extensive business contacts. While this may be the case, Rees and Gray (1982) found evidence to suggest that neither father's occupation, educational level, nor income were related to the adolescent's employment status. However, Rees and Gray (1982) did find that sibling's employment status was strongly related to the target adolescents' employment status, especially if the two were of the same sex (e.g., if her sister worked, then chances were better that she also worked). Rees and Gray (1982) speculate that this pattern is a product of siblings serving as information networks. In any event, it does not appear that family income is strongly related to the quality or quantity of employment contacts. Another factor that may help explain the higher employment/population rate among adolescents from middle-income families is, as Lewin-Epstein indicates, that such families tend to live in suburbs where there tend to be more employment opportunities for adolescents (e.g., shopping malls, fast-food restaurants).

Before we consider characteristics of the adolescents' jobs, we should mention that employment status also varied according to the type of school program. Except for female sophomore students, those in vocational programs were more likely to be employed than either those in college preparatory or general programs. This may be due to a greater interest in work for those enrolled in vocational programs, or, as Lewin-Epstein suggests, to the work and experience orientations of vocational programs. Most likely, it is a combination of both. As we have seen, adolescents' employment status tends to vary according to such factors as grade level, race, sex, place of residence, family characteristics, and school program.

Lewin-Epstein's (1981) study also explored various aspects of the jobs that adolescents hold. As might be expected, there was wide variation according to such characteristics as type of job, number of hours worked, and wages earned. Among the sophomore students the most popular types of jobs were babysitting, food service, and odd jobs. For the senior students the most popular jobs were store clerk/salesperson and food service. Clerical/office work, manual labor, and skilled trade were the other more common types of jobs. Babysitting and odd jobs (the most common types of jobs for sophomores) were among the least popular jobs for the senior students. The difference between sophomores and seniors is not surprising. However, as Lewin-Epstein points out, jobs such as food service or store clerk offer much more exposure to the world of work in terms of organizational structure, supervising relations, and co-worker interactions than do such jobs as babysitting or odd jobs. In other words, the jobs that seniors hold tend to be more structured and adult-like than those held by the sophomore students.

As we have seen, characteristics of student employees as well as of student jobs vary to a large extent. Lewin-Epstein's study suggests that older students are more involved in the world of work, especially in terms of time spent, wages earned, and interaction with the employer's organizational structure than younger students. However, it remains to be seen whether adolescents typically progress from relatively low structured and low time-demand employment to high structured and high time-demand employment, or whether they typically "jump into" employment of the latter type. In other words, do adolescents generally take "small steps" into the world of work, or are they "thrown in"? More research is needed. However, in line with our previous discussion about optimizing vocational development, the former would be preferable to the latter pattern.

We now turn to the effect of employment on adolescents. With few exceptions, the effects of part-time employment on adolescents have been the subject of optimistic speculation based on the "work is good" assumption (e.g., work creates social and personal responsibility; work keeps kids out of trouble). Hamilton and Crouter (1980) conclude in their review of the research on the effects of work on adolescents, "we find some evidence that adolescent work experience enhances the socialization (to adulthood) process, but little evidence that it provides either career knowledge or job-related skills that prove advantageous over time" (p. 331). This is not to say that work does not have a positive impact on adolescents, but rather that few studies have been done to test the impact.

One notable exception is a research project on the costs and benefits of early work experience on adolescent development conducted by Greenberger, Steinberg, and their colleagues. Starting in October, 1978, these researchers collected information concerning employment history and family background characteristics from 3,100 tenth and eleventh grade students in four high schools in Orange County, California. It was found that 36% of the students were currently working, 39% had never worked, and those who worked spent an average of 20 to 24 hours per week working (Steinberg et al., 1982). A group of students who were not initially employed were followed for a period of about one and a half years, during which time several of those students became employed. Thus, these researchers were able to look at 75 adolescents before and after they began work and determine what changes in the adolescents were associated with work.

Before discussing the results of this research project, it is necessary to caution the reader on two counts. First, since this is the only extensive study of its kind, the results need to be replicated with a different group of adolescents before definitive conclusions can be made. Secondly, as they point out (Steinberg et al., 1982), the researchers were mainly interested in first-time employees and only those employed in the private, part-time labor force. In other words, their results may not pertain to those adolescents who have worked previously in a number of jobs or to those who work in different settings (e.g., career-education programs, family-owned businesses).

Among the "benefits" of working, it was found that working facilitated the development of personal responsibility. For example, workers were found to have more self-reliance and a greater work orientation (e.g., more able to successfully complete tasks and take pride in doing so) than non-workers (Steinberg, Greenberger, Vaux, & Ruggiero, 1981). In addition, there was some evidence that working may encourage adolescents to better understand others (Steinberg, Greenberger, Jacobi, & Garduque, 1981). Also, working was associated with greater knowledge about the world of work and other practical matters (e.g., money, consumer transactions), especially among academically marginal students (Steinberg, Greenberger, Jacobi, & Garduque, 1981). Finally, for girls, working was associated with increased autonomy (Steinberg et al., 1982).

The "costs" of working were found to be more extensive than are generally assumed. In general, work was found to be associated with decreased involvement with non-work activities, specifically with school, family, and peers. For example, compared to non-workers, workers had higher absentee rates, participated less in extracurricular activities, enjoyed school less, spent less time on homework, and earned lower grades (especially among marginal students) (Steinberg, Greenberger, Garduque, & McAuliffe, 1982; Steinberg et al., 1982). These patterns were the more likely to occur the more hours per week the adolescent worked. In addition, workers tended to spend less time in family activities (Greenberger et al., 1980), and working tended to decrease feelings of family closeness in the adolescents, especially for females working long hours (Steinberg et al., 1982). It was found, however, that working just a few hours a week led to an increase in the adolescents' feelings of family closeness (Steinberg et al., 1982). Finally, working led to a decrease in emotional closeness with peers (Steinberg et al., 1982).

Other "costs" of working included the association of work with more negative and cynical attitudes about work, as well as increased tolerance of unethical business practices (Steinberg, Greenberger, Vaux, & Ruggiero, 1981). In addition, certain aspects of the adolescents' health appear to be adversely affected by work. For example, workers were found to have higher rates of cigarette, alcohol, and drug use than non-workers (Greenberger, Steinberg, & Vaux, 1981). Again, the more hours the adolescent worked, the greater chance for this pattern to occur. In fact, one common thread running through these studies is that working long hours (e.g., more than 15 to 20 hours per week) tends to increase the likelihood of negative effects (Steinberg et al., 1982).

Considering the relatively limited scope of information on the costs and benefits of adolescent employment, caution must be exercised in drawing firm conclusions and in applying them to adolescents in general. What we do know is that adolescence is a time during which the vocational identity of individuals takes shape. Very likely, the price paid as well as the benefits obtained from employment affect the vocational developmental process. A key to understanding how work affects adolescents' vocational development is the adolescents' motivations, something that past research has not attended to.

Our view is that the majority of adolescents do not seek part-time jobs in order to gain experience in their anticipated vocations. In other words, while they may seek general knowledge and experience of the inner-workings of the world of work, they generally are not looking for specific occupational training—and it is a good thing that they are not, for, as Greenberger, Steinberg, and Ruggiero (1981) found, most of the part-time jobs available to adolescents involve highly routine and repetitive work with few opportunities for creativity, decision-making, or learning.

However, there are exceptions, and some adolescents actively seek and find jobs that will provide them with some first-hand experience in their anticipated vocational choice. For example, consider two adolescents employed at a gas station. One aspires to be a mechanic, and the other has aspirations outside the mechanical domain and is employed solely for the income. The first one may have more mechanical aptitude, may take more interest in the job, and may even receive more mechanical experience and responsibility than the second adolescent. We would expect that the job would differently affect the two adolescents' vocational development. The first may become more interested in, and sure of, his or her vocational choice and may even encounter full-time job offers, while the second may decide that he or she never wants to work in a gas station, or anything like it, again. This, however, is only a good guess. Obviously, more research is needed before the complex relationships between adolescent work and vocational development are sufficiently understood to be translatable into concrete advice for adolescents or guidelines for their parents or teachers.

One important issue that we have not addressed thus far is how working affects the future employment of students. Among adolescents who drop out of school, those who worked part-time while in school fare better in terms of future employment prospects than do those who did not work during school (Stevenson, 1978). In addition, even among those who graduate from high school, part-time work during school seems to increase the chances of being employed and, to a lesser extent, of earning higher wages for up to four years following graduation (Meyer & Wise, 1982). However, as Meyer and Wise (1982) point out, it may not be work experience per se that enhances future employment. Rather, there may be some personality factor or strong work-ethic that is common for individuals across adolescence and adulthood (e.g., those strongly oriented toward work during adolescence may also be the same during adulthood). In fact, as Meyer and Wise indicate, how hard the adolescent "works" as a student (e.g., as indicated by grades and class rank) is also highly predictive of his or her future occupation success. Another way to look at the affect of employment on the future success of adolescents is to consider what happens when they *do not* work—the subject of the next section.

Youths Who Do Not Work

To put the youth unemployment issue in perspective, it is useful to group all youths into one of four categories (remember the youth population refers to those aged 16–24): (1) non-employed, (2) part-time employed or part-time unemployed, (3) full-time employed, and (4) full-time unemployed. Those non-employed are neither working nor looking for work. Those who are part-time employed or unemployed are working or looking for work on a part-time basis. These first two groups usually consist of those who are in some type of school (e.g., high school, vocational-technical school, college) and who are supported, at least to some extent, by their parents. The third group, youths employed on a full-time basis, generally consists of those who have completed at least some form of secondary education. The large majority of the nation's youths are contained in these three groups. For example, in reference to 1976 data on males aged 16–19, Feldstein and Elwood (1982) stated: "More than 90% of all male teenagers are either in school, working, or both. Most unemployed teenagers are either in school or seeking only part-time work. Only 5% of teenage boys are unemployed, out of school, and looking for full-time work" (p. 19). This 5% figure describes the fourth group—the full-time unemployed youths.

This is not to say that youth unemployment is a small problem, neither in magnitude nor effect. Rather, the point is that youth unemployment is concentrated in a specific population—especially those who have dropped out of school. In addition, as Table 2 illustrates, youth unemployment is a major problem for 16–19 year olds and minorities. Table 2 provides the 1980 un-

Table 2
Percent of Labor Force Unemployed
by Age, Race, and Sex (1980)

Age & Race	Male	Female
All Workers (Aged 16–65 and over)	6.9	7.4
16–19 Yrs.	18.2	17.2
20–24 Yrs.	12.5	10.3
White (Aged 16–65 and over)	6.1	6.5
16–19 Yrs.	16.2	14.8
20–24 Yrs.	11.1	8.5
Other Races (Aged 16–65 and over)	13.3	13.1
16–19 Yrs.	34.9	36.8
20–24 Yrs.	22.4	21.9

Source: U.S. Bureau of the Census, 1981.

employment rates according to age, sex, and race (keep in mind that many of the 16–19 year olds were seeking only part-time employment).

There are several reasons why youth unemployment is concentrated among school drop-outs, 16 to 19 year olds, and minorities, ranging from discriminatory practices to ineffective schools, from an unstable labor market to incompetence. One reason why high school drop-outs have such a hard time getting a job is the stigma associated with dropping out. As Garbarino and Asp (1981) note, a high school diploma is often viewed as a prerequisite for full personhood. And it is not because the drop-out is any less qualified than the graduate. To the employer, graduating from school is not as much an indication of what one knows as it is an indication of what one has mastered and tolerated. As Squires (1979) points out, graduating from school (high school or college) requires, to some extent, the ability to follow the "rules"— often the same type of "rules" that employers have.

The major issue, as we see it, with youth unemployment is the affect it has on the future prospects of young people. This issue is usually addressed in terms of whether the unemployed youths get jobs in the future and how much money they make if they do get jobs. And the general finding is that unemployed youths, especially those who drop out of school, are destined for a life of poor job prospects and low wages (e.g., Stevenson, 1978). Corcoran (1982) analyzed data from the National Longitudinal Survey of Young Women, a national sample of 5,159 women between the ages of 14 and 24 who were interviewed annually from 1968 to 1973 and again in 1975. She found that six out of seven women spent some time working but also a significant amount of time not working in the four years following completion of school. Many young women did not work for prolonged periods of time. Corcoran found that they had to pay a price: (1) the odds of any woman's being employed were found to be 148 times higher if she worked the previous year than if she did not; (2) evidence was found that early non-work (two years or more) resulted in 3% to 5% lower wages as late as 10 years after school completion.

Elwood (1982) analyzed a similar data set from the National Longitudinal Survey of Young Men. His conclusions are similar to those of Corcoran. Concentrating his analyses on a subsample of out of school 16- to 19-year-old men, he concludes that there are, indeed, long-term effects of being out of work. He, too, finds that being out of work will be reflected in lower wages indefinitely and reduced work time in any year following unemployment. Elwood stresses, however, that there is little evidence to suggest that instances of early unemployment set off a vicious cycle of recurrent unemployment.

But there is another way to address this issue. As we have stressed, adolescence is an important time in the formulation of a vocational identity. Attempting to formulate that identity without some full-time work-related experience is a difficult task indeed. (While college youths may be in the same position, they at least are moving toward career goals and, if they graduate, will have credentials that facilitate getting a job.) In addition, unemployed out-of-school youths eventually get jobs, but as we have seen, the economic impact of waiting for three or four years is not erased once a job is found.

It is also possible, however, that long term unemployment, especially during adolescence and young adulthood, serves to "short-circuit" vital developmental processes. Discouragement, cynicism, involvement in criminal activities, and the development of a "welfare ethic" may all be difficult to ascertain but possible outcomes. A recent study by Guerney (1980), while exploratory in nature, confirms the deleterious nature of unemployment in Australian school drop-outs. Unemployed males showed considerably greater mistrust than employed males; both males and females revealed a significantly lower sense of usefulness and accomplishment when compared to an employed cohort. Finally, Guerney also reports that in another study he found lower self-esteem in unemployed than in employed youths, a finding also supported to some extent by Gade and Peterson (1980) among American youths. Guerney concludes that these psycho-social consequences of youth unemployment may represent merely a delay in the completion of developmental tasks vital to a successful transition from school to work roles. Nevertheless, for unemployed youths the mere fact of long-term unemployment may force the compromising, or even sacrificing, of vocational interests and aspirations, leading them to a situation of taking whatever job they can get, often at a level substantially below that warranted by aptitudes and abilities. In our view, this does not constitute optimal vocational development.

To Work or Not to Work

In the previous sections we have observed that there are identifiable consequences for young people stemming from both the experience of work as well as the experience of unemployment. Furthermore, we have seen that these consequences may vary according to whether the work is part-time, while attending school, or full-time. Generally, we have concluded that much more research needs to be carried out to establish what really causes one set of consequences as opposed to another. Preliminary findings do suggest, however, that positive work experiences in high school or even junior high school can greatly facilitate the transition from school to the world of work, while lack of employment after leaving school can result in decreased earnings potential and possibly lower-level employment eventually.

The decision of whether young people should be encouraged to seek work while in school is not quite as clear-cut. When dealing with individual adolescents, as would be the case for teachers, counselors, or parents, it is essential to take into account each person's individual characteristics. This should involve the posing of a number of pertinent questions, such as:

1. Is the adolescent physically capable of managing the demands of the job?
2. Is it likely that the job will build and enhance the adolescent's commitment to work? (For example, some years ago it was commonly accepted that working for a certain state agency involved nothing more strenuous than simply showing up for work.)
3. Is it possible to ensure that employment will not interfere with school work? (Some adolescents so enjoy the consequences of employment that they quit school to devote more time to their jobs, frequently, with negative long-term consequences.)
4. Can work be arranged in such a way that it does not disrupt important peer relationships, including those with the opposite sex? (Some work situations may allow for replacing peer relationships lost at school with age-appropriate relationships at work—but others may not provide for this.)
5. Is the adolescent emotionally mature enough to handle the pressure at work? (Often, work experiences represent the initial opportunities to assume important responsibility for the welfare of others or for important economic consequences, such as destroying an expensive machine, ruining a production run, or alienating an important customer.)
6. Is the adolescent sufficiently conscientious and reliable to have a good chance of experiencing the positive reinforcement or rewards that are offered to workers with such qualities? (Being fired from a first job clearly would be detrimental in most cases.)

Seeking answers to those and similar questions requires, undoubtedly, a certain amount of study and thoughtful consideration. The task brings us right back to the first section of our chapter, in which we discussed current theories of vocational and career development. Those theories, each in its own way, guide the way in which we think about careers, and they often direct us in selecting the individual characteristics and behaviors that should be the focus of our concerns. Ultimately, a thorough understanding of the individual adolescent and his/her circumstances, on the one hand, and comprehensive knowledge regarding the world of work, on the other, will ensure that adolescents can choose and initiate careers in which they can flourish as adults. We trust that our chapter will contribute toward this end.

SOURCES OF HELP

The reader may recall that we previously observed that career development in adolescence can be facilitated (1) through the availability of timely and relevant career information, (2) through sensitive and sensible assistance with decision-making, and (3) through the provision of early positive work experiences. In the following pages we shall outline how help can be obtained to further career development and also to locate employment.

1. Career Information

There are many ways in which individuals acquire information about careers. Certainly the oldest method of acquiring career information is through passing it from generation to generation, usually from father to son. This still operates to some extent in Western societies and remains the principal means of disseminating career information in many less developed societies. In the United States, however, the most comprehensive and probably the most widely used sources of career information are published by the United States government through the Department of Labor's Bureau of Labor Statistics. Among the great number of informational pamphlets and volumes listed by the U.S. Government Printing Office, two are particularly noteworthy: the *Dictionary of Occupational Titles* (4th ed., 1977), and the *Occupational Outlook Handbook* (1980–81). It may be useful to briefly discuss the information they contain.

The *Dictionary of Occupational Titles* (DOT) provides detailed definitions of more than 20,000 occupations. These occupations are described in a way analogous to a job description; the essential requirements, i.e., tasks or services performed are followed by tasks which may or may not be required of members of the occupation in question. Furthermore, the DOT provides logically and programmatically organized groupings of occupations that have common characteristics. Finally, the Department of Labor occasionally issues supplements to the DOT which address occupational classification issues of various kinds. A particularly useful recent supplement (U.S. Department of Labor, 1979) is titled *Guide for Occupational Exploration.* It lists occupational groups by types of qualifications (both personal and educational/technical) needed by workers to enter specific vocational areas.

The *Occupational Outlook Handbook* is more restricted in scope (it lists only about 900 occupations) but is much more detailed and timely than the DOT. Perhaps most importantly, it is issued in revised form every two years, thus providing an invaluable and timely information resource for individuals wishing to learn about specific occupations and occupational groups. The information provided by the *Occupational Outlook Handbook* includes descriptions of the nature of the work performed in a given occupation, the likely places of employment, training and other qualifications needed, the outlook for employment in the occupation, likely earnings and working conditions, and listings of additional sources of information.

The above informational resources are readily available and relatively inexpensive. There are many other publications by commercial publishers that provide a combination of occupational information and advice about careers. One notable example is the recent best seller *What Color Is Your Parachute?* by Bolles (1977). Although the information provided in the various publications can be very helpful to individuals in the process of making career decisions, such individuals may frequently need some assistance in evaluating the plethora of career information and in making good career decisions.

2. Decision-Making Assistance

Making career decisions is serious business. It is also a very complex process that continues from childhood to old age. Our focus is on adolescence—when the convergence of predispositions, attitudes, and abilities interact with family and other environmental factors to produce the initial important career decisions. Because of the pivotal nature of adolescent and young adult career decisions, much of the available assistance in career decision-making processes is concentrated on youth. Most frequently, decision-making assistance takes the form of vocational guidance or career counseling, but many more informal sources of help play an important role in career decision-making.

Parents, teachers, and other role models are often important influences on decision making. Sometimes they are aware of it and conduct themselves accordingly, and sometimes they are unaware of the significance of their actions. In any case, it is desirable to keep in mind that it is the young person him/herself who needs to live with any decision made; thus, undue influence is to be avoided, and a focus on modeling and teaching problem-solving skills should be preferred.

Vocational guidance specialists and career counselors, of course, have special skills and special tools to assist in career decision-making. They are trained in the development of counseling relationships which promote learning and problem-solving. Perhaps most importantly, they can use instruments to assess vocational interests, work values, career maturity, and personality, on the one hand, and aptitudes and abilities, on the other. Through proper utilization of such instruments and through assistance provided in the evaluation of all relevant information, individuals are able to make well-informed and reasonable career decisions. Although different counselors may pursue somewhat different avenues in their specific approach to career counseling, they are all interested in facilitating effective decisions which actually help individuals to have a solid chance to achieve their career objectives.

Two questions should be raised in connection with career counseling or vocational guidance: "Is a counselor really necessary?" and "How can one locate a qualified counselor?" The answer to the first question depends upon the life circumstances of the individual. Clearly, some people do not need professional assistance either because they are able to make satisfactory decisions on their own or because they utilize the informal network of resources (e.g., parents, friends, other relatives) to obtain assistance. People who need professional assistance in vocational or career decision-making are usually individuals who, for some reason, cannot use informal assistance or who have particular needs, conflicts, or uncertainties regarding their career options and, hence, their career choices.

The second question, pertaining to the identification of qualified counselors, can be answered in a variety of ways. The most common location for career counselors is in the nation's secondary schools. The Federal government, especially during the late fifties and sixties, implemented a number of programs, such as the National Defense Education Act (NDEA) of 1958, which sponsored and supported the training of school counselors (Srebalus, Marinelli, & Messing, 1982). Many of these counselors have specialized in career planning, and they actively assist students in junior and senior high schools in career decision making. Typically, such counselors have access to the tools of career counseling, including career information, vocational interest inventories, aptitude tests, and other psychometric devices to assist students and facilitate their career development.

3. Finding a Job

Finding a job as an adolescent, even in these times of high unemployment, may not be all that difficult. This depends, of course, on whether the adolescent is seeking full- or part-time employment, and whether he or she is looking for career-specific employment, or "just a job." As we stated, food-service and retail establishments tend to employ adolescents on a part-time basis. The employee turnover rate tends to be relatively high in these establishments, thus job openings occur frequently. Of course, communities vary in the number and types of jobs open to adolescents. The best ways to locate these types of jobs are through want-ads and word-of-mouth. For information about government-sponsored and school-based career education programs, the adolescent should check with his or her high school guidance counselor.

Trying for a job and actually getting a job are often two different matters. There are several "how-to" books on getting jobs; however, as we previously mentioned, *What Color Is Your Parachute?* (Bolles, 1977) is one of the better books. Bolles provides information on guidelines for résumé writing and for displaying the appropriate attitude and appearance during job interviews. Furthermore, Bolles provides a listing of various manuals and agencies devoted to helping young people find and land jobs.

Of course, one should not forget about such job-getting virtues as creativity, ambition, and perseverance. Sometimes a job can be created. For example, the junior author of this chapter banded together with a few other "broke" high school students one summer in an effort to find work. Eventually, the group decided on painting house numbers on the curbs in the suburbs, for minimal "donations." While this enterprising pursuit involved such hassles as getting approval from various city commissions, dealing with very large dogs, and avoiding a few disturbed suburb-dwellers, it proved to be a fun and profitable summer.

ANNOTATED REFERENCES

Bolles, R. N. *What Color Is Your Parachute? A Practical Manual for Job Hunters and Career Changes.* Berkeley, CA: Ten Speed Press, 1977.

For those interested in some good, practical information on making career decisions and finding a job, this is one of the better "how to" guides. Included in the book is information on various professional resources (including addresses and phone numbers) available to those who need job-related help.

Cole, S. "Send Our Children to Work?" *Psychology Today,* July 1980, 44–68.

This article provides an easy-to-read discussion about working during adolescence. The costs and benefits of working for both the adolescent and the family are discussed.

Herr, E. L., & Cramer, S. H. *Career Guidance through the Life-span: Systematic Approaches.* Boston: Little, Brown, 1979.

This book is a comprehensive, well-documented review of career guidance in all its complexity and diversity. An essential resource for teachers and guidance personnel, but also most useful for parents and students with a serious interest in learning about procedures and resources for career development.

Osipow, S. H. *Theories of Career Development* (3rd ed.). Englewood Cliffs, NJ: Prentice-Hall, 1983.

This popular volume, now in its third edition, is essential reading for the serious student of career development. All major theories of career development are examined and critically evaluated. In addition, a valuable review of issues pertaining to the effects of "minority group" membership is included in the third edition, as is a chapter on the career development of women.

Rist, R. C. (Ed.). *Confronting Youth Unemployment in the 1980s: Rhetoric versus Reality.* New York: Pergamon Press, 1980. (This is a special issue of the journal *Children and Youth Service Review*, 1980, Volume 2, Numbers 1 & 2.)

This book gives an excellent review of the youth unemployment problem, including federal policy issues, youth employment program evaluation, and a critical review of the youth unemployment literature. In addition, there is a chapter by Lawrence Steinberg and Ellen Greenberger concerning part-time employment of adolescents.

Srebalus, D. J., Marinelli, R. P., & Messing, J. K. *Career Development: Concepts and Procedures.* Monterey, CA: Brooks/Cole, 1982.

This book is a goldmine of useful, practical, up-to-date information for any person interested in career development for any reason. Written from the perspective of professional career counselors, the book addresses career development theory and counseling theory in a manner suitable for educated lay persons. Moreover, strategies of career exploration and career action are detailed with particular reference to sources of information and help. Finally, each chapter concludes with a section on recommended readings and learning activities.

REFERENCES

Bandura, A. *Principles of Behavior Modification.* New York: Holt, Rinehart & Winston, 1969.

Beilin, H. "The Application of General Developmental Principles to the Vocational Area." *Journal of Counseling Psychology*, 1955, 2, 1, 53–57.

Blau, P. M., & Duncan, D. D. *The American Occupational Structure.* New York: Wiley, 1967.

Bolles, R. N. *What Color Is Your Parachute? A Practical Manual for Job Hunters and Career Changes.* Berkeley, CA: Ten Speed Press, 1977.

Bühler, C. *Der menschliche Lebenslauf als psychologiches Problem.* Leipzig: Hirzel, 1933.

Charles, D. C. "Historical Antecedents of Life-span Developmental Psychology." In L. R. Goulet & P. B. Baltes (Eds.), *Life-span Developmental Psychology: Research and Theory.* New York: Academic Press, 1970, 23–52.

Corcoran, M. "The Employment and Wage Consequences of Teenage Women's Non-employment." In R. B. Freeman & D. A. Wise (Eds.), *The Youth Labor Market Problem: Its Nature, Causes, and Consequences.* Chicago: University of Chicago Press, 1982.

Dudley, G. A., & Tiedeman, D. V. *Career Development: Exploration and Commitment.* Muncie, IN: Accelerated Development, 1977.

Elwood, D. T. "Teenage Unemployment: Permanent Scars or Temporary Blemishes." In R. B. Freeman & D. A. Wise (Eds.), *The Youth Labor Market Problem: Its Nature, Causes, and Consequences.* Chicago: University of Chicago Press, 1982.

Feldstein, M., & Elwood, D. T. "Teenage Unemployment: What Is the Problem?" In R. B. Freeman & D. A. Wise (Eds.), *The Youth Labor Market Problem.* Chicago: University of Chicago Press, 1982.

Gade, E., & Peterson, L. "A Comparison of Working and Non-working High School Students on School Performance, Socioeconomic Status, and Self-esteem." *The Vocational Guidance Quarterly,* 1980, *29*, 65–69.

Garbarino, J., & Asp, C. E. *Successful Schools and Competent Students.* Lexington, MA: Lexington Books, 1981.

Ginzberg, E. "Toward a Theory of Occupational Choice: A Restatement." *Vocational Guidance Quarterly,* 1972, *20*, 136–169.

Ginzberg, E. "The Job Problem." *Scientific American,* 1977, *237*, 43–51.

Ginzberg, E. *Good Jobs, Bad Jobs, No Jobs.* Cambridge, MA: Harvard University Press, 1979.

Ginzberg, E., Ginsburg, S. W., Axelrad, S., & Herma, J. R. *Occupational Choice: An Approach to a General Theory.* New York: Columbia University Press, 1951.

Goldstein, B., & Oldman, J. *Children and Work: A Study of Socialization.* New Brunswick, NJ: Transaction Books, 1979.

Grandy, T. G., & Stahmann, R. F. "Family Influence on College Students' Vocational Choice: Predicting from Holland's Personality Types." *Journal of College Student Personnel,* 1974, *15*, 404–405.

Greenberger, E., Steinberg, L. D., & Ruggiero, M. "A Job Is a Job Is a Job . . . Or Is It? Behavioral Observations in the Adolescent Workplace." *Work and Occupation,* 1982, *9*, 79–96.

Greenberger, E., Steinberg, L. D., & Vaux, A. "Adolescents Who Work: Health and Behavioral Consequences of Job Stress." *Developmental Psychology,* 1981, *17*, 691–703.

Greenleaf, B. K. *Children Through the Ages.* New York: Harper and Row, 1978.

Guerney, R. M. "The Effects of Unemployment on the Psycho-social Development of School-leavers." *Journal of Occupational Psychology*, 1980, *53*, 205–213.

Haller, A. D., & Portes, A. "Status Attainment Processes." *Sociology of Education*, 1973, *46*, 51–91.

Haller, A. D., & Woelfel, J. "Significant Others and Their Expectations: Concepts and Instruments to Measure Interpersonal Influence on Status Aspirations." *Rural Sociology*, 1972, *37*, 591–622.

Hamilton, S. F., & Crouter, A. C. "Work and Growth: A Review of Research on the Impact of Work Experience on Adolescent Development." *Journal of Youth and Adolescence*, 1980, *9*, 323–338.

Harris, D. B. "Comments delivered at the Symposium on Career Development and Vocational Maturity." Eastern Psychological Association, Boston, April 27, 1972.

Havighurst, R. J. "Youth in Exploration and Man Emergent." In H. Borow (Ed.), *Man in a World of Work*. Boston: Houghton Mifflin, 1964.

Havighurst, R. J., & Neugarten, B. L. *Society and Education* (4th ed.). Boston: Allyn and Bacon, 1975.

Herr, E. L., & Cramer, S. H. *Career Guidance Through the Life-span: Systematic Approaches*. Boston: Little, Brown, 1979.

Holland, J. L. *Making Vocational Choices: A Theory of Careers*. Englewood Cliffs, NJ: Prentice-Hall, 1973.

Holland, J. L., & Gottfredson, G. D. "Using a Typology of Persons and Environments to Explain Careers: Some Extensions and Clarifications." In D. H. Montross & C. H. Shinkeman (Eds.), *Career Development in the 1980s: Theory and Practice*. Springfield, IL: Charles C. Thomas, 1981.

Hollingshead, A. B. *Elmstown Youth*. New York: Wiley, 1949.

Huston-Stein, A. P., & Higgins-Trenk, A. "Development of Females from Childhood Through Adulthood: Career and Feminine Orientations." In P. B. Baltes (Ed.), *Life-span Development and Behavior*. New York: Academic Press, 1978.

Jordaan, J. P. "Exploratory Behavior: The Formation of Self and Occupational Concepts." In D. Super, R. Starishevsky, N. Matlin, & J. P. Jordaan (Eds.), *Career Development: Self-concept Theory*. New York: College Entrance Examination Board, 1963.

Kaestle, C. F., & Vinovskis, M. A. *Education and Social Change in Nineteenth-century Massachusetts*. New York: Cambridge University Press, 1980.

Kett, J. F. *Rites of Passage: Adolescents in America, 1970 to the Present*. New York: Basic Books, 1977.

Krumboltz, J. D. "A Social Learning Theory of Career Decision Making." In A. M. Mitchell,G. B. Jones, & J. D. Krumboltz (Eds.), *Social Learning and Career Decision-making*. Cranston, RI: Carroll Press, 1979.

Lewin-Epstein, N. *Youth Employment During High School*. Washington, DC: National Center for Education Statistics, 1981.

Meyer, R., & Wise, D. "High School Preparation and Early Labor Force Experience." In R. Freeman & D. Wise (Eds.), *The Youth Labor Market Problem: Its Nature, Causes and Consequences*. Chicago: University of Chicago Press, 1982.

Mitchell, A. M., Jones, G. B., & Krumboltz, J. D. (Eds.). *Social Learning and Career Decision-making*. Cranston, RI: Carroll Press, 1979.

Mortimer, J. T. "Patterns of Intergenerational Occupational Movements: A Smallest Space Analysis." *American Journal of Sociology*, 1974, 5, 1278–1295.

Osipow, S. H. *Theories of Career Development* (3rd ed.). Englewood Cliffs, NJ: Prentice-Hall, 1983.

Panel on Youth of the President's Science Advisory Committee. *Youth: Transition to Adulthood*. Chicago: University of Chicago Press, 1974.

Pounds, R. L., & Bryner, J. R. *The School in American Society* (2nd ed.). New York: Macmillan, 1973.

Roe, A. *The Psychology of Occupations*. New York: Wiley, 1956.

Srebalus, D. J., Marinelli, R. P., & Messing, J. K. *Career Development: Concepts and Procedures*. Monterey, CA: Brooks/Cole, 1982.

Sherraden, M. W. "Youth Employment and Education: Federal Programs from the New Deal through the 1970s." In R. C. Rist (Ed.), *Confronting Youth Unemployment in the 1980s: Rhetoric versus Reality*. New York: Pergamon Press, 1980.

Steinberg, L. D., & Greenberger, E. "The Part-time Employment of High School Students: A Research Agenda." In R. C. Rist (Ed.), *Confronting Youth Unemployment in the 1980s: Rhetoric versus Reality*. New York: Pergamon Press, 1980.

Steinberg, L. D., Greenberger, E., Garduque, L., & McAuliffe, S. High School Students in the Labor Force: Some Costs and Benefits to Schooling and Working." *Education and Policy Analysis*, 1982, 4, 363–372.

Steinberg, L. D., Greenberger, E., Garduque, L., Ruggiero, M., & Vaux, A. "Effects of Working on Adolescent Development." *Developmental Psychology*, 1982, 18, 385–395.

Steinberg, L. D., Greenberger, E., Jacobi, M., & Garduque, L. "Early Work Experience: A Partial Antidote for Adolescent Egocentrism." *Journal of Youth and Adolescence*, 1981, 10, 141–157.

Steinberg, L. D., Greenberger, E., Vaux, A., & Ruggiero, M. "Effects of

358 *Experiencing Adolescents*

Early Work Experience on Adolescent Occupational Socialization."
Youth and Society, 1981, *12*, 403–422.

Stevenson, W. "The Relationship Between Early Work Experience and
Future Employabilty." In A. Adams & G. Mangum (Eds.), *The Lin-
gering Crisis of Youth Unemployment*. Kalamazoo, MI: Upjon Institute for Employment Research, 1978.

Squires, G. D. *Education and Jobs: The Imbalancing of Social Ma-
chinery*. New Brunswick, NJ: Transaction Books, 1979.

Super, D. E. "A Theory of Vocational Development." *American Psychologist*, 1953, *8*, 185–190.

Super, D. E. *The Psychology of Careers*. New York: Harper & Row, 1957.

Super, D. E. "Self-concepts in Vocational Development." In D. E. Super,
R. Stavishevsky, N. Matlin, & J. P. Jordaan (Eds.), *Career Develop-
ment: Self-concept Theory*. New York: CEEB Research Monograph
No. 4, 1963.

Super, D. E. "A Life-span Life-space Approach to Career Development."
Journal of Vocational Behavior, 1980, *16*, 282–298.

Super, D. E. "A Developmental Theory: Implementing a Self-concept."
In D. H. Montross & C. J. Shinkman (Eds.), *Career Development in
the 1980s: Theory and Practice*. Springfield, IL: Charles C. Thomas,
1981.

Super, D. E., Starishevsky, R., Matlin, N., & Jordaan, J. P. *Career
Development: Self-concept Theory*. New York: College Entrance
Examination Board, 1963.

Tiedeman, D. V. "Decisions and Vocational Development: A Paradigm
and Its Implications." *Personnel and Guidance Journal*, 1961, *40*,
15–21.

Tiedeman, D. V., & O'Hara, R. P. *Career Development: Choice and
Adjustment*. Princeton: College Entrance Examination Board, 1963.

Tyack, D. B. *Turning Points in American Educational History*. Waltham,
MA: Blaisdell, 1967.

U.S. Bureau of the Census. *Characteristics of the Population*. Washington, DC: U.S. Government Printing Office, 1940.

U.S. Bureau of the Census. *Census of the Population: 1970* (Final
Report PC(2)-6A, Employment Status and Work Experience). Washington, DC: U.S. Government Printing Office, 1973.

U.S. Bureau of the Census. *Fertility of American Women: June 1978*
(Current Population Reports, Series P-20, No. 341, October 1979).
Washington, DC: U.S. Government Printing Office, 1979.

U.S. Bureau of the Census. *Statistical Abstract of the United States: 1981*
(102d edition). Washington, DC, 1981.

U.S. Department of Labor. *Dictionary of Occupational Titles* (4th ed.).
Washington, DC: U.S. Government Printing Office, 1977.

U.S. Department of Labor. *Guide for Occupational Exploration.* Washington, DC: U.S. Government Printing Office, 1979.

U.S. Department of Labor. *Occupational Outlook Handbook* (1980–81 ed.). Washington, DC: U.S. Government Printing Office, 1980.

U.S. Office of Education. *Digest of Educational Statistics, 1972.* U.S. Bureau of the Census, Series P-23, No. 44, March, 1973.

Vondracek, F. W., & Lerner, R. M. "Vocational Role Development in Adolescence." In B. B. Wolman (Ed.), *Handbook of Developmental Psychology.* Englewood Cliffs, NJ: Prentice-Hall, 1982.

Vondracek, F. W., Lerner, R. M., & Schulenberg, J. E. "The Concept of Development in Vocational Theory and Intervention." *Journal of Vocational Behavior,* 1983, *23,* 179–202.

Wilensky, H. L. "Varieties of Work Experience." In H. Borow (Ed.), *Man in a World at Work.* Boston: Houghton Mifflin, 1964.

Woelfel, J. "Significant Others and Their Role Relationships to Students in a High School Population." *Rural Sociology,* 1972, *37,* 86–97.

Work-Education Consortium. *Work and Service Experience for Youth.* Washington, DC: Manpower Institute, 1978.

Young, A. M. "Students, Graduates, and Dropouts in the Labor Market, October 1975." *Monthly Labor Review,* 1976, *99,* 37–41.

Young, A. M. "The Difference a Year Makes in the Nation's Youth Work Force." *Monthly Labor Review,* 1979, *102*(10), 34–38.

Young, A. M. "School and Work Among Youth During the 1970s." *Monthly Labor Review,* 1980, *103,* 44–47.

Young, A. M. "Labor Force Patterns of Students, Graduates, and Dropouts, 1981." *Monthly Labor Review,* 1982, *105,* 39–42.

11. HANDICAPPED ADOLESCENTS
M. Bernadette Reidy and Susan M. McHale

PART I: ISSUES AND FINDINGS

In the preceding chapters, the experience of adolescence has been described as a time of transition—a period between childhood and adulthood, when major physical, psychological, and social changes prepare adolescents for the roles they will later assume in the larger society. Although much has been written about this period of life with regard to the characteristics and problems of the typical adolescent, little information has been gathered about handicapped adolescents, their needs, or their concerns.

For handicapped adolescents, the transitions of this age period are in some ways similar to those of their nonhandicapped peers. Nonetheless, for these youngsters—adolescents who cannot function according to age-based expectations in the areas of cognitive, physical, communicative, perceptual-motor, or social abilities— the tasks of the adolescent period present unique challenges. In this chapter we consider the potential effects of various disabling conditions on three important tasks of the adolescent period: the development of the self-concept, the establishment of social relationships with peers, and the growth of sexuality and heterosexual relationships.

As we will see, the constraints imposed by different handicapping conditions—in terms of adolescents' cognitive, social, and emotional abilities—may give rise to a special set of problems for handicapped teens to face. For instance, at a time when society expects youth to exhibit more self-reliance, independence, and other adult-like behaviors, handicapped adolescents may lack the opportunity, experience, or abilities to do so. Similarly, during adolescence, when youth increasingly seek the social approval and acceptance of their peers, atypical adolescents who cannot conform to group standards, who are "different" because of appearance or capabilities, or who have few effective social skills may find their social overtures to age-mates met with rejection.

In addition to these concerns are the potential difficulties caused by the physical changes and related developments of secondary sexual characteristics and sexual drives during this period. For example, in the case of some handicapped youth, hormonal development may proceed at a normal rate, producing physical and emotional changes. These changes, however, will not be in synchrony with the delayed social and/or cognitive abilities of these youngsters, and consequently, the adjustments required during puberty may be even more difficult for them. Beyond this, the newly developing sexuality of handicapped adolescents may draw increased attention to the uncertainty of their futures, raising questions about whether they will be capable of secure, intimate relationships or the care and raising of their own children. Finally, for those handicapped adolescents who may be physically dependent upon family members, their increased size and strength can cause problems with physical caregiving, especially as their parents become older. In short, the world of the handicapped adolescent can be an especially confusing and difficult place to live.

How can these adolescents learn to cope with the difficulties that arise as a function of their handicaps? In an effort to answer this question, our first task in this chapter is to describe what is known, with regard to youngsters who display different handicapping conditions, about three components of development that we discuss in this chapter: self-concept, peer relations, and sexuality. Ideally, we would discuss the various problems in these domains that are faced by adolescents with different kinds of disabilities. As yet, however, the research literature on handicapped adolescents is scanty and does not provide systematic information about the consequences of particular handicapping conditions. As such, in our review we have made use of available studies to draw inferences about the problems facing handicapped youngsters in general, as well as about the unique challenges facing adolescents with particular kinds of disabilities. We hope that this information can serve as a starting point for parents to understand the particular concerns and problems of their handicapped adolescent. And, in understanding their difficulties, parents may begin to seek appropriate ways of helping them cope with the demands of the teenage years.

For purposes of this chapter, the term "handicapped" will refer to such disorders as mental retardation, autism, physical disabilities, and visual or hearing impairments. We have excluded from our discussion information about adolescents whose primary disorder is a specific learning disability or emotional disturbance. As mentioned, some of the research information presented in this chapter may allude specifically to one type of handicap but not another. It is not our intent in the use of examples to ignore the literature on youngsters with other handicaps. Rather, these omissions reflect the state of the art of research in this field. We will find, however, that research pertaining to adolescents with one form of handicap has implications, in some cases, for the development of youngsters with other handicapping conditions. As an example, the knowledge that educable mentally retarded adolescents have low self-esteem because of failure in school may lead us to suspect that other children who fail in school also will have lower self-esteem—regardless of whether their failure is due to deafness, blindness, a physical impairment, or some other form of disability. Thus we will often make use of data pertaining to youngsters with one handicapping condition to draw inferences about the needs of adolescents with other kinds of disabilities.

THE DEVELOPMENT OF THE SELF-CONCEPT

Most people would argue that in order to be happy and to perform effectively in everyday life, people need to believe that they are worthwhile and competent, as well as respected and accepted by others. A positive attitude about oneself is a personal evaluation of one's attributes, abilities, and behaviors and can be referred to as a positive self-concept.

During adolescence, self-concept, or the way in which teenagers perceive and evaluate their present and future abilities and accomplishments, depends upon, to a large extent, the young person's ability to meet certain standards or expectations. These may include being accepted by peers, achieving academic and vocational goals, becoming comfortable with newly developing sexuality, and growing increasingly more independent and self-sufficient.

Challenges for Handicapped Adolescents

For the handicapped adolescent, these struggles are the same—although their ability to resolve them successfully may not be comparable to that of their nonhandicapped peers. As a result, some handicapped youngsters may acquire overly negative views of themselves. Specifically, researchers have uncovered problems in self-concept with blind and visually impaired (Meighan, 1971), deaf (Meadow, 1976), physically handicapped (Goldberg, 1981; Starr, 1982), and mentally retarded (Robinson & Robinson, 1976) young persons.

In the search for the reasons that underlie handicapped adolescents' negative self-concepts, one avenue has explored the connection between school achievement or failure and self-esteem (Coopersmith, 1959, 1967; Richmond & Dalton, 1973; Rubin, Docke & Sandidge, 1977; Tolor, Tolor, & Blumin, 1977). Increasingly, such studies have provided empirical support for the notion that handicapped students' beliefs about their abilities or shortcomings affect not only their feelings of self-worth but also their subsequent performance. Although this chapter does not specifically address the problems of learning disabled adolescents, research on this population of students has implications for other handicapped students who must learn to cope with each day's successes and failures. For example, Bryan and Pearl (1979) have discovered that learning disabled students are more likely than non-disabled peers to have negative self-concepts and to believe that they cannot succeed in school. Other investigators also have observed that learning disability syndromes usually are accompanied by feelings of frustration and futility (Minde, Lewin, Weiss, Lavigeur, Douglas, & Sykes, 1971). For most of these youngsters, even special instruction and training seem to have little effect on their feelings of anxiety and frustration, and they continue to be unwilling to attempt even those tasks at which they can be successful (Bluestein, 1967; Sabatino, 1976). Similarly, in severely underachieving deaf adolescents, the experience of failure or frustration can lead to a sense of "learned helplessness" in which these adolescents come to believe that they cannot succeed on future problems (McCrone, 1979).

In other words, many handicapped children and adolescents *expect* to fail. Such expectations of failure can lead to low self-esteem and a decrease in the person's motivation to try again (Seligman, 1975). Abramson and his associates (1979) have stated that "many handicapped youths [are] in a no-win situation. Parents, peers, teachers, and employers may expect more from the adolescent than he is actually capable of providing, thus creating an opportunity for the youth to fail. Also likely is that these significant others will expect too little, thereby not challenging the individual and causing him to perform at a lower level than is possible" (p. 560–561). Minde (1979) provides support for the link between parental expectations and emotional development in handicapped adolescents in a study of the coping styles of cerebral palsied teenagers. In this report, Minde found that these adolescents with severe psychiatric problems were either from disturbed families or had parents who perceived the cerebral palsied adolescent as either completely normal (thus leading to overly high expectations) or totally and permanently crippled (leading to unnecessarily low expectations).

The first of these unrealistic expectations, expectations which are too high, may come about when parents assume that the visible physical growth and the development of secondary sexual characteristics during adolescence are accompanied by similar developments in mental and social skills. Particularly for those adolescents whose physical development may be age-appropriate and whose handicap is not obvious, there may be a tendency to be less tolerant of age-inappropriate behavior. For instance, in the case of mentally retarded individuals, the dependent behaviors which were permitted at younger ages and the sometimes embarrassing behaviors which were overlooked in childhood no longer may be acceptable. Instead, the expectation may be that mentally retarded adolescents, because they have developed the sexual characteristics of this age group, also should be mentally and emotionally more mature. Here is a case in which overly optimistic views of a handicapped adolescent's abilities can lead to unrealistically high expectations which, in turn, can set the stage for failure.

At the other end of the continuum are those parents and teachers who may underestimate a handicapped student's abilities. For example, Chapman and Boersma (1979) report that mothers of learning disabled students generalize their children's failures from one situation to another and expect that their children will not be successful even in areas in which these children are not disabled and actually could succeed. Interestingly, a study of the beliefs of learning disabled children regarding their successes and failures had corresponding findings—that is, the children themselves believe that they cannot succeed even in areas in which they do not exhibit a disability (Pearl, Bryan, Donahue, 1979).

This issue of parent/teacher expectations and their effects on student performance has been discussed widely in the education and psychology literatures. In 1968, Rosenthal and Jacobson reported an experiment in which teachers were told that certain students in their classroom would "blossom" during the year and demonstrate especially high achievement while certain other children would move along at an average rate. Unknown to the teachers, the children in each group were not really different in their ability levels. The findings of the study revealed the power of "self-fulfilling prophecies": measures of the students' achievement at the end of the school year suggested that students performed according to the way they were expected to perform. That is, students who were expected to perform well actually did perform better than those who were expected to show average levels of performance, and these findings suggest that students perform in accordance with the way they are expected to perform. Other studies indicate that the reason for this may be that an adult's expectations are communicated to children in the classroom through the adult's overt behavior, for instance, by teachers giving children less praise or providing them with less stimulation. Similarly, such expectations may be communicated to handicapped adolescents at home through the verbal or nonverbal behavior of their parents. If handicapped adolescents are told through the words or actions of others that they lack the ability to master a skill, they may be less likely to even try to achieve such a goal.

How Parents Can Help

Parents can help their handicapped adolescents develop a better sense of self-worth and competence by establishing realistic expectations for them. By providing disabled adolescents with an accurate idea of what they can or cannot do, parents can avert unnecessary failures. Furthermore, atypical teenagers may have more confidence to explore and attempt difficult activities if parents can assure them that their efforts ultimately will be successful. Parents can help their youngsters achieve success by setting goals which are only slightly more difficult than what the disabled youngster can already accomplish. By breaking a task down into manageable small steps and structuring activities so that steps can be mastered one at a time, parents can assist their children to gain mastery over complicated activities.

Unrealistic expectations, whether too high or too low, often may be the result of erroneous beliefs about the characteristics of a handicapping condition. The same diagnosis of cerebral palsy can imply a certain set of abilities and limitations for one person but a different set for another. Discussing the unique strengths and weaknesses of their own child with professionals who come into contact with him or her (e.g., teachers, psychologists, counselors, and physicians) may help parents to establish the most realistic standards for their child.

Because the self-concept is, to a large degree, a reflection of how one appears in the eyes of another (Mead, 1934), it also is important for parents to model for their child the kind of self-image they would like him or her to have. Parents who feel sorry for their child, for instance, may give their child the idea that he is a pitiful individual. Likewise, parents who see their child almost exclusively in terms of her handicap may foster this image as the child's primary view of herself. In contrast, parents who see a child's handicap as only *one* of his or her characteristics demonstrate another (more differentiated) self-image for the child. In this regard, it may be important for parents to help their youngsters find *labels* to describe who they are and what they are like. A child who is confined to a wheel chair may be "a great reader," "a basketball trivia expert," or "a kid who can make friends with anyone," rather than only "being cerebral palsied." The labels that parents supply can be used by youngsters in the process of identity formation that takes place in adolescence. Moreover, teens can use these ideas about themselves when forming peer relationships, to help their friends and classmates see them in these more positive and differentiated ways. As we will see, exhibiting a positive image of oneself can be extremely important in regard to another fundamental component of the adolescent's life—social relationships with other youngsters—a topic to which we now turn.

SOCIAL RELATIONSHIPS

Youngsters' affiliation with the peer group reaches its peak in mid-adolescence. Through interactions with other youngsters, adolescents seek to define who they are, to test out various social roles and obtain feedback about their performance, and to develop further their sense of social worth and self-esteem. As such, Hartup (1976) has identified positive peer interactions as a determining factor in youngsters' popularity among agemates as well as an important force in their emotional and moral development. Other investigators (e.g., Schmuck & Schmuck, 1975) also have suggested that acceptance by one's peers strongly influences one's self-evaluation which, in turn, affects self-concept and academic achievement. Indeed, the evidence is overwhelming that the quality of peer relationships affects social and psychological development as well as academic success.

Challenges for Handicapped Adolescents

The implications of research findings on the importance of peer relations for social and intellectual development may be particularly important in the case of handicapped adolescents who sometimes have problems in making friends. Several studies, for example, have demonstrated that nonhandicapped students are less accepting of youngsters who are mentally retarded (Ballard, Corman, Gottlieb, & Kaufman, 1978; Gottlieb, 1974, 1975; Gottlieb & Budoff, 1973; Sheare, 1974), speech handicapped (Woods & Carrow, 1959), autistic (Bemporad, 1979), blind (Jones,

Lavine, & Shell, 1972), and physically handicapped (Richardson, 1971).

The recognition of the significant role peers play in all aspects of development and these findings about the negative quality of peer relations between handicapped and nonhandicapped youngsters provided a basis for the mainstreaming clauses of Public Law 94-142 (The Education for All Handicapped Children Act). In mainstreamed school programs, handicapped students are integrated with nonhandicapped peers in regular classroom settings. One assumption underlying this strategy is that placement in the same classroom will provide opportunities for more social contact and acceptance between the two groups of students.

A number of studies on the social status of mainstreamed students, however, have yielded disappointing results. Even when they are in the same classroom, handicapped and nonhandicapped students do not necessarily seek social contact with one another, particularly when youngsters are simply placed in the same classroom without instructions or support for interacting together (Bruininks, 1978; Bryan, 1978; Gottlieb, Semmel, & Veldman, 1978; Iano, Ayers, Heller, McGettigan, & Walker, 1974). Several reasons have been suggested for this lack of social involvement, and these will be described below in terms of either direct or indirect results of youngsters' handicapping conditions.

1. *Direct influences of handicaps on peer relations.* A handicapping condition can directly impede peer interactions between handicapped and nonhandicapped adolescents because of the functional limitations inherent in the disability and, with some handicapping conditions, the abnormalities of the individual's appearance. In the case of functional limitations, it is not difficult to understand the dilemma of blind, deaf, or physically handicapped adolescents who may have problems getting to and participating in "normal" teenage activities such as a Saturday night movie at a downtown theatre, a dance, athletic events, or a party at someone's home across town. For these individuals, their handicaps affect more than their ability to see, hear, or use certain body parts. Youngsters who are blind or physically impaired, for instance, also may have problems participating in sports, games, dances, and other activities requiring physical movement and coordination. In the same way, deaf teenagers are impaired not

only in their ability to hear, but also in their ability to communicate with others, thus limiting their social exchanges with non-disabled persons in their world.

These impacts are undoubtedly obvious to anyone who has much contact with these youngsters; yet, there are other effects, equally important, which may be overlooked. These are the influences of physical appearance on interpersonal relationships. Teenagers place a lot of significance on their own appearance and on that of their peers. This should not be surprising, because adolescence is a time when the development of secondary sexual characteristics draws attention to one's "maleness" or "femaleness" and, hence, the roles and friendships between the sexes.

What happens when we find the appearance of another to be "different"? Stephen Richardson, well-known for his work on appearance and stigma in handicapped persons, has noted that "handicaps such as facial disfigurement, the absence or deformity of a limb, a bent spine, involuntary drivelling, and grimaces, awkwardness of gait, and involuntary unusual movements lead to differences in static appearances, movement and nonverbal behavior" (1969, p. 1053). Richardson suggests that because these appearances are strange and unfamiliar, they constitute a disruption in what we expect people to look like. This, in turn, can have a negative effect on one's social reactions to the person with atypical physical features (Richardson, 1969). For example, in a large study of 420 preadolescent nonhandicapped students, Richardson (1971) asked the students to rank order, from most-liked to least-liked, pictures of children with and without handicaps. The pictures used differed in terms of whether the child shown had a physical handicap and in terms of what kind of handicap the child had. The general findings of this study were that the preferences given by the students, in descending order from most-liked to least-liked, were: (1) a nonhandicapped child, (2) a child with a facial disfigurement, (3) a child using a wheelchair, (4) a child with crutches and leg braces, (5) an obese child, and (6) a child with an amputated limb.

These results suggest both that the social stigma associated with physical handicaps varies in severity depending on the nature of the handicap and that students who are not impaired tend to agree in their reactions to different disabilities (Richardson,

1971). In the adolescent peer group, the visible cues of a handicapping condition can serve as constant reminders that the youngster is "different." This may be particularly important during this age period, because being different in adolescence can mean being isolated from the peer group.

The problem of social isolation may be exacerbated because of the way handicapped youngsters themselves evaluate others who also have handicaps. One study, for instance, found that handicapped adolescents evaluate disabled peers as a group much more negatively than they evaluate nonhandicapped peers or even themselves (Parish, Baker, Arnheart, & Adamchak, 1980). The fact of handicapped children's awareness and acceptance of the social stigma associated with a handicapping condition also is evidenced by research showing that many youngsters lie about their special class placement (Jones, 1972).

What are the implications for the handicapped adolescent who is rejected by nonhandicapped age-mates and who may perceive disabled peers negatively? Although we have no documented answers to this question, it would seem probable that atypical adolescents who assume the negative values of their normal peers toward handicapped individuals as a whole, and yet, are rejected themselves by this group, could set the stage for their own social isolation. Given this, it would seem that both nonhandicapped and handicapped youngsters could profit from experiences designed to generate more acceptance of persons who are "different."

2. *Indirect influences of handicaps on peer relations.* Functional restrictions and atypical physical appearance are the more direct and obvious ways in which a handicap can impede interpersonal relationships. In recent years, however, research on the actual behaviors which comprise the social exchanges of handicapped children and adolescents has found that more subtle factors also may play a crucial role in determining the success of these youngsters' social interactions. Such studies have focused primarily on the handicapped individual's ability or inability to use socially acceptable behaviors to establish, maintain, and enhance interpersonal relationships.

Much of the impetus behind this interest in the social skills of handicapped youngsters has come from the research literature that has identified specific social behaviors that lead to group acceptance or rejection in nonhandicapped children and adolescents. Popular children, these studies show, are those who more often engage in positive social behaviors (such as giving attention, affection, and approval to others), who communicate effectively, and who can initiate positive interactions with peers (Asher, Oden, & Gottman, 1976; Gottman, Gonso, & Rasmussen, 1975). Conversely, unpopular children are more likely to be impulsive and physically assaultive (Feshbach, 1970), quarrelsome, and prone to use physical aggression as a means of solving disagreements (Asher, Renshaw, Geraci, & Dor, 1979).

Although much of this research has been conducted on nondisabled populations, the implications of these findings may well be the key to defining those specific behaviors which predict social acceptance or rejection of handicapped children and adolescents. Because it is likely that those behaviors which lead to poor peer acceptance of nonhandicapped persons will also result in rejection for handicapped individuals, a careful study of these factors may lead to appropriate intervention programs geared toward training handicapped youngsters in desirable social behavior (Gresham, 1981). In addition, investigating the social interactions of handicapped children who are popular versus unpopular with their peers could provide important information about what social behaviors may be most effective for making friends.

In recent years, the list of what behaviors constitute "good social skills" for nonhandicapped children has expanded rapidly. Some researchers have focused on a child's ability to give and receive positive reinforcers (such as smiles, praise, tangible objects, and affection) as an important element of social skills (Keller & Carlson, 1974). Others have discussed the ability to communicate accurately and effectively (Asher & Parke, 1975); still others have added to this list the ability to be assertive and to express one's opinions and feelings (Rinn & Markle, 1979). Several authors have further identified a category of social skills labeled "prosocial behaviors" which includes such behaviors as generosity, altruism, sharing, sympathy, and other "actions that are intended to aid or benefit another person or group of people without the actor's anticipation of external rewards" (Mussen & Eisenberg-Berg, 1977, p. 2).

Although all of these components of social skills are considered to be crucial ingredients of competent and effective social behavior, two additional abilities have been considered particularly fundamental to the development and use of other social skills. These include the abilities of role-taking (to put oneself in another's place to understand his needs, assess his intentions, and coordinate one's own behavior with his) and social discrimination (to determine which social behaviors are appropriate to use under what circumstances).

Researchers consider role-taking ability to be a particularly important basis of interpersonal activities, and as such, several investigations have focused on handicapped youngsters' abilities in this regard. Volpe (1976), for instance, studied the development of role-taking skills in orthopedically handicapped children and pre-adolescents and found these children to be inferior in this area as compared to normal children. Volpe suggested that role-taking ability is dependent upon a person's experiences with others—through such experiences one can learn the attributes and expectancies of certain roles. If one's experiences are restricted, either by virtue of the functional limitations of a handicap or through rejection by others, a person may have no opportunities to learn what is required in different social roles. Not knowing the attributes or expectations of a role thus means not being able to take on the perspective of a person in that role. This, in turn, can impair the success of social exchanges.

Other investigators have reported role-taking distortions in mentally retarded (Affleck, 1976; DeVries, 1970) and autistic individuals (Feffer & Gourevitch, 1960). In autistic adolescents, for instance, certain characteristic behaviors such as a lack of empathy, rigidity in behaviors and social responses, and social distancing in which the adolescents focus on themselves and exclude others (Mesibov, 1983) are particularly incompatible with role-taking ability. Similar behaviors have been reported in deaf youngsters. Meadow (1976) notes that deaf individuals lack the complex language necessary to understand explanations about the emotions of others and, thus, cannot understand how their behavior either positively or negatively affects others. Furthermore, since role-taking requires being able to accommodate oneself to the needs, thoughts, feelings, intentions, and desires of another, adolescents who are deaf may be further impeded by their problems in responding flexibly to changing social situations and environments (Meadow, 1976).

Closely related to role-taking ability is the ability to make social discriminations, that is, the ability to choose adaptive social behaviors at appropriate times (Miller & Schloss, 1982). Positive social behaviors will not always have positive consequences if they are utilized at the wrong time or circumstances. A youngster who has learned to joke and tease his peers can turn such social skills into aversive behaviors if he overdoes them or engages in these activities at the wrong time or place. Similarly, a youngster may be successful in communicating a need or desire to another, but such a skill may backfire if the communication is directed toward the wrong person in the wrong setting.

How Parents Can Help

Parents of handicapped and nonhandicapped students alike need to be aware of the role of negative values and perceptions when the atypical adolescent is isolated from his or her peer group. Richardson (1971), in discussing ways in which adults can help improve the social reactions of others to handicapped individuals, suggests sensitizing nonhandicapped peers to what it is like to be handicapped as well as educating them to be aware of their own feelings toward their atypical age-mates. Consistent with this suggestion, after the implementation of P.L. 94-142, a number of educational programs were initiated in mainstreamed classrooms across the country. Such programs involved turning nonhandicapped students into "handicapped" youngsters for a day. Some students were confined to wheelchairs. Others were blindfolded. Some were asked to wear earplugs while teachers and peers mouthed conversations silently to them. Still others were given as their assignments, reading material with strange letters or words which made no sense.

The effects of these programs have been quite positive in that many nonhandicapped students report a greater awareness of the problems of handicapped individuals and more acceptance of disabled students in the classroom. These short-term programs, however, do not seem to affect youngsters' social relationships outside the immediate academic setting. Part of the reason for this may be continuing prejudices, either conscious or unconscious, despite increased awareness. As we noted in the discussion of self-concept development, parents and teachers can model unconsciously negative attitudes and expectations about atypical students, and such negative values can have an adverse influence on nonhandicapped adolescents' perceptions of their atypical peers. Richardson (1969), for example, found that high school seniors and their parents held the same preference rankings for certain types of handicaps. This suggests that adults do influence the values of their children toward atypical individuals. Clearly, school students are not the only members of society whose consciousness about handicapped persons needs to be raised.

As discussed earlier, a major step in the process of changing the atittudes of others begins with both the awareness of, and changes in, biased attitudes within ourselves. Parents need to be aware of the expectations they hold for their atypical child or adolescent, how these expectations may influence their own behavior, and how such behavior may signal subtle messages to both handicapped and nonhandicapped adolescents. Likewise, the parents of a handicapped child or adolescent need to serve as the primary advocate for their child by assisting teachers, counselors, and other adults to develop realistic expectations for the handicapped individual.

These efforts to model positive attitudes toward handicapped persons are important. Nonetheless, parents need to be aware that modeling is only one component of the process of changing attitudes. What also is necessary is to provide for positive exchanges between handicapped and nonhandicapped youngsters in such a way that nonhandicapped adolescents can discover commonalities between themselves and their atypical age-mates. These mutual concerns or interests, in turn, may lead to increased positive reactions to, and interactions with, one another. Evidence now exists that the *way* we structure interpersonal situations between handicapped and nonhandicapped individuals has a significant impact on whether this goal is achieved (Ballard, Corman, Gottlieb, & Kaufman, 1977; Johnson, Rynders, Johnson, Schmidt, & Haider, 1979; Martino & Johnson, 1979).

A recent study by Rynders, Johnson, Johnson, and Schmidt (1980) provides an excellent illustration of this point. These authors contend that the acceptance or rejection of handicapped students by nonhandicapped peers is greatly dependent upon the way in which teachers structure learning situations in the classroom. For instance, teachers can structure situations to be either cooperative, competitive, or individualized. In a cooperative situation, students can obtain their own goals only if other students in their group cooperatively achieve their goals. In a competitive situation, students can obtain their own goals only if other students in the group fail to reach their goals. Lastly, in an individualistic situation, whether one student reaches his or her goal is completely independent of the performance of others.

Rynders and his associates applied these three types of situations to a series of bowling games involving Downs Syndrome and nonhandicapped teenagers. In the cooperative situation, where the success of the group depended upon the performance of each person whether handicapped or not, the Downs Syndrome adolescents received much more praise, encouragement, and support from their nonhandicapped peers. Interestingly, even though the performance of the Downs Syndrome students detracted from the overall group performance, nonhandicapped students in the cooperative group made more statements of liking toward their handicapped team members and evaluated them more positively than did nonhandicapped students in the other two conditions.

In discussing their findings, Rynders et al. hypothesized that attitude changes resulting from cooperation may arise from feeling positively about the efforts of someone else aiding us in reaching a goal. Although, initially, positive feelings are directed toward the *efforts* of the other person, eventually, the feelings are transferred directly to that person. It is important to note that whether or not the handicapped youngsters are successful in their efforts, the mere fact that they attempt to aid their nonhandicapped peers seems to be the more crucial factor in attitude change, at least on a short-term basis.

It also is plausible that, in this study, the nonhandicapped youngsters in the cooperative group discovered similarities between themselves and their handicapped teammates. These similarities may have included their common goals, common attitudes toward the game, or supportive behavior toward all team members. Asher, Oden, and Gottman (1977) have proposed that if a nonhandicapped student can find a similarity between him or herself and a disabled student, acceptance of that youngster could result. The findings of Rynders and his colleagues (1980), as well as the results of similar investigations (Ballard, Corman, Gottlieb, & Kaufman, 1977; Chenault, 1967; Lilly, 1971; McDaniel, 1970), provide support for this claim.

DEVELOPMENT OF SEXUAL IDENTITY

Every adolescent is faced with the task of developing a stable sense of his or her own sexuality. During this time of life, the testing of sexual roles, the establishment of intimacy, and the tentative beginnings of commitment provide a foundation for later loving and intimate relationships.

For most adolescents, the task of developing a sexual identity, though certainly not easy, is facilitated by daily exposure to sexual role models, either in the form of persons they know in everyday life or through such media as television, magazines, or popular novels. Additionally, nonhandicapped teenagers have numerous opportunities to discuss and even explore various aspects of sexual behavior and sexual roles with peers.

Challenges for Handicapped Adolescents

For handicapped adolescents, the task of developing a stable sexual identity presents several unique problems. For instance, despite the fact that these adolescents also are exposed to the same masculine or feminine models as their non-disabled peers, these youngsters may have a more difficult time finding models with whom they can personally identify. It is rare that these teenagers see, either in person or in the media, handicapped adults who are portrayed as competent social and sexual beings. At the same time, these teenagers may be socially isolated from nonhandicapped peers and thus denied normal opportunities to discuss and explore sexual feelings. Contact with similarly disabled teenagers, when it does occur, may be unenlightening because these teens may be equally inexperienced, misinformed, or unsure about their sexual feelings and behaviors.

Although a lack of appropriate sexual models and occasions for sexual experimentation may underlie many of the handicapped adolescent's problems with sexual identity, other factors also may influence sexual adjustment. Among the most critical are the negative social attitudes and myths about the disabled and their sexuality, the problems of handicapped adolescents in obtaining appropriate sex education, and poor body images caused by their perceptions of themselves as different or unattractive.

Myths and misconceptions about the sexuality of handicapped individuals. The first of these factors, unfounded myths about the sexuality of the handicapped, can be the most insidious and pervasive of the negative influences on the atypical adolescent's development of a sexual sense of him or herself. Several such myths abound:

Myth #1: The handicapped adolescent is asexual. This misconception is based on an overemphasis on the person's disability as the sole defining characteristic of the person. In essence, this myth ignores all other physical, social, or psychological needs or wishes of the disabled person and focuses entirely on the problems directly related to a handicapping condition. Here, an assumption is made that an impairment or delay in one area of functioning affects all other aspects of development, including sexual feelings and capabilities. Overwhelmingly, the literature on disabilities and sexuality tells us that such beliefs are, indeed, myths. This holds true for autistic (Mesibov, 1982), blind (Foulke & Uhde, 1974, 1976), deaf (Fitz-Gerald & Fitz-Gerald, 1978), mentally retarded (Hall, 1975), and cerebral palsied adolescents (Cornelius, Chipouras, Makas, & Daniels, 1982).

Myth #2: The sexual urges of handicapped adolescents are stronger and more uncontrollable than those of their nonhandicapped peers. Usually applied to mentally retarded or autistic adolecents, this myth stands in contrast to the first, and stems from a misunderstanding about the sexual expression of disabled individuals. Parents of males fear that their sons may be overcome by unrestrainable urges and be driven to crimes involving sexual assault; in contrast, parents of females fear that their daughters will engage in irresponsible and promiscuous sexual behaviors.

In reality, the urges of handicapped teens are probably very similar to those of their nonhandicapped peers; however, misconceptions about their behavior can arise when "uncontrollable" behavior is confused with "inappropriate" behavior—that is, behavior expressed in the wrong place or toward the wrong people. The real basis of this myth, therefore, is the inability of these handicapped adolescents to discriminate acceptable circumstances in which to express affectionate or sexual behaviors. For example, a mentally retarded adolescent may masturbate in public, indiscriminately touch or express affection toward others, undress in public, or engage in a number of other actions which may be interpreted as resulting from "insatiable sexual urges." Likewise, "a person with autism might only be unzipping his fly in public as preparation for the bathroom, [but] the public might very well see this as exposing oneself with very severe recrimination and restrictions resulting" (Mesibov, 1982, p. 8).

In short, if a nonhandicapped adolescent masturbates or undresses in the privacy of the bathroom or bedroom, we would not consider these behaviors deviant. On the other hand, when these same behaviors are exhibited by a disabled adolescent in a public place or in view of others, they are considered to be abnormal. An additional element to this problem may be that when a retarded child caresses and kisses strangers, we may consider the child to be cute, loving, friendly, and sociable. Yet, when this same child grows up to be an adolescent expressing these same behaviors, he or she is regarded as seductive, promiscuous, or sexually assaultive. These youngsters may have to be taught explicitly that certain kinds of behaviors are no longer acceptable because they are growing up.

Myth #3: Adolescents with certain types of handicaps do not need sex education because they are incapable of sexual activity. This myth usually refers to persons with more limiting handicaps such as severe and profound mental retardation, cerebral palsy, and various types and degrees of paralysis such as those which result from spinal cord injury. In each case, the literature differs regarding the sexual capabilities of these individuals.

In the case of severely retarded persons, for example, Wolfensberger (cited in Cornelius, Chipouras, Makas, Daniels, 1982) reports less intense and less frequent sexual urges, whereas in the profoundly retarded, impotence is more common. Although impotence may impede penile-vaginal intercourse, it does not preclude other forms of pleasurable stimulation such as masturbation.

For cerebral palsied individuals, genital functioning per se is not affected by their disorder, although the physical expression of sexuality may be. Cornelius and her associates (1982) state that "petting, masturbation, and mutual masturbation may be restricted by paralysis, stiffness, or deformity of the hands and arms. Spasms and athetoid movements are often accentuated by emotional excitement . . . Coitus [intercourse] may also be affected by these same physical problems. . . . Spasms can cause involuntary muscular contractions which make intercourse extremely difficult" (p. 149). Yet, given appropriate sexual counseling and whatever personal or environmental adaptations may be needed by a cerebral palsied person, such disabled individuals can engage in sexual activity (Cornelius et al., 1982; Robinault, 1978).

While the varying levels and extent of injury makes sweeping generalizations about specific sexual activity in spinal cord injury victims inappropriate, several authors have indicated that all of these individuals are capable of some form of satisfying sexual activity (Cole, 1975; Cornelius et al., 1982; Singh & Magner, 1975). An excellent review of this literature is provided by Cornelius and associates (1982) in which they conclude that pleasurable sexual experiences, varying from masturbation, to erotic stimulation of nongenital body areas, to intercourse, are possible for spinal cord injured victims.

Nigro (cited in Robinault, 1978, p. 111), in discussing the marriage of two severely multihandicapped people, notes that, "Making love is, for handicapped people as for others, a very private and uniquely worked out practice. If their disability is such that they can engage in sex in the standard or conventional way, they have no more problems than able-bodied people in working toward a good sexual adjustment. If their physical disability prevents them from the usual practices, either because of physical distortions or because of impairment in sexual function, this need not be a barrier to achieving sexual satisfaction. . . . I don't want to imply that no serious problems in this area may arise, but it is apparent that a loving, determined, and resourceful couple, regardless of their handicap can find an acceptable way of fulfilling their sexual needs."

Myth #4: Handicapped adolescents should be discouraged from involvement with members of the opposite sex since they cannot get married. Although most parents feel comfortable with the idea of marriage for blind or deaf individuals, parents are less positive, more apprehensive, and, often, strongly opposed to marriages involving persons who are mentally retarded, autistic, or cerebral palsied. Some of this concern and disapproval may arise from beliefs that these handicapped individuals are always children in the sense that they are devoid of sexual feelings and in need of constant care and attention. Other reservations are based on concerns about the handicapped person's ability to function independently, to be financially self-sufficient, and to bear and raise children. While these problems warrant careful consideration, they are not unresolvable dilemmas for many handicapped persons.

As an example, current trends in community living programs for handicapped teens and adults have made possible a variety of supervised or semi-supervised residential options for mentally retarded and, in some communities, cerebral palsied individuals. At present, the majority of these alternative living arrangements are supervised group homes. However, in recent years, there has been an increase in the number of semi-supervised apartments in which individuals live independently except for supervisory visits every few days by the sponsoring agency's staff. Such living arrangements might be appropriate residential accommodations for couples in which both members are disabled and still in need of minimal supervision. Additionally, the increased availability of sheltered and semi-sheltered employment opportunities as well as the growing number of business and industry work programs for handicapped individuals provide for increased self-sufficiency in disabled persons. Lastly, though it is not a minor concern, the development of effective contraception has made possible the option of childless marriages for those couples who may not have the abilities to raise children.

Each of these issues, of course, deserves far greater consideration than can be undertaken here. Yet, parents must remain aware that intimate relationships and marriage can be viable options for many handicapped persons. In fact, a wealth of recent literature indicates that marriage, even for the most severely handicapped, can be a means of emotional and sexual satisfaction, mutual

support, increased independence, and comfortable companionship (Hall, 1975; Kempton & Forman, 1976; Mattison, 1973; Rosen,
1972).

Sex education. Persons who make sex education for handicapped adolecents their concern are faced with a number of important considerations. As previously noted, not the least of these
is the uncertainty (for instance, of parents, teachers, and counselors) about how a particular disability may affect an individual's
sexuality. Several resources on this topic for parents and handicapped individuals are included in Annotated References at the
end of this chapter.

Another concern of those responsible for the sex education of
handicapped adolescents is that they may not know how to modify
the information they wish to present according to the needs of a
particular individual. For example, in deaf adolescents, limitations in the ability to communicate with others are the major
obstacle in sex education (Fitz-Gerald & Fitz-Gerald, 1977). Even
if parents and teachers are familiar with sign language, they may
not be familiar with the sexual vocabulary of sign well enough to
provide accurate information or answer specific questions (Cornelius et al., 1982).

Similarly, in the case of congenitally blind adolescents, the
inability to see the human body and society's prohibitions against
exploring one's own or another's body by touch can result in poor
comprehension of human anatomy, especially of the opposite
sex. Foulke and Uhde (1974, 1976 cited in Cornelius et al., 1982)
report that even blind adolescents who have learned precise sexual
terminology or who can define sexual activity using the appropriate vocabulary may still have a limited conceptualization of
the physiological aspects of sexuality. One blind student, for
example, could accurately define sexual terms such as "intercourse" but, when urged to elaborate, exhibited some confusion
by stating that a woman's vagina could be found just under her
right breast.

For mentally retarded and autistic adolescents, the question
becomes not only one of how to modify the information given,
but, also, how much information to give. As Mesibov (1982)
notes: "The amount of assistance needed may vary greatly among
individuals. . . . For example, one person might simply need

instruction on managing himself in public, while another would need a thorough sex education course including heterosexual relationships" (p. 2).

The dilemma of how much to teach and how to teach it is not an easy one to resolve. Several resources for parents are provided at the end of this chapter, and parents will need to adapt such information to their own child's particular needs and learning strengths or weaknesses.

Body image. The sexual identity problems of handicapped adolescents are not limited to a lack of accurate sexual knowledge. Equally important is one's body image and awareness of one's self as a sexual being.

For the physically disabled teenager, adolescent standards for physical wholeness, attractiveness, and strength may seem impossible ideals. During this period of development, atypical adolescents may become even more conscious of their being "different," and more uncertain of the limitations their disability might place on sexual capacities or expressions. Having cerebral palsy, spina bifida, paralysis, or other bodily deformities presents teenagers with the task of reconciling their perception of their appearances and physical limitations with the images they see in "normal" adolescents. Additionally, because non-disabled individuals tend to avoid touching persons with physical handicaps such as cerebral palsy (Geiger & Knight, 1975), a lack of affection and normal physical contact can provide a message of dislike and disapproval to a disabled youngster. Consequently, what can result from unfavorable comparisons and feelings of being repugnant is the incorporation of a body image of distortion and abnormality into one's self-concept.

In a similar way, blind adolescents, who cannot see their bodies and the locations and functioning of the various parts in relation to one another, may have extreme difficulty forming positive body images (Cook-Clampert, 1981). Furthermore, not being able to see the various shapes, sizes, structures, and features of others in their environment, blind adolescents cannot compare and evaluate their own appearances against those of others. Hence, the usual self-doubts adolescents have about being pretty or handsome, well-proportioned, or sexually attractive can remain unresolved for these teenagers.

How Parents Can Help

In prior sections we discussed setting realistic expectations for, and promoting positive attitudes about, handicapped adolescents. When considering possible ways in which parents can assist their disabled teenagers to develop positive sexual identities, many of these prior suggestions also apply. First, parents need to examine their own attitudes about the sexuality of their handicapped adolescent. This may be difficult for parents to do since the sexual development which occurs during these years may be a reminder to parents of the uncertainty of their adolescent's impending adulthood. Yet, if parents view sexual development negatively and consider it to be abnormal or shameful, their child may come to consider it in the same light.

A second means of promoting a positive sexual identity for disabled adolescents is to provide them with accurate information about their sexual capabilities and realistic expectations for their sexual functioning. Parents can achieve this by first educating themselves about the sexuality of disabled persons and by then communicating this information as honestly and accurately as possible to their handicapped teenager.

PART II: SOURCES OF HELP

The following groups provide information on various handicaps for parents, teachers, and other professionals. Many also provide referral for parents needing diagnostic and treatment services for their children.

Action for Brain Handicapped Children
300 Wilder Building
St. Paul, MN 55102

American Association on Mental Deficiency
5201 Connecticut Avenue, NW
Washington, DC 20015

American Cleft Palate Education Foundation
331 Salk Hall
University of Pittsburgh
Pittsburgh, PA 15261

American Foundation for the Blind
15 West 16 Street
New York, NY 10011

American Speech and Hearing Association
10801 Rockville Pike
Rockville, MD 20852

Association for Children with Learning Disabilities
5225 Grace Street
Pittsburgh, PA 15236

Association for the Education of the Visually Handicapped
1919 Walnut Street, Fourth Floor
Philadelphia, PA 19107

Council for Exceptional Children
1920 Association Drive
Reston, VA 22091

Cystic Fibrosis Foundation
41 East 42 Street
New York, NY 10036

Epilepsy Foundation of America
1828 L. Street, NW
Suite 406
Washington, DC 20036

March of Dimes Birth Defects Foundation
1275 Mamaroneck Avenue
White Plains, NY 10605

Muscular Dystrophy Association of America
810 Seventh Avenue
New York, NY 10019

National Association for Retarded Citizens
2709 Avenue E East
Arlington, TX 76010

National Clearinghouse for Mental Health Information, National Institute of Health
Bethesda, MD 20014

National Easter Seal Society for Crippled Children and Adults
2023 W. Ogden Avenue
Chicago, IL 60636

National Society for Children and Adults with Autism
1234 Massachusetts Avenue, NW
Suite 1017
Washington, DC 20005

Spina Bifida Association of America
P.O. Box 266
Newcastle, DE 19720

United Cerebral Palsy Association, Inc.
66 East 34 Street
New York, NY 10016

ANNOTATED REFERENCES

Allen, P., & Lipke, L. A. *Your Changing Body: A Guided Self-exploration.*
Grand Rapids, MI: Institute for the Development of Creative Child
Care, 1974.
This kit of sex-education materials for blind children and adolescents
includes audio-tapes and a parent's teaching guide. The tapes instruct
the blind individual in exploring his or her own body while focusing on
the similarities and differences between the male and female bodies.

Cornelius, D. A., Chipouras, S., Makas, E., & Daniels, S. M. *Who Cares?
A Handbook on Sex Education and Counseling Services for Disabled
People.* (2nd Edition). Baltimore, MD: University Park Press, 1982.
Although primarily written for professionals involved in sex education, counseling and therapy for handicapped individuals, this book
provides a wealth of information and resources for parents and handicapped individuals. Contents include a discussion of the myths and
attitudes toward the sexuality of handicapped persons, a chapter written
specifically for handicapped individuals, and excellent reviews of the
research literature on sexuality in hearing and visually impaired, cerebral
palsied, mentally retarded, and spinal cord injured individuals.

Exceptional Parent (296 Boylston St., Third Floor, Boston, MA 02116)
This magazine is published bi-monthly and addresses many issues of
concern to parents of handicapped children, adolescents, and adults.

Articles include information on pertinent topics such as residential care, training and education, dating and marriage for the handicapped, and other themes important to parents.

Hopper, C. E., & Allen, W. A. *Sex Education for Physically Handicapped Youth.* Springfield, IL: Charles C. Thomas, 1980.
This book is written in an easy-to-read form, specifically for physically disabled teenagers. Information is provided on a variety of topics including physical development, dating, reproduction, venereal disease, marriage, masturbation, and homosexuality.

Meyers, R. *Like Normal People.* New York: Signet, 1979.
This is a true story about Roger and Virginia Meyers, both of whom are mentally retarded and who overcome numerous obstacles to marry and build a life together.

Woodward, J. *Signs of Sexual Behavior: An Introduction to Some Sex-related Vocabulary in American Sign Language.* Silver Spring, MD: T. J. Publishers, Inc., 1979.
This book will serve as a valuable resource for parents and teachers of deaf children and adolescents in helping them to communicate with the hearing impaired about sexual development and activity.

REFERENCES

Abramson, M., Ash, M. J., & Nash, W. R. "Handicapped Adolescents: A Time for Reflection." *Adolescence*, 1979, *14*, 557–565.

Affleck, G. G. "Role-taking Ability and the Interpersonal Competencies of Retarded Children." *American Journal of Mental Deficiency*, 1976, *80*, 312–316.

Asher, S. R., Oden, S. L., & Gottman, J. M. "Children's Friendships in School Settings." In L. G. Katz (Ed.), *Current Topics in Early Childhood Education* (Vol. 1). Norwood, NJ: Ablex, 1977.

Asher, S. R., & Parke, R. D. "Influence of Sampling and Comparison Processes on the Development of Communication Effectiveness." *Journal of Educational Psychology*, 1975, *67*, 64–75.

Asher, S. R., Renshaw, P. D., Geraci, R. L., & Dor, A. K. *Peer Acceptance and Social Skill Training: The Selection of Program Content.* Paper presented at the biennial meeting of the Society for Research in Child Development, San Francisco, 1979.

Ballard, M., Corman, L., Gottlieb, J., & Kaufman, M. J. "Improving the Social Status of Mainstreamed Retarded Children." *Journal of Educational Psychology*, 1978, *69*, 605–611.

Bemporad, J. R. "Adult Recollections of a Formerly Autistic Child." *Journal of Autism and Developmental Disorders*, 1979, *9*, 179–197.

Bluestein, V. W. "Factors Related to and Predictive of Improvement in the Schools." *Psychology in the Schools*, 1967, *4*, 272–276.

Bruininks, V. L. "Actual and Perceived Peer Status of Learning Disabled Students in Mainstream Programs." *Journal of Special Education*, 1978, *12*, 51–58.

Bryan, T. S. "Social Relationships and Verbal Interactions of Learning Disabled Children." *Journal of Learning Disabilities*, 1978, *11*, 107–115.

Bryan, T., & Pearl, R. "Self-concepts and Locus of Control of Learning Disabled Children." *Journal of Clinical Child Psychology*, 1979, *8*, 223–226.

Chapman, J. W., & Boersma, F. J. "Learning Disabilities, Locus of Control, and Mother Attitudes." *Journal of Educational Psychology*, 1979, *71*, 250–258.

Chenault, J. "Improving the Social Acceptance of Unpopular Mentally Retarded Pupils in Special Classes." *American Journal of Mental Deficiency*, 1967, *72*, 455–458.

Cole, T. "Sexuality and the Spinal Cord Injured." In R. Green (Ed.), *Human Sexuality: A Health Practitioner's Text*. Baltimore: Williams & Wilkins Co., 1975.

Cook-Clampert, D. "The Development of Self-concept in Blind Children." *Journal of Visual Impairment and Blindness*, 1981, *75*, 233–238.

Coopersmith, S. "A Method for Determining Types of Self-esteem." *Journal of Abnormal and Social Psychology*, 1959, *59*, 87–94.

Coopersmith, S. *The Antecedents of Self-esteem*. San Francisco: Freeman, 1967.

Cornelius, D. A., Chipouras, S., Makas, E., & Daniels, S. M. *Who Cares? A Handbook on Sex Education and Counseling Services for Disabled People*. (2nd ed.). Baltimore, MD: University Park Press, 1982.

DeVries, R. "The Development of Role-taking as Reflected by Behavior of Bright, Average, and Retarded Children in a Social Guessing Game." *Child Development*, 1970, *41*, 759–770.

Dweck, C. S., & Repucci, N. D. "Learned Helplessness and Reinforcement Responsibility in Children." *Journal of Personality and Social Psychology*, 1973, *25*, 109–116.

Feffer, M. H., & Gourevitch, V. "Cognitive Aspects of Role-taking in Children." *Journal of Personality*, 1960, *28*, 383–396.

Feshbach, S. "Aggression." In P. H. Mussen (Ed.), *Carmichael's Manual of Child Psychology*. (3rd ed., Vol. 2). New York: Wiley, 1970.

Fitz-Gerald, D., & Fitz-Gerald, M. "Behind the Times." *SIECUS Report*, 1977, *6*, 3–5.

Fitz-Gerald, D., & Fitz-Gerald, M. "Sexual Implications of Deafness." *Sexuality and Disability*, 1978, *1*, 57–69.

Foulke, E., & Uhde, T. "Do Blind Children Need Sex Education?" *New Outlook for the Blind*, 1974, *68*, 193–200, 209.

Foulke, E., & Uhde, T. "Sex Education and Counseling for the Blind." *Medical Aspects of Human Sexuality*, 1976, *10*, 51–52.

Geiger, R. C., & Knight, D. E. "Sexuality of People with Cerebral Palsy." *Medical Aspects of Human Sexuality*, 1975, *9*, 70–83.

Goldberg, R. T. "Toward an Understanding of the Rehabilitation of the Disabled Adolescent." *Rehabilitation Literature*, 1981, *42*, 66–74.

Gottlieb, J. "Public, Peer, and Professional Attitudes toward Mentally Retarded Persons." *Studies in Learning Potential*, 1974, *4*, 20–39.

Gottlieb, J. "Attitudes toward Retarded Children: Effects of Labeling and Behavioral Aggressiveness." *Journal of Educational Psychology*, 1975, *67*, 581–585.

Gottlieb, J., & Budoff, M. "Social Acceptability of Retarded Children in Nongraded Schools Differing in Architecture." *American Journal of Mental Deficiency*, 1973, *78*, 15–19.

Gottlieb, J., Semmel, M. I., & Veldman, D. J. "Correlates of Social Status Among Mainstreamed Mentally Retarded Children." *Journal of Educational Psychology*, 1978, *70*, 396–405.

Gottman, J., Gonso, J., & Rasmussen, B. "Social Interaction, Social Competence, and Friendship in Children." *Child Development*, 1975, *46*, 709–718.

Gresham, F. M. "Social Skills Training with Handicapped Children: A Review." *Review of Educational Research*, 1981, *51*, 139–176.

Hall, J. E. "Sexuality and the Mentally Retarded." In R. Green (Ed.), *Human Sexuality: A Health Practitioner's Text*. Baltimore: Williams & Wilkins, 1975.

Hartup, W. W. "Peer Relations and the Behavioral Development of the Individual Child." In E. Schopler & R. J. Reichler (Eds.), *Psychopathology and Child Development*. New York: Plenum, 1976.

Ians, R. P., Ayers, D., Heller, H. B., McGettigan, J. F., & Walker, S. "Sociometric Status of Retarded Children in an Integrative Program." *Exceptional Children*, 1974, *40*, 267–271.

Johnson, R., Rynders, J., Johnson, D. W., Schmidt, B., & Haider, S. "Producing Positive Interaction Between Handicapped and Non-handicapped Teenagers Through Cooperative Goal Structuring: Implication for Mainstreaming." *American Educational Research Journal*, 1979, *16*, 161–168.

Jones, R. L. "Labels and Stigma in Special Education." *Exceptional Children*, 1972, *38*, 553–564.

Jones, R. L., Lavine, K., & Shell, J. "Blind Children Integrated in Classrooms with Sighted Children: A Sociometric Study." *New Outlook for the Blind*, 1972, *66*, 75–80.

Keller, M. F., & Carlson, P. M. "The Use of Symbolic Modeling to Promote Social Skills in Preschool Children with Low Levels of Social Responsiveness." *Child Development*, 1974, *45*, 912–919.

Kempton, W., & Forman, R. *Guidelines for Training in Sexuality and the Mentally Retarded*. Philadelphia: Planned Parenthood Association of Southeastern Pennsylvania, 1976.

Lilly, M. S. "Improving Social Acceptance of Low Sociometric Status, Low Achieving Students." *Exceptional Children*, 1971, *37*, 341–347.

Martino, L., & Johnson, D. W. "Cooperative and Individualistic Experiences Among Disabled and Normal Children." *Journal of Social Psychology*, 1979, *107*, 177–183.

Mattison, J. "Marriage and Mental Handicap." In F. F. De La Cruz & G. D. LaVeck (Eds.), *Human Sexuality and the Mentally Retarded*. New York: Brunner/Mazel, 1973.

McDaniel, C. O., Jr. "Participation in Extracurricular Activities, Social Acceptance, and Social Rejection Among Educable Mentally Retarded Students." *Education and Training of the Mentally Retarded*, 1970, *5*, 4–14.

Mead, G. H. *Mind, Self, and Society*. Chicago: University of Chicago Press, 1934.

Meadow, K. P. "Personality and Social Development of Deaf Persons." *Journal of Rehabilitation of the Deaf*, 1976, *9*, 1–12.

Meighan, T. *An Investigation of the Self-concept of Blind and Visually Handicapped Adolescents*. New York: American Foundation for the Blind, 1971.

Mesibov, G. B. *Sex Education for People with Autism: Matching Programs to Levels of Functioning*. Paper presented at the meeting of the National Society for Children and Adults with Autism, Omaha, NE, July 1982.

Mesibov, G. B. "Current Perspectives and Issues in Autism and Adolescence." In E. Schopler & G. B. Mesibov (Eds.), *Autism in Adolescents and Adults*. New York: Plenum Press, 1983.

Miller, S. R., & Schloss, P. J. *Career-vocational Education for Handicapped Youth*. Rockville, MD: Aspen Systems Corporation, 1982.

Minde, K. K. "Coping Styles of 34 Adolescents with Cerebral Palsy." In S. Chess & A. Thomas (Eds.), *Annual Progress in Child Psychiatry and Child Development*. New York: Brunner/Mazel, 1979.

Minde, K., Lewin, D., Weiss, G., Lavigeur, H., Douglas, V., & Sykes, E. "The Hyperactive Child in Elementary School: A 5-year Controlled Follow-up." *Exceptional Children*, 1971, *38*, 215–221.

Mussen, P., & Eisenberg-Berg, N. *Roots of Caring, Sharing, and Help: The Development of Prosocial Behavior in Children.* San Francisco: W. H. Freeman, 1977.

Parish, T. S., Baker, S. K., Arheart, K. L., & Adamchak, P. G. "Normal and Exceptional Children's Attitudes Toward Themselves and One Another." *The Journal of Psychology,* 1980, *104*, 249–253.

Pearl, R., Bryan, T., & Donahue, M. "Learning Disabled Children's Attributions for Success and Failure." Unpublished manuscript, University of Illinois at Chicago Circle, 1979.

Richardson, S. A. "The Effect of Physical Disability on the Socialization of a Child." In D. A. Goslin (Ed.), *Handbook of Socialization Theory and Research.* New York: Rand McNally & Company, 1969.

Richardson, S. A. "Research Report: Handicap, Appearance, and Stigma." *Social Science and Medicine,* 1971, *5*, 621–628.

Richmond, B. O., & Dalton, J. L. "Teacher Ratings and Self-concept Reports of Retarded Pupils." *Exceptional Children,* 1973, *40*, 178–183.

Rinn, R. C., & Markle, A. "Modification of Skill Deficits in Children." In A. S. Bellack & M. Hersen (Eds.), *Research and Practice in Social Skills Training.* New York: Plenum Press, 1979.

Robinault, I. P. *Sex, Society, and the Disabled: A Developmental Inquiry into Roles, Reactions, and Responsibilities.* Hagerstown, MD: Harper & Row, 1978.

Robinson, H. B., & Robinson, N. M. *The Mentally Retarded Child: A Psychological Approach.* New York: McGraw-Hill, 1976.

Rosen, M. "Psychosexual Adjustment of the Mentally Handicapped." *Sexual Rights and Responsibilities of the Mentally Retarded.* Proceedings of the Conference of the American Association on Mental Deficiency, Newark, DE, 1972.

Rosenthal, R., & Jacobsen, L. *Pygmalion in the Classroom.* New York: Holt, Rinehart and Winston, 1968.

Rubin, R. A., Dorle, J., & Sandidge, S. "Self-esteem and School Performance." *Psychology in the Schools,* 1977, *14*, 503–507.

Rynders, J. E., Johnson, R. T., Johnson, D. W., & Schmidt, B. "Producing Positive Interaction Among Downs Syndrome and Nonhandicapped Teenagers through Cooperative Goal Structuring." *American Journal of Mental Deficiency,* 1980, *85*, 268–273.

Sabatino, D. A. (Ed.). *Learning Disabilities Handbook: A Technical Guide to Program Development.* DeKalb, IL: Northern Illinois University Press, 1976.

Schmuck, R. A., & Schmuck, P. A. *Group Processes in the Classroom.* Dubuque, IA: Wm. C. Brown, 1975.

Seligman, M. E. P. *Helplessness.* San Francisco: Freeman, 1975.

Sheare, J. B. "Social Acceptance of EMR Adolescents in Integrated Programs." *American Journal of Mental Deficiency*, 1974, *78*, 678–682.

Singh, S. P., & Magner, T. "Sex and Self: The Spinal Cord-injured." *Rehabilitation Literature*, 1975, *36*, 2–7.

Starr, P. "Physical Attractiveness and Self-esteem Ratings of Young Adults with Cleft Lip and/or Palate." *Psychological Reports*, 1982, *50*, 467–470.

Tolor, A., Tolor, B., & Blumin, S. S. "Self-concept and Locus of Control in Primary-grade Children Identified as Requiring Special Educational Programming." *Psychological Reports*, 1977, *40*, 43–49.

Volpe, R. "Orthopedic Disability, Restriction, and Role-taking Activity." *The Journal of Special Education*, 1976, *10*, 371–381.

Woods, F. J., & Carrow, M. A. "The Choice-rejection Status of Speech Defective Children." *Exceptional Children*, 1959, *25*, 279–283.

Author Index

Subject Index